BEGINNER'S
STEP-BY-STEP
CODING
COURSE

BEGINNER'S
STEP-BY-STEP
CODING
COURSE

LEARN COMPUTER PROGRAMMING THE EASY WAY

DK

Penguin Random House

DK DELHI

Senior editor	Suefa Lee
Project art editor	Sanjay Chauhan
Project editor	Tina Jindal
Art editors	Rabia Ahmad, Simar Dhamija, Sonakshi Singh
Assistant editor	Sonali Jindal
Jacket designer	Tanya Mehrotra
DTP designer	Jaypal Chauhan
Pre-production manager	Balwant Singh
Senior managing editor	Rohan Sinha
Managing art editor	Sudakshina Basu

DK LONDON

Project editor	Miezan van Zyl
Project art editor	Francis Wong
Managing editor	Angeles Gavira Guerrero
Managing art editor	Michael Duffy
Associate publishing director	Liz Wheeler
Publishing director	Jonathan Metcalf
Art director	Karen Self
Jacket design development manager	Sophia MTT
Producer (pre-production)	Gillian Reid
Senior producer	Meskerem Berhane

First published in Great Britain in 2020 by
Dorling Kindersley Limited,
DK, One Embassy Gardens, 8 Viaduct Gardens,
London SW11 7BW

The authorised representative in the EEA is Dorling
Kindersley Verlag GmbH. Arnulfstr. 124, 80636 Munich, Germany.

A CIP catalogue record for this book is
available from the British Library.

ISBN: 978–0–2413–5873–3

Printed in China

For the curious
www.dk.com

CONTRIBUTORS

Clif Kussmaul is Principal Consultant at Green Mango Associates, LLC, where he designs and implements research projects, faculty development workshops, and classroom activities. Formerly, he taught for 20 years at college level and worked full and part time in software development and consulting. Craig was a Fulbright Specialist at Ashesi University and a Fulbright-Nehru Scholar at the University of Kerala. He has received multiple grants from the US National Science Foundation, Google, and other sources to support his work with Process Oriented Guided Inquiry Learning (POGIL), Free and Open Source Software (FOSS), and other topics in computer science education.

Sean McManus writes and co-writes inspiring coding books, including *Mission Python, Scratch Programming in Easy Steps, Cool Scratch Projects in Easy Steps,* and *Raspberry Pi For Dummies*.

Craig Steele is a specialist in computer science education who helps people develop digital skills in a fun and creative environment. He runs Digital Skills Education, and is a founder of CoderDojo in Scotland, which runs free coding clubs for young people. Craig has run digital workshops with the Raspberry Pi Foundation, Glasgow Science Centre, Glasgow School of Art, and the BBC micro:bit project.

Dr Claire Quigley studied Computing Science at Glasgow University, where she obtained a BSc and PhD. She has worked in the Computer Laboratory at Cambridge University and at Glasgow Science Centre. She is currently STEM Co-ordinator with Glasgow Life, and lectures part-time at the Royal Conservatoire of Scotland, working with BEd Music students. Claire has been involved in running CoderDojo Scotland since its initial session in 2012.

Dr Tammy Pirmann is a computer science professor at the College of Computing and Informatics at Drexel University in Philadelphia, Pennsylvania. She is an award-winning educator, recognized for her focus on equity in computer science education and for promoting guided inquiry in secondary computing education. She was the co-chair of the Computer Science Teachers Association's Standards Committee and an advisor on the K12 CS Framework.

Dr Martin Goodfellow is a Lecturer in the Computer and Information Sciences department at the University of Strathclyde. He has also developed educational computer science content and workshops for other organizations worldwide, including Google, Oracle, CoderDojo Scotland, Glasgow Life, Makeblock, and the BBC.

Jonathan Hogg is an audiovisual artist who has spent the last decade constructing works out of combinations of software, electronics, sound, light, wood, plastic, and metal. He often works with young people, running creative and technical workshops. Prior to art, Jonathan designed and developed software in the London finance industry. He began his career researching and teaching Computing at the University of Glasgow. The only constant in all of this has been Python.

David Krowitz learnt to program in the early 1980's on a Commodore VIC-20 plugged into a portable black-and-white TV set. He has been studying and practising computer programming ever since. Nowadays, Dave spends his time building microservice architecture for businesses, whilst expounding his love for object-oriented design patterns and software architecture. See dotpusher.com for more info.

CONTENTS

FOREWORD   10

About this book   12

INTRODUCTION

What is programming?   16

Coding in the real world   18

Working as a software developer   20

Programming languages   22

SCRATCH

What is Scratch?	**28**
Scratch interface	**30**
Sprites	**32**
Coloured blocks and scripts	**34**
Output using movement	**36**
Output using looks and sounds	**38**
Managing program flow	**40**
Manipulating data	**42**
Logic and decisions	**44**
Input	**46**
Sending messages	**48**
Using functions	**50**
PROJECT: Travel translator	**52**
PROJECT: Logic puzzle	**64**
PROJECT: Asteroid dodge	**80**

PYTHON®

What is Python?	**94**
Installing Python	**96**
Using IDLE	**98**
Variables in Python	**100**
Data in Python	**102**
Logic operators and branching	**104**
Input and output	**106**
Loops in Python	**108**
Functions	**112**
Libraries	**116**
PROJECT: Team allocator	**118**
Debugging	**130**
PROJECT: Project planner	**134**
Objects and classes	**156**
PROJECT: Budget manager	**158**
Pygame Zero	**176**
PROJECT: Knight's quest	**178**

WEB TECHNOLOGIES

How the Web works — 206

Code editors — 208

Exploring basic HTML — 210

HTML forms and hyperlinks — 212

Build a better website — 214

PROJECT: Build a web page — 216

Cascading Style Sheets — 234

CSS selectors — 236

CSS styling — 238

Responsive layouts — 240

PROJECT: Styling the web page — 242

What is JavaScript? — 264

Variables and data types — 266

Logic and branching — 270

Input and output — 272

Loops in JavaScript — 274

Functions in JavaScript — 278

JavaScript debugging — 280

Object-oriented JavaScript — 282

Libraries and frameworks — 284

Graphic user interfaces — 286

PROJECT: Animating the web page — 288

PROJECT: Responsive website — 304

Other programming languages — 344

GLOSSARY — 348

INDEX — 352

ACKNOWLEDGMENTS — 360

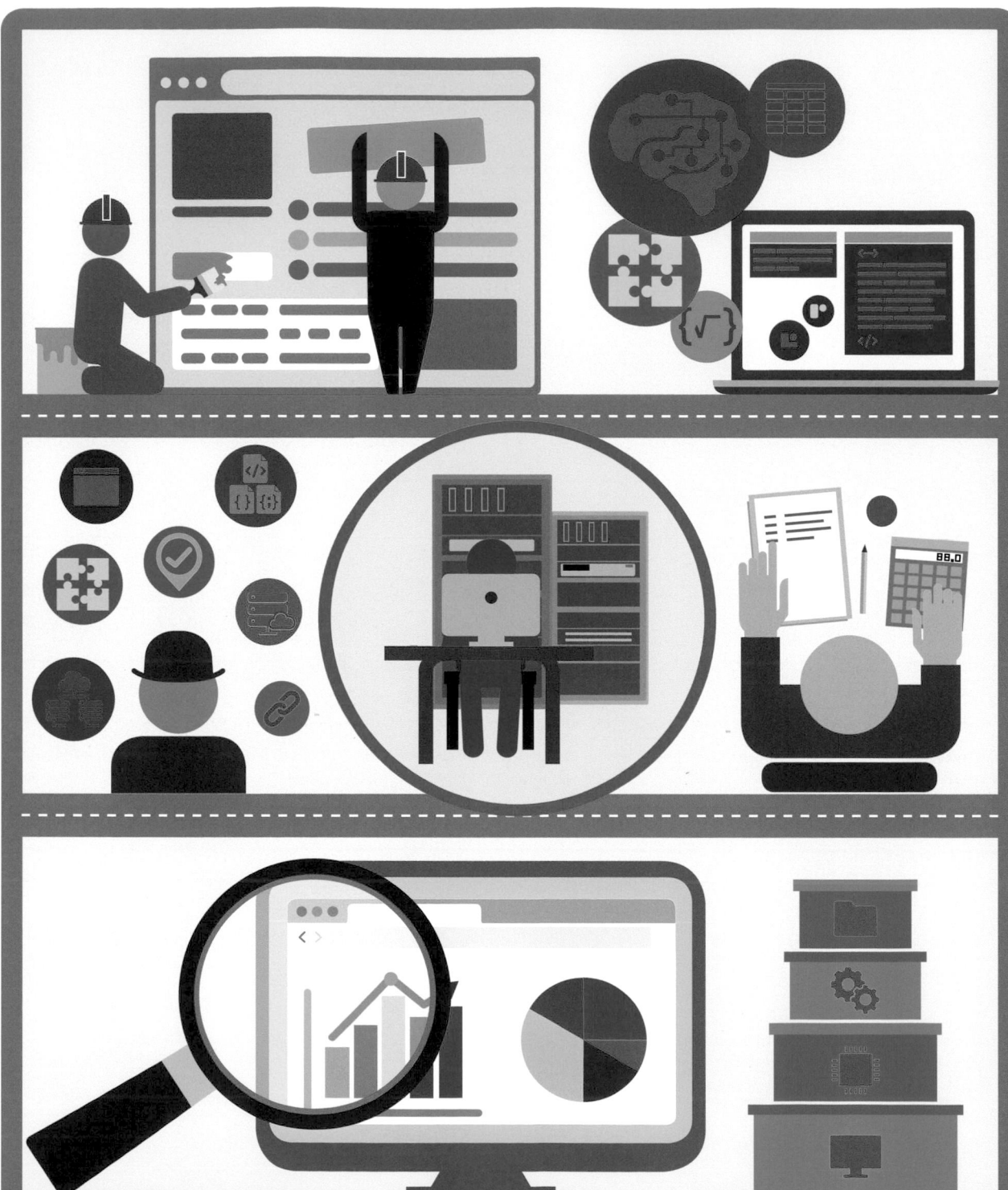

Foreword

If you've ever asked a teenager for help with your computer, you'll probably have felt the crushing weight of self-doubt as you realize you understood less than half of what they just said. That same "helpful teen" would most likely scoff at the idea of a book – made out of honest-to-goodness old-fashioned paper – on the subject of learning to code. "Just Google it, there are loads of tutorials on Youtube!" they might say.

But not everyone is high-bandwidth, multi-screen ready. Plus, when you are carefully stepping through the creation of your first lines of code, a physical page with your fingertip planted firmly on the next step can act as a valuable lifeline to the tangible world.

If you're reading this as a teenager yourself, congratulations on discovering life beyond YouTube! You're about to find out that the creators of this guide are exactly the kind of industry-defining professionals whose content channels, blogs, and social media posts you'd end up on if you did decide to Google "learning to code".

As a life-long gamer and computing enthusiast I've been reporting on technology for almost a quarter of a century. In that time, I've witnessed seismic changes in the way we interact with the world. A.I., big data, automation, e-commerce – all now intrinsic parts of our daily routines even if we aren't always aware of them.

Technology is no longer a niche topic. In fact, today, every industry could be considered a tech industry, which leads to a simple choice: get with it or get left behind.

Starting at the absolute beginning, this guide will introduce the jargon and tools you'll need to get programming in the most popular and versatile software languages. The pages are also peppered with interesting facts about coding and careers, together with step-by-step projects to get you going. Even if you decide not to become the next Mark Zuckerberg, the skills you'll learn will be a great asset when talking to technology professionals and will also help develop your own logic and problem-solving abilities.

It was an ancient Greek philosopher who first noted the irony "the only constant in life is change", and this has never been more true than in the world of computing. Maybe you're looking for a different career or want to learn a new skill to support a hobby or passion project? Or perhaps you just want to be able to talk to your tech-obsessed teenager in a language that will impress them!

For those curious about coding, this guide is full of straightforward information, in easily digestible bites, written by some of the leading educators and experts in their field. There is jargon, but it's jargon you'll understand as you get to it. Is learning about coding essential? No. Will it help you understand and feel more comfortable in the world we now live? I think so. Could it lead to a new and amazing career direction? Definitely, if that's what you want.

There is still a desperate shortage of technology professionals in the workforce. Opportunities exist, but they are not going to come looking for you unless you speak at least a bit of their language.

Kate Russell
Technology reporter, author, and gamer

About this book

How this book works

Divided into three chapters, this book teaches the fundamentals of five programming languages: Scratch, Python, HTML, CSS, and JavaScript; the last three are grouped under Web Technologies. The book defines the basic concepts of each programming language and builds on them with the help of detailed projects that you can try on your own.

Concepts

Each chapter contains the basic programming concepts of the language. These are explained with the help of practical code examples that you can try out to understand the concept better.

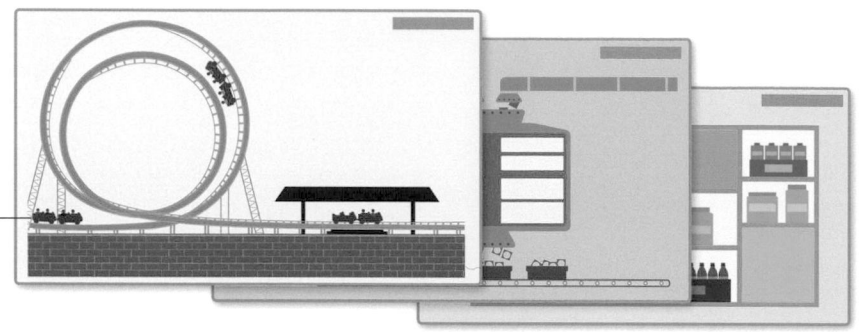

Illustrations help you understand and learn concepts

Projects

The projects in this book teach you how to create games, planners, apps, and websites. Each project starts with a brief overview of what you will learn in the project, how to plan the project, and what you will need to create it. Simple step-by-step instructions guide you through the project and explain every aspect of the code, with the help of detailed annotations.

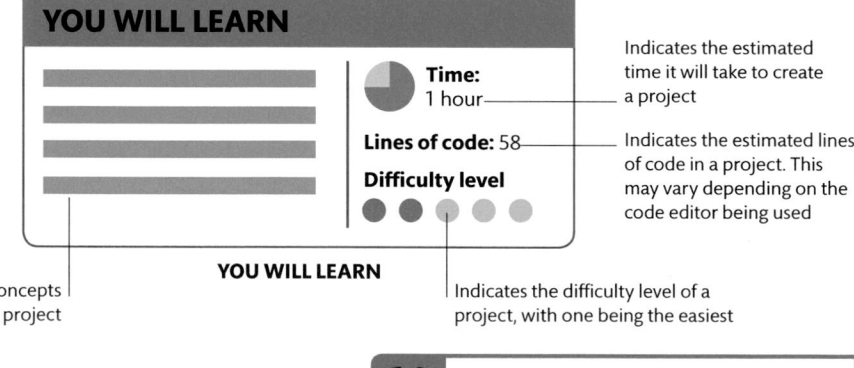

YOU WILL LEARN

Time: 1 hour

Lines of code: 58

Difficulty level

Indicates the estimated time it will take to create a project

Indicates the estimated lines of code in a project. This may vary depending on the code editor being used

YOU WILL LEARN

This box highlights the concepts being used in a project

Indicates the difficulty level of a project, with one being the easiest

Projects are broken down into smaller sections with clear steps to make learning easier

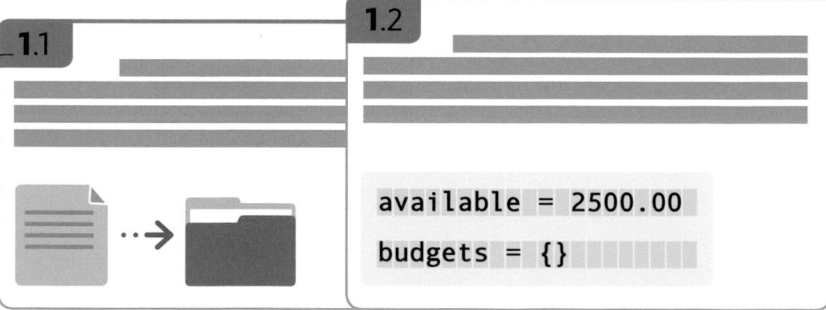

1.1

1.2

```
available = 2500.00
budgets = {}
```

STEP-BY-STEP

Hacks and tweaks

The "Hacks and tweaks" section at the end of each project provides tips on how to tweak existing bits of code, or add new functionalities to it.

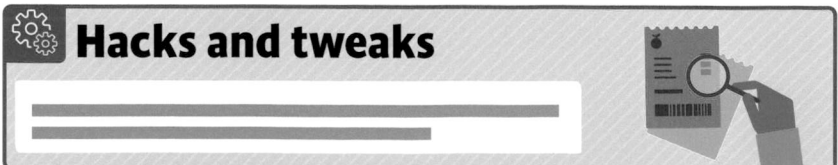

Hacks and tweaks

Coding elements in the book
Icons, colour-coded windows with grids, and flowcharts that explain the program structure help you work your way through the projects.

Icons
The "Save" icon will remind you to save the program at a particular point in the project. The "HTML", "CSS", and "JS" icons indicate which web file you need to write the code in.

SAVE **HTML** **CSS** **JS**

Python code windows
Python uses two different windows – the shell window and the editor window – for writing code. To differentiate between the two, this book uses different colours. This will help you know which window you should type the code in.

Each block of the grid represents a single space in the code

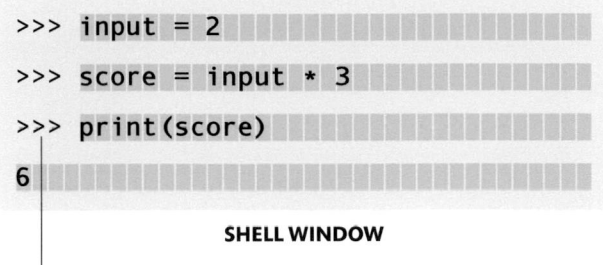

```
>>> input = 2
>>> score = input * 3
>>> print(score)
6
```

SHELL WINDOW

```
def reset_game():
    global score, charms
    score = 0
    charms = 0
```

EDITOR WINDOW

These chevrons appear only in the shell window. Type in the code at the >>> prompt

Every indent (spaces at the start of a line) equals four empty grid blocks. All subsequent indents will be in multiples of four

Web languages code window
The code for all the Web languages is written in green-coloured windows in this book. A special visual element, a turnover arrow, is used to indicate code being split over two lines. This element is not part of the actual code and has only been introduced in the book to help explain the flow of code in a block.

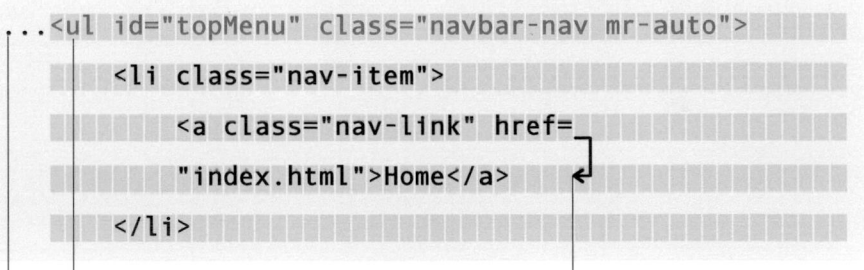

```
...<ul id="topMenu" class="navbar-nav mr-auto">
        <li class="nav-item">
            <a class="nav-link" href=
            "index.html">Home</a>
        </li>
```

CODE WINDOW FOR WEB LANGUAGES

In this book, ellipses are used at the start of a line of code to indicate an extended indent, usually more than eight grid blocks

Grey code indicates an existing line of code in the program. It is used to identify the line below or above which the new code must be added

The placement of the arrow indicates if a space needs to be added before it. In instances where there will be no space, no empty grid blocks are left between the arrow and the code

---

DK website for code
The resource pack for the projects in this book (except the "Hacks and tweaks" sections and the projects created in Scratch) have been hosted on **www.dk.com/coding-course**. This includes code in its original format (.py, .html, .css, .js) and images for all the games and websites.

www.dk.com/coding-course

Go to this url to download the Coding Course Resource Pack

INTRODUCTION

What is programming?

Computers and electronic devices need software (or programs) to tell them what to do. Programming, or coding, is the art of writing these instructions. Though some people are professional programmers, coding can also be a hobby.

Computer programs are everywhere

Programming is not just about conventional computer systems anymore. The world has become increasingly digital, and almost everything runs on software. Programs are now incorporated into devices such as mobile phones and tablets, labour-saving equipment around the home, and even in transportation systems.

BECOMING A CODER

After learning the basics of programming, these tips can be used to develop coding skills further.

- **Practice:** Write and experiment with code
- **Read code:** A lot can be learned by studying other people's programs
- **Learn multiple languages:** Learning the different ideas and concepts of other languages can help programmers choose the most suitable language for each project
- **Publish projects:** Putting work online and getting feedback on it from other coders helps you to write better code

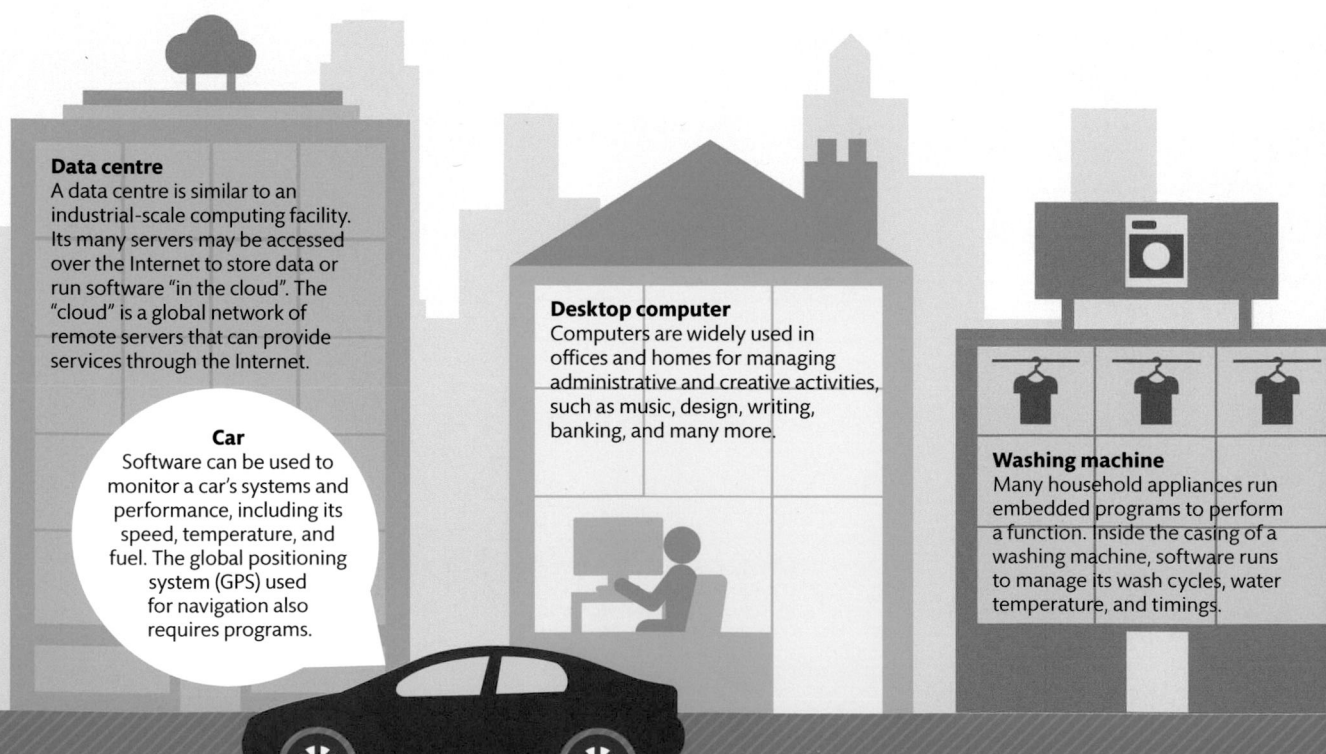

Data centre
A data centre is similar to an industrial-scale computing facility. Its many servers may be accessed over the Internet to store data or run software "in the cloud". The "cloud" is a global network of remote servers that can provide services through the Internet.

Car
Software can be used to monitor a car's systems and performance, including its speed, temperature, and fuel. The global positioning system (GPS) used for navigation also requires programs.

Desktop computer
Computers are widely used in offices and homes for managing administrative and creative activities, such as music, design, writing, banking, and many more.

Washing machine
Many household appliances run embedded programs to perform a function. Inside the casing of a washing machine, software runs to manage its wash cycles, water temperature, and timings.

What is a computer program?

A program is a set of instructions that a computer follows to perform a task. Programs can be extremely complex, and there can be several different layers of programs working together. Microsoft Windows, for example, is made up of millions of lines of instructions.

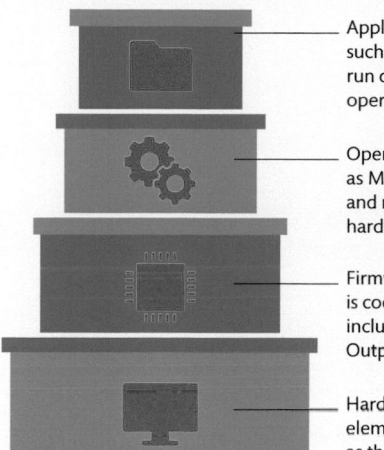

Applications software, such as word processors, run on top of the operating system

Operating systems, such as Microsoft Windows and macOS manage the hardware and software

Firmware is software that is coded into the hardware, including the Basic Input/ Output System (BIOS)

Hardware includes the physical elements of a computer, such as the monitor

Thinking like a computer

To write a program it is necessary to understand how a computer processes instructions. This means that tasks need to be broken down into smaller chunks so that the computer can understand the instructions. For example, a robot cannot simply be asked to "make some toast". It is necessary to program precise and detailed instructions for each step.

1. Open breadbin
2. Remove loaf
3. Open bag
4. Remove slice
5. Insert in toaster
6. Remove slice
7. Insert in toaster
8. Push down plunger
9. Wait until toast pops up

Instead of repeating the same instruction twice, it will be shorter and clearer to say "Do this twice: remove slice, insert in toaster" in a program

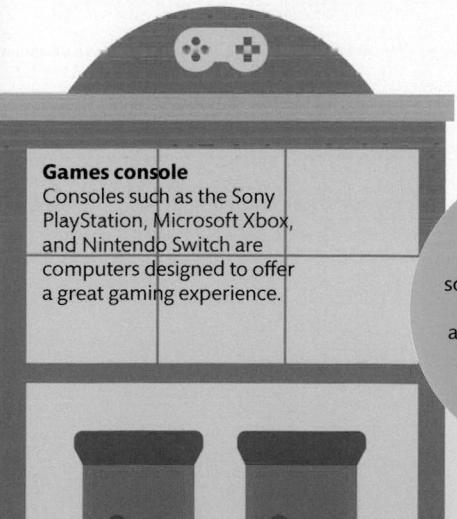

Games console
Consoles such as the Sony PlayStation, Microsoft Xbox, and Nintendo Switch are computers designed to offer a great gaming experience.

Camera
Modern cameras use software to change settings, capture images digitally, and enable users to review and delete photographs.

Factory equipment
Factories can be highly automated. Assembly line robots, planning and control systems, and quality-control cameras all require programs to operate.

Managers and office workers

Many businesses create and use specialized software. Software engineers develop complex software systems, but managers and office workers often write short programs to solve problems or automate tasks that might take hours or days by hand. For example, they might write code to query databases, format information, analyse data, control equipment, customize websites, or add features to word processors and spreadsheets. Some programming languages are specifically designed for these purposes (see pp.344–47).

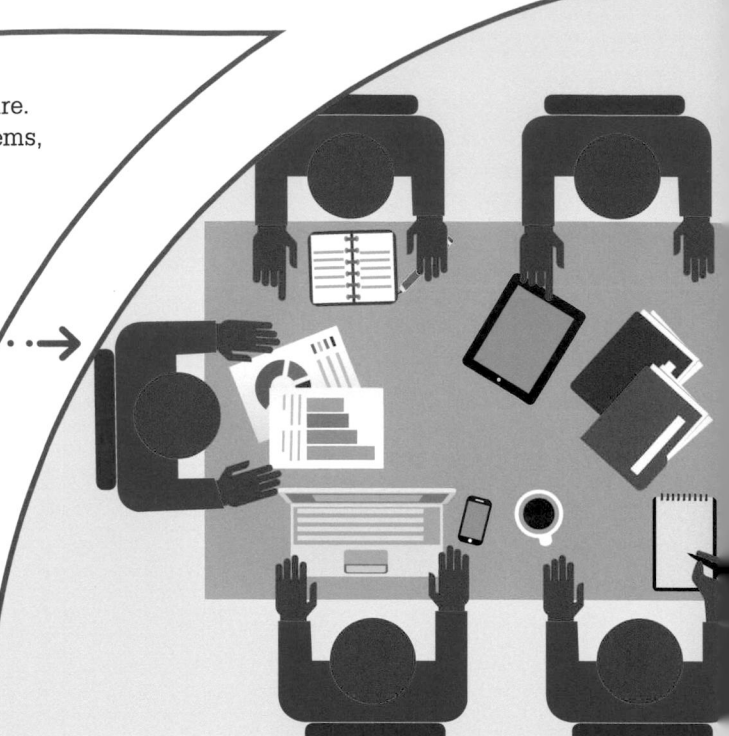

Artists and hobbyists

Coding can support many forms of creativity. Artists can create software to make music or visual art that changes as people interact with it. Hobbyists might create software for games, interactive stories, to direct simple robots, control lighting, or do tasks around the home.

Coding in the real world

Coding is used in nearly every aspect of modern life and work. Basic knowledge of coding helps people to use software more effectively, create simple programs, and communicate with other software developers.

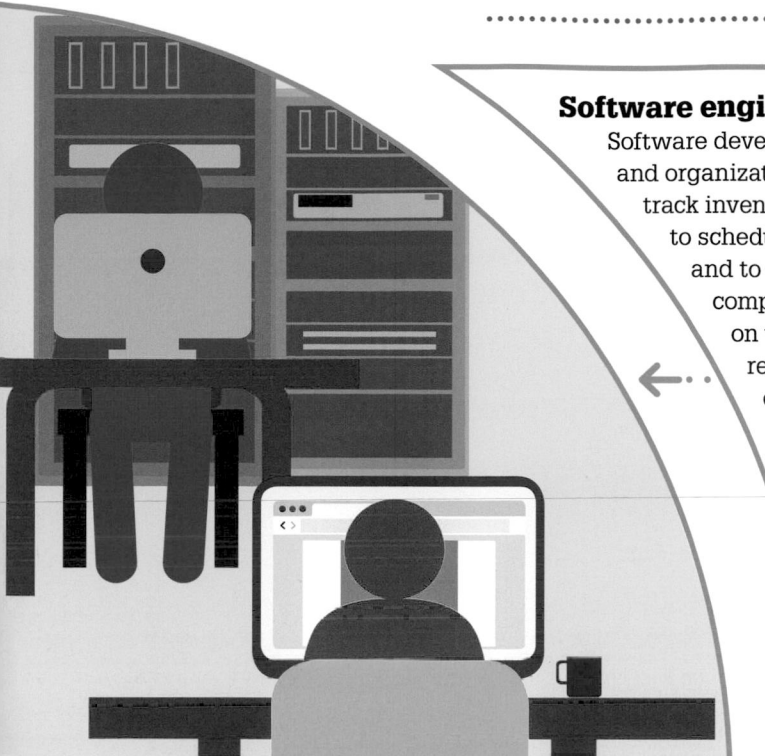

Software engineers and web developers

Software developers work for many different businesses and organizations. Businesses require software to track inventory and place orders with suppliers, to schedule employees and track work hours, and to send mailings to customers. Insurance companies use software to set pricing based on the number and cost of events, and to review and approve policies. Websites often combine existing programs with custom coding for special features. Software engineers play key roles in developing systems that suit a client's needs.

Scientists and researchers

Code can also be used to create experiments, analyse data, and create medical reports. For example, brain scientists might use software to display shapes or words to a patient, to record brain activity, and to analyse the data to learn what parts of the brain are most active.

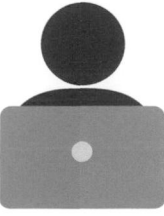

25,000,000
WORKERS ACROSS THE WORLD **ARE SOFTWARE DEVELOPERS**

Working as a software developer

Writing a simple program might seem straightforward, but it can be surprisingly difficult. Developing large, reliable software systems is even more complex, and requires teams of software developers with a variety of specialized skills and roles.

Analyse

In this phase, developers decide what the software must do. They might study existing systems, design new processes, or interview people to understand how they will use the system. This also defines other constraints or requirements. For example, how much data must the system handle, how quickly must it respond, and what should it do when problems occur? The resulting documents could range from a few pages to hundreds or more.

Test

Developers check whether the software works correctly, and fix any problems they find during the testing phase. This is often the longest and least predictable phase, and a common reason for delays and extra costs. There are many types of tests – unit tests check if individual functions are correct, functional tests check individual components, integration tests check if components work together, and system tests check the entire system.

Overview

Software development involves four phases: analyse, design and plan, build, and test. These phases, however, can be structured in a variety of ways. A waterfall model steps through each phase once, which seems simple, but often leads to problems. An iterative model cycles through the phases several times, building part of the system in each cycle. An agile model cycles through each phase many times, adding different features in each cycle.

Design and plan

In this phase, developers decide how the software will work and how it will be created. This can include deciding on which language to use, sketching user interfaces, designing databases, subdividing it into pieces, and specifying the files and even the individual functions to be created. Developers also need to estimate the time, effort, materials, and cost to create the system, and a schedule for who will do which tasks at what time.

Build

In the build phase developers create the software, including user interfaces, databases, code, and documentation for users and programmers. This means that coding is just one part of one phase of software development, and in some ways the easiest and most predictable. As each piece is built, developers might inspect or review the code to see how well it is written, and then integrate it into the larger system.

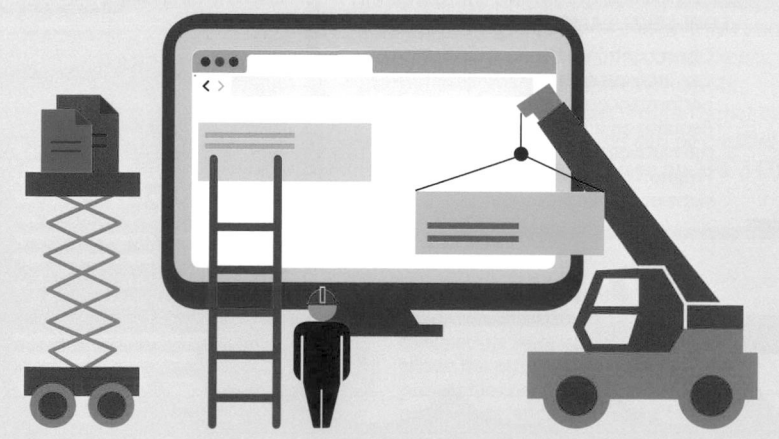

Types of programming language

Many different philosophies or paradigms have been used to design programming languages over the years. Since they are not mutually exclusive, programming languages often embody several core ideas. They can also be used in different ways depending on the programmer's preferred approach. Python, for example, can be used for both object-oriented and procedural programming. JavaScript can be used for event-driven and object-oriented programming. The best approach or the best programming language to use often depends on the programmer's preference. Below are some of the ways that programming languages can be defined and classified.

IMPERATIVE PROGRAMMING

These languages require a list of instructions for the computer to carry out. The programmer has to first work out how the task can be completed, and then provide step-by-step instructions to the computer. Imperative languages are common and include Python (see pp.94–95), C, C++, and Java.

```
user = input("What's your name? ")
print("Hello", user)
```

INPUT IN PYTHON

Python program to greet a user by name

```
What's your name? Sean
Hello Sean
```

OUTPUT IN PYTHON

DECLARATIVE PROGRAMMING

In declarative programming, programmers tell the computer what result they want, without needing to say how it will be achieved. In the Wolfram Language, for example, a word cloud based on the words in Wikipedia's Music page can be created using a single line. Other declarative languages include SQL, which is used for databases.

```
WordCloud[WikipediaData["music"]]
```

INPUT IN WOLFRAM

OUTPUT IN WOLFRAM

EVENT-DRIVEN PROGRAMMING

The event-driven programming concept is one where the program listens for certain things to happen, and then starts the appropriate program sequence when they do. For example, a program might react to user actions, sensor input, or messages from other computer systems. JavaScript (see pp.264–65) and Scratch (see pp.28–29), among others, can be used to write event-driven programs.

Creates a web page button

```
<input type="button" value="Click me!"
onClick="showMessage();">
```

Runs the **showMessage()** JavaScript instructions when the button is clicked

This icon has been used in the book to indicate code being split into two lines

CHOOSING A LANGUAGE

Sometimes, programmers' choice of language may be dictated by the hardware they are using, the team they are programming with, or the kind of application they want to create. Often, they will have a choice. Here are some popular languages that can be considered.

PYTHON

A flexible language, it emphasizes ease of understanding in the code.

SCRATCH

A great first programming language, Scratch is perfect for simple games.

JAVA

Widely used in financial services, small devices, and Android phones.

JAVASCRIPT

The language used by web pages for interactivity.

PROCEDURAL PROGRAMMING

This type of programming is based on functions, which contain reusable chunks of program. Functions can start other functions at any time, and can even start themselves again. They make programs easier to develop, test, and manage. Many popular programming languages, such as Java and Python (see pp.94–95) support procedural programming.

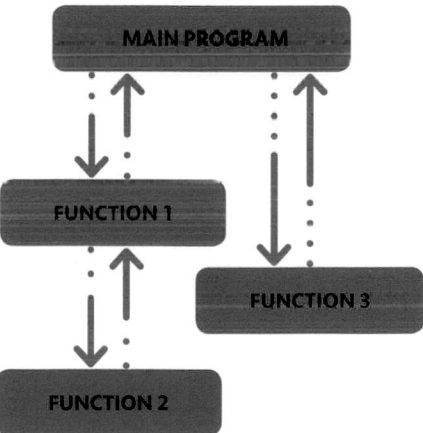

MAIN PROGRAM

FUNCTION 1

FUNCTION 3

FUNCTION 2

OBJECT-ORIENTED PROGRAMMING

In object-oriented programming, the idea is that data and the instructions related to it are stored together in "objects". Objects can interact with each other to achieve the program's objectives. The aim is to make code more modular, so it is easier to manage, and is more reusable. Many popular programming languages, such as C++, JavaScript, and Python support object-oriented programming.

OBJECT

Data for this object

Instructions for this object

Interfaces for communicating

VISUAL PROGRAMMING LANGUAGES

These languages make it easier to develop software using drag-and-drop interfaces, so a programmer can create software more quickly and with fewer errors. Visual Basic, for example, includes tools to design user interfaces visually. Scratch (see pp.28–29) is another highly visual language, often used to learn programming.

A Scratch program to react when a button is clicked

when this sprite clicked

say (Button was clicked!) for (2) seconds

SCRATCH

What is Scratch?

Scratch is a visual programming language that does not require users to type code. Instead, they build programs using coloured blocks that represent instructions. Scratch focuses on the creative aspect of coding, and allows users to create interactive games, stories, and other visual applications.

Features

Scratch has a number of features that make it an ideal programming language for beginners. The use of ready-made blocks of code sets it apart from most other programming languages.

Community
Scratch allows users to connect with others through a built-in Scratch community. Users can share their programs for others to play with, modify, and remix. They can also learn by studying others' projects.

Drag and drop
Scratch blocks can be dragged and dropped in the Code Area to build programs. There is very little typing, so users are less likely to make errors.

Powerful language
Scratch is easy to use, but includes core concepts used in professional coding languages. It therefore provides a good all-round introduction to programming.

Jigsaw design
Instruction blocks snap together like jigsaw pieces, so users cannot connect them in wrong ways. Nonsensical combinations are typically impossible, so errors in logic are minimized.

Learning to program with Scratch

Scratch was created by the Lifelong Kindergarten group at the Massachusetts Institute of Technology (MIT) in the US. It was first launched in 2007.

Scratch was designed to be fun and easy to use for beginners, and to help them understand basic concepts and avoid errors. It is therefore widely used in education. Scratch has a highly visual interface with coloured blocks of code that join together to form scripts, which can include images and sounds to create action on screen. Scratch provides a powerful platform (see pp.30–31) for exploring programming.

Built-in assets
Scratch comes with a pre-installed library of sounds and images (called sprites – see pp.32–33) that makes it easy to start coding right away. Other programming languages lack in this regard as images need to be created or uploaded before writing a program.

Colour coding
Instruction blocks for movement, sound, control, and sensing (among others) are colour coded, so they can be easily identified and read when creating a program.

Hardware support

The latest version of Scratch works on computers with Windows, macOS, and Linux. It can even be used on tablets. Scratch projects can use extensions to interact with hardware devices.

Raspberry Pi
Scratch can use a Raspberry Pi to connect to other sensors or motors.

micro:bit
Scratch can be used with a BBC micro:bit, which has a built-in LED display, buttons, and tilt sensors.

Lego®
Scratch can connect to Lego® WeDo and Lego® Mindstorms™ to work with motors, sensors, and robots.

Webcam
Scratch can access a webcam to layer images on a live video feed to create simple augmented reality applications.

GETTING SCRATCH

The Scratch developer environment is required for using Scratch. It can be accessed both online and offline.

In your browser
Visit the Scratch website at *https://scratch.mit.edu/* and click Join Scratch to create an account.

Offline
Scratch can be downloaded and used without an Internet connection at *https://scratch.mit.edu/download*.

Scratch interface

The screen layout, or interface, in Scratch can be used to build programs, edit them, and view the output in the same screen. The interface is divided into several sections, each serving a particular purpose. This book uses Scratch 3.0 – the latest version of Scratch.

Understanding the screen layout

The Scratch interface is divided into the following sections:

- **Blocks Palette:** This contains the instructions, or code blocks, required to build a program
- **Code Area:** The instruction blocks are assembled here to create a script
- **Stage:** Allows the user to interact with the program
- **Sprite List:** Displays and manages all the images, or sprites, used in a program
- **Stage Info:** Manages the background images

BLOCKS PALETTE
CODE AREA
STAGE
SPRITE LIST
STAGE INFO

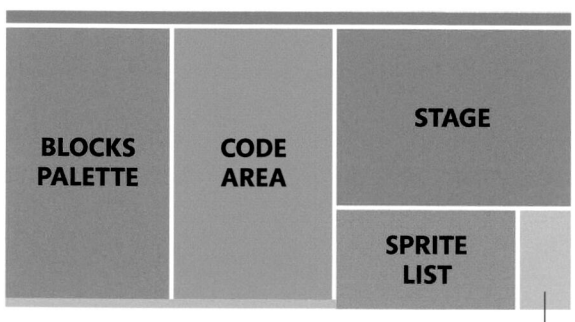

VERSIONS OF SCRATCH

There have been three versions of Scratch so far, each with a different screen layout. New features and instruction blocks were added at each update of the interface. These features may not work on earlier versions.

- **Scratch 1.4:** The interface was similar to Scratch 3.0, but the Code Area was called Scripts Area.
- **Scratch 2.0:** The Stage was on the left of the screen. Introduced sprite cloning and reorganized some blocks into the Events category.
- **Scratch 3.0:** Introduced Blocks Palette extensions, and moved the Pen blocks into them.

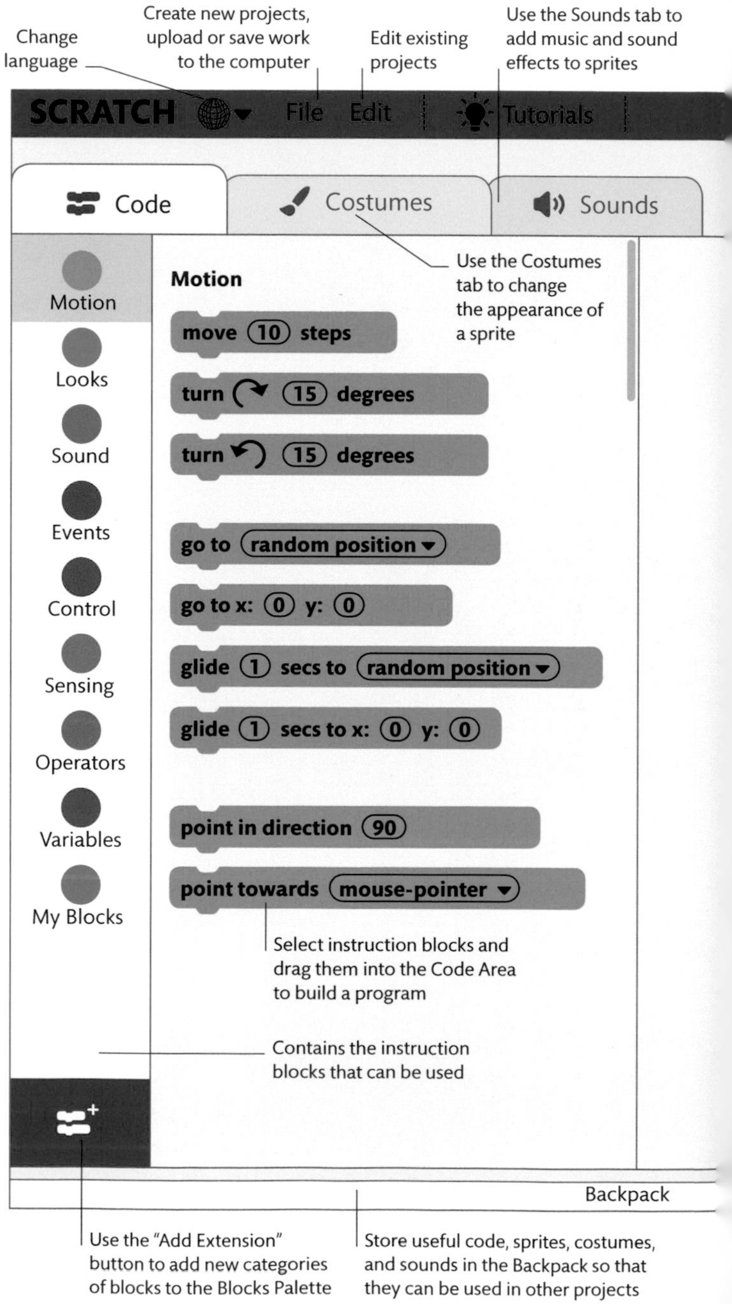

Change language
Create new projects, upload or save work to the computer
Edit existing projects
Use the Sounds tab to add music and sound effects to sprites
SCRATCH
File
Edit
Tutorials
Code
Costumes
Sounds
Use the Costumes tab to change the appearance of a sprite
Motion
Looks
Sound
Events
Control
Sensing
Operators
Variables
My Blocks
Motion
move 10 steps
turn 15 degrees
turn 15 degrees
go to random position
go to x: 0 y: 0
glide 1 secs to random position
glide 1 secs to x: 0 y: 0
point in direction 90
point towards mouse-pointer
Select instruction blocks and drag them into the Code Area to build a program
Contains the instruction blocks that can be used
Backpack
Use the "Add Extension" button to add new categories of blocks to the Blocks Palette
Store useful code, sprites, costumes, and sounds in the Backpack so that they can be used in other projects

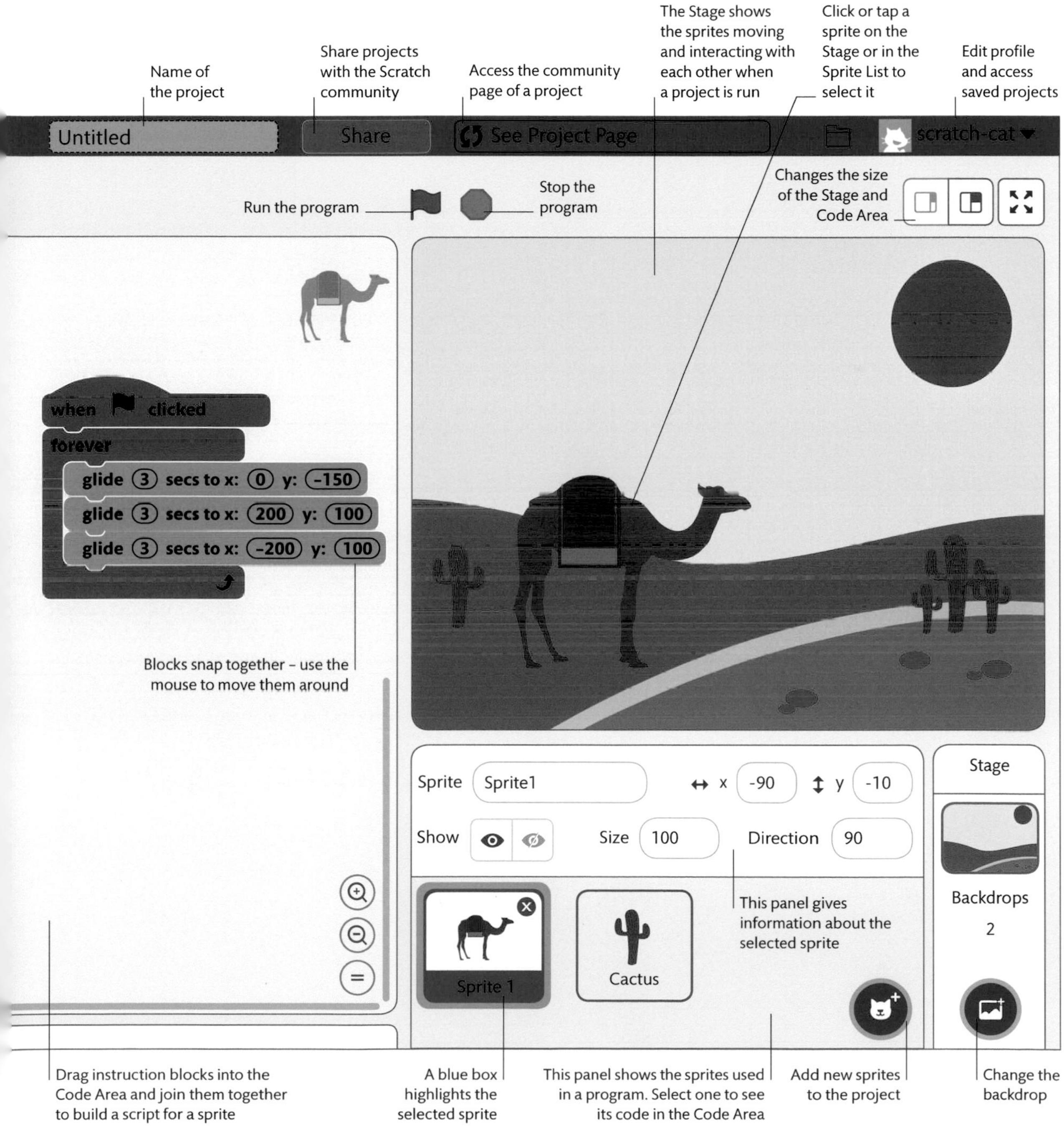

Name of
the project

Share projects
with the Scratch
community

Access the community
page of a project

The Stage shows
the sprites moving
and interacting with
each other when
a project is run

Click or tap a
sprite on the
Stage or in the
Sprite List to
select it

Edit profile
and access
saved projects

Untitled

Share

See Project Page

scratch-cat ▼

Run the program

Stop the
program

Changes the size
of the Stage and
Code Area

when ⚑ clicked

forever

glide 3 secs to x: 0 y: -150

glide 3 secs to x: 200 y: 100

glide 3 secs to x: -200 y: 100

Blocks snap together – use the
mouse to move them around

Sprite Sprite1   ↔ x -90   ↕ y -10

Show 👁 👁   Size 100   Direction 90

Stage

⊕
⊖
=

Sprite 1

Cactus

This panel gives
information about the
selected sprite

Backdrops
2

Drag instruction blocks into the
Code Area and join them together
to build a script for a sprite

A blue box
highlights the
selected sprite

This panel shows the sprites used
in a program. Select one to see
its code in the Code Area

Add new sprites
to the project

Change the
backdrop

Sprites

Sprites are the basic components of Scratch. Similar to characters in a video game, they can move around the Stage, change their appearance, and interact with other sprites. Each sprite uses one or more images and is controlled by scripts.

How do sprites work?

Most sprites have multiple images, called costumes, which can be used to animate them in a program. The Cat sprite, for example, has two costumes that show its legs in different positions. Switching between the costumes makes it look like the cat is walking on the Stage. Scratch comes with a preloaded library of sprites that can be used and modified in a program.

Default sprite
Every project starts with the Cat sprite. Delete it by clicking the "x" on its thumbnail in the Sprite List.

Creating a sprite

Scratch allows its users to add or create their own images. The Choose a Sprite button on the bottom right of the Sprite List reveals options to add, create, or upload sprites in a project.

Upload
Users can include their own images and upload them to the Scratch interface to be used as sprites. This includes images, such as photographs, which may be required to create or personalize games.

Surprise
Scratch also has an option to add a random sprite from the Sprite library. It can be a quick way to add sprites to experiment with, or to generate new game ideas.

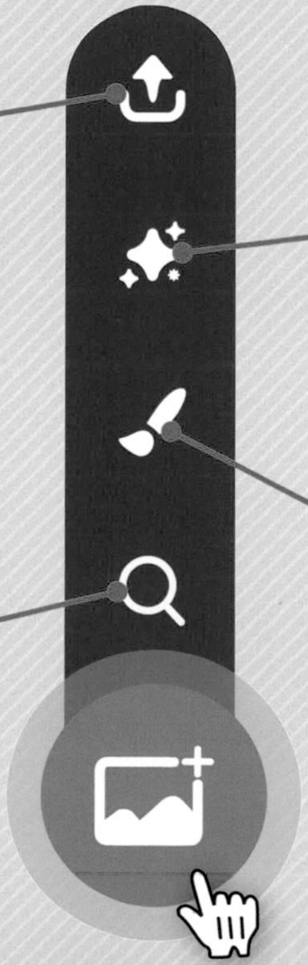

Choose a Sprite
Scratch contains a large library of sprites that can be used. The sprites are divided into categories such as Animals, People, and Fantasy. Hovering over a sprite in the library cycles through its costumes.

Paint
Users can create their own images in Scratch's Paint Editor (shown on the right). This editor is quite versatile and can be used to edit the costumes of existing sprites in the Sprite library.

Painting a sprite's costume

The Paint Editor in Scratch can be used to make new sprites or create additional costumes. By default, the editor uses the vector mode, which stores images as shapes and lines, making them easier to edit. The user can switch to the bitmap mode, which stores the colour of every bit in the image. The Paint Editor shown below is in the vector mode.

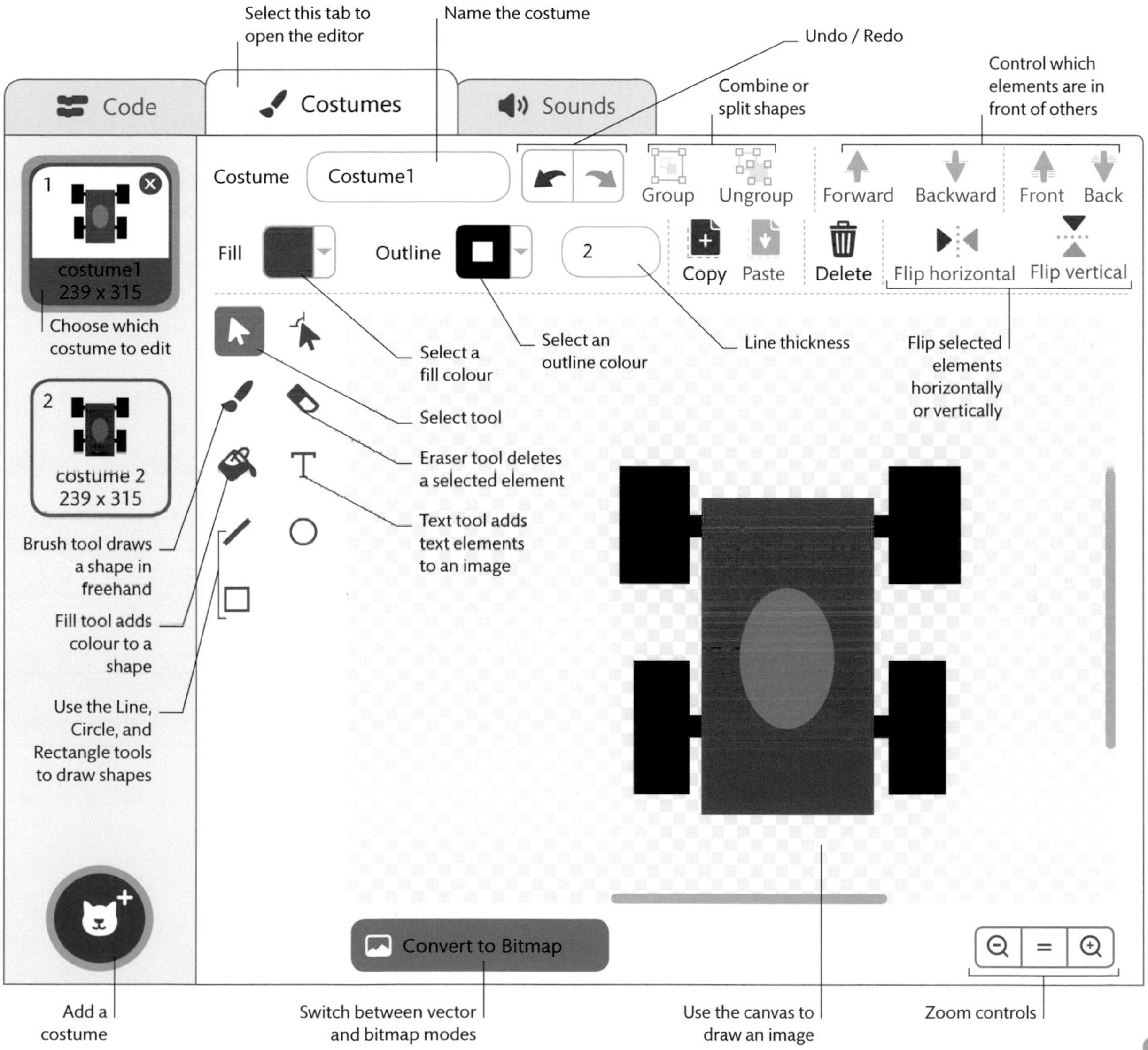

Select this tab to open the editor

Name the costume

Undo / Redo

Combine or split shapes

Control which elements are in front of others

Code   Costumes   Sounds

Costume   Costume1

Group   Ungroup   Forward   Backward   Front   Back

1
costume1
239 x 315

Choose which costume to edit

Fill   Outline   2

Copy   Paste   Delete   Flip horizontal   Flip vertical

2
costume 2
239 x 315

Brush tool draws a shape in freehand

Fill tool adds colour to a shape

Use the Line, Circle, and Rectangle tools to draw shapes

Select a fill colour

Select an outline colour

Select tool

Eraser tool deletes a selected element

Text tool adds text elements to an image

Line thickness

Flip selected elements horizontally or vertically

Add a costume

Convert to Bitmap

Switch between vector and bitmap modes

Use the canvas to draw an image

Zoom controls

Coloured blocks and scripts

Scratch instructions come in colour-coded blocks that can be assembled into chunks of program called "scripts". These blocks can be used for collecting input, processing information, and displaying the output on screen.

Program flow

A program can receive information (input), do something with it (process it), and then deliver the result (output). In a game, the input can be the player's key presses, and the output is the movement on screen. A program may receive input from users, other computer systems, or sensors. Output, on the other hand, can be given on the screen, by a printer, or by sending information to another system.

In Scratch, instructions in a program are built through code blocks. These instructions always run from top to bottom, unless told otherwise.

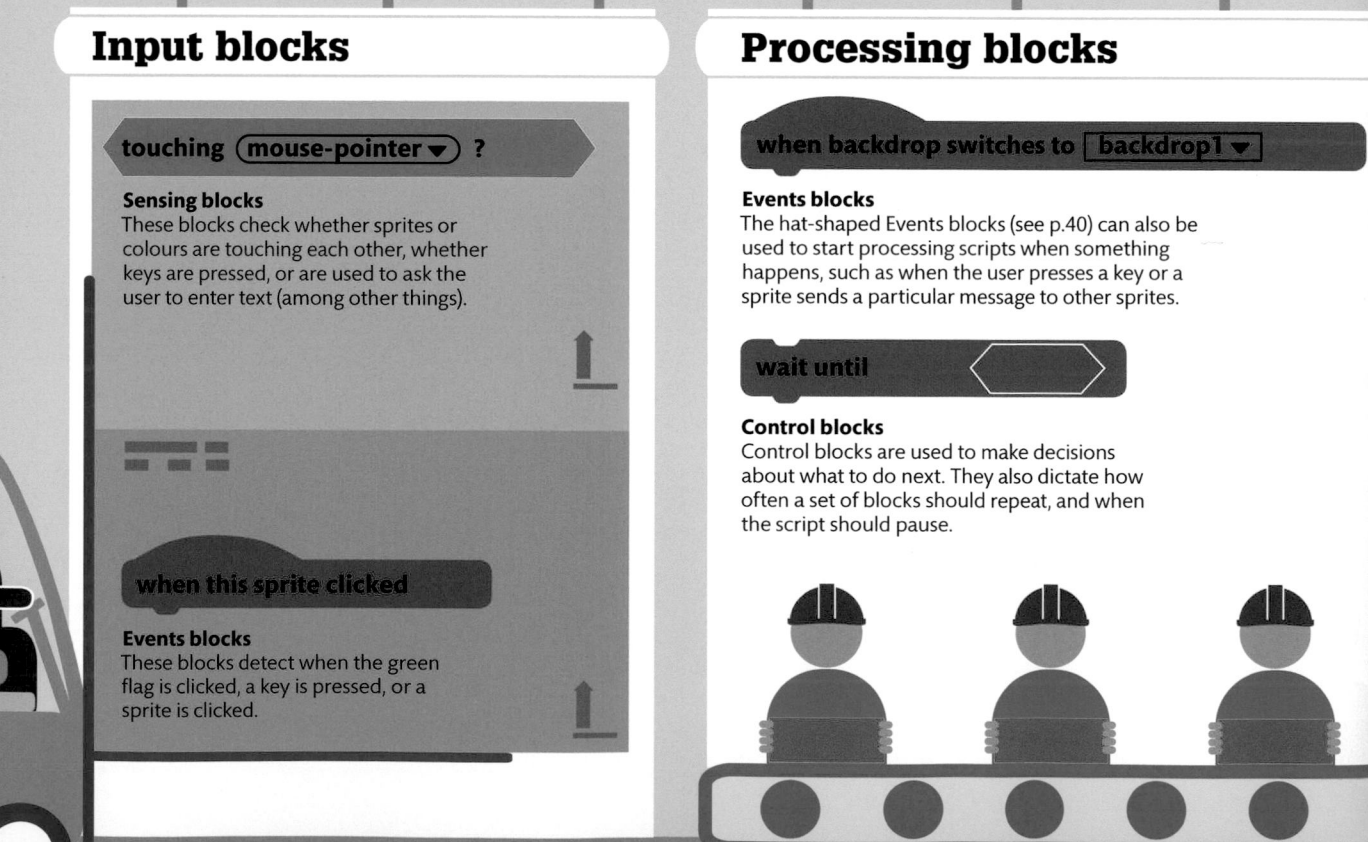

Input blocks

touching (mouse-pointer ▼) ?

Sensing blocks
These blocks check whether sprites or colours are touching each other, whether keys are pressed, or are used to ask the user to enter text (among other things).

when this sprite clicked

Events blocks
These blocks detect when the green flag is clicked, a key is pressed, or a sprite is clicked.

Processing blocks

when backdrop switches to [backdrop1 ▼]

Events blocks
The hat-shaped Events blocks (see p.40) can also be used to start processing scripts when something happens, such as when the user presses a key or a sprite sends a particular message to other sprites.

wait until

Control blocks
Control blocks are used to make decisions about what to do next. They also dictate how often a set of blocks should repeat, and when the script should pause.

Using the Blocks Palette

The Blocks Palette can be found on the extreme left of the Scratch interface. It contains nine different types of blocks and an "Add Extension" button that can be used to add more blocks to the palette. The blocks can be accessed by switching between the coloured categories and scrolling through the list of blocks that appear.

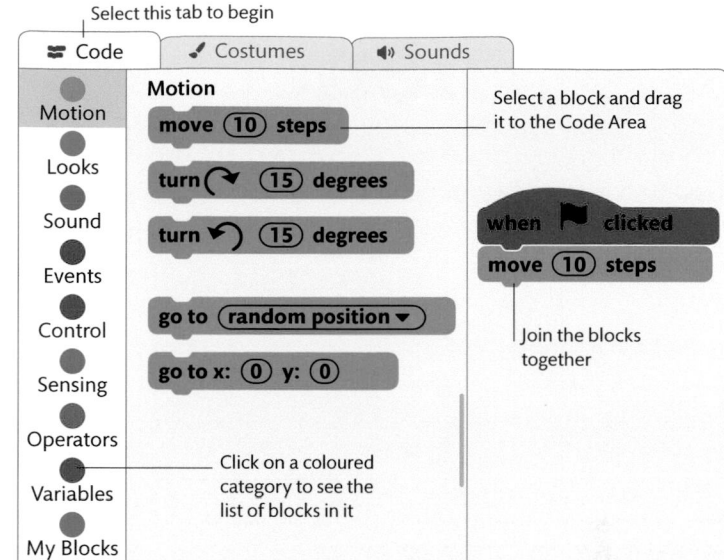

Select this tab to begin

Select a block and drag it to the Code Area

Join the blocks together

Click on a coloured category to see the list of blocks in it

Creating scripts

To create a script, click or press a block and drag it into the Code Area. Drop the block below another block and they will snap together to make a script. If the blocks fail to snap together, it means they cannot be used that way, or they are not close enough to attach.

Output blocks

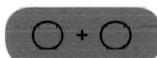

Operators blocks

These blocks are used for maths, and comparing numbers and pieces of text, as well as analysing text. They can also be used to generate random numbers, and are great for adding surprises to a game.

Variables blocks

Variables blocks are used to store information, such as the current score of a game. They can also be used to store text. Certain blocks in this category can increase or decrease a variable's number.

Motion blocks

Motion blocks display the output of a program by moving and controlling the sprites on the Stage.

Looks blocks

These blocks can alter a sprite's costume, change the background image, and display information in a speech bubble. They can also change a sprite's size and visibility, and apply special effects.

Sound blocks

Sound blocks are used to add sound effects to a program. They provide audio output by replaying recorded sounds.

Output using movement

Scratch is an ideal language for programming simple games and applications that move images around the screen. It has a set of blue Motion blocks that can be used to control a sprite's movement.

Coordinates

In Scratch, any position on the Stage can be pinpointed using the x and y coordinates. The x axis runs from -240 on the left to 240 on the right, and the y axis runs from -180 at the bottom to 180 at the top. When writing a program, coordinates can be used to place a sprite in a particular position.

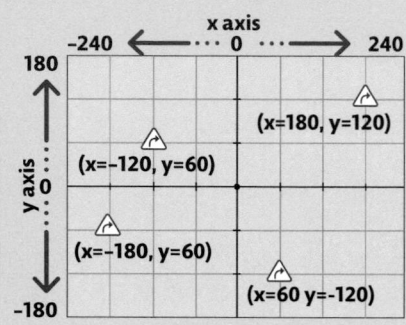

x and y grid
The Stage here has been marked with grid lines every 60 steps. Try these positions in the Motion blocks (below) for moving a sprite using coordinates.

Moving sprites using coordinates

These Motion blocks can be used to move a sprite to a particular position on the Stage using coordinates. The **go to x: y:** block and **set x to** and **set y to** blocks are often used to set a sprite's starting position.

---

go to x: (0) y: (0)

Set sprite position
Makes a sprite jump to a particular point on the Stage. The numbers in the block can be edited to choose different coordinates.

glide (1) secs to x: (0) y: (0)

Move sprite in given time
This block smoothly moves the sprite to a particular point. The time taken for this journey can be specified in the input area for seconds.

---

change x by (10)

Alter x position
Changes the x position by the number in the block, without changing the y position. It is used to move a sprite sideways.

set x to (0)

Change x position
Moves the sprite to a particular x position, without changing its y position. The sprite will jump straight there.

change y by (10)

Alter y position
Changes the y position by the specified number, without changing the x position.

---

set y to (0)

Change y position
Moves the sprite to a particular y position, without changing its x position. As with the similar x block, the sprite jumps straight there.

x position

Show x position
This block does not move a sprite, but shows the sprite's x position when clicked. Drop it into other blocks to use this coordinate in a script.

y position

Show y position
Does not move a sprite, but shows its y position. It can also be used with other blocks. For example, a sprite can be made to say its y position (see p.38).

Moving sprites using directions

Scratch calls each position on the Stage a step. A sprite can be moved by pointing it in a particular direction and then making it walk forwards. The direction 90 degrees will make a sprite face right. This is the default direction for most sprites.

move (10) steps

Move sprite
This block moves the sprite 10 steps across the Stage. However, since this is just one movement, the sprite will appear to jump, not walk.

turn ↺ (15) degrees

Rotate sprite anticlockwise
This block changes the sprite's direction by 15 degrees the other way. The value in the degrees input can be changed by the user.

turn ↻ (15) degrees

Rotate sprite clockwise
Changes the sprite's direction by 15 degrees clockwise. As with all blocks with input areas, the number of degrees can be changed as required.

point in direction (90)

Change sprite's direction
Sets the sprite's direction to a specific number. The direction numbers are measured from 0 at the top to 180 going clockwise, and -180 going anticlockwise.

Drawing with pen blocks

Each sprite has a pen, which it can use to draw a line as it moves around the Stage. The thickness (or size) and colour of the line can be changed as required. The **pen down** block is used to draw, while the **pen up** block turns off the pen. The Pen blocks are an extension in Scratch 3.0. They can be found under the Add Extension section of the Blocks Palette.

Stops the sprite drawing as it moves to the start position

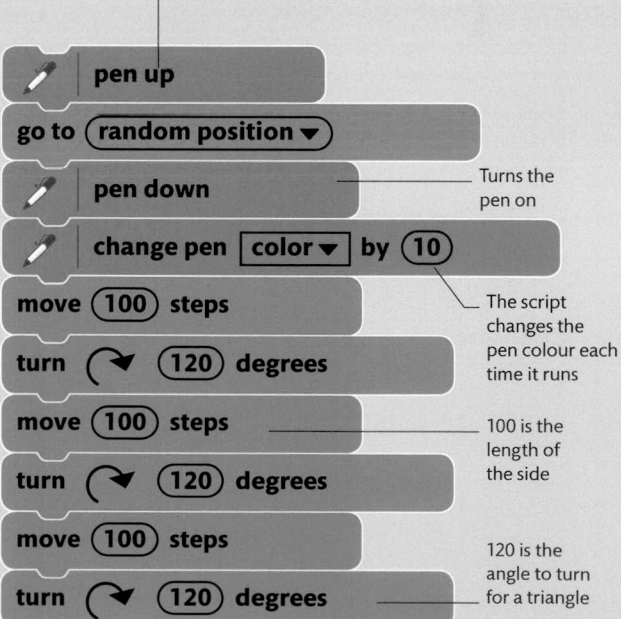

Turns the pen on

The script changes the pen colour each time it runs

100 is the length of the side

120 is the angle to turn for a triangle

Drawing a triangle
Try this script to draw a triangle using the pen and movement blocks. Click on the script to run it. The **erase all** block in the Blocks Palette can be used to wipe the Stage.

Output using looks and sounds

In a game, sprites often mutate or play sound effects to tell players what is going on. Changing a sprite's appearance or playing sounds can be useful in other programs as well. It can be used to warn users or get their attention to look at something important.

Displaying messages

In Scratch, sprites can display messages through speech and thought bubbles. These are created using the **say** and **think** blocks from the Looks section of the Blocks Palette. The holes in these blocks can be used to change the message to be displayed, or to drop another round-ended block in it.

Speech bubble
This block displays a speech bubble containing "Hello!" until a new **say** or **think** block is used.

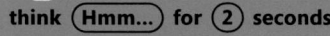

Timed speech bubble
Using this block, a message can be displayed for two seconds before it disappears. Both the message and its duration can be changed.

think (Hmm...)

Thought bubble
This block uses a thought bubble to display a message until a new **say** or **think** block is used.

think (Hmm...) for (2) seconds

Timed thought bubble
This displays a thought bubble that disappears after two seconds. Again, it is possible to change both the message and its duration.

Changing a sprite's appearance

The Looks blocks can be used to show a sprite's reaction to a game event by giving it special effects. They can also help to display a message. There are even blocks to make a sprite visible or invisible on the Stage.

clear graphic effects

Remove effects
In Scratch, each sprite can have its own special effects. This block removes all special effects applied to a sprite.

switch costume to (costume1 ▼)

Change costume
This block changes a sprite's costume to a particular image. The menu can be used to choose which costume to display.

set size to (100) %

Change size
Makes the sprite's size a particular percentage, considering its default size to be at 100 per cent.

hide

Hide sprite
Makes a sprite invisible on the Stage. It can still move around using the Motion blocks.

next costume

Show next costume
Useful for animation, it switches to a sprite's next costume or goes back to the first one, depending on the sprite's current costume.

change (color ▼) **effect by** (25)

Change effect
Increases (or decreases) a special effect using a positive (or negative) number. Both the number and special effect can be changed.

show

Show sprite
Makes a sprite visible on the Stage if it has previously been made invisible with the hide block.

change size by (10)

Alter size
Changes the sprite's size by the percentage entered in the block. Using a negative number shrinks the sprite.

set (color ▼) **effect to** (0)

Set effect
Used to give special effects a particular value, no matter what the current value is. Used with 0, this turns off the effect.

MUSIC BLOCKS

The Music blocks in Scratch are an extension, and need to be added using the Add Extension button on the bottom left of the Blocks Palette. They make it possible for programmers to use blocks to play musical notes. It is not necessary to know the number for each note, since clicking the hole for the note number will display a piano keyboard to help enter the required music.

Scratch's **set instrument** block has 21 built-in instruments

```
set tempo to (120)
set instrument to ((20) Synth Lead ▼)
play note (60) for (0.25) beats
play note (62) for (0.25) beats
play note (64) for (0.25) beats
play note (62) for (0.25) beats
play note (67) for (1) beats
```

Playing sounds

Sounds are a great way to provide feedback in a game or as an alert in a program. Before a sound can be used, it has to be added to the sprite from the **Choose a Sound** button under the Sounds tab. Programmers can either use a sound from the Scratch Sound library, or can record or upload a sound of their own.

```
play sound (Meow ▼) until done
```

Pause script to play sound
Sets a sound to play, and then pauses the script until it is finished. The menu in the block can be used to choose a different sound.

```
start sound (Meow ▼)
```

Play sound in background
Starts playing a sound, but does not pause the script. The sound plays in the background while the script runs.

```
stop all sounds
```

Stop all sounds
This block stops all the sounds, no matter which sprite started them, or how many sounds are playing.

```
change | pitch ▼ effect by (10)
```

Alter pitch
Changes the pitch of a sound effect. Positive numbers make the pitch higher and negative ones make it lower. The stereo setting can be adjusted as well.

```
set | pitch ▼ effect to (100)
```

Reset pitch
Resets the pitch or changes it to a value specified by the programmer. It can also be used to adjust the stereo left/right setting.

```
clear sound effects
```

Remove sound effects
This block resets all of the sound effects previously applied to sprites or backdrops.

Managing program flow

When writing code, programmers not only have to tell the computer what to do, but also when to do it. In Scratch, the Control and Events blocks are used to manage when an instruction is carried out.

Event-driven programming

In event-driven programming, the program's actions are started by events, such as user input, sensor input (see pp.46–47), or messages sent by other programs or parts of the program. The Events section of the Blocks Palette contains blocks that can start scripts when something happens. Also called hat blocks due to their shape, these Events blocks provide many more ways to start scripts than simply clicking on them.

Use green flag to start
Provides an easy way for users to start the program. Copies of this block can be used to start multiple scripts simultaneously.

Use mouse click to start
This block starts the attached script when the sprite is clicked. It is ideal for creating on-screen buttons for users to click on.

Use sounds to start
When the microphone detects a volume more than 10 (on a scale of 0 to 100), the script can be activated.

Use message to start
Scripts can send messages to each other (see pp.48–49). This block starts a script when a particular message is received.

Use key press to start
Starts a script when a key is pressed. The menu in the block can be used to select the required key.

Use background to start
This block is particularly useful in story-based projects. It enables scripts to start when the scene (or background image) changes.

Making a clickable drum

This example uses an Events block to make a simple clickable drum. When the drum is clicked or tapped on the Stage, the script plays a sound and briefly changes the image (or costume) to show that it is playing.

2 **Add the script**
Select the Code tab and add the following script to the Drum Kit sprite. The sprite already has the required sound. Click the sprite on the Stage to hear it play, and see its playing costume for half a second.

The blue highlight indicates this is the selected sprite

1 **Add the Drum Kit sprite**
Hover over the Choose a Sprite icon in the Sprite List and select the magnifying glass to see the library. Sprites are listed alphabetically. Scroll down to find the Drum Kit sprite and click or tap on it to add it.

Drum Kit

This costume indicates that the Drum Kit is playing

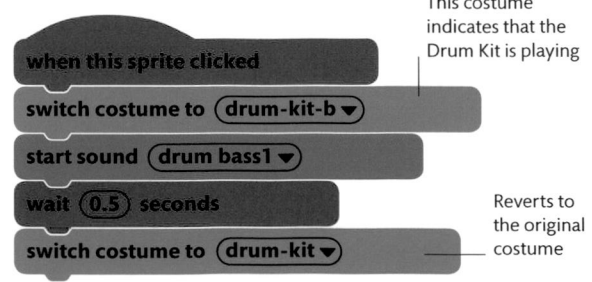

Reverts to the original costume

Using loops to repeat

A loop is a part of a program that needs to be repeated. In Scratch, these blocks are placed within the bracket of a **repeat** block, so that Scratch knows where the repeating section starts and ends. The bracket automatically stretches to make room for longer sets of instructions.

Repeating forever

Sometimes a program needs to repeat forever, until explicitly stopped. For example, a simple animation or game can play indefinitely. The **forever** block repeats a set of instructions without ending. This block has no nub to join other blocks underneath it, since it never ends. To end the script, click the red Stop button. A **stop all** block may also be used to stop the script.

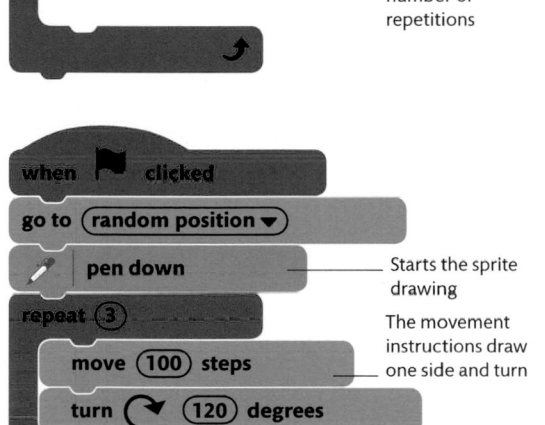

It is possible to change the number of repetitions

Starts the sprite drawing

The movement instructions draw one side and turn

This marks the end of the repeating section

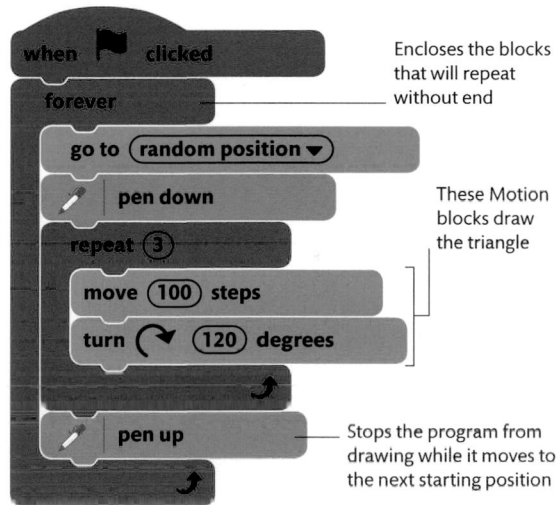

Encloses the blocks that will repeat without end

These Motion blocks draw the triangle

Stops the program from drawing while it moves to the next starting position

Drawing a triangle
In the previous example of drawing a triangle (see p.37), three copies of the instructions for moving and turning were added. The script above, however, uses a loop, which is much easier to read and write.

Drawing infinite triangles
This script will draw triangles in random positions forever. As shown above, a repeat loop can be placed within a forever loop. A loop inside a loop is called a nested loop.

INTRODUCING DELAY

It is not always desirable to have a program run as fast as possible. In many cases, a program may need to be slowed down so that users can easily see what is going on and have time to respond. Games are often artificially slowed down in order to ensure that players can keep up.

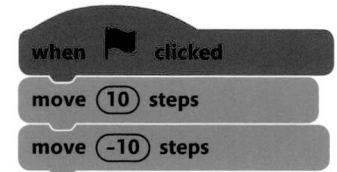

Normal movement
In this example, the program runs so fast that the sprite's movements are not visible. Nothing seems to happen.

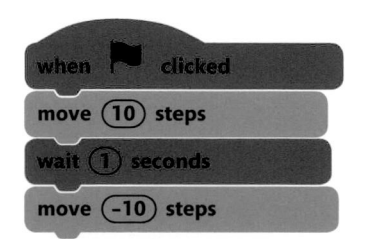

Delayed movement
Introducing a **wait** block makes it possible to see the sprite move from right to left and back again.

Manipulating data

Programs are often used to manage and process data. This data is either provided by the user or collected from other computer systems. In Scratch, the Operator blocks are used to manipulate numbers and text stored in variables.

Variables

Many programming languages use variables to store information. A variable can store one piece of information, either text or a number. In a game, for example, two variables might be used to store the player's name and score.

1 **Make a variable**
To create a variable in Scratch, select Variables in the Blocks Palette and click on the Make a Variable button. Give the new variable a meaningful name, such as score, so that the code is easy to understand. Usually, variables need to be created for all sprites, which means that all sprites can see and change the variable.

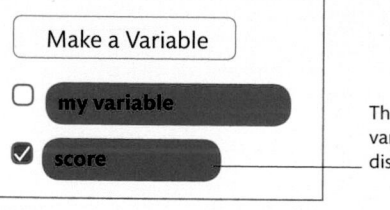

The new variable will be displayed here

2 **Use blocks with your variable**
Use the **set [variable name]** block to reset the variable's value. For example, **set score to 0**. The **change [variable name] by** block can be used to increase or decrease the value.

 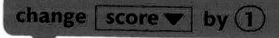

Strings

Programmers often call a piece of text in a program a "string". For example, a string can be a name, an answer to a question, or an entire sentence. In Scratch, any variable can store a number or a string, and it can store different values at different times.

`join (apple) (banana)`

Join strings
This block can be used to join two strings. The strings are joined without a space, so the result for this example will be "applebanana". Variable blocks can also be used in place of words typed into the block.

`letter (1) of apple`

Extract letters
This block extracts one letter from a string. In this example, the first letter of the string "apple" is extracted.

`length of (apple)`

Count a string
The number of characters in a string can be counted using this block. The result for the block can be viewed by clicking on it. It can also be dropped into other blocks to use in a script.

`(apple) contains (a) ?`

Check strings
This block checks whether the second string input is in the first one, and gives the answer as true or false. It is also possible to check for more than one letter: **apple contains app?**

LISTS

A list is used to store similar pieces of information, such as a list of names. In Scratch, a list can be created from the Variables section of the Blocks Palette. List positions are used for inserting and deleting items. For example, the **delete 2 of [list name]** block can be used to remove the second item from a list.

Numbers

Operator blocks are a core part of Scratch, and can be used for arithmetic operations, comparisons, and to pick random numbers. Some operator blocks even work with strings.

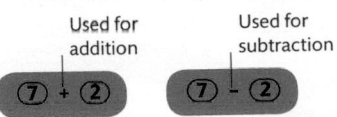

Used for addition — `(7) + (2)`

Used for subtraction — `(7) - (2)`

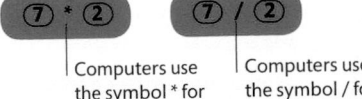

`(7) * (2)`

Computers use the symbol * for multiplication

`(7) / (2)`

Computers use the symbol / for division

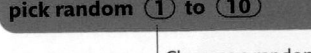

`pick random (1) to (10)`

Chooses a random number between 1 and 10

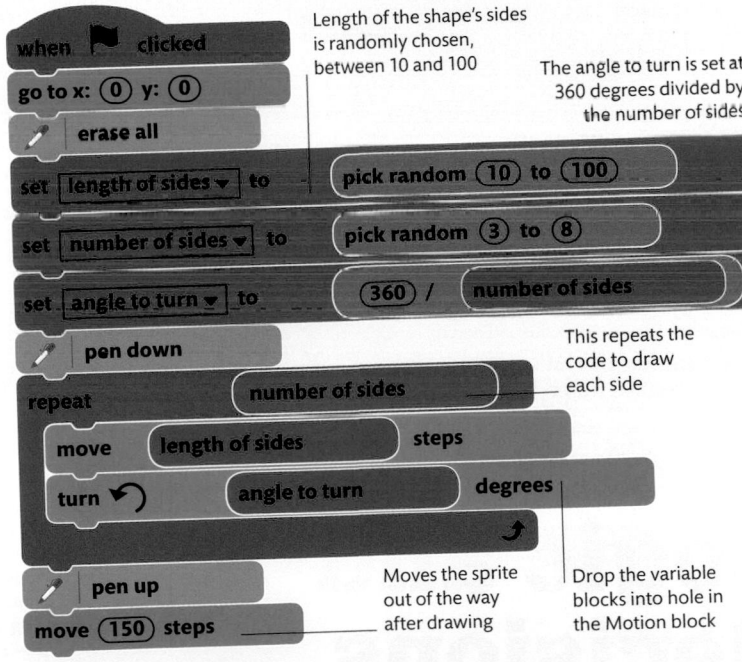

```
when 🏁 clicked
go to x: (0) y: (0)
🖊 erase all
set  length of sides ▼  to  pick random (10) to (100)
set  number of sides ▼  to  pick random (3) to (8)
set  angle to turn ▼  to  (360) / number of sides
🖊 pen down
repeat          number of sides
    move    length of sides      steps
    turn ↺       angle to turn       degrees
🖊 pen up
move (150) steps
```

Length of the shape's sides is randomly chosen, between 10 and 100

The angle to turn is set at 360 degrees divided by the number of sides

This repeats the code to draw each side

Moves the sprite out of the way after drawing

Drop the variable blocks into hole in the Motion block

Drawing random shapes

The program above draws a random shape each time the green flag is clicked. Start by making the variables **length of sides**, **number of sides**, and **angle to turn**. Click the green flag several times to create random art.

Sending messages

One of the ways that programs, or parts of a program, can interact with each other is by sending messages. Scratch has a dedicated Events block – the broadcast block – for this purpose.

Understanding broadcasts

Broadcast blocks make it possible to send a message from a script that can be seen by all other scripts for all other sprites in a program. Scripts can be set to start when they receive the broadcast message, either for the same sprite (see p.47), or for different sprites. The **when I receive** block is triggered in response to an incoming message, while the **broadcast** block allows sprites to send messages to other sprites.

1. All sprites listen for any broadcasts all the time

Using broadcasts

In Scratch, a single broadcast can trigger multiple sprites to run their scripts. In the example below, when the Speaker sprite is clicked, it starts playing music and also broadcasts a message. This message then triggers the other sprites. When the music ends, another message is sent, which makes the Ballerina sprite stop dancing.

1 **Add new sprites**
Start a new project and delete the default Cat sprite. Then choose the Ballerina, Butterfly 2, and Speaker sprites from the library. Click the Choose a Sprite icon and use the Search box in the Sprite library to find them.

Ballerina

Butterfly 2

Speaker

2 **Send the broadcast**
Click Speaker in the Sprite List and add the following script to it. Find the broadcast blocks in the Events section of the Blocks Palette and click the menu to enter a new broadcast message.

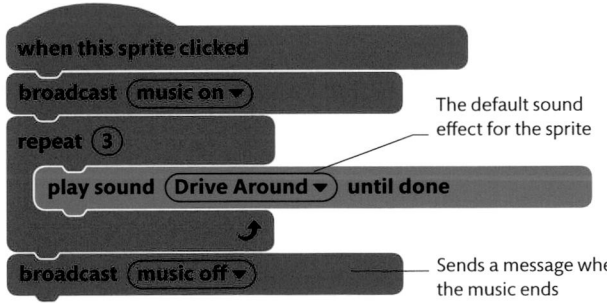

The default sound effect for the sprite

Sends a message when the music ends

3 **Trigger the Butterfly 2 sprite**
Next, click and drag the Butterfly 2 sprite on the Stage to move it away from the speaker. Add this script to Butterfly 2. When it receives the message indicating the music has started, the butterfly will fly towards the speaker.

Moves the Butterfly sprite to the Speaker

2. When one sprite sends a broadcast, it is picked up by any sprite that may be listening for that message

3. The sprites can use that incoming message to start their own scripts

SENSIBLE MESSAGES

The default name for a broadcast message in Scratch is **message1**, but this can be renamed by the user. To make a program easier to understand, it is advisable to change the message to something relevant. The menu in the broadcast blocks can be used to choose a new message name.

4 **Trigger the Ballerina sprite**
Select the Ballerina sprite in the Sprite List and add these two scripts. A variable is used to store whether the Ballerina should be dancing or not. When the music begins, this variable is set to "yes" and the ballerina starts dancing. The dance moves repeat until the dancing variable is set to "no". This happens when the Speaker broadcasts the "music off" message. The outcome is that the ballerina starts dancing when the music starts, and stops when it ends.

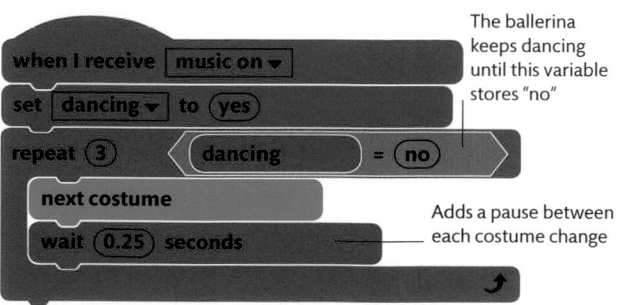

The ballerina keeps dancing until this variable stores "no"

Adds a pause between each costume change

When the music stops, the variable is set to "no"

WHY BROADCAST?

Broadcasts can be used for several purposes in Scratch programs. Here are some of the most popular uses of broadcasting:

• **Synchronization:** Broadcasts can be used to trigger several scripts across several sprites to start at the same time, so that they can be synchronized as a group.
• **Making other sprites move:** Though a sprite can only move itself, it can also tell other sprites when it is time for them to move. For example, clicking the Speaker sprite also triggers the other sprites to move.
• **Enforcing a sequence:** It is possible to make sure scripts run in the right order by using broadcasts to trigger them. The **broadcast and wait** block sends a message, but the script does not continue until every script that receives the message is finished.

Using functions

A function is part of a program that performs a particular task and can be reused. Functions make code easier to read, write, and test. In Scratch, each block is a function, and users can define new blocks.

How the program flows

When a script is run, Scratch carries out one instruction block at a time, from top to bottom. When the instruction is a function, Scratch remembers its place in the script, and switches to run the instructions in the function. When the function ends, Scratch picks up the main script where it left off. Functions can be used by multiple scripts, and can accept information for processing.

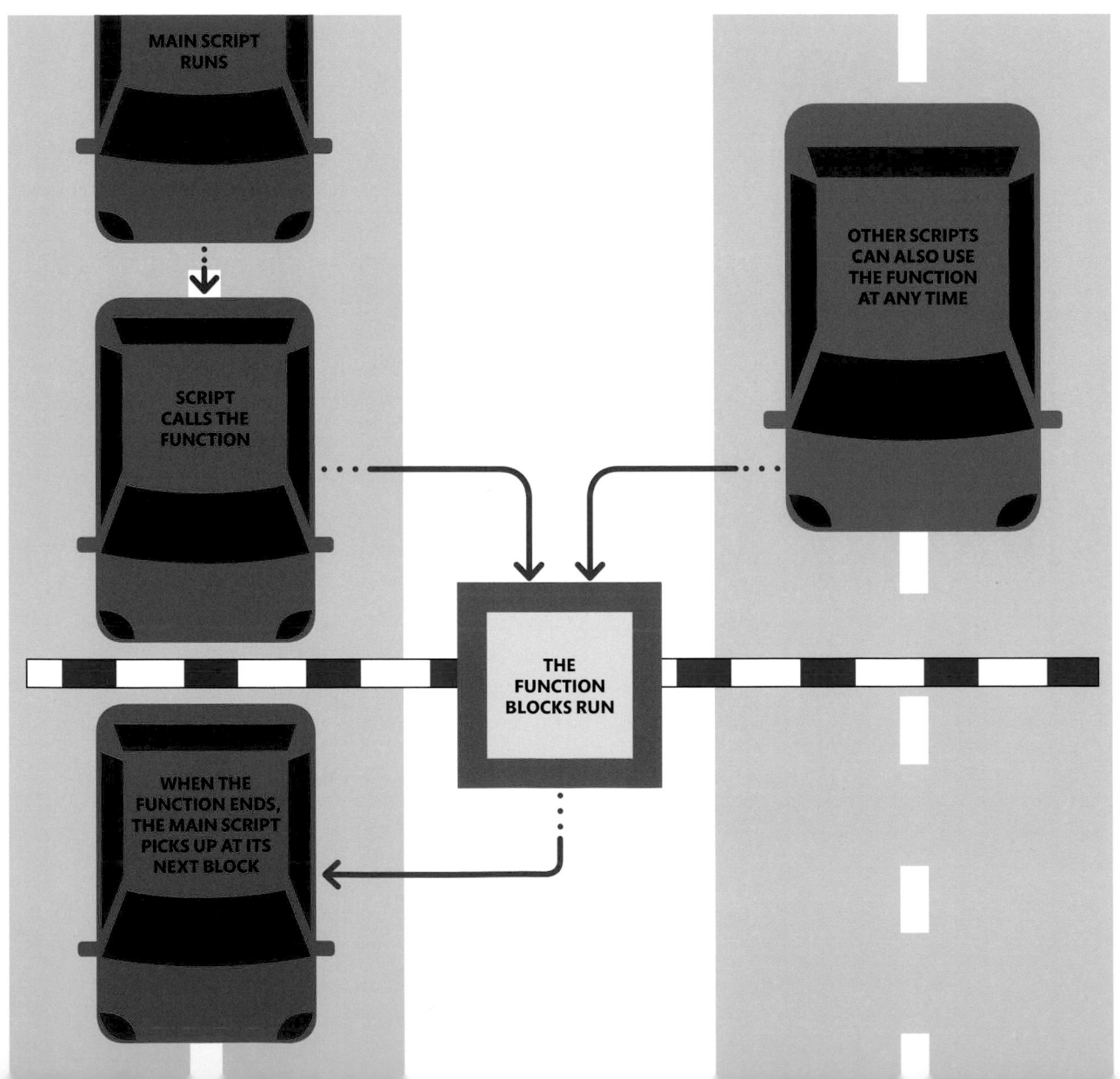

MAIN SCRIPT RUNS

OTHER SCRIPTS CAN ALSO USE THE FUNCTION AT ANY TIME

SCRIPT CALLS THE FUNCTION

THE FUNCTION BLOCKS RUN

WHEN THE FUNCTION ENDS, THE MAIN SCRIPT PICKS UP AT ITS NEXT BLOCK

Define your own blocks

To avoid repeating chunks of code multiple times, Scratch allows users to create their own blocks. Each new block can be made up of several instructions. The example below illustrates how to create a function to draw a triangle, and then use it to draw triangles of three different sizes, stacked on top of each other. The end result looks like a fir tree.

1 **Make a new block**
Go to the My Blocks section of the Blocks Palette and select the Make a Block button. Name the block "draw a triangle of size".

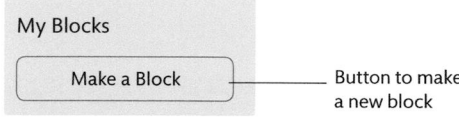

My Blocks

Make a Block ———— Button to make a new block

2 **Add and name an input**
Select the option to add a text input. A new input area will appear in the block. Name this "length" and click OK.

draw a triangle of size (length)

3 **Define your script**
Add the following instructions to the **define** block. The number the function receives goes into the **length** block. To use it in the script, drag this variable block from the **define** block into the **move 10 steps** block.

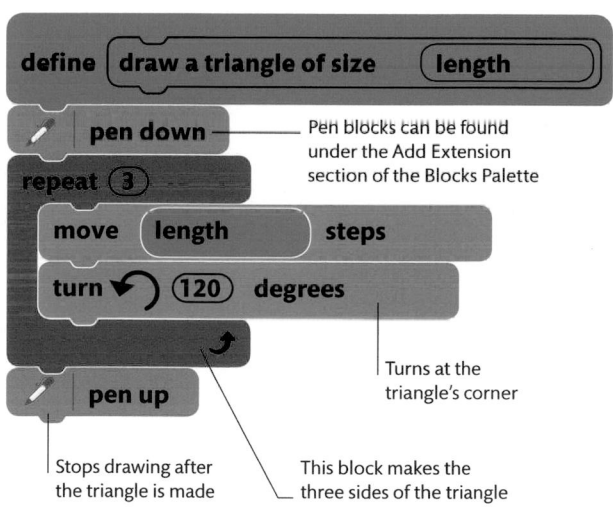

define (draw a triangle of size (length))

pen down ——— Pen blocks can be found under the Add Extension section of the Blocks Palette

repeat (3)

move (length) steps

turn ↺ (120) degrees ——— Turns at the triangle's corner

pen up

Stops drawing after the triangle is made

This block makes the three sides of the triangle

4 **Using the new block**
The new block can now be used in a program. Add this script to the Code Area, and when the green flag is clicked, Scratch will draw three triangles.

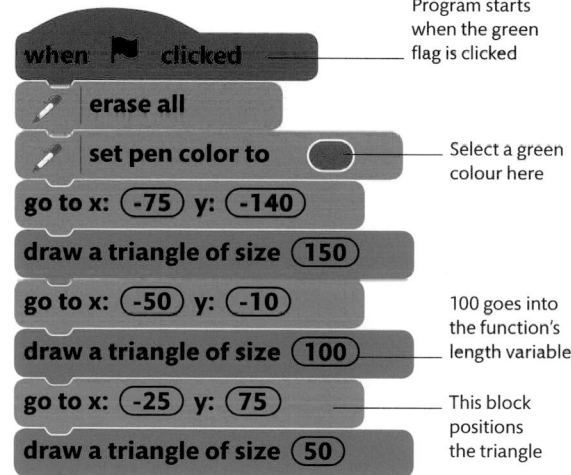

when ⚑ clicked ——— Program starts when the green flag is clicked

erase all

set pen color to ◯ ——— Select a green colour here

go to x: (-75) y: (-140)

draw a triangle of size (150)

go to x: (-50) y: (-10)

draw a triangle of size (100) ——— 100 goes into the function's length variable

go to x: (-25) y: (75) ——— This block positions the triangle

draw a triangle of size (50)

WHY USE FUNCTIONS ? • • •

Nearly all programming languages use functions in some way. Here are some advantages of using functions:
• Once a function is written, it can be reused in other programs.
• When each function has a meaningful name, programs are easier to read.
• When functions are reused, programs tend to be shorter.

• It is easier to write and test many small functions rather than one large program.
The example above would be longer, more complicated, and harder to understand if each instance of "draw a triangle" were replaced by all of the blocks in the function.

Travel translator

Travellers like to use translation apps to help them communicate in foreign languages. Using Scratch's extension blocks, this project will create a simple text translator. You can use it to translate any text into dozens of different languages. This can be the perfect app for your next holiday.

How the app works

To use this app, users first need to select a language they want to translate the text into. The program then prompts the user to type in the phrase to be translated. Once the user enters a phrase, the app displays the translated text in the chosen language on the screen.

Translating languages

This project uses the Scratch's Translate extension to convert one language into another. The blocks in this extension use the Google Translate API for the translations, so make sure you are connected to the Internet when using the app.

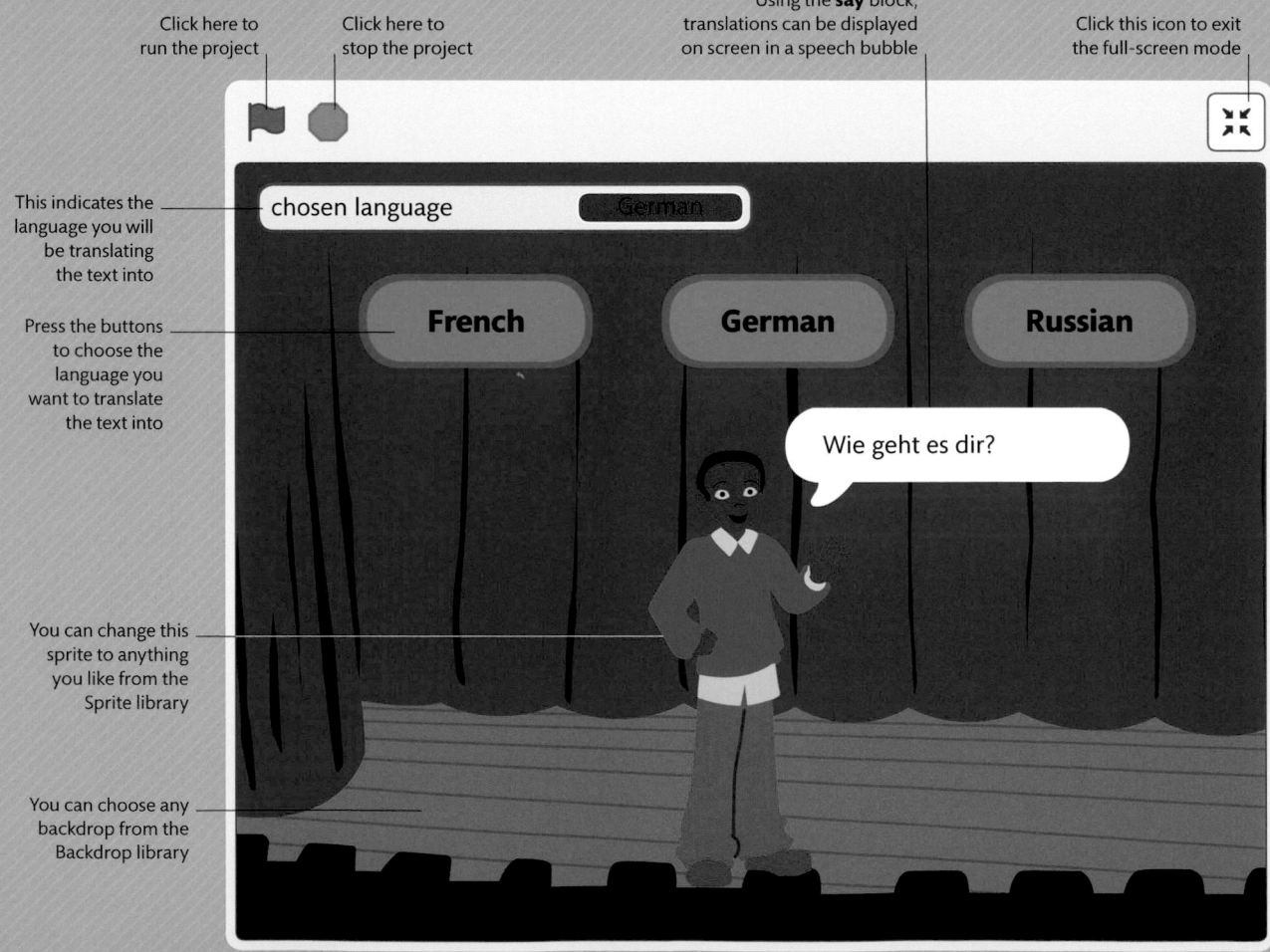

Click here to run the project

Click here to stop the project

Using the **say** block, translations can be displayed on screen in a speech bubble

Click this icon to exit the full-screen mode

This indicates the language you will be translating the text into

chosen language   German

Press the buttons to choose the language you want to translate the text into

French   German   Russian

Wie geht es dir?

You can change this sprite to anything you like from the Sprite library

You can choose any backdrop from the Backdrop library

YOU WILL LEARN

› How to add and code sprites
› How to use the Paint Editor
  to change a costume
› How to add Scratch extensions
  to a project

Time:
15–20 mins

Difficulty level

●●●●●

WHERE THIS IS USED

Good translation apps need to be accurate with their translations. The code used in this project can be reused to translate from a list of languages available in Scratch. You can also experiment by adding blocks that speak the translation out loud so you don't need to worry about your pronunciation.

Program design

Programmers often use flowcharts – a graphical representation of an algorithm – to structure their programs and to show how they work. Each step is shown in a box, with an arrow leading to the next step. Sometimes, a step could have multiple arrows leading onwards, depending on the answer to that step.

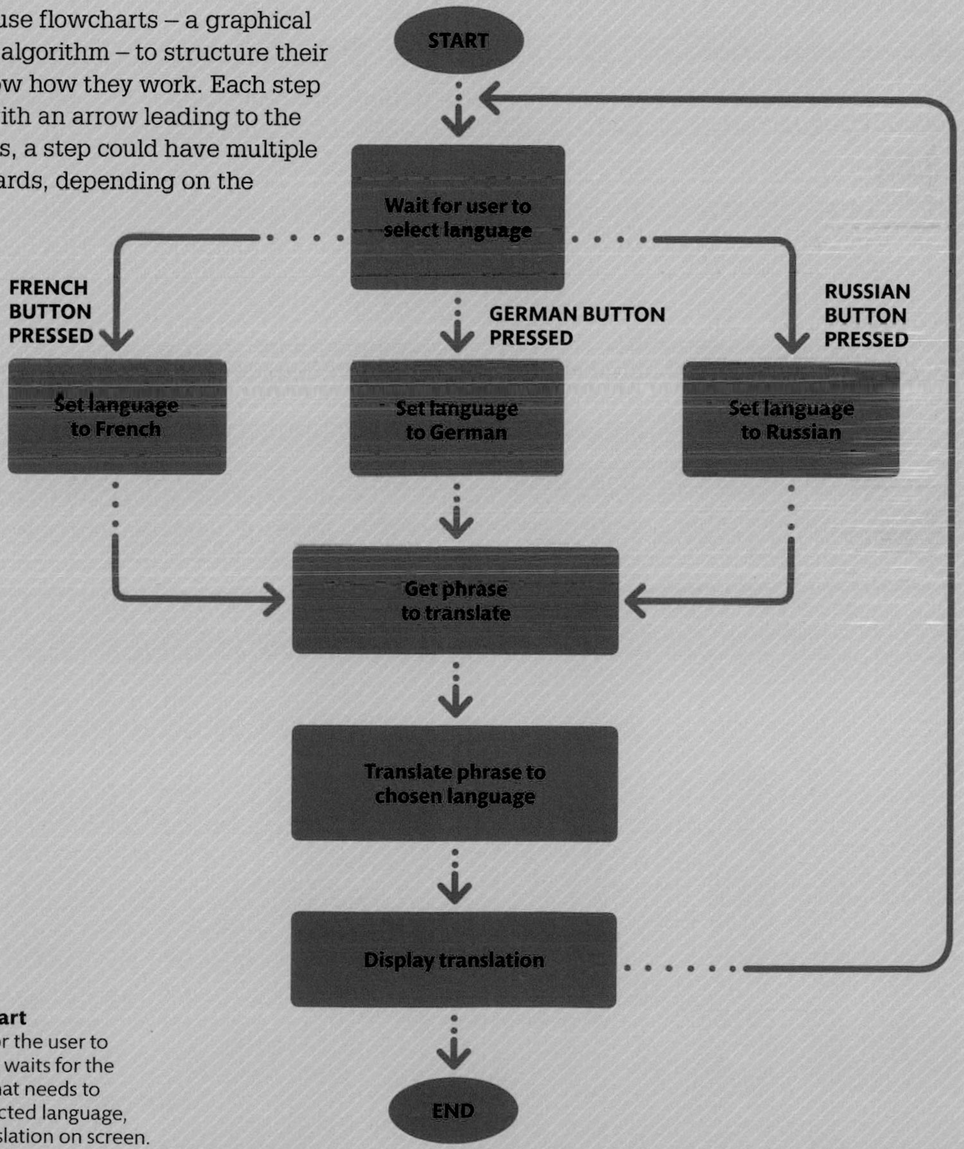

START

Wait for user to select language

FRENCH BUTTON PRESSED

GERMAN BUTTON PRESSED

RUSSIAN BUTTON PRESSED

Set language to French

Set language to German

Set language to Russian

Get phrase to translate

Translate phrase to chosen language

Display translation

END

Travel translator flowchart
First, this program waits for the user to choose a language. It then waits for the user to enter the phrase that needs to be translated into the selected language, before displaying the translation on screen.

1.6 **TRY IT OUT**
Now run the code and see what happens. Click the green flag on the top left corner of the Stage to start the code. The red stop sign next to it will stop the code.

Devin will say whatever you have typed in

Type in a phrase and press the tick icon to test the project

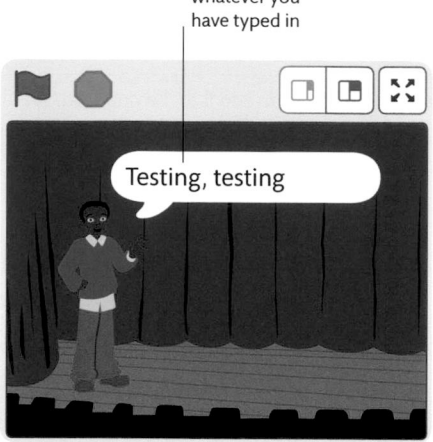

2 Adding a language

At the moment Devin can only speak in English – the default language. To proceed with the program, you need to add another language that Devin can translate the text into. The next few steps will help you create a button for the language, and will then add the Translate blocks to begin translating.

2.1 **ADD A BUTTON**
Start by adding a button to select a different language. Click the Choose a Sprite icon in the Sprite List and find the sprite called "Button2". Select it to add it to the project, then drag it to the top left of the Stage. Rename the sprite by clicking the text box in the information panel and typing the word "French".

Type here to rename the sprite, so you know which language it is for

This gives the position of a sprite on the Stage

Drag the button to a corner on the Stage

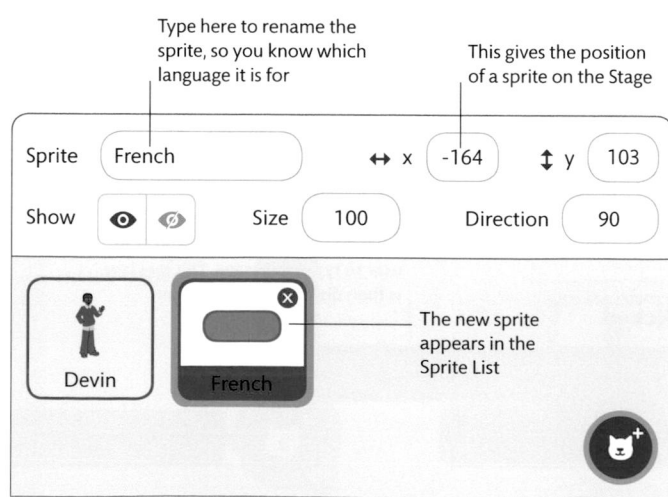

The new sprite appears in the Sprite List

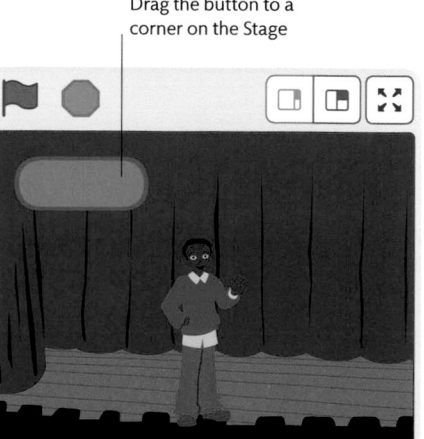

2.2 EDIT THE BUTTON SPRITE'S COSTUME

You can change the way a sprite looks by changing its costume. Select the Button2 sprite to modify it, and then click on the Costumes tab at the top left of the interface. This will open Scratch's Paint Editor. You can use this editor to draw your own costumes for the sprites, or edit the selected ones. The Text tool lets you add text to an image. Select the Text tool icon and click inside the button. Then type "French". This creates a label for the button. You can change the font using the drop-down menu, or the colour of the text using the Fill option, if you want.

Click here to open the Paint Editor for editing a costume

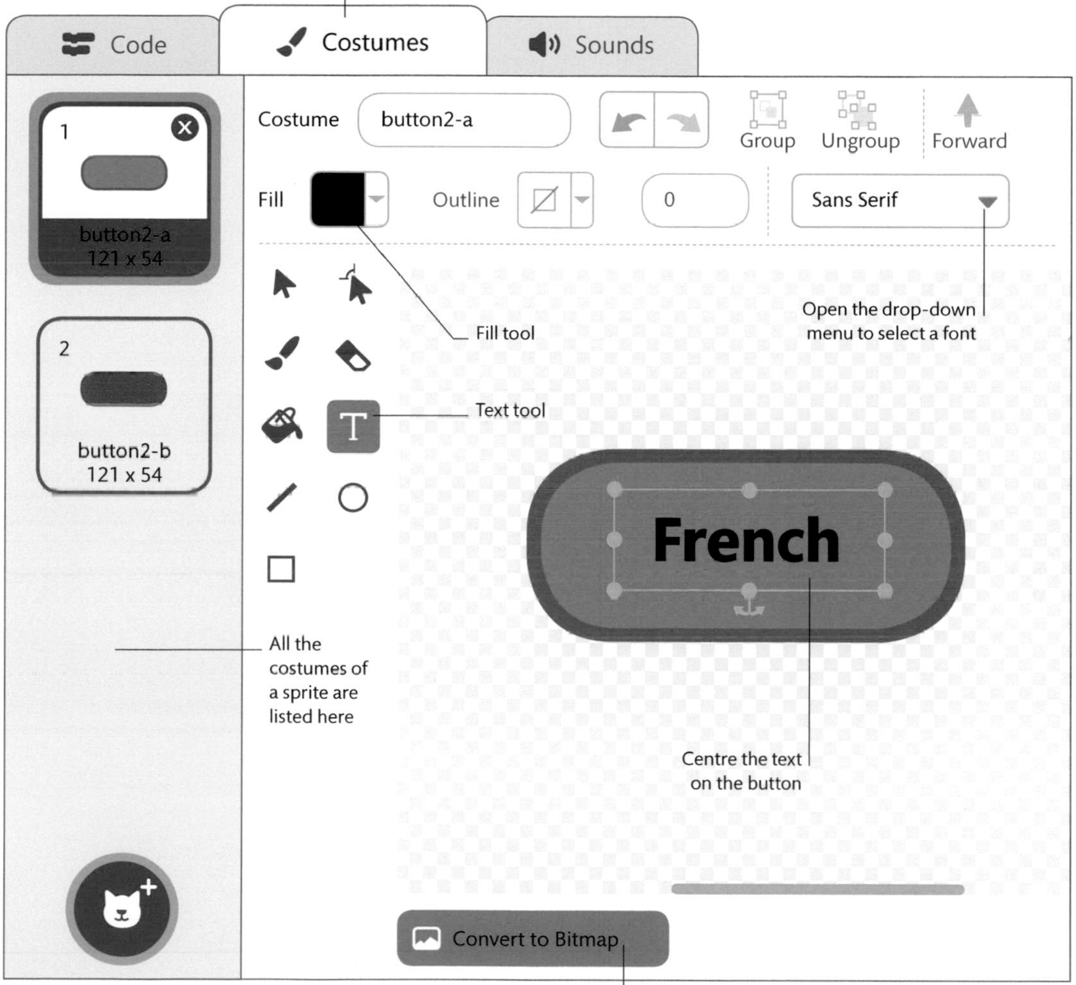

Code | Costumes | Sounds

Costume | button2-a | Group Ungroup Forward

Fill | Outline | 0 | Sans Serif

1
button2-a
121 x 54

2
button2-b
121 x 54

Fill tool

Open the drop-down menu to select a font

Text tool

All the costumes of a sprite are listed here

French

Centre the text on the button

Convert to Bitmap

This changes the mode from vector to bitmap and vice versa. You are currently working in the vector mode

2.3 CREATE A VARIABLE

You can now add some more code to the project. Select the French sprite and then click on the Code tab at the top left of the interface. Go to Variables in the Blocks Palette and click the Make a Variable button. A dialogue box will pop up to create a new variable. Name this variable "chosen language" and select OK.

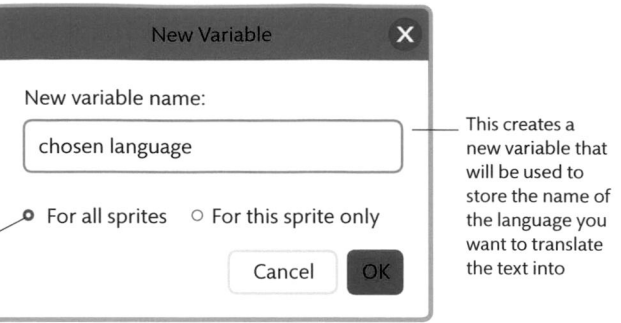

New Variable

New variable name:

chosen language

● For all sprites ○ For this sprite only

Cancel   OK

This creates a new variable that will be used to store the name of the language you want to translate the text into

Make sure this option is selected, so Devin can use this variable

2.4 SET CHOSEN LANGUAGE TO FRENCH

Next, add these blocks of code to the French sprite. When the user clicks on the sprite, it will set the chosen language variable to French. This will help keep track of the language you want to translate the text into later.

You can find these blocks in the yellow and orange sections of the Blocks Palette

when this sprite clicked

set chosen language ▼ to French

Type in the name of the language here

2.5 ADD AN EXTENSION BLOCK

It is now time to start translating. You will need to add some extra blocks to do this. Select the Add Extension button at the bottom of the Blocks Palette. You will see a selection of extra extensions that you can add to your projects. Choose the extension called "Translate". This will add some extra blocks to your palette in a section called Translate.

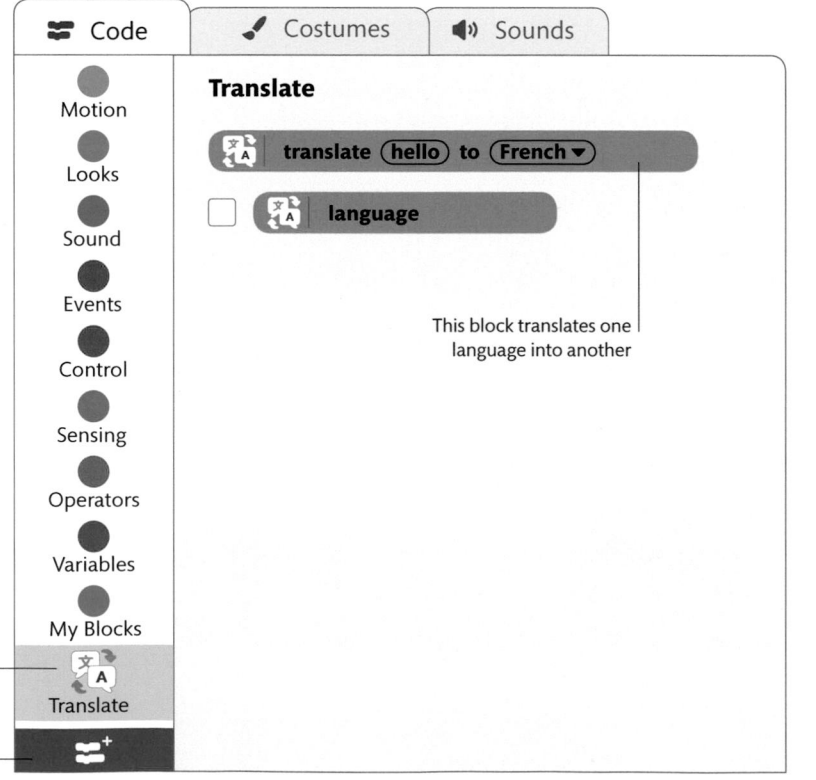

🔀 Code   🖌 Costumes   🔊 Sounds

Motion

Looks

Sound

Events

Control

Sensing

Operators

Variables

My Blocks

Translate

Translate

translate (hello) to (French ▼)

☐ language

This block translates one language into another

Every new section is added at the bottom of the Blocks Palette

Click here to open the Scratch extensions

EXTENSION BLOCKS

Scratch's extension blocks allow projects to communicate with hardware or software outside of the Scratch environment. Selecting an extension will add more blocks to the Palette for you to use.

Music
Use these extension blocks to make music using a variety of instruments and drum sound effects.

Pen
This extension enables a sprite to draw across the screen like a pen. It could be used to create a painting app.

Video sensing
These blocks let you connect Scratch to your webcam. They can be used to detect movement in front of the camera.

Text to speech
Use this extension to make your projects talk. These blocks use Amazon Web Services (an online tool) to read text out loud.

Translate
These blocks let you translate text into a lot of different languages – this is the extension you are using in the current project.

Makey Makey
This lets you connect everyday objects to your computer. These blocks allow you to use connected objects to control your games.

micro:bit
The micro:bit is a palm-sized gadget that you can control with the code blocks in this extension.

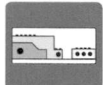
LEGO® BOOST
These blocks are designed to make it easy for children (or people new to coding) to build a set of interactive robots.

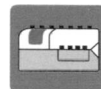
LEGO® Education WeDo 2.0
The WeDo extension blocks are used to control simple robotic projects built with LEGO blocks.

LEGO® MINDSTORMS™ EV3
These extension blocks are used to make projects that control more advanced robots built with LEGO blocks.

GoDirect Force & Acceleration
This extension lets you use an external sensor to record forces and acceleration and send the information to your Scratch project.

2.6 UPDATE DEVIN'S CODE

You can now use the new Translate blocks. Click on Devin and change the code to look like this. If the chosen language is set to French, then Devin will translate the text into French.

Find this block in the Operators section, then drag and drop the **chosen language** variable in the first hole, and type French in the second hole

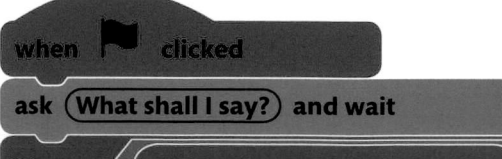

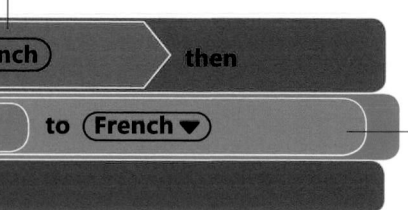

Update the purple block with this Translate block

2.7 **TRY IT OUT**
Test the code. Press the French button, and then click the green flag to run the project. Next, type a phrase you want to translate and click the tick icon to enter it.

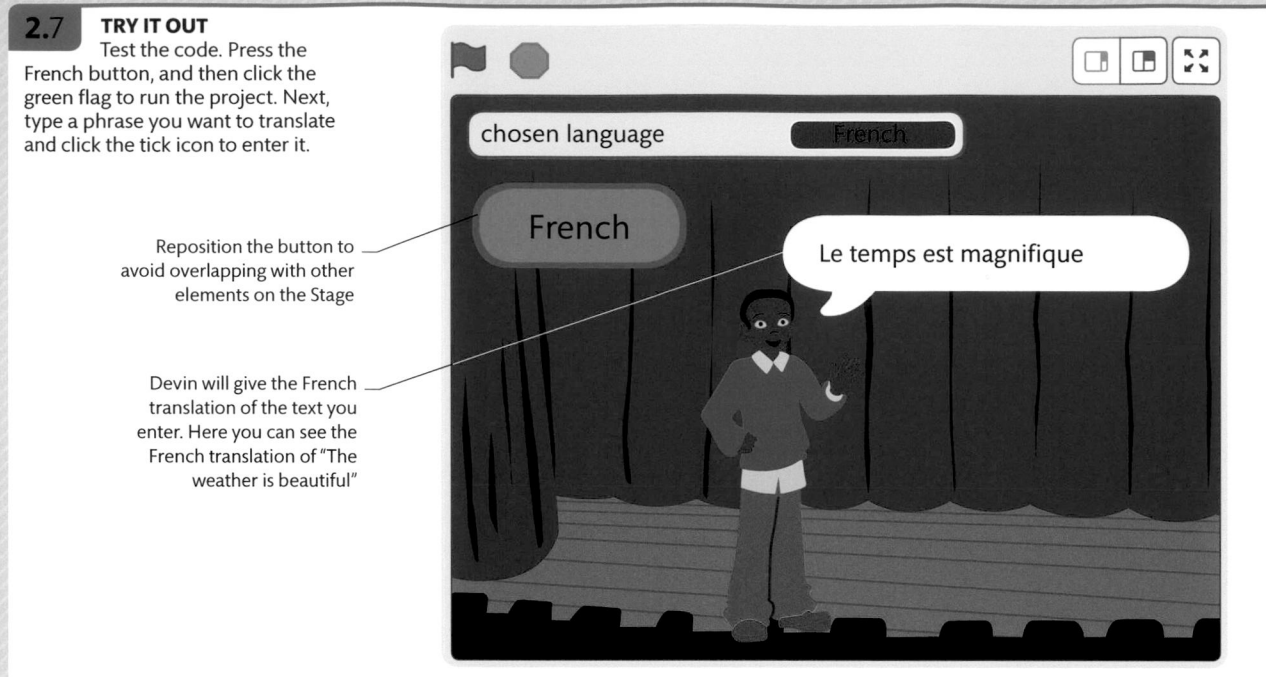

Reposition the button to avoid overlapping with other elements on the Stage

Devin will give the French translation of the text you enter. Here you can see the French translation of "The weather is beautiful"

chosen language   French

French

Le temps est magnifique

3 **Adding more languages**
You can increase the complexity of the app and make it more useful by adding more languages to the project. Start by creating buttons for each new language and then adding the Translate blocks, just like before. You can add as many languages as you like.

3.1 **CREATE MORE BUTTONS**
In this step you will make a few more buttons so you can translate into other languages. Scratch makes it easy to do this. Right click on the French sprite in the Sprite List and choose "duplicate". This creates a copy of the sprite and all the code associated with it. Create two duplicates and rename them German and Russian. You can choose other languages if you like.

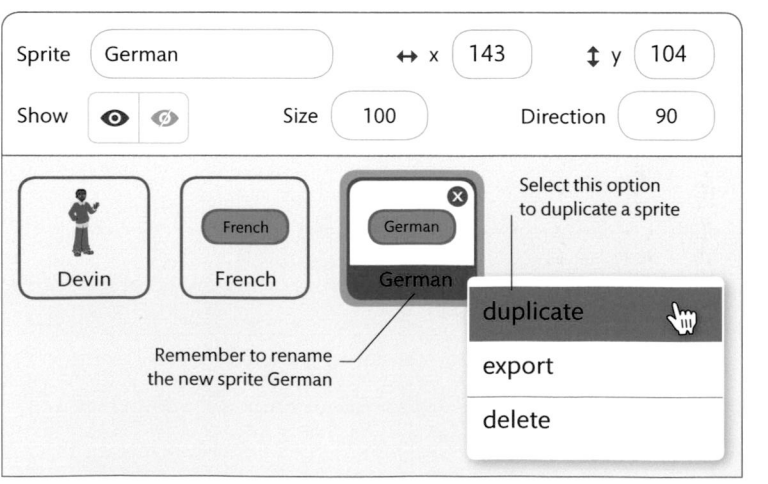

| Sprite | German | | | ↔ x | 143 | ↕ y | 104 |
| Show | 👁 🚫 | | Size | 100 | | Direction | 90 |

Devin   French   German

French   German

Select this option to duplicate a sprite

Remember to rename the new sprite German

duplicate
export
delete

3.2 EDIT THE NEW BUTTONS

You now need to make some changes to the code for each of these new sprites. Edit the code for the German and Russian buttons to look like this.

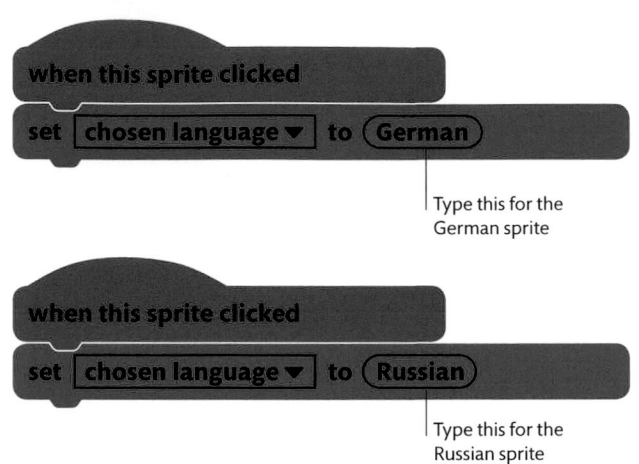

when this sprite clicked

set chosen language ▼ to German

Type this for the German sprite

when this sprite clicked

set chosen language ▼ to Russian

Type this for the Russian sprite

3.3 UPDATE THE COSTUMES

Next, you will also need to edit the costumes for these new sprites so their label reads German and Russian, and not French. Remember to click on the Costumes tab to open the Paint Editor and then use the Text tool. Make sure you are in the vector mode.

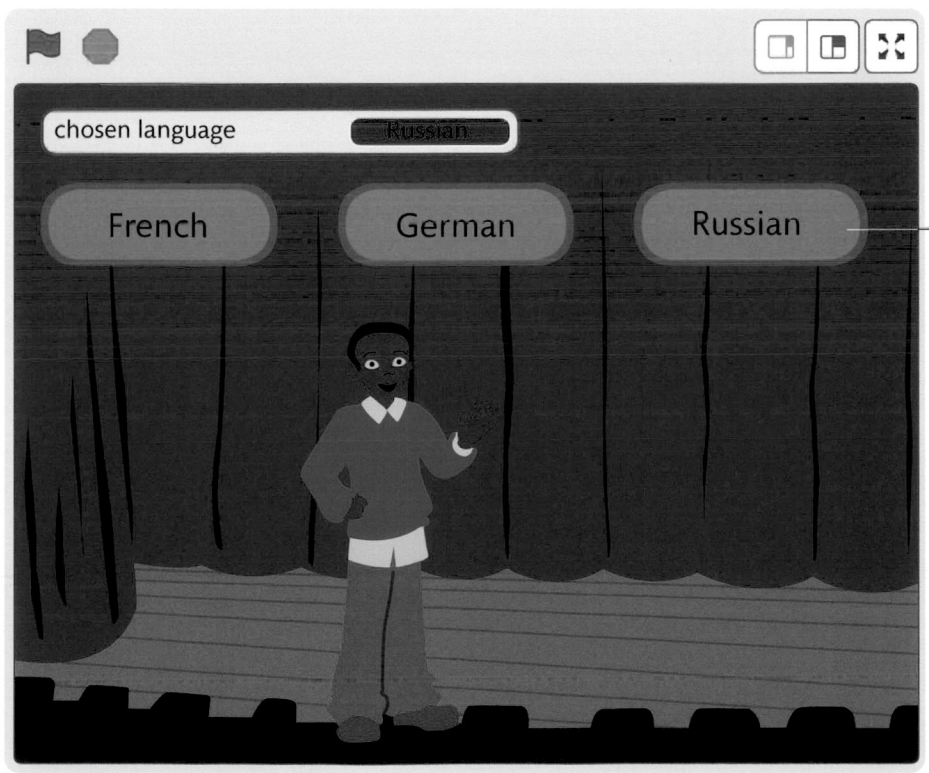

chosen language   Russian

French   German   Russian

Drag the buttons to the top of the Stage and align with the button for French

3.4 UPDATE DEVIN'S CODE

Finally, click on Devin in the Sprite List and edit the code to get the correct translations. You can duplicate the original code by right clicking on it and selecting "duplicate". Then just make the edits so it matches the code shown here.

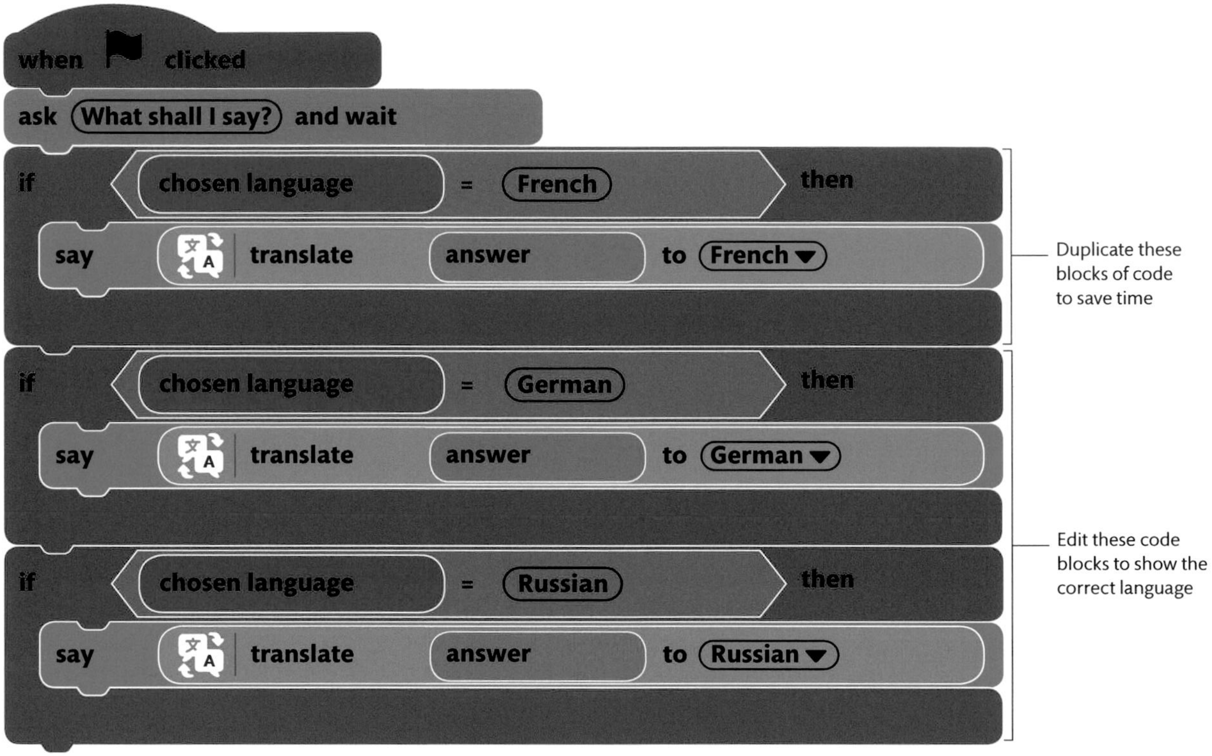

```
when 🏳 clicked

ask (What shall I say?) and wait

if < chosen language = (French) > then
    say [🔤 translate (answer) to (French ▾)]
```
— Duplicate these blocks of code to save time

```
if < chosen language = (German) > then
    say [🔤 translate (answer) to (German ▾)]
```

```
if < chosen language = (Russian) > then
    say [🔤 translate (answer) to (Russian ▾)]
```
— Edit these code blocks to show the correct language

3.5 TRANSLATE NOW

Congratulations! You have now successfully created your first app. Just click on the green flag and start translating.

BONJOUR

HELLO

HOLA

AHOJ

⚙ Hacks and tweaks

Multilingual
Create additional buttons and code blocks so you can translate more languages. Scratch's Translate blocks allow you to choose from dozens of different languages. Which ones would you like to add?

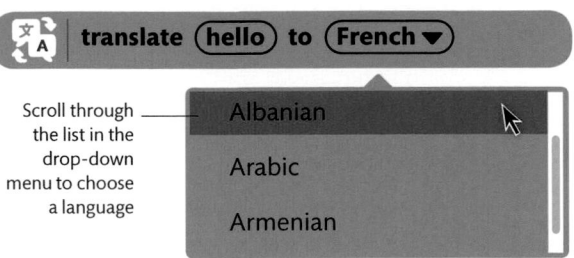

Scroll through the list in the drop-down menu to choose a language

Common phrases
"Hello", "How are you?", "How much is this?" – these common phrases are useful all over the world. Can you adapt your code and use the Translate blocks to see the translations for these useful phrases without having to type them in? You might want to add some dedicated buttons to do this.

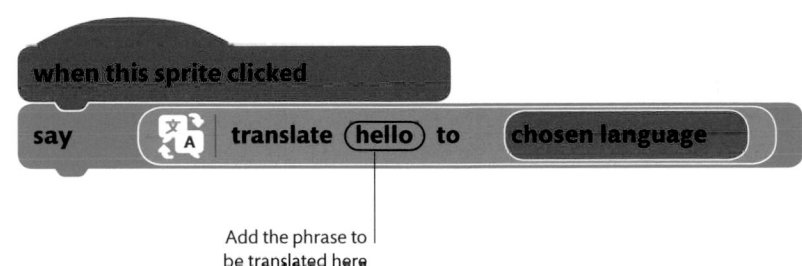

Add the phrase to be translated here

Speak it
There is another Scratch extension called "Text to Speech" that can be used to read text out loud. Tweak your code so that the phrases are read out loud. You can then listen and learn how to pronounce the words.

Text to Speech

Scratch has five different voices that you can choose from

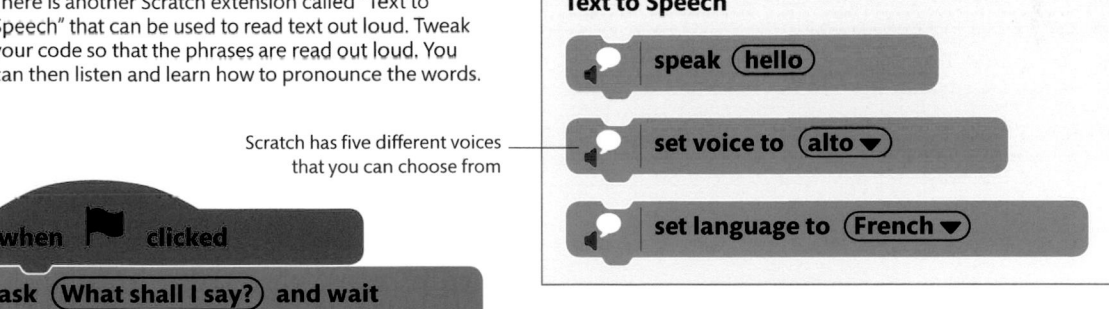

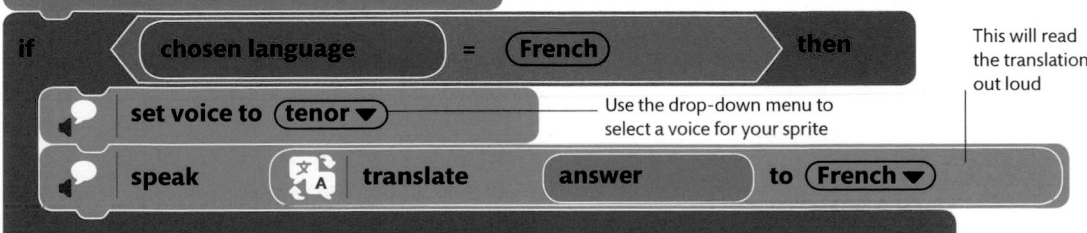

Use the drop-down menu to select a voice for your sprite

This will read the translation out loud

Logic puzzle

Puzzles are a great way to stimulate your brain and help develop logical thinking and cognitive skills. This project uses loops and Scratch's Operators blocks to create a complex logic puzzle. The program checks the code each time a sprite moves.

What is the puzzle?

The aim of the puzzle is to transport a lion, a donut, and a rooster from one side of a river to the other. You can only fit one sprite in the boat at a time. However, if left unattended together, the lion will eat the rooster, and the rooster will eat the donut. The challenge is to work out the logic and get everything over to the other side of the river, safely.

Complex logic
The complexity in the puzzle arises from the restrictions on what sprites can be transported at the same time, or what sprites may be safely left together.

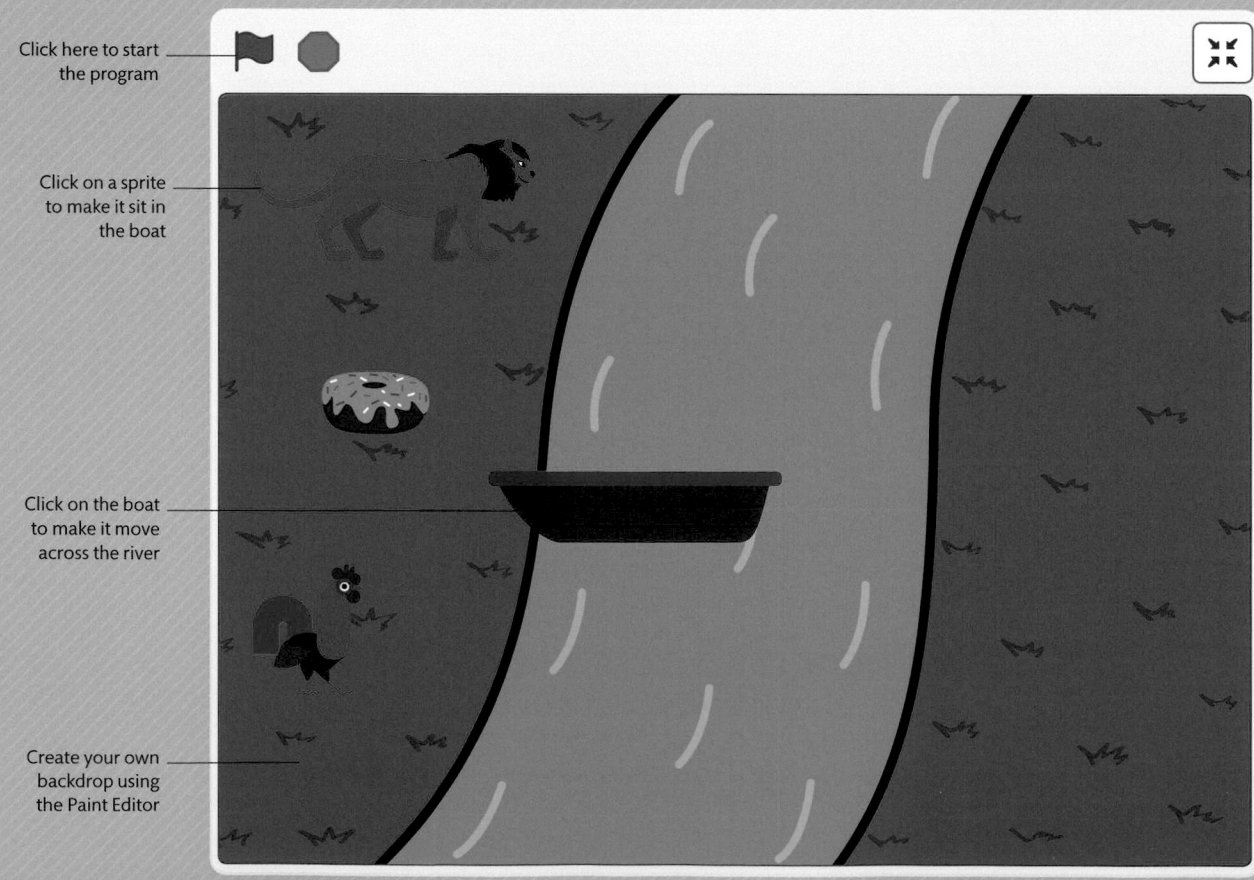

Click here to start the program

Click on a sprite to make it sit in the boat

Click on the boat to make it move across the river

Create your own backdrop using the Paint Editor

YOU WILL LEARN

> How to use the Paint Editor to create backdrops and sprites
> How to create a simulation
> How to add complex logic to a project

Time:
20–25 mins

Difficulty level
●●●●○○

WHERE THIS IS USED

Computer programs can simulate real-world problems and situations. By using code, it is possible to investigate and test different ways of solving a problem, often much more quickly than it would be to test it in the real world.

Program design

The program waits for the user to select a sprite. Once the selection has been made, the user attempts to move the sprite across the river. The program then checks to see if any of the rules have been broken using one continuous loop. If a rule is broken then it is game over. If the user gets all the sprites across the river correctly, then the puzzle is solved.

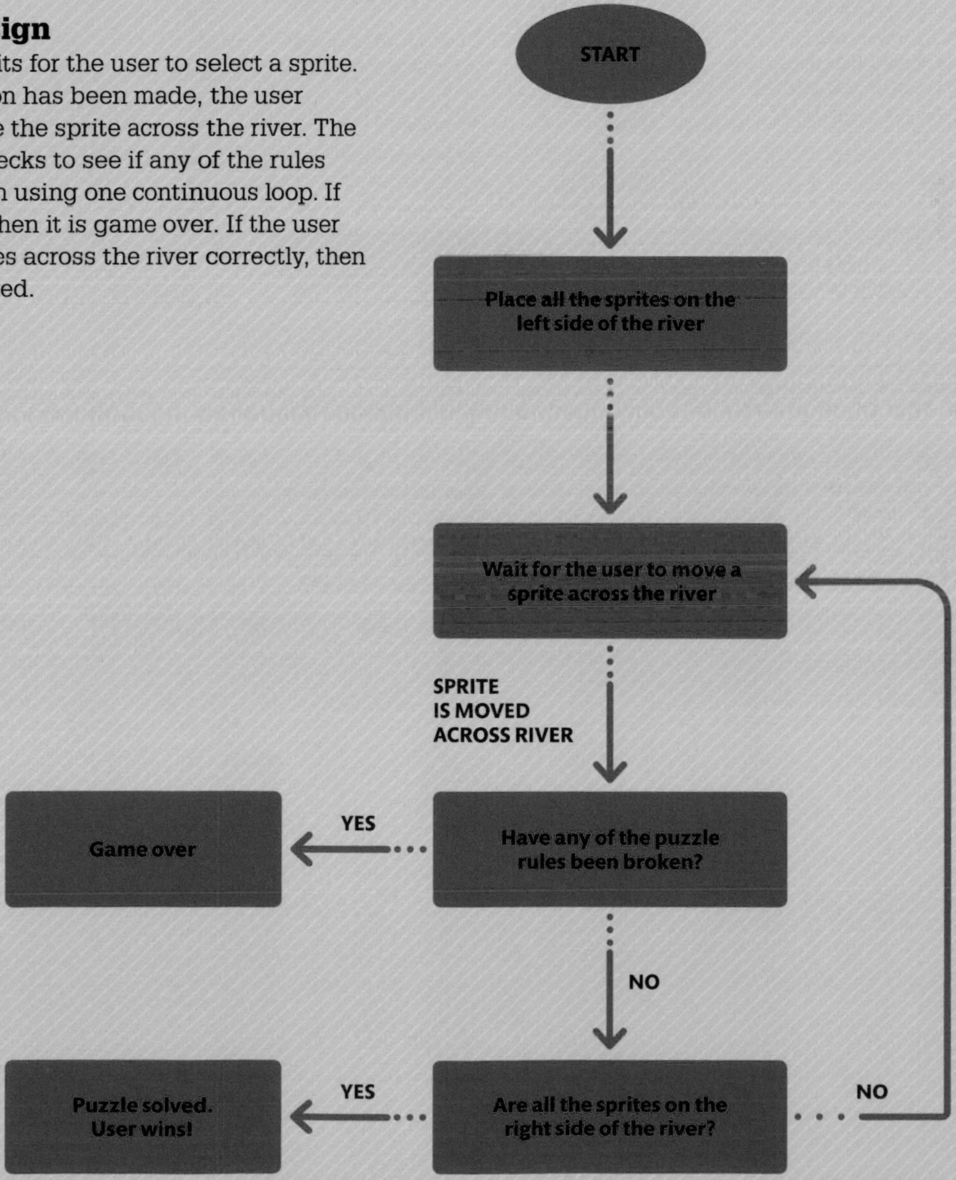

START

Place all the sprites on the left side of the river

Wait for the user to move a sprite across the river

SPRITE IS MOVED ACROSS RIVER

Have any of the puzzle rules been broken?

YES → Game over

NO

Are all the sprites on the right side of the river?

YES → Puzzle solved. User wins!

NO

2.2 CREATE THE VARIABLES

With the Lion sprite still highlighted, go to the Variables section of the Blocks Palette and create two new variables for this sprite. Call them "lion side" and "lion onboard". If you need to rename or delete a variable, right click or Ctrl + click on it.

Variables

Make a Variable

☐ **boat capacity**

☐ **boat moving**

☐ **boat side**

Make sure these ——— ☐ **lion onboard** ——— This will be true if the lion is on the boat
boxes are unchecked

☐ **lion side** ——— This will be used to track which side of the river the lion is on

2.3 PLACE THE LION

Next, add these code blocks to the Lion sprite to position it on the left-hand side of the river when the project starts. Remember, you might need to adjust the x and y values to suit your backdrop.

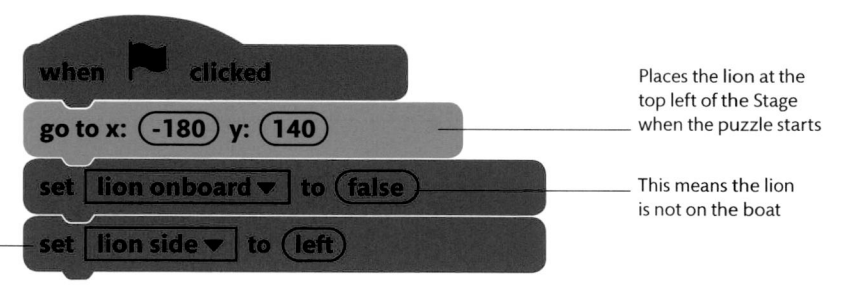

when 🚩 clicked

go to x: (-180) y: (140) ——— Places the lion at the top left of the Stage when the puzzle starts

set lion onboard ▼ to (false) ——— This means the lion is not on the boat

Puts the lion on the ——— set lion side ▼ to (left)
left-hand side of the river

2.4 GET ON THE BOAT

When the user clicks the lion, it must move onto the boat. Add this code to do that. Click on the green flag to try it out.

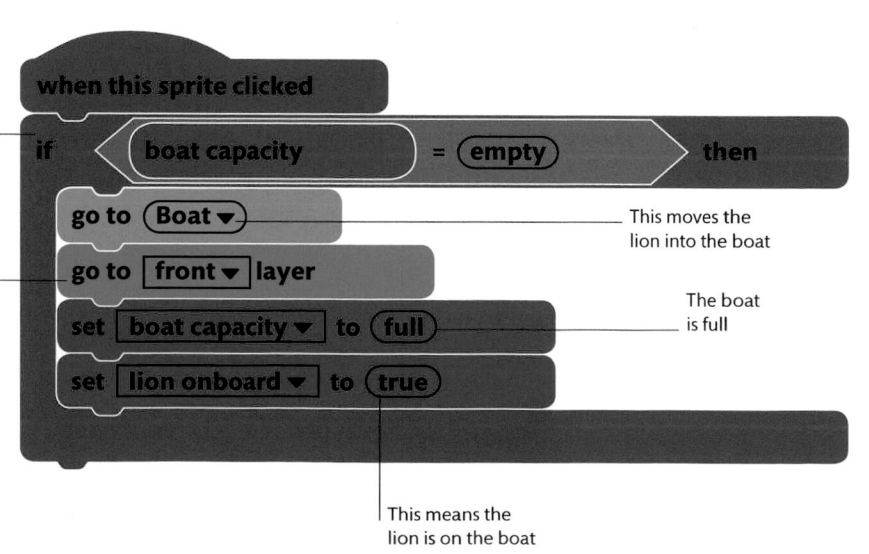

These blocks are run only if the ——— when this sprite clicked
boat is empty. This prevents more
than one object from being inside
the boat at the same time ——— if ⟨ boat capacity = (empty) ⟩ then

go to (Boat ▼) ——— This moves the lion into the boat

Find this block in the ——— go to front ▼ layer
Looks section of the Blocks
Palette. It ensures that the Lion
sprite stays in front of the boat ——— set boat capacity ▼ to (full) ——— The boat is full

set lion onboard ▼ to (true)

This means the
lion is on the boat

2.5 MOVE THE LION WITH THE BOAT

When the boat moves across the river, the lion needs to move with it. This will make it seem like the lion is sailing to the other side of the river. Add the following code to the Lion sprite to do this, then run the code. See if you can move the lion across the river in the boat and then back again.

Click on the lion to move it along with the boat

These blocks are run when the user clicks on the Boat sprite

```
When I receive  boat is moving ▼

if < lion onboard = (true) > then

    repeat until < boat moving = (false) >

        go to (Boat ▼)
        go to [front ▼] layer

    if < boat side = (right) > then

        go to x: (165) y: (99)
        set [lion side ▼] to (right)

    else

        go to x: (-180) y: (140)
        set [lion side ▼] to (left)

    set [boat capacity ▼] to (empty)
    set [lion onboard ▼] to (false)
```

This loop runs only if the lion is on the boat

The lion moves along with the boat until the boat stops

If the boat ends up on the right, this moves the lion to the grassy area on the right-hand side of the river and updates the variables

If the boat ends up on the left, this moves the lion to the grassy area on the left-hand side of the river and updates the variables

Ensures the boat is empty

This means the lion is no longer on the boat

3 Add more sprites

The next step is to add more characters to increase the complexity of the project. You need to code the new sprites in exactly the same way as the lion in the previous steps. Then you can add some rules that will constantly check if the correct logic has been applied to solve the puzzle.

3.1 ADD A DONUT

Go to the Sprite library and look for the Donut sprite. Select it to add it to the project. It is a big sprite, so change its size to 50 in the information panel.

Donut

3.2 COPY CODE FROM THE LION

The code for the donut is very similar to the code for the lion. Luckily, Scratch makes it easy to reuse code. Click on the Lion sprite and find the blocks of code you made in steps 2.3, 2.4, and 2.5. Drag and drop all of those blocks onto the Donut sprite in the

Sprite List. This will create a copy of all the blocks for the Donut sprite. The blocks may get copied on top of each other, but you can right click in the Code Area and select Clean up Blocks to set them in order.

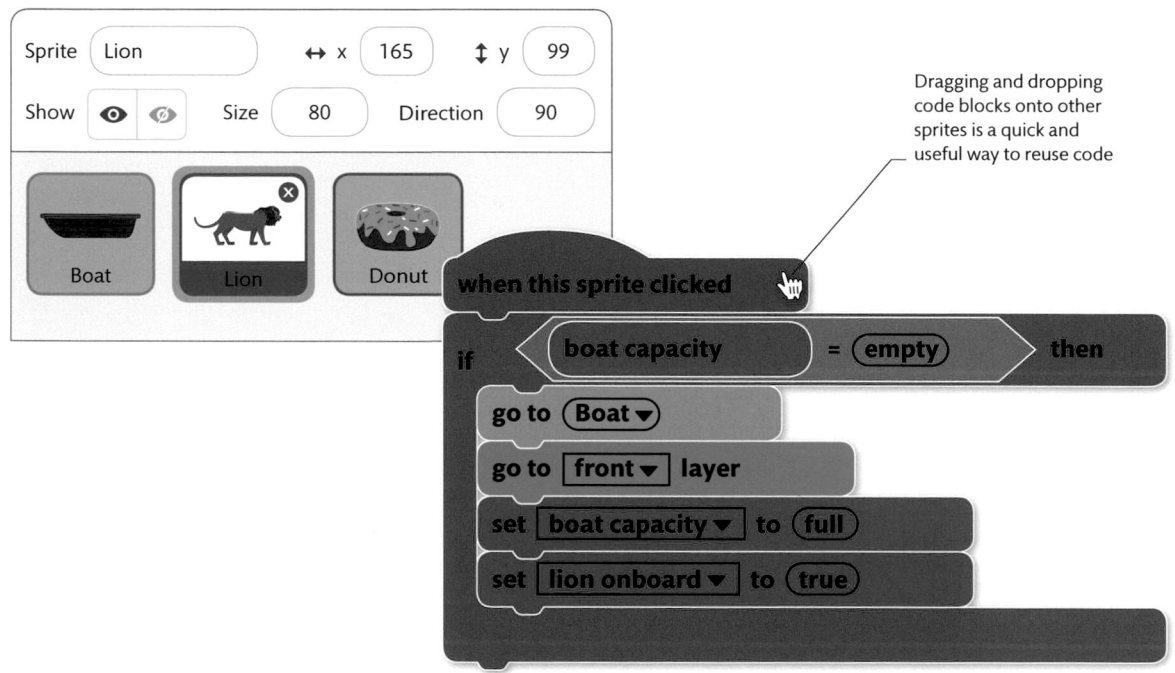

Dragging and dropping code blocks onto other sprites is a quick and useful way to reuse code

3.3 UPDATE THE CODE

Now select the Donut sprite. You will see the blocks you just copied across. Update the code to make it work for the donut. First, create two new variables, **donut side** and **donut onboard**, then edit the code blocks to look like this. Make sure you uncheck the boxes next to the new variables.

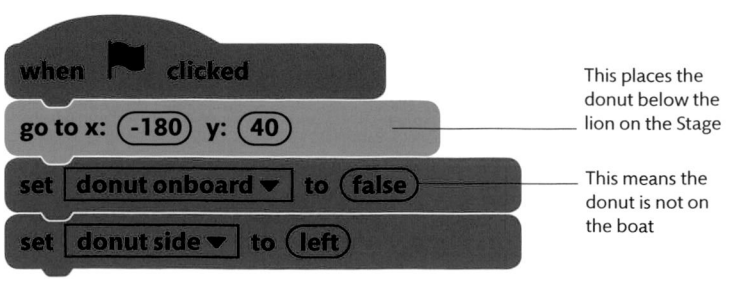

This places the donut below the lion on the Stage

This means the donut is not on the boat

when this sprite clicked

if < boat capacity = empty > then

go to (Boat ▼)

go to [front ▼] layer

set [boat capacity ▼] to (full)

set [donut onboard ▼] to (true) ——— Update this block with the correct variable for the donut

When I receive [boat is moving ▼]

if < donut onboard = true > then ——— This loop runs only if the donut is on the boat

repeat until < boat moving = false >

go to (Boat ▼)

go to [front ▼] layer

if < boat side = right > then

go to x: (190) y: (0)

set [donut side ▼] to (right)

If the boat ends up on the right, this moves the donut to the grassy area on the right-hand side of the river and updates the variables

else

go to x: (-180) y: (40) ——— Update these coordinates for the donut

set [donut side ▼] to (left)

If the boat ends up on the left, this moves the donut to the grassy area on the left-hand side of the river and updates the variables

set [boat capacity ▼] to (empty)

set [donut onboard ▼] to (false)

3.4 ADD THE ROOSTER

Now add the final sprite to the program. Go to the Sprite library and look for the "Rooster" sprite. Select it and make sure you reduce its size to 50 in the sprite information panel.

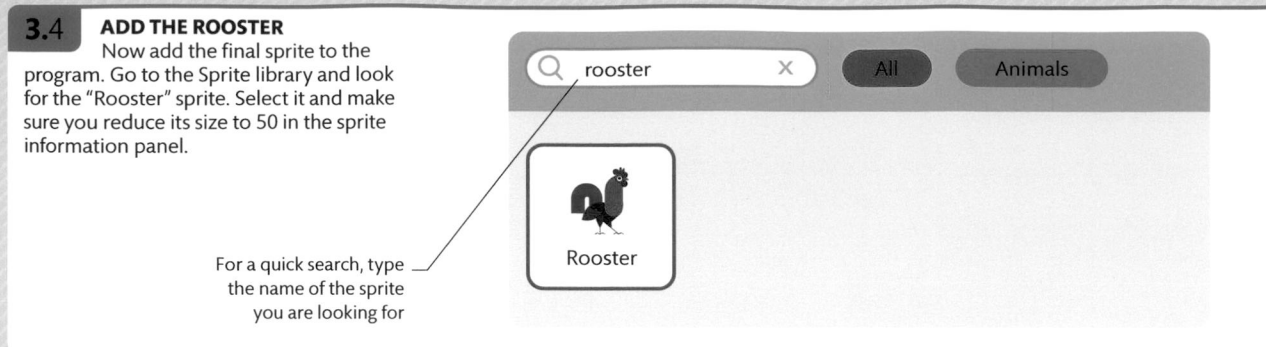

For a quick search, type the name of the sprite you are looking for

3.5 COPY CODE FROM THE LION

Next, add code to the Rooster. Just like you did for the Donut, drag and drop all the code blocks from the Lion sprite onto the Rooster in the Sprite List.

This will make a copy of all the blocks. Right click anywhere in the Code Area and select Clean up Blocks to view the code blocks in an order.

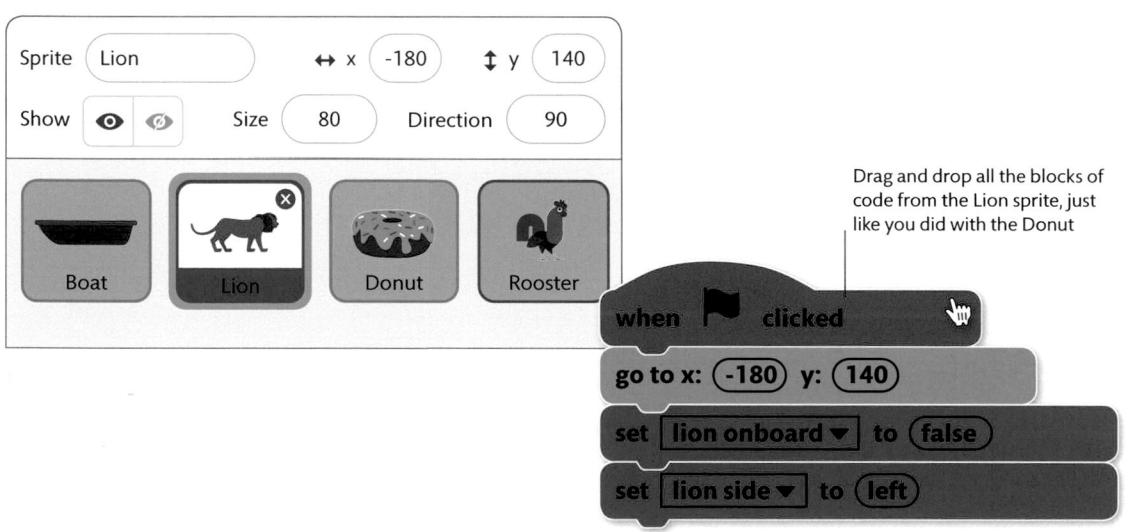

Drag and drop all the blocks of code from the Lion sprite, just like you did with the Donut

```
when ⚑ clicked
go to x: (-180) y: (140)
set lion onboard ▼ to (false)
set lion side ▼ to (left)
```

3.6 UPDATE THE CODE

Now you will need to edit the code you just copied. Remember to create two new variables **rooster side** and **rooster onboard**, and make sure you uncheck the boxes next to the variables. The edited code for the Rooster sprite should look like this.

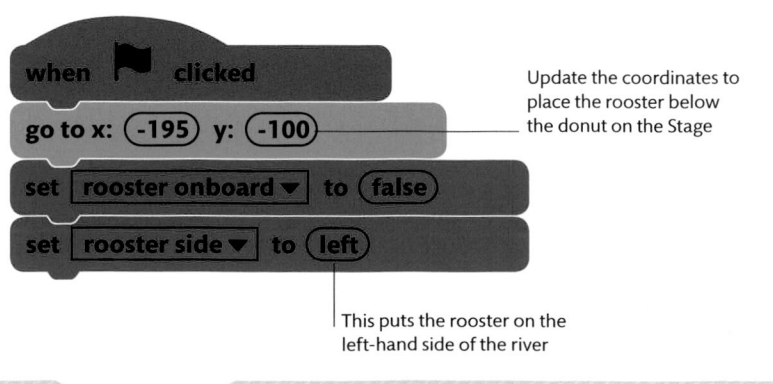

```
when ⚑ clicked
go to x: (-195) y: (-100)
set rooster onboard ▼ to (false)
set rooster side ▼ to (left)
```

Update the coordinates to place the rooster below the donut on the Stage

This puts the rooster on the left-hand side of the river

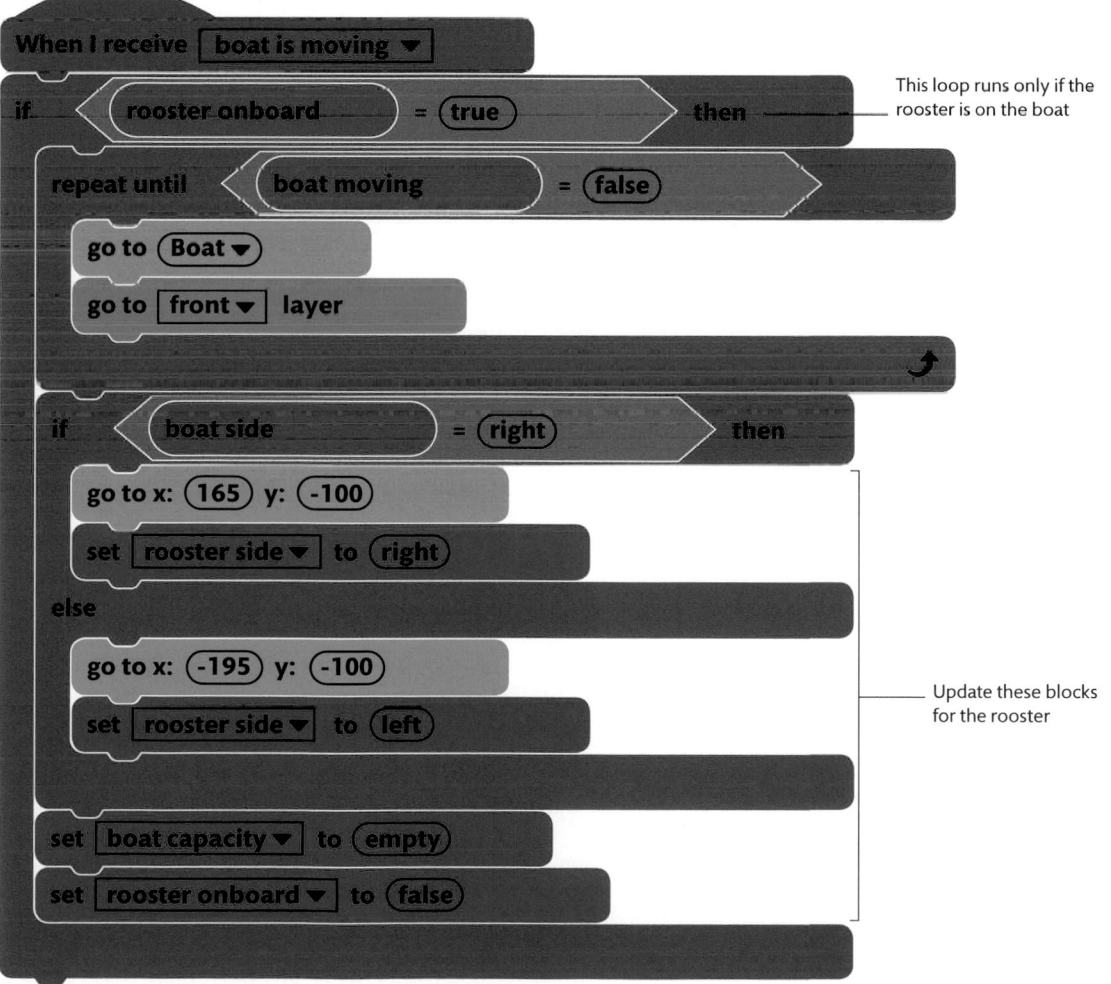

when this sprite clicked

if ⟨ boat capacity = empty ⟩ then

go to Boat ▼

go to front ▼ layer

set boat capacity ▼ to full

set rooster onboard ▼ to true

Update this block with the correct variable for the rooster

When I receive boat is moving ▼

if ⟨ rooster onboard = true ⟩ then

This loop runs only if the rooster is on the boat

repeat until ⟨ boat moving = false ⟩

go to Boat ▼

go to front ▼ layer

if ⟨ boat side = right ⟩ then

go to x: 165 y: -100

set rooster side ▼ to right

else

go to x: -195 y: -100

set rooster side ▼ to left

Update these blocks for the rooster

set boat capacity ▼ to empty

set rooster onboard ▼ to false

3.7 ADD THE RULES

At this point, you should be able to move the objects back and forth across the river. Now it is time to introduce the rules of the puzzle. Add these code blocks to the Boat sprite. They will check the sides to see if any of the rules are being broken, or if the user has successfully solved the puzzle.

Click on the drop-down menu and choose "New message" to create this message

```
when I receive [check sides ▾]

if < (lion side) = (right) > and < (donut side) = (right) > and < (rooster side)
    say (Win: Everything is on the right side of the river)

if < (lion side) = (left) > and < (donut side) = (right) > and < (rooster side)
    say (Lose: The Lion eats the rooster)

if < (lion side) = (right) > and < (donut side) = (left) > and < (rooster side)
    say (Lose: The Lion eats the rooster)

if < (lion side) = (right) > and < (donut side) = (left) > and < (rooster side)
    say (Lose: The rooster eats the donut)

if < (lion side) = (left) > and < (donut side) = (right) > and < (rooster side)
    say (Lose: The rooster eats the donut)
```

If the lion and rooster are left alone on the left-hand side then it is game over

If the lion and rooster are left alone on the right-hand side then it is game over

If the rooster and donut are left alone on the left-hand side it will be against the rules

If the rooster has been left alone with the donut on the right-hand side, it will be against the rules

Hacks and tweaks

Design your own scenario
Use the Paint Editor to change the sprites' costumes and the project's backdrop to create a whole new scenario for this puzzle. Maybe it could be set in space, and you need to transport aliens from one space station to another, but you cannot leave certain types of alien together. Use the Sprite and Backdrop library to come up with more ideas.

Experiment with other sprites and backdrops to create different scenarios

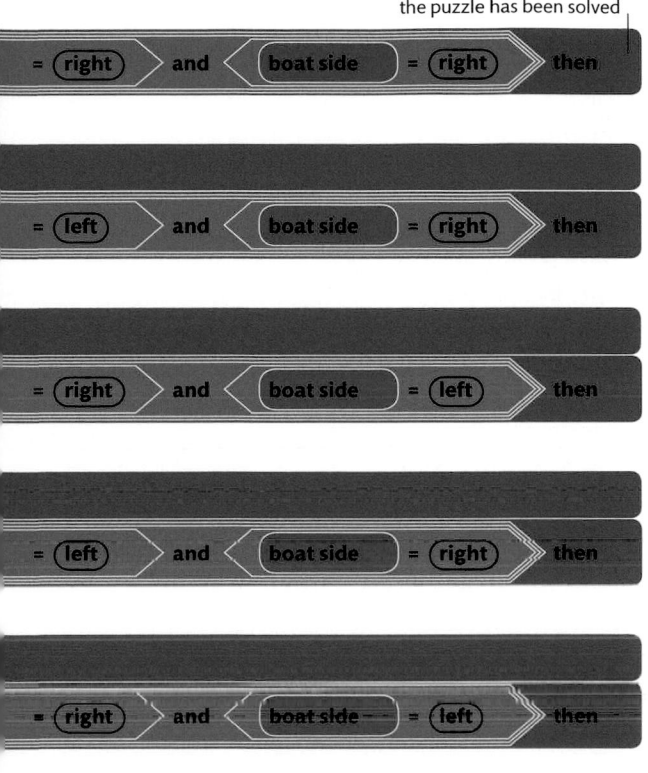

If every sprite is on the
right-hand side of the river then
the puzzle has been solved

```
= ( right )  and  ( boat side  = ( right )  then
```

```
= ( left )  and  ( boat side  = ( right )  then
```

```
= ( right )  and  ( boat side  = ( left )  then
```

```
= ( left )  and  ( boat side  = ( right )  then
```

```
= ( right )  and  ( boat side  = ( left )  then
```

3.8 ENFORCE THE RULES

Finally, these rules need to be checked at all times. Just update the blocks of code you added in step 1.7 with a few new blocks. Then run the code and test the logic.

Find these blocks of code in the Boat sprite

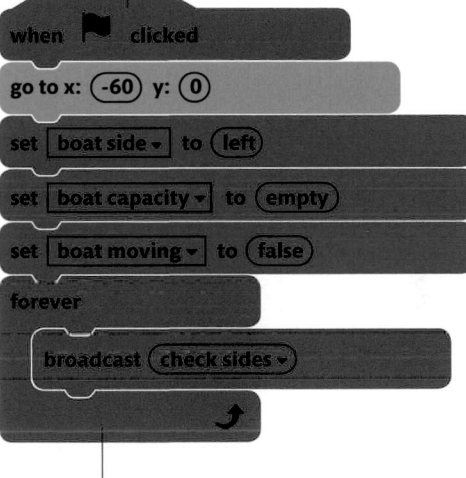

```
when [flag] clicked
go to x: (-60) y: (0)
set [boat side ▾] to (left)
set [boat capacity ▾] to (empty)
set [boat moving ▾] to (false)
forever
    broadcast (check sides ▾)
```

The forever loop will constantly check the sides to see if any of the rules have been broken

Count the moves

Can you add a variable that counts how many "moves" the player has made so far? You will need to add a new variable called **moves** and set it to increase by one every time someone clicks on the boat.

Add this block to the code created in step 1.8 to increase the number of moves

```
change [moves ▾] by (1)
```

Background music

Many puzzle games have simple background music to help the player focus. To add music, select the Backdrops icon at the bottom right of the screen, then click the Sounds tab. Go to the Choose a sound icon at the bottom left and look for "Dance Chill Out". Then add this code to make the sound play forever.

You can pick any sound of your choice from the Sound library

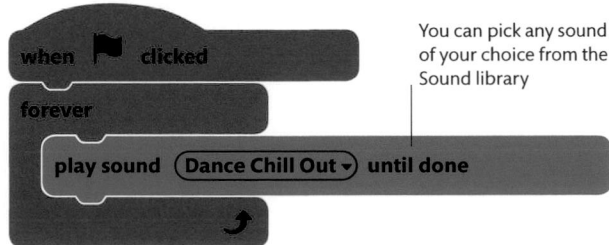

```
when [flag] clicked
forever
    play sound (Dance Chill Out ▾) until done
```

Asteroid dodge

In this Scratch project, you will create a side-scrolling game with animated sprites. This is a great way to get started with game development. The finished game will test your concentration and the speed of your reflexes.

How the game works

The game lets a player use the up and down arrow keys to navigate a rocketship around asteroids. The "Warp Speed" slider controls the speed of the game, and the rate at which asteroids appear increases as the game progresses. Any contact between the rocketship and an asteroid ends the game.

Moving obstacles
The project creates an illusion of motion by moving the obstacles along the x-axis and making them appear at random intervals.

Use the slider to increase the speed

Click here to exit the full-screen mode

Click here to run the project

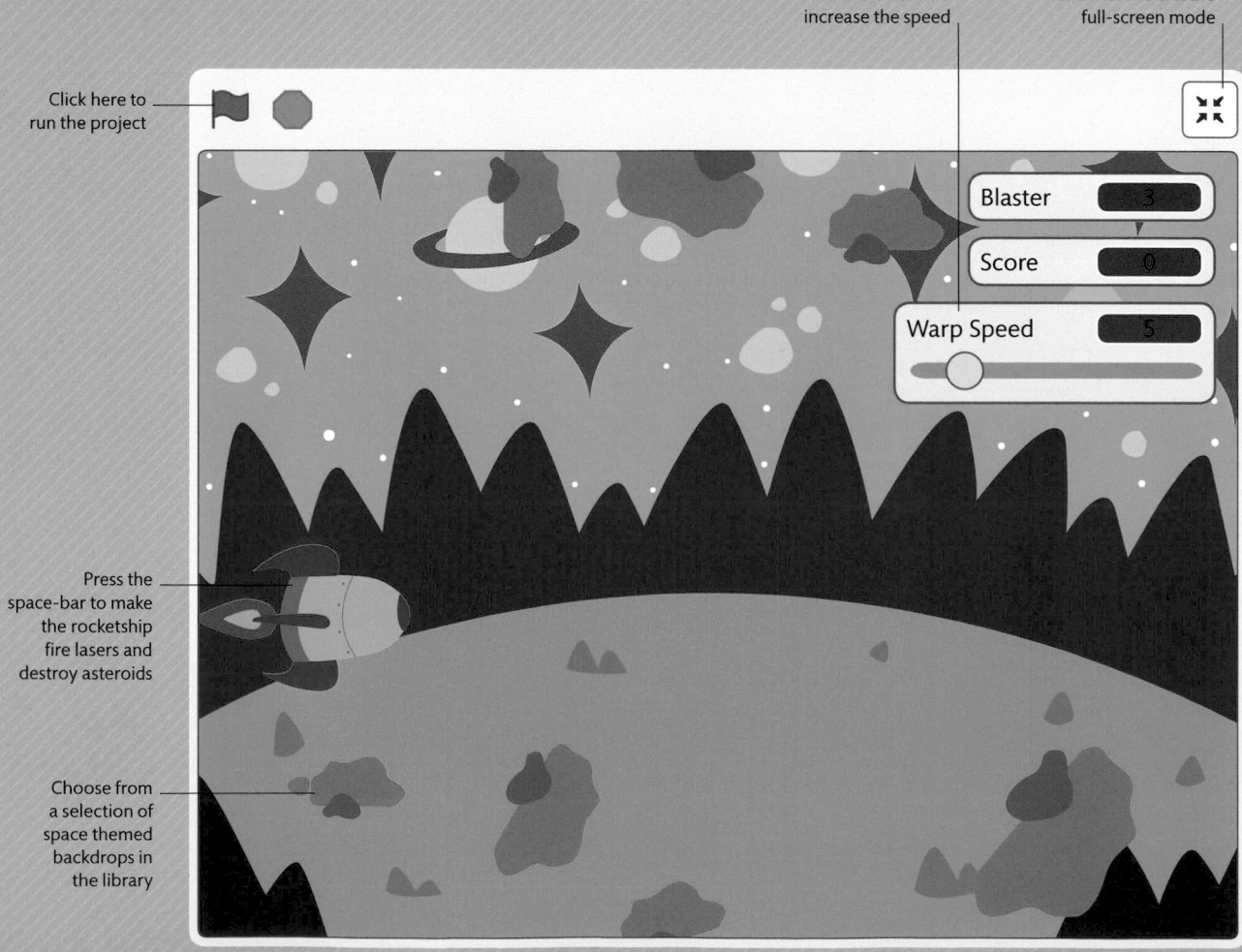

Blaster   3
Score   0
Warp Speed   5

Press the space-bar to make the rocketship fire lasers and destroy asteroids

Choose from a selection of space themed backdrops in the library

YOU WILL LEARN

> How to create a side-scrolling game

> How to use loops to create continuous game play

> How to create a game that increases in difficulty as it progresses

Time:
20–25 mins

Difficulty level

WHERE THIS IS USED

In this game, the background and other objects move across the screen to make it seem like the player is moving. This popular approach is called a side-scrolling game, and can be adapted for racing or shooting games.

Program design

The program uses one main loop to check which key is being pressed to move the rocket up or down the screen. It fires a laser to destroy asteroids if the space-bar is pressed. Using this main loop, the code continually checks if any rocks have touched the rocket to end the game.

```
                    START

Move rocketship          Up arrow
up screen      ← YES     key pressed?
                            │ NO

Move rocketship          Down arrow
down screen    ← YES     key pressed?
                            │ NO

Fire laser and           Pressed space-bar?
destroy asteroids ← YES
                            │ NO

Game over     ← YES      Touched rock?     NO →
```

1 Prepare for launch

This project requires a few basic elements to get started. The sprites and backdrop will create the space setting for the game, and variables will add functionality.

1.1 ADD SPRITES

Start a new project and delete the default Cat sprite. Then add the two new sprites required for this game: Rocketship and Rocks. You can find them in the Sprite library.

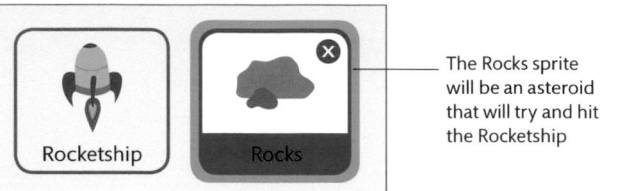

The Rocks sprite will be an asteroid that will try and hit the Rocketship

1.2 PREPARE THE BACKDROPS

You will need two backdrops for this game. First, click on Choose a Backdrop in the Stage section at the bottom right of Scratch. Then select Space to add the first backdrop for this game. You can pick any other backdrop from the "Space" category if you want.

Click here to add a new backdrop

Choose a Backdrop

The new backdrop can be viewed under the Backdrops tab

1.3 PAINT IT RED

To create the second backdrop, go to the Backdrops tab and click on the original backdrop1. Click on the Convert to Bitmap button, and use the Fill tool to paint the backdrop red. Finally, click the Space backdrop again so it will be selected as the default background.

Click here to make Space the default backdrop

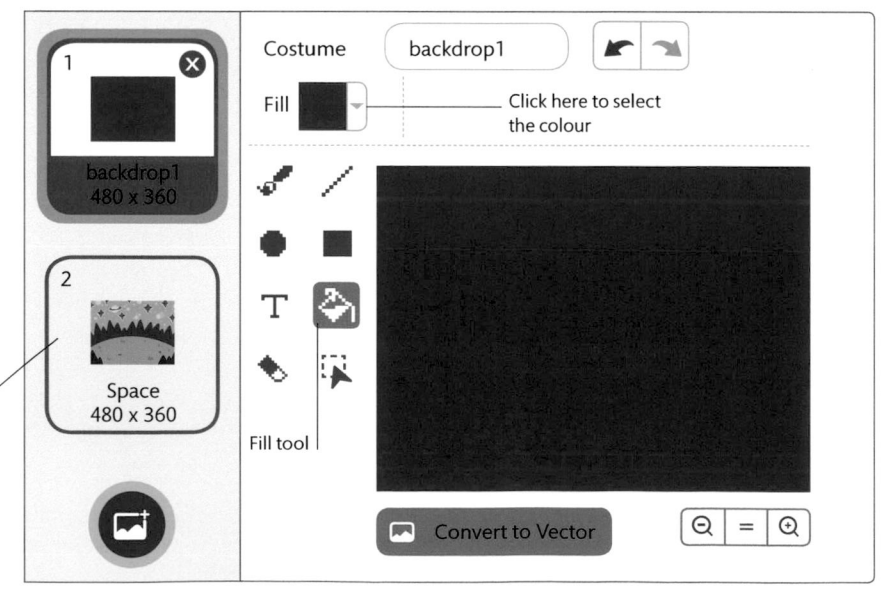

Click here to select the colour

Fill tool

1.4 CREATE VARIABLES

Use the Make a Variable button in the Variables section to create all the variables required for this project. Make sure the check-boxes for the variables **Blaster**, **Score**, and **Warp Speed** are ticked so that they show on screen.

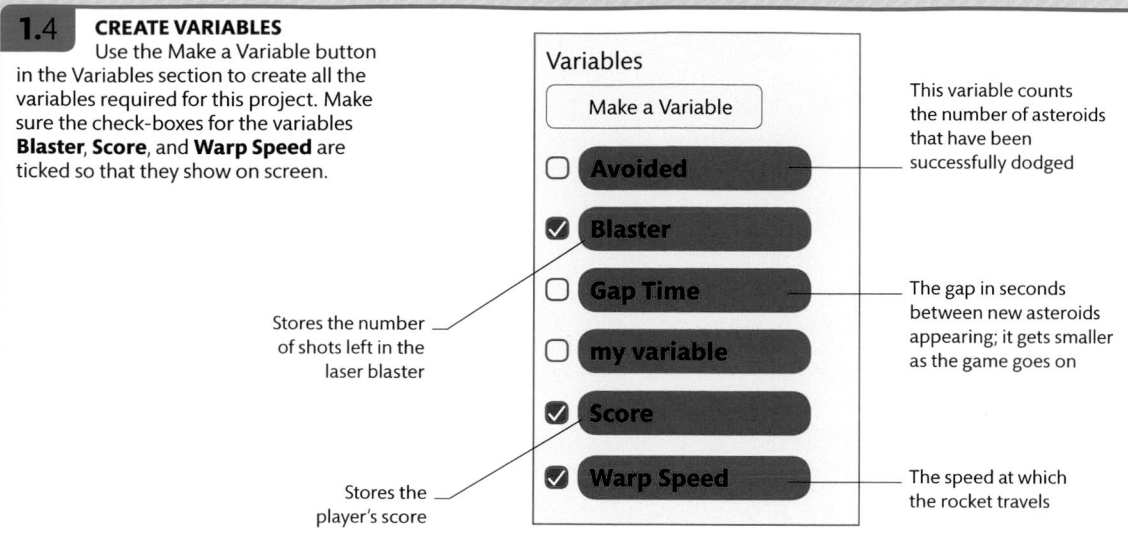

Variables

Make a Variable

☐ Avoided — This variable counts the number of asteroids that have been successfully dodged

☑ Blaster

☐ Gap Time — The gap in seconds between new asteroids appearing; it gets smaller as the game goes on

☐ my variable

☑ Score

☑ Warp Speed — The speed at which the rocket travels

Stores the number of shots left in the laser blaster

Stores the player's score

2 Code the rocketship

Now that the basic elements required for the project are ready, you can begin coding. Start by adding code for the Rocketship sprite. The next few steps will add steering controls for the rocket, make it move through space, and also add a blaster gun for firing the laser.

2.1 PREPARE THE ROCKET

Select the Rocketship sprite in the Sprite List and then add these code blocks for it. This will set up the rocketship for the game.

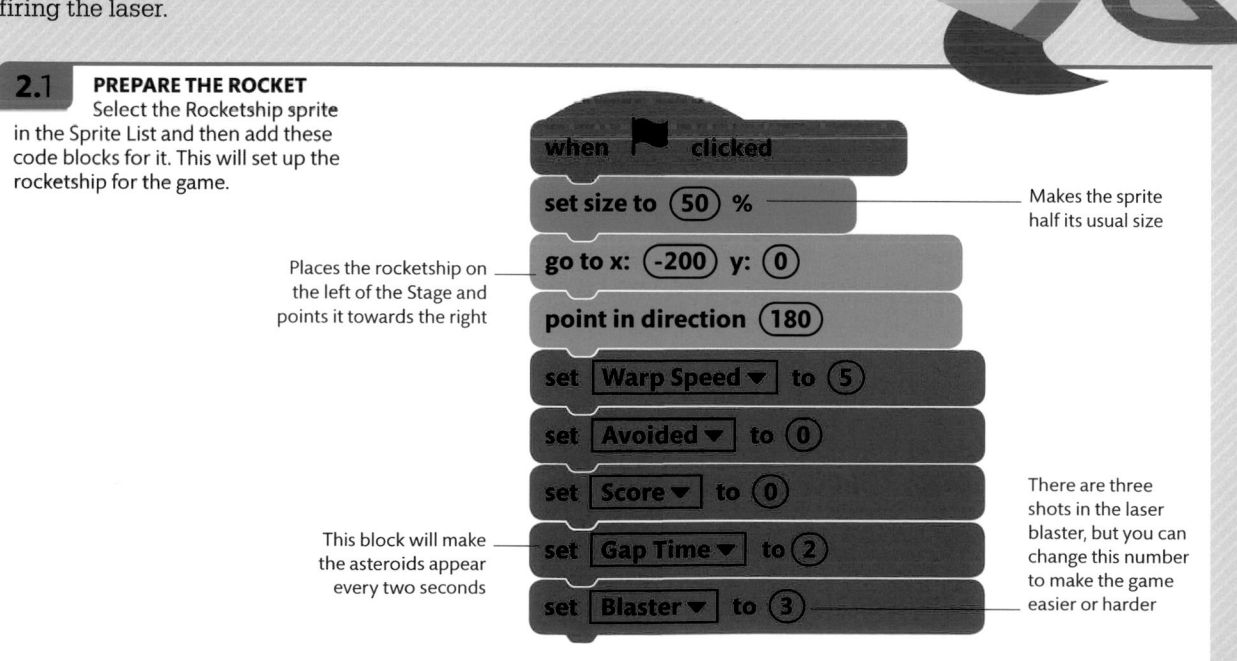

```
when 🏳 clicked

set size to 50 %

go to x: -200 y: 0

point in direction 180

set Warp Speed ▼ to 5

set Avoided ▼ to 0

set Score ▼ to 0

set Gap Time ▼ to 2

set Blaster ▼ to 3
```

Makes the sprite half its usual size

Places the rocketship on the left of the Stage and points it towards the right

This block will make the asteroids appear every two seconds

There are three shots in the laser blaster, but you can change this number to make the game easier or harder

2.7 UPDATE THE SCORE

Now add these blocks of code. This will increase the score by one each time five asteroids are avoided. Then, it reduces the Gap Time – this means new asteroids will appear more often.

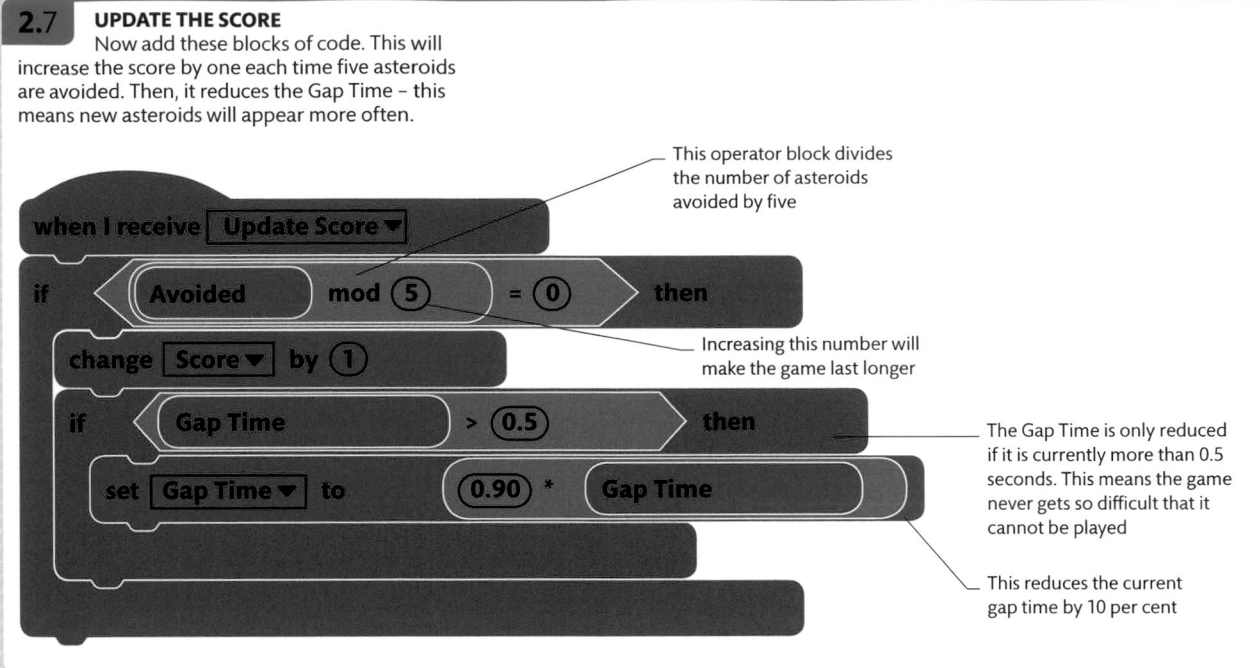

This operator block divides the number of asteroids avoided by five

Increasing this number will make the game last longer

The Gap Time is only reduced if it is currently more than 0.5 seconds. This means the game never gets so difficult that it cannot be played

This reduces the current gap time by 10 per cent

3 Code the asteroids

Once the rocketship is prepared, you need to program the asteroids. The code in the next few steps will make a stream of asteroids move across the screen, making them fly across space. An explosion will also be added to indicate the asteroids being hit by the blaster gun.

3.1 CREATE THE ASTEROIDS

To write the code for the asteroids, click on the Rocks sprite and add this code. The forever loop means that once the game is started, asteroids keep getting created.

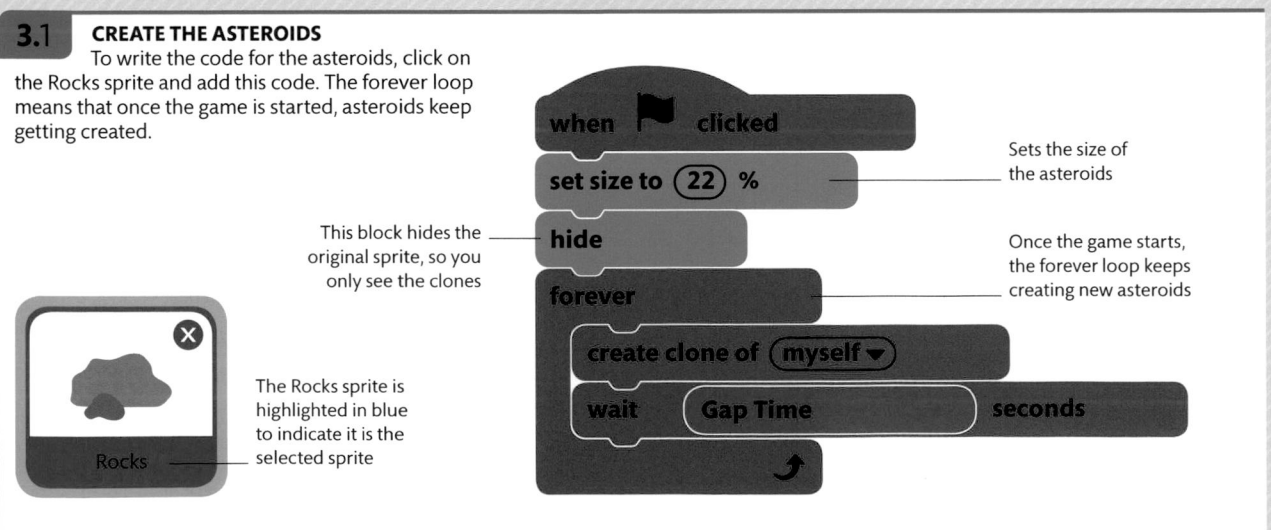

This block hides the original sprite, so you only see the clones

The Rocks sprite is highlighted in blue to indicate it is the selected sprite

Sets the size of the asteroids

Once the game starts, the forever loop keeps creating new asteroids

3.2 MAKE THE ASTEROIDS MOVE

To create the illusion of the rocketship moving, the rocks will move across the screen. Once they reach the left side, they vanish. The random blocks are used so that each asteroid starts at different positions at the right side of the screen. This way the player cannot guess where the next one will appear, making the game more challenging. Add this code to the Rocks sprite to make this happen.

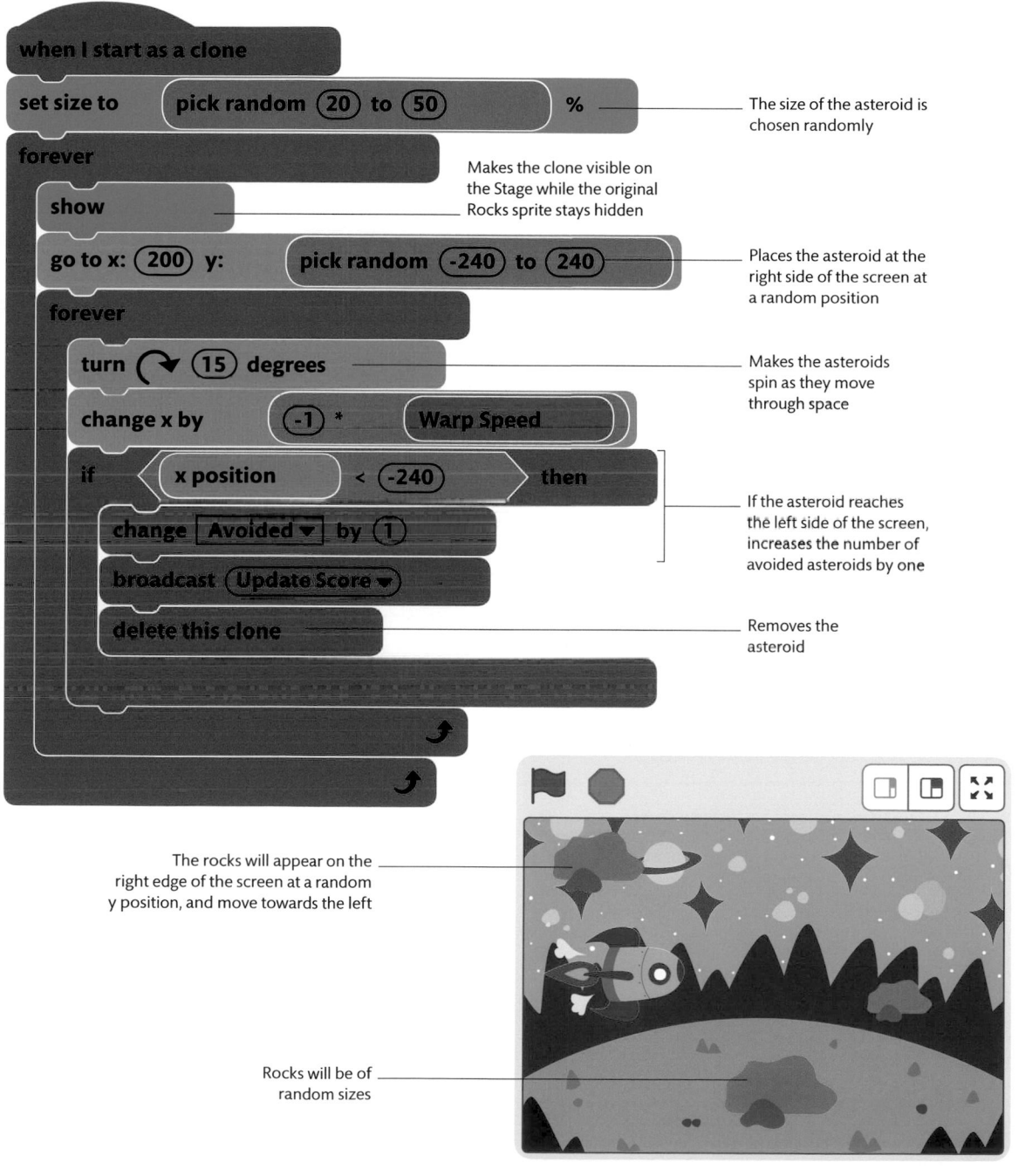

when I start as a clone

set size to pick random (20) to (50) %
— The size of the asteroid is chosen randomly

forever

show
— Makes the clone visible on the Stage while the original Rocks sprite stays hidden

go to x: (200) y: pick random (-240) to (240)
— Places the asteroid at the right side of the screen at a random position

forever

turn ↻ (15) degrees
— Makes the asteroids spin as they move through space

change x by (-1) * Warp Speed

if < x position < (-240) > then
— If the asteroid reaches the left side of the screen, increases the number of avoided asteroids by one

change Avoided ▼ by (1)

broadcast Update Score ▼

delete this clone
— Removes the asteroid

The rocks will appear on the right edge of the screen at a random y position, and move towards the left

Rocks will be of random sizes

3.3 REMOVE ASTEROIDS

Now it is time to add some code to fire the blaster gun. When this program is run it will destroy the asteroids when the blaster is fired. Add these blocks to the Rocks sprite and then test it out. Remember that you only have three shots.

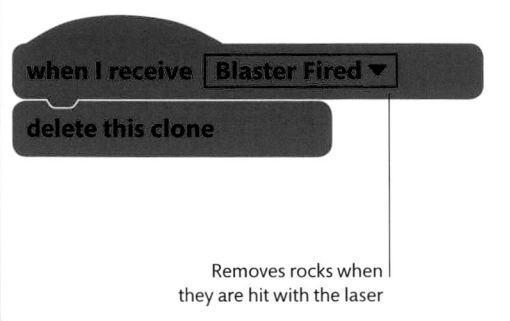

```
when I receive  Blaster Fired ▼
delete this clone
```

Removes rocks when they are hit with the laser

3.4 CREATE AN EXPLOSION SPRITE

Next, add one more sprite to create an explosion when the asteroids hit the rocketship. Choose "Paint" from the Choose a Sprite menu at the bottom right of the Sprite List, and name the sprite "Explosion".

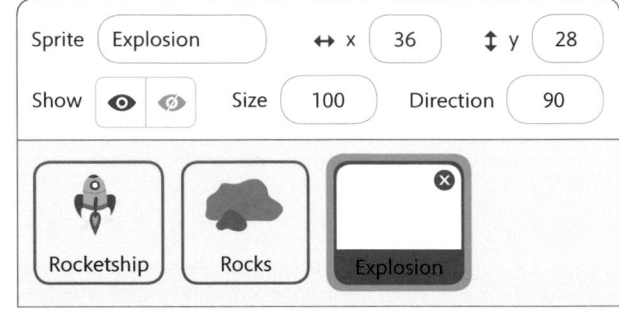

Sprite	Explosion	↔ x	36	↕ y	28
Show	👁 👁̸	Size	100	Direction	90

Rocketship · Rocks · Explosion

3.5 PAINT THE EXPLOSION

Use the Paint Editor to draw a large fireball effect. You can use the Brush, Fill, and Text tools to create a large, colourful explosion.

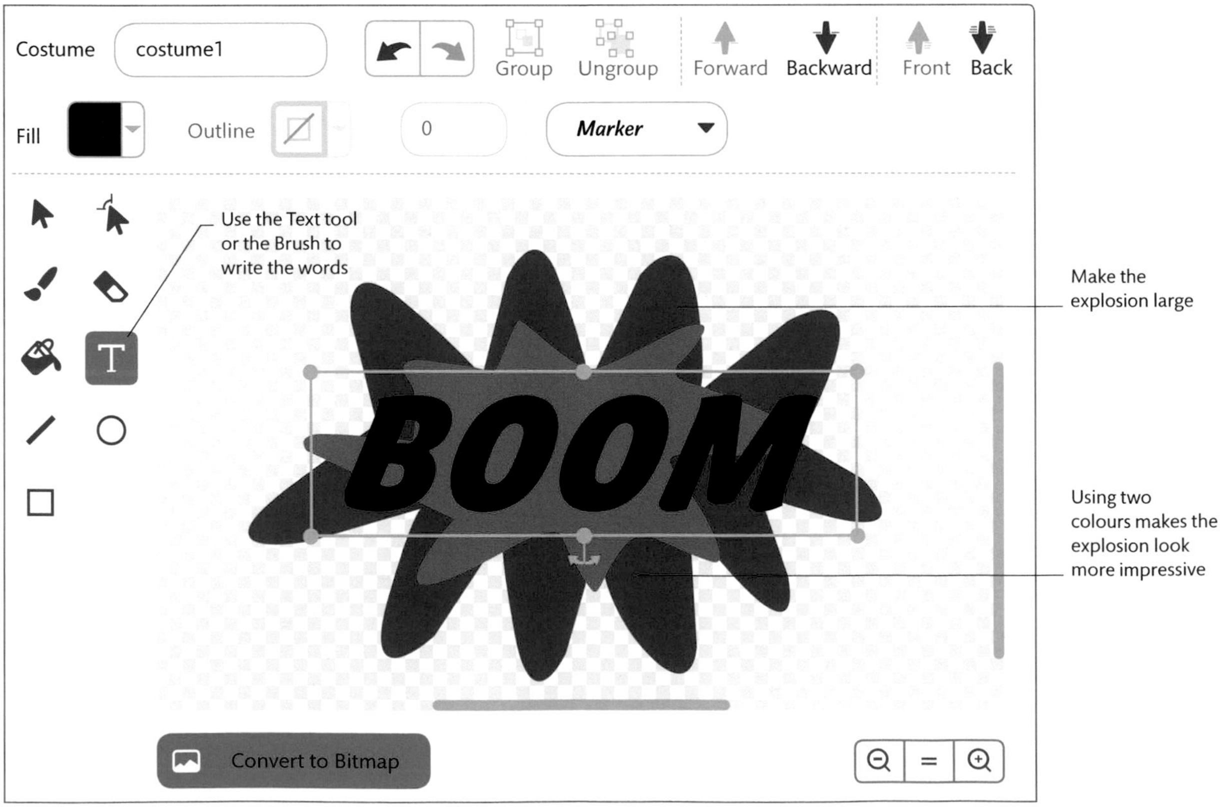

Costume	costume1		Group	Ungroup	Forward	Backward	Front	Back

Fill ▮ ▼   Outline ⊘ ▼   0   Marker ▼

Use the Text tool or the Brush to write the words

Make the explosion large

BOOM

Using two colours makes the explosion look more impressive

Convert to Bitmap   ⊖ = ⊕

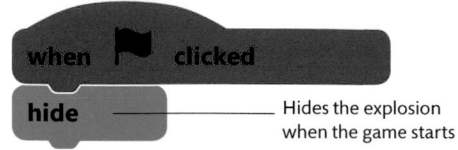

3.6 HIDE EXPLOSION

When the game starts, you do not want the explosion to be visible on the screen. Add this code to the Explosion sprite to hide it.

when ⚑ clicked

hide ———————— Hides the explosion when the game starts

3.7 GAME OVER

Next, add these blocks of code to the Explosion sprite. This will make the explosion appear in the middle of the screen when the Game Over message is broadcast and then stops the game.

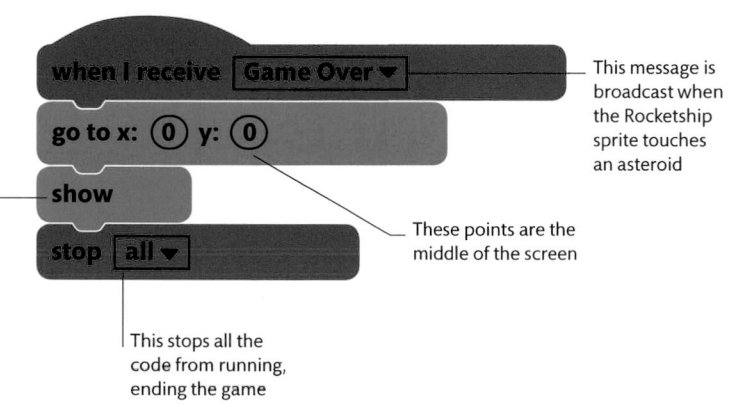

when I receive Game Over ▼ ———— This message is broadcast when the Rocketship sprite touches an asteroid

go to x: ⓪ y: ⓪

This is the opposite of the **hide** block, so it displays the explosion ———— show

These points are the middle of the screen

stop all ▼

This stops all the code from running, ending the game

3.8 WARP SPEED SLIDER

One final touch is to right click on the **Warp Speed** variable at the top right of the screen and choose "slider". This means that the player can now adjust the speed of the game by moving the slider left and right. The game is now ready to play. See how far you can guide the rocketship, and do not forget to use the blaster when you need to. You can even adjust the Warp Speed slider and see how fast you can go.

Blaster   3
Score   0
Warp Speed   5

normal readout

large readout

slider

Choose the slider option from the drop-down menu

Hacks and tweaks

Add a cheat code to refill your blaster gun
Adding your own cheat codes is a fun way to personalize a project. Add this code to the Rocketship sprite so that when you press the x key, the blaster is refilled with three more shots. You can also try to create a sprite that appears every 20 asteroids, and increases the number of blaster shots by one if it touches the spaceship.

Change this number to increase or decrease the number of shots to be refilled

Deep space spectrum
Add this code to the backdrop and it will make the background cycle through a spectrum of colours, creating a fantastic intergalactic light show.

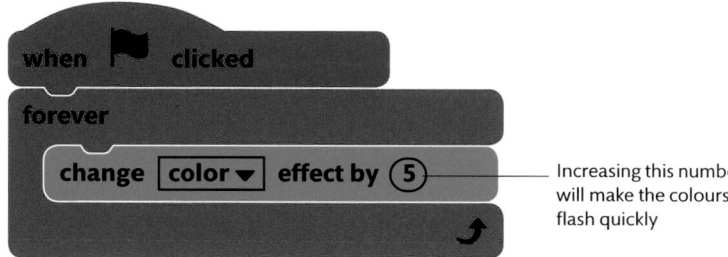

Increasing this number will make the colours flash quickly

Run the code to see the changing colours of the backdrop

Unidentified flying objects

You can easily add other objects for the rocketship to dodge. Just add a new costume to the Rocks sprite and then amend the code as shown here. This will make dogs fly through space.

These new blocks will change the Rocks costume into flying space dogs once every 10 times the code is run

The space dog is added to the Rocks costumes

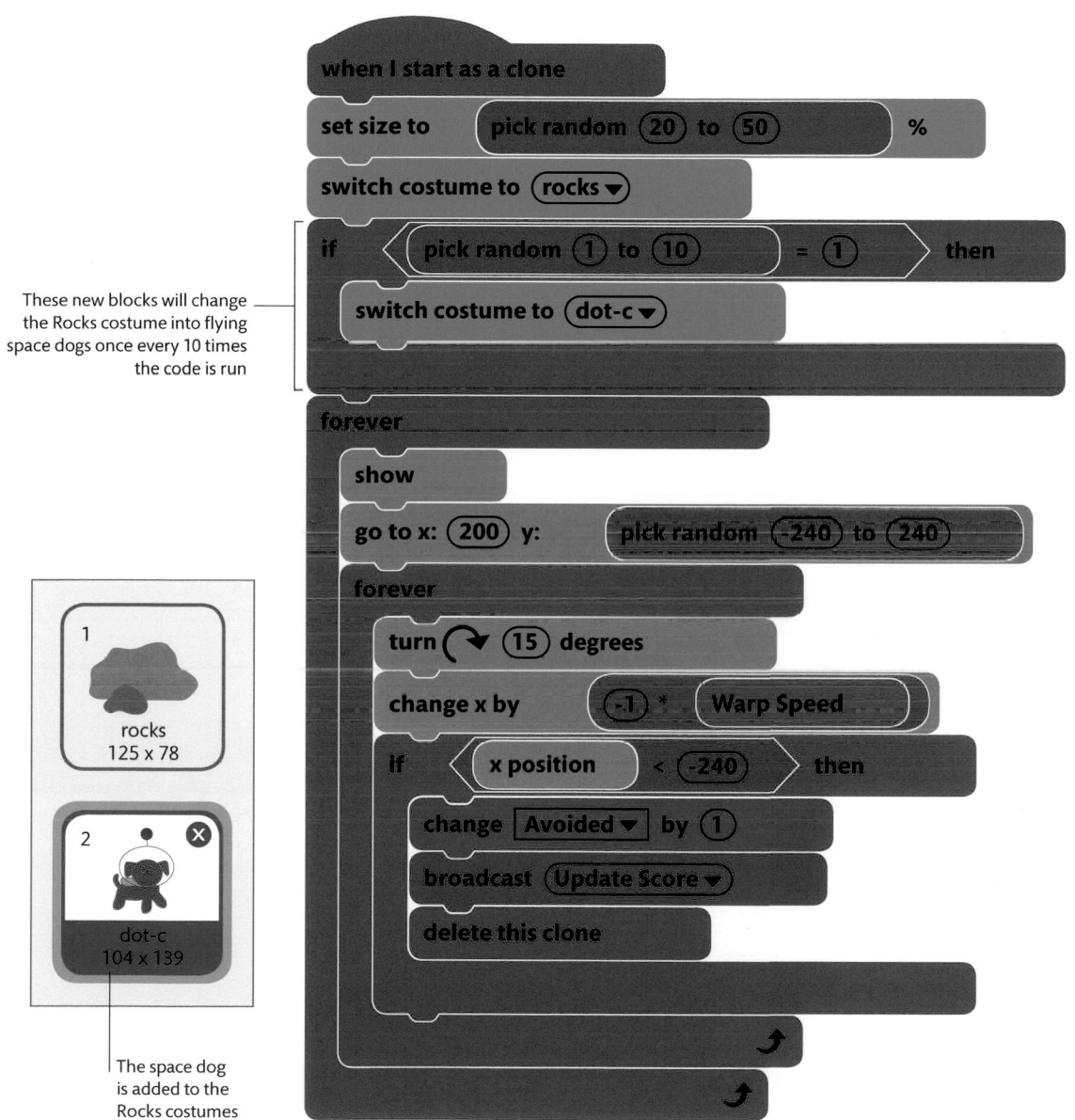

```
when I start as a clone
set size to pick random (20) to (50) %
switch costume to (rocks ▼)
if < pick random (1) to (10) = (1) > then
    switch costume to (dot-c ▼)

forever
    show
    go to x: (200) y: pick random (-240) to (240)
    forever
        turn ↻ (15) degrees
        change x by ( (-1) * Warp Speed )
        if < x position < (-240) > then
            change [Avoided ▼] by (1)
            broadcast (Update Score ▼)
            delete this clone
```

1
rocks
125 x 78

2
dot-c
104 x 139

PYTHON

What is Python?

Python is one of the world's most popular programming languages. It is extremely versatile, and can be used in many real-world situations. A text-based language, the readability and clear layout of its code makes Python less daunting for beginners.

Why use Python?

Created by Dutch programmer Guido van Rossum, Python was released in 1991. It was designed as a high-level language that would appeal to programmers familiar with the C language (see p.347) and the Unix operating system. Python lends itself to writing a wide range of programs, and is used by many schools and universities to teach programming.

The syntax (arrangement of words and symbols forming the code) in Python is close to English syntax, which supports its goal of producing readable code. In addition, Python also forces programmers to lay out their code in a structured way. This is a useful skill to develop as it makes it easier for the programmer to debug the code, and also improves readability for other users.

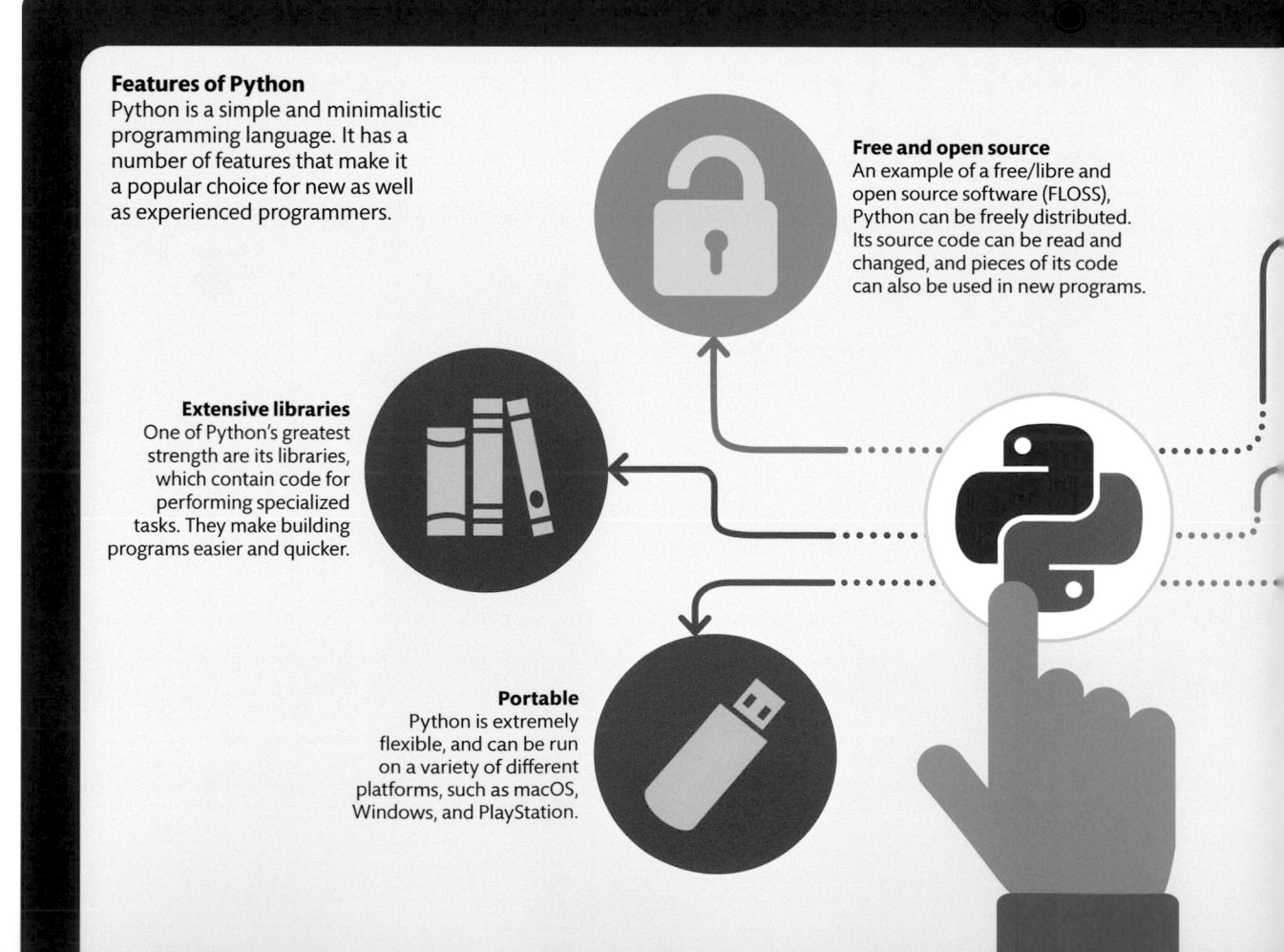

Features of Python
Python is a simple and minimalistic programming language. It has a number of features that make it a popular choice for new as well as experienced programmers.

Free and open source
An example of a free/libre and open source software (FLOSS), Python can be freely distributed. Its source code can be read and changed, and pieces of its code can also be used in new programs.

Extensive libraries
One of Python's greatest strength are its libraries, which contain code for performing specialized tasks. They make building programs easier and quicker.

Portable
Python is extremely flexible, and can be run on a variety of different platforms, such as macOS, Windows, and PlayStation.

How it works

A Python program, usually called a script, is a text file containing words, numbers, and punctuation that correspond to instructions. These instructions are formed of certain fixed patterns of words and symbols, which the programmer types in. IDLE (Integrated Development and Learning Environment) is a free app that is installed with Python. Designed for beginners, it includes a basic text editor that allows the user to write, edit, and save code before running a program.

ENTER CODE　　　**SAVE**　　　**RUN**

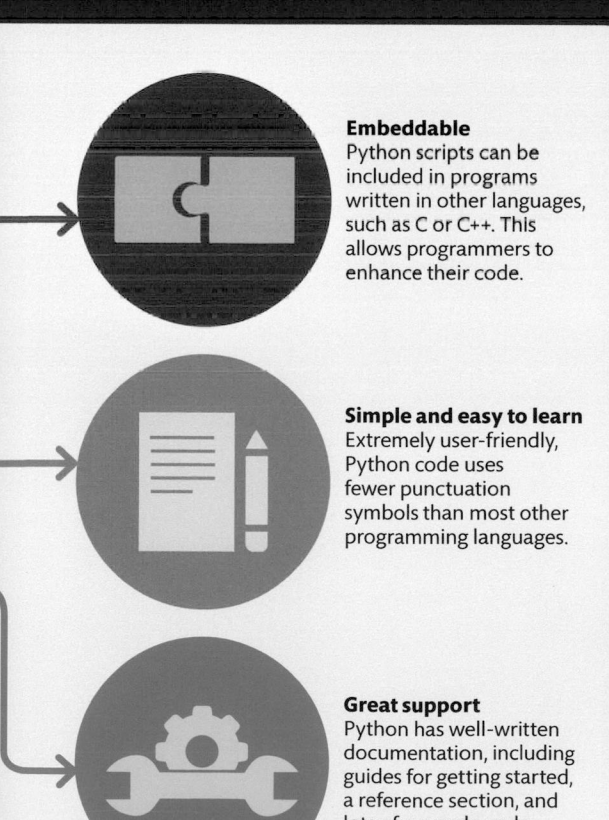

Embeddable
Python scripts can be included in programs written in other languages, such as C or C++. This allows programmers to enhance their code.

Simple and easy to learn
Extremely user-friendly, Python code uses fewer punctuation symbols than most other programming languages.

Great support
Python has well-written documentation, including guides for getting started, a reference section, and lots of example code.

APPLICATIONS

Python is a general-purpose programming language that can be used to create systems for a variety of purposes. This, along with its many specialist libraries, makes it useful in fields as diverse as business, medicine, science, and media.

Game development
Python has various modules and libraries that support game development. These include *pygame*, for 2D games, and *PySoy*, a cloud-based 3D game engine.

Space
Software engineers have used Python to create tools for NASA's Mission Control Centre. These tools help the crew prepare for and monitor the progress of each mission.

Business
Python's easy syntax makes it ideal for building large applications. It has become especially popular with the rise of Fintech (financial technology).

Scientific computing
Python has libraries that can be used in specific areas of science, such as *PyBrain* for machine learning and *pandas* for data analysis.

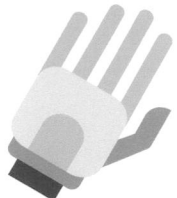

Web development
Python is used by software developers for automated tasks, such as build control and testing. It can also be used to create web applications.

Installing Python

It is important to download the right version of Python. This book uses the current version: Python 3. It is free and can be easily downloaded from the Python website. Follow the instructions that match your operating system.

Python on Windows

Before you install Python, you need to find out if your system has a 32-bit or 64-bit architecture. To do that, click the Start menu, right-click This PC, and choose Properties. A computer's architecture indicates how its microprocessor handles data at the lowest level. A 64-bit processor provides higher performance, as it can handle more data at once than a 32-bit processor.

FLYING CIRCUS

Python is not named after the snake, as many people think, but after the British television series *Monty Python's Flying Circus*. Guido van Rossum, who created the language, was a big fan of the programme, and Python was a title that stuck. There are numerous references to Monty Python's sketches in Python's official documentation.

1 Go to the Python website
Go to *www.python.org* and click on Downloads in the menu bar on top. A list of operating systems will appear on screen. Select Windows.

> https://www.python.org

4 Open IDLE
Once the installation process is complete, go to the Applications folder and find IDLE inside the Python folder. You can also search for it in the Start menu. Double-click on IDLE to open Python's shell window. You will see IDLE's menu at the top of the window.

2 Download an installer
Find the most recent Python installer, which should start with 3. Be sure to select an x86 installer for 32-bit machines and x86-64 installer for 64-bit machines. Either the web-based or executable installer will work.

The website could have a more recent version of Python

- Python 3.7.3 - 2019-03-25
  - Download Windows x86-64 web-based installer
  - Download Windows x86 web-based installer

3 Run the installer
Once downloaded, double-click the installer file and follow the instructions that appear on screen. Remember to tick the box on the initial prompt that says "Add Python to Path".

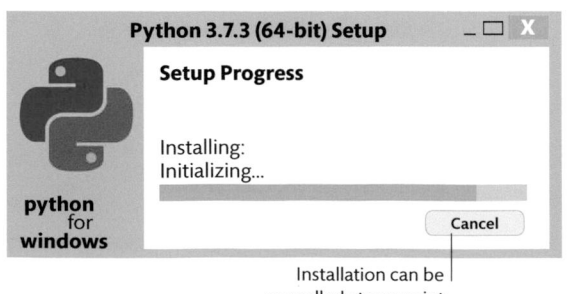

Python 3.7.3 (64-bit) Setup

Setup Progress

Installing:
Initializing...

Cancel

python for windows

Installation can be cancelled at any point

Python on a Mac

Before you install Python, you need to check which operating system
your Mac uses. This will tell if your system has a 32-bit or 64-bit
architecture. To find out, click the Apple icon in the top left of the screen
and select About this Mac from the drop-down menu. If the processor is
an Intel Core Solo or Intel Core Duo it means your system has a 32-bit
architecture, otherwise it has a 64-bit architecture.

1 Go to the Python website
Go to *www.python.org*. Hover the cursor over the
Downloads tab in the menu bar on top to generate a list
of operating systems. Select the macOS option to find
the installers suited to Mac computers.

https://www.python.org

4 Open IDLE
Once the installation is complete, open the
Applications folder from the Finder window's sidebar and
find IDLE in the Python folder that appears. Double-click
on IDLE to open Python's shell window and check that
installation has been successful.

2 Download an installer
Find the most recent Python 3 installer that matches
your operating system and select it. The **Python.pkg** file
will download to your system automatically.

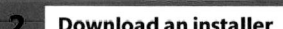

Choose this installer
for 64-bit machines

- Python 3.7.3 - 2019-03-25
  - Download macOS 64-bit Installer
  - Download macOS 64-bit/32-bit installer

Choose this installer
for 32-bit machines

3 Run the installer
Once downloaded, double-click the **.pkg** file
and follow the instructions that appear. The installation
process on a Mac computer is very straightforward.
It will only ask you to agree to the licencing requirements
and confirm the installation location (usually the
Macintosh Hard Disk).

Select Continue to proceed
with the installation

Shell window

The shell window is opened as soon as IDLE is launched. It can be very useful to try out ideas in this window as it gives instant feedback. However, as the shell cannot save code it is not practical to use this window to evaluate more than a few lines of code at a time.

The shell window shows the version of Python it is running

```
                              Python 3.7.0 Shell

Python 3.7.0 (v3.7.0:1bf9cc5093, Jan 26 2019, 23:26:24
[Clang 6.0 (clang-600.057)] on darwin
Type "copyright", "credits" or "license()" for more information
>>>
```

This information depends on the operating system being used

Editor window

The editor window can be opened by selecting New File or Open from IDLE's File menu. This window allows programmers to type in much longer and more complex series of instructions and save them in files. Python file names are easy to identify as they end with .py.

A Python file displayed in the editor window

```
                          helloworld.py

print("Hello world!")
```

COLOURS IN THE CODE

To make code easier to read and errors easier to spot, IDLE displays the text in the editor and shell windows using different colours. The colour used for each word depends on its role in the code.

COLOURS IN THE CODE		
Code	**Colour**	**Example**
Built-in commands	Purple	print()
Symbols, names, and numbers	Black	25
Text within quotes	Green	"Hello world!"
Errors	Red	pront()
Keywords	Orange	if, else
Output	Blue	Hello world!

Using IDLE

Python's Integrated Development and Learning Environment (IDLE) interface has two windows for carrying out different tasks. The shell evaluates short commands immediately, while the editor window allows programmers to enter and save longer programs in files.

Running a program using IDLE

To run a program from IDLE, the file containing it must first be opened in the editor window. If it runs successfully, the shell window displays the output of the code, otherwise the relevant error message appears.

```
                         Python 3.7.0 Shell

Python 3.7.0 (v3.7.0:1bf9cc5093, Jan 26 2019, 23:26:24
[Clang 6.0 (clang-600.057)] on darwin
Type "copyright", "credits" or "license()" for more information
>>>
======== RESTART: /Users/tinajind/Desktop/helloworld.py ========
Hello world!
>>>
```

Common errors

As well as being case-sensitive, Python is also very strict about the layout and spelling of code. It requires sections of code to be indented by four spaces from the line above, in order to make the code more readable. These features often trip up new programmers. IDLE helps spot and fix errors with pop-up information boxes and error messages (see pp.130–33) in the shell window.

```
num = 4
1f (nut == 5):
    print("Hello world!")
```

Here "num" has accidentally been typed as "nut"

The mistake in code results in this error message

```
Traceback (most recent call last):
  File "/Users/tinajind/Desktop/helloworld.py",
line 2, in <module>
    if (nut == 5):
NameError: name 'nut' is not defined
>>>
```

Data in Python

Python programs work with various data types. These types determine what can be done with different data items, and how they are input, output, and stored. Errors in Python code are often the result of forgetting to consider a value's type and what it allows.

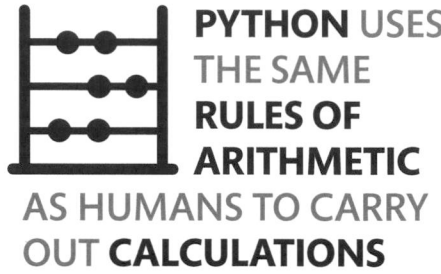

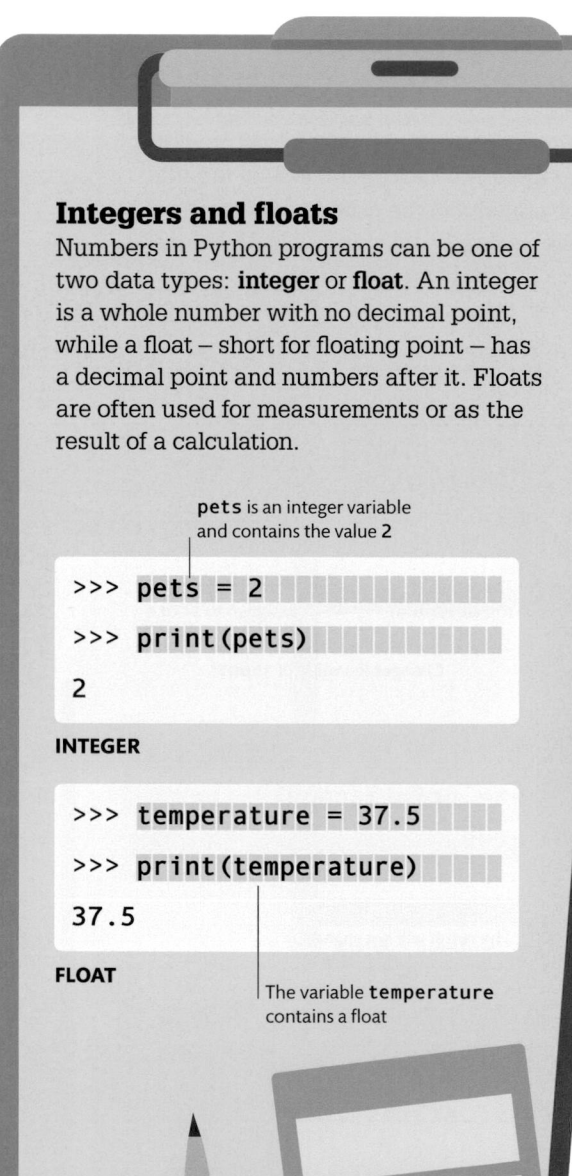

Integers and floats

Numbers in Python programs can be one of two data types: **integer** or **float**. An integer is a whole number with no decimal point, while a float – short for floating point – has a decimal point and numbers after it. Floats are often used for measurements or as the result of a calculation.

`pets` is an integer variable and contains the value 2

```
>>> pets = 2
>>> print(pets)
2
```

INTEGER

```
>>> temperature = 37.5
>>> print(temperature)
37.5
```

FLOAT

The variable `temperature` contains a float

Arithmetic operators

Numbers and variables containing numbers can be combined using addition, subtraction, multiplication, and division. The symbols for these processes are called arithmetic operators. While addition and subtraction use familiar symbols, multiplication and division are slightly different and are shown as * and / respectively.

ARITHMETIC OPERATORS	
Symbol	**Meaning**
+	Addition
-	Subtraction
*	Multiplication
/	Division

Calculations

These Python commands use arithmetic operators to calculate the tax owed on an item costing £8.00.

This variable contains `price` as a float

The result will be stored in the variable `tax`

```
>>> price = 8.00
>>> tax = price * (20/100)
>>> print(tax)
1.6
```

The output is the value stored in the variable `tax`

Characters and strings

The data type Python uses for text is known as **string**. Made up of individual letters, numbers, or symbols called characters, strings must always have quotation marks at the beginning and the end. Python allows both single and double quotation marks in its code.

Strings

The variable **forename** contains a string made up of the characters of the word Alan.

```
>>> forename = "Alan"
>>> forename
'Alan'
```

THE LEN() FUNCTION

In a lot of programs it can be very useful to know the length of a **string** or a **list**. Python has a built in **len()** function that can be used for both tasks. Remember that the length of a **string** will also count spaces and punctuation.

```
>>> len("Hello Alan")
10
```

Combining strings

Combining two or more strings to make a new one is called concatenation. Python uses the + symbol to do this. It is important to change any values with different data types into strings before concatenating them.

```
>>> happy = "happy birthday to you "
>>> name = "Emma "
>>> song = happy + happy + "happy \
birthday dear " + name + happy
>>> song
'happy birthday to you happy
birthday to you happy birthday
dear Emma happy birthday to you'
```

The variable **song** now contains a personalized version of "Happy Birthday"

Casting

It is sometimes necessary to change the data type of a value for a particular task, for example, when combining an integer and string. This is called **casting**, and Python provides functions, such as **str()** and **int()**, to allow it.

Change integer to string

```
>>> age = 25
>>> print ("Your age is " + str(age))
Your age is 25
```

Lists

It is often useful to be able to group items together in a program. Python provides the **list** data type for this. A list can contain items that have the same data type or a variety of data types. To create a list, the values are enclosed in square brackets and are separated by commas.

The string **"two"** enclosed in double quotes

```
>>> my_list = [1, "two", \
              3, 5, 7.4]
>>> my_list
[1, 'two', 3, 5, 7.4]
```

Single quotes do not affect the value

Backslash splits code over two lines

Accessing items

To allow programmers to access items in a list, Python numbers each one. Typing the name of the list followed by the item number inside square brackets retrieves the relevant item. Python numbers the items in a list starting at 0.

```
>>> my_list[0]
1
>>> my_list[2]
3
```

First item in the list **my_list**

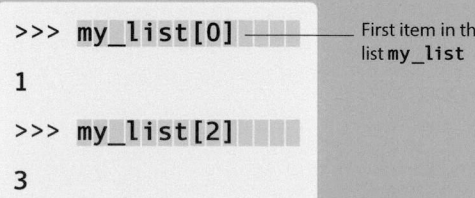

Logical operators and branching

Booleans, another data type in Python, have only two possible values: True or False. Booleans allow programmers to write branching statements that control which parts of a program are run.

= AND ==

It is important to distinguish between Python's two different equals signs. A single equals "=" means that a value is being assigned to a variable. A double equals sign "==" is a logical comparison to see whether or not the values on either side of it are equal.

Logical operators

Logical operators are symbols that allow a program to make comparisons between values. Any comparison that uses logical operators is called a Boolean expression and the result is a Boolean value. Logical operators are similar to arithmetic operators (see p.102), but produce Boolean values rather than numbers.

LOGICAL OPERATORS	
Symbol	**Meaning**
<	Less than
>	Greater than
==	Equal value
!=	Not equal value

Equality
A Boolean expression containing a double equals sign is True if the values on either side of it are equal.

Checks if the values on each side are equal

```
>>> 3 == 9
False
```

Less than
An expression containing the < symbol is True if the value on the left is less than the value on the right.

Checks if the value on the left is smaller

```
>>> 3 < 5
True
```

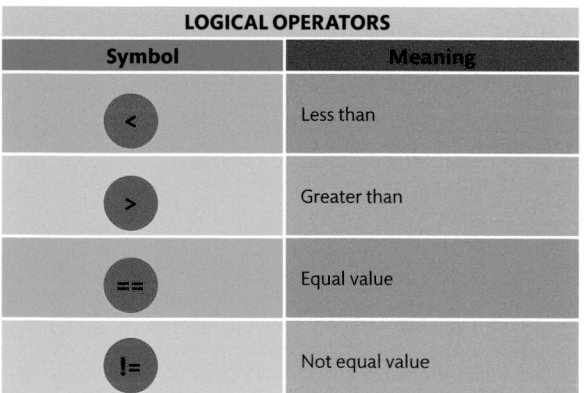

```
>>> oranges = 5
>>> apples = 7
>>> oranges != apples
True
```

Stores the value 5 in the variable **oranges**

Values in **oranges** and **apples** are not equal

Not equal
Logical operators also work with variables. This example stores values in two variables then checks for the stored values being unequal.

Boolean operators

Boolean expressions can be combined using the Boolean operators "and", "or", and "not". They allow programmers to build more complex expressions that can deal with several different variables.

```
>>> (oranges < 10) and (apples > 2)
True
```
For this to be True, both expressions must be True

```
>>> (oranges < 10) or (apples == 3)
True
```
Only one expression has to be True for this statement to be True

Putting "not" in front of a True expression results in the value False

```
>>> not(apples == 7)
False
```

More than two branches
When there are more than two possible paths through the code, the **elif** command – short for **else-if** – is used. It is possible to have several **elif** branches between the **if** branch and the **else** branch.

This comparison is the first condition

If the first condition is True this is printed

```python
quiz_score = 9
if quiz_score > 8:
    print("You're a quiz champion!")
elif quiz_score > 5:
    print("Could do better!")
else:
    print("Were you actually awake?")
```

This is the second condition

If the second condition is True this line is printed

If both conditions are False this line is the output

One branch
The most straightforward branching command has only a single branch that the computer takes if the condition is True. This is called an **if** statement.

```python
temperature = 25
if temperature > 20:
    print("Switch off heating")
```

This comparison is the condition

If the condition is True the code runs

Two branches
A situation where a program should do one thing if a condition is True, and another if it Is False needs a command with two branches. This is an **if-else** statement.

```python
age = 15
if age > 17:
    print("You can vote")
else:
    print("You are not old \
enough to vote")
```

The comparison is the first condition

If the condition is True, this line is printed

If the condition is False this line is printed

A backslash is used to split a long line of code over two lines without affecting the output

Branching

Computer programs often contain code that should only be run in certain situations. To allow for this programmers create branches in the code. The decision about which branch to take depends on the result of a Boolean expression. This helps programmers tailor a program's behavior to different inputs or environments.

Loops in Python

Programs often contain blocks of code that are repeated several times. Rather than typing the same lines over and over again, programmers use loops. The type of loop they choose depends on a number of factors.

For loop

If a programmer knows the number of times a block of code will be repeated, a **for** loop is used. The code that gets repeated is called the body of the loop and each execution is called an iteration. The body is always indented from the **for** statement and begins exactly four spaces from the start of the next line. Indentation can also be done manually.

Loop variable

This example loop counts from one to three, printing each number on a new line, followed by a line saying "Go!". The loop variable keeps track of loop iterations. It takes the value of each item in **range(1,4)** in a set order, starting with the first value for the first iteration.

```
for counter in range(1,4):
    print(counter)
print("Go!")
```

This is like a list that has the values 1, 2, 3

This statement is the loop body

For loop with a list

To process a list using **for** loop there is no need to use the **range()** function. Python can simply set the value of the loop counter to each item in the list in turn. In this example, the loop prints out each name in the list **red_team**.

```
red_team = ["Sue", "Anna", "Emily", "Simar"]

print("The Red Team members are:")
for player in red_team:
    print(player)
```

player is the temporary loop counter

While loops

Another type of loop in Python is the **while** loop. It is used when a programmer does not know how many times a loop will run and cannot use a **for** loop. The number of iterations in this loop depends on user input.

This question will appear, asking for user input

```
answer = input("Should I keep going? (y/n)")
while answer == "y":
    answer = input("Should I keep going? (y/n)")
```

The question is asked again

Loop condition

A **while** loop includes a question called a loop condition, the answer to which is either True or False. The body of the loop is executed only if the loop condition on that iteration is True. If the loop condition is False, the **while** loop ends.

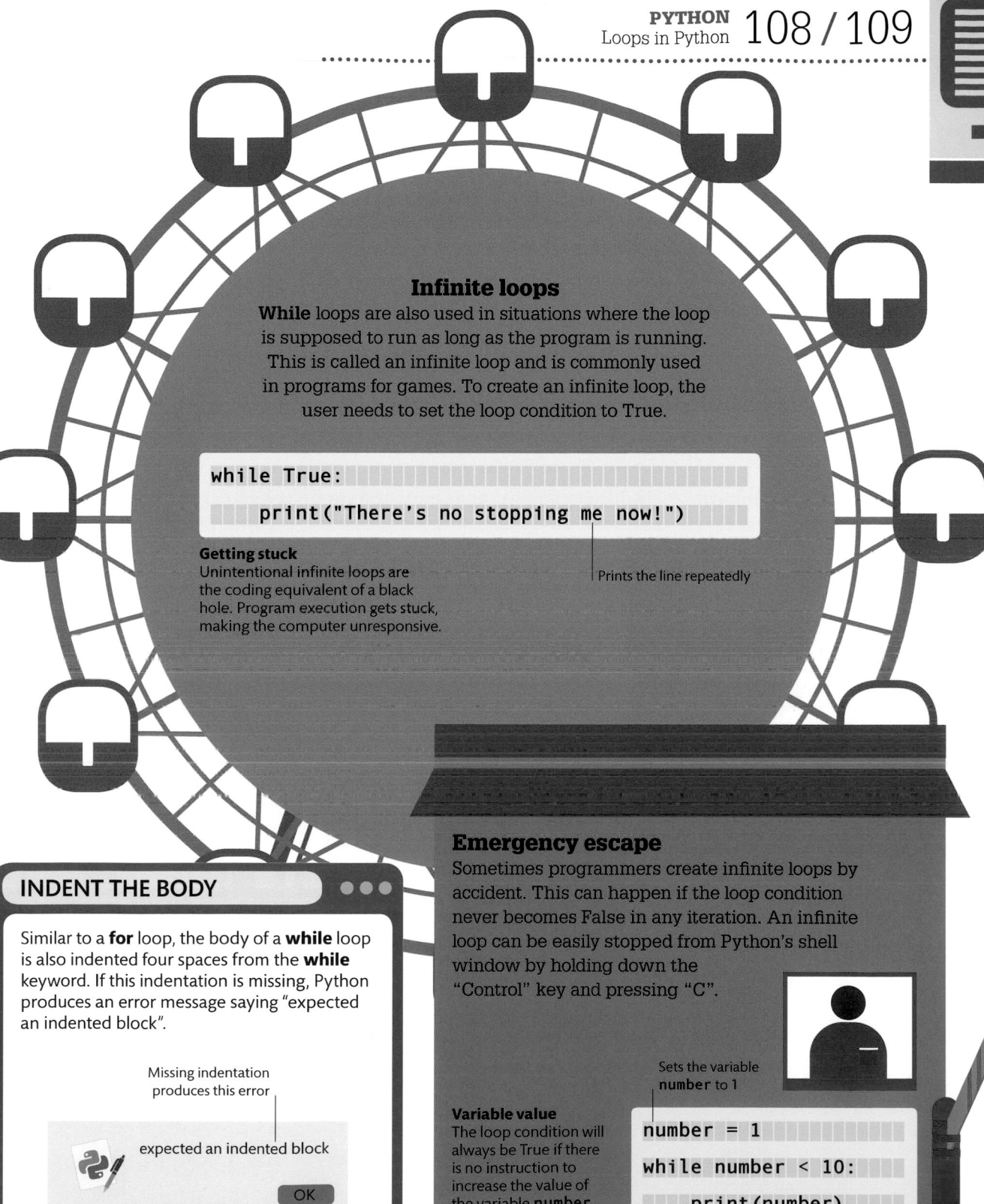

Infinite loops

While loops are also used in situations where the loop is supposed to run as long as the program is running. This is called an infinite loop and is commonly used in programs for games. To create an infinite loop, the user needs to set the loop condition to True.

```
while True:
    print("There's no stopping me now!")
```

Getting stuck
Unintentional infinite loops are the coding equivalent of a black hole. Program execution gets stuck, making the computer unresponsive.

Prints the line repeatedly

Emergency escape

Sometimes programmers create infinite loops by accident. This can happen if the loop condition never becomes False in any iteration. An infinite loop can be easily stopped from Python's shell window by holding down the "Control" key and pressing "C".

INDENT THE BODY

Similar to a **for** loop, the body of a **while** loop is also indented four spaces from the **while** keyword. If this indentation is missing, Python produces an error message saying "expected an indented block".

Missing indentation produces this error

```
expected an indented block

                        OK
```

Variable value
The loop condition will always be True if there is no instruction to increase the value of the variable **number** in the loop body.

Sets the variable **number** to 1

```
number = 1
while number < 10:
    print(number)
```

Functions

Pieces of code that carry out a specific task are called functions. If the task is executed often, it is possible to separate it from the main code to avoid typing identical instructions multiple times. Breaking the code into sections this way also makes it easier to read and test the program.

Using functions

Using a function is also known as "calling" it. Most of the time, this is as simple as typing the function's name followed by a pair of brackets. If the function takes a parameter it goes inside the brackets. A parameter is a variable or value that is given to the function to allow it to carry out its task.

Defining a function
When a function is defined (see pp.114–15), it always has the keyword "def" and the function's name at the start of the code block.

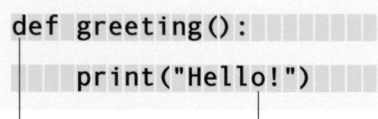

```
def greeting():
    print("Hello!")
```

The keyword **def** tells Python that this block of code is a function

The parameter of the function

POST OFFICE

A **METHOD** IS A **FUNCTION** THAT CONTAINS SOME **CODE** TO **CARRY OUT A TASK**

Built-in functions

Python includes a range of built-in functions that enable the completion of basic tasks. These include getting input from the user, displaying output on screen, simple arithmetic, and determining the length of a string or list. The examples below can all be tried in IDLE's shell window.

input() function's parameter is a question that prompts the user for input

```
>>> name = input("What is your name? ")
What is your name? Tina
>>> print("Hello " + name)
Hello Tina
```

User inputs response

print() function's parameter is a string that is displayed on screen

Number to be rounded

```
>>> pi = 22/7
>>> pi
3.142857142857143
>>> round(pi, 2)
3.14
```

Decimal places

input() and print()
The **input()** function gets data from the user, and the **print()** function displays it as output on the screen. The parameter for **input()** is displayed on screen to prompt the user.

round()
This function rounds off a float to a specific number of decimal places. It takes two parameters – the number to be rounded, and the number of decimal places to shorten it to.

Calling another way

Built-in functions, such as **print()** or **len()**, can be easily called because they accept parameters of various types. A method is a function associated with a particular object, and can only be used on that object (see pp.156–57). Calling a method is different from calling a built-in function. A method call has the object's name, a dot, and the method name followed by a pair of brackets.

Object name

upper() method
This method transforms all the lowercase letters in a string to uppercase letters. The **upper()** method can only be used with strings.

```
>>> city = "London"
>>> city.upper()
'LONDON'
```

The bracket may take a parameter

Method name

Adding to a list
The list method **append()** adds a value to the end of a list. It has one parameter – the value that needs to be appended to the list.

```
>>> mylist = [1,2,3,4]
>>> mylist.append(5)
>>> print(mylist)
[1, 2, 3, 4, 5]
```

The new value is added to the end of the list

Creating functions

Python has a Standard Library that contains a lot of ready-made functions. Most programs, however, include functions that have to be specifically made for them. In Python, creating a function is known as "defining" it.

Defines a function that takes a temperature in Celsius and prints it in Fahrenheit

This formula converts Celsius to Fahrenheit

```
def print_temperature_in_Fahrenheit(temperature_in_Celsius):
    temperature_in_Fahrenheit = temperature_in_Celsius * 1.8 + 32
    print(temperature_in_Fahrenheit)
```

Prints the temperature in Fahrenheit

A function that completes a task
Some functions simply carry out a task without returning any information to the code that called them. This is similar to sending a letter by normal post. A postal worker delivers the letter and completes his task, but does not inform the sender that it has been delivered.

Top-down coding

In Python, functions are normally defined at the top of the program, before the main code. This is because it is important to define a function before it is called, either by another function or by the main part of the code.

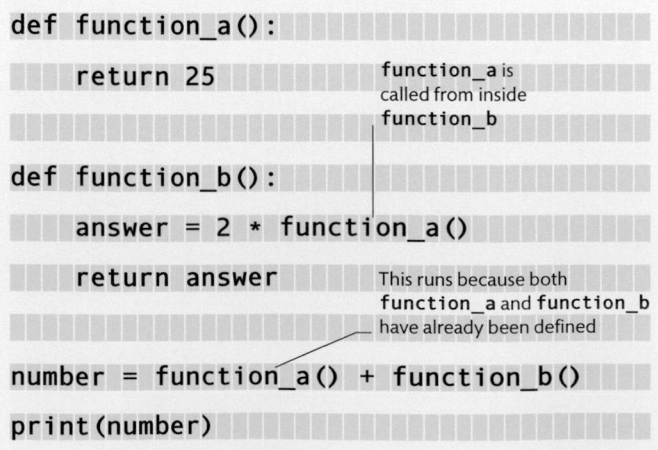

```
def function_a():
    return 25

def function_b():
    answer = 2 * function_a()
    return answer

number = function_a() + function_b()
print(number)
```

function_a is called from inside function_b

This runs because both function_a and function_b have already been defined

Order of definition
Since the main part of the code calls both `function_a` and `function_b`, they must be defined at the start of the program. As `function_a` relies on `function_b`, `function_a` must be defined before `function_b`.

```
def count_letter_e(word):
    total_e = 0
    for letter in word:
        if letter == "e":
            total_letter_e = total_letter_e + 1
            return total_letter_e


user_name = input("Enter your name: ")
total_es_in_name = count_letter_e(user_name)
print("There are " + str(total_es_in_name) + "E's in your name")
```

Defines a function that counts and returns the number of times the letter "e" appears in a particular word

This loop examines each letter in the word being investigated

Asks users to enter their name, and then stores it in the variable **user_name**

A function that returns a value
There are also functions that carry out a task and produce a value, which is then returned to the code that called them. This enables the calling code to store the value in a variable, if necessary.

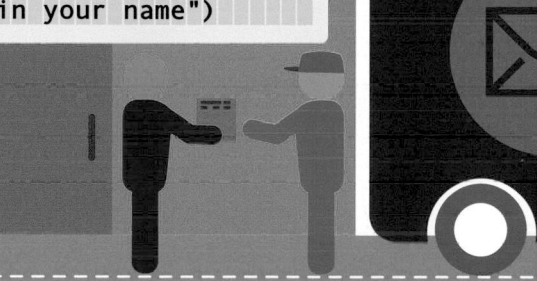

Local and global variables

A global variable is declared in the main part of the code and is visible everywhere. A local variable, on the other hand, is declared inside a function and is only visible there. For example, global variables are like divers, visible to everyone under the sea, including people in submarines. Local variables, however, are like people in the submarines: only visible to other people in that submarine. Global variables can be read by other functions in the code, but local variables cannot. The code will return an error message if a local variable is used outside of its function. A function must declare the global variable it intends to use or else Python will create a new local variable with the same name.

```
def reset_game():
    global score, charms, skills
    score = 0
    charms = 0
    skills = 0
```

reset_game()
This function resets a game by setting the value of the global variables **score**, **charms**, and **skills** back to **0**.

Declares the global variables that this function will be using

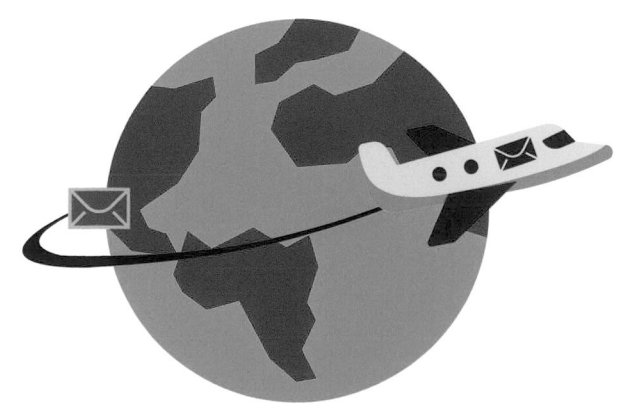

Libraries

A Python library is a collection of files, known as modules, that are available for other programmers to use. These modules contain code for common programming tasks, ranging from interacting with hardware to accessing web pages.

Built-in modules

The library that comes with every installation of Python is called the Python Standard Library. It contains modules, such as **Tkinter** and **turtle**, which are available without the need to download or install any additional code.

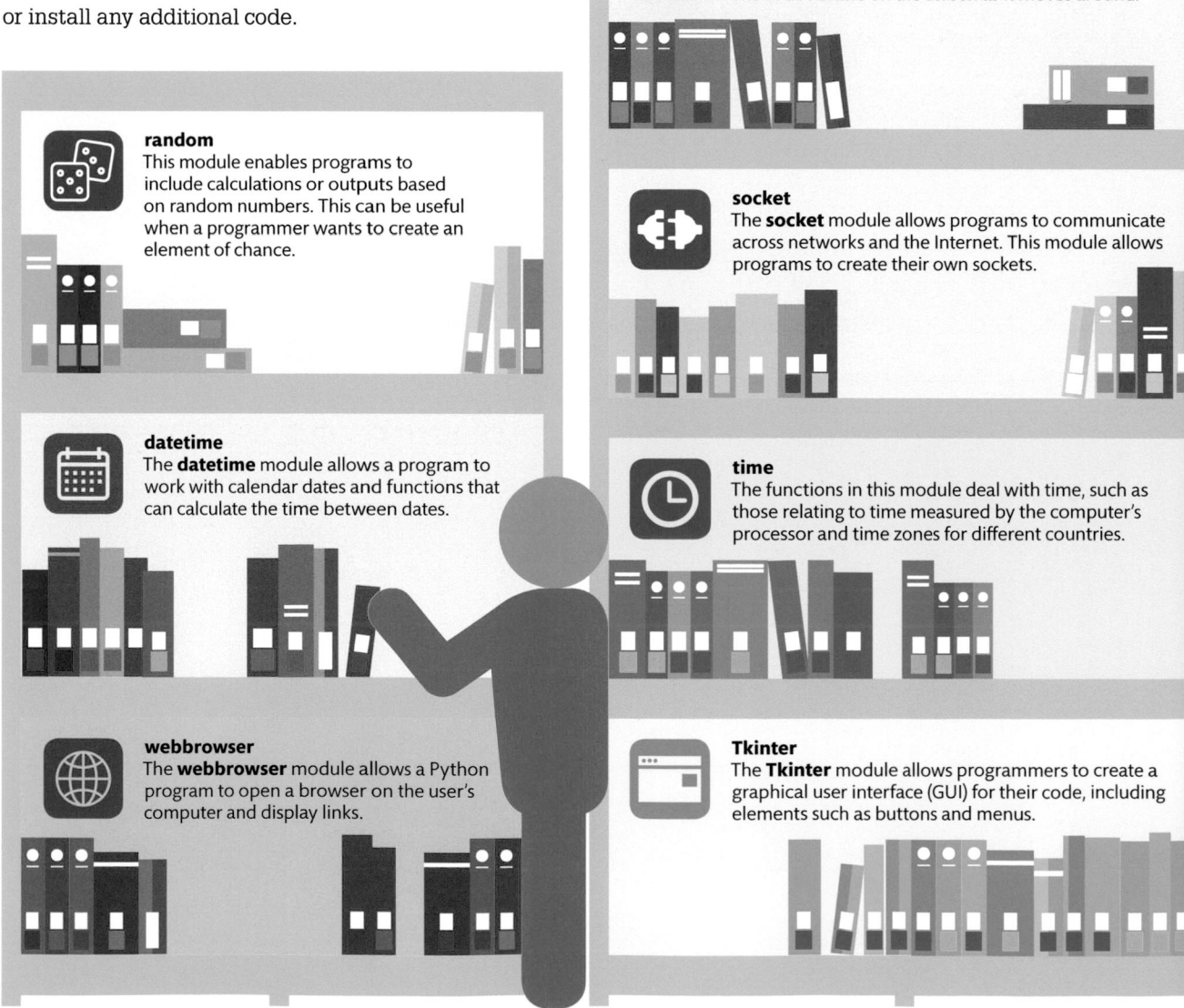

turtle
This Python module recreates the turtle-shaped robot from the programming language Logo. The robot draws on the screen as it moves around.

random
This module enables programs to include calculations or outputs based on random numbers. This can be useful when a programmer wants to create an element of chance.

socket
The **socket** module allows programs to communicate across networks and the Internet. This module allows programs to create their own sockets.

datetime
The **datetime** module allows a program to work with calendar dates and functions that can calculate the time between dates.

time
The functions in this module deal with time, such as those relating to time measured by the computer's processor and time zones for different countries.

webbrowser
The **webbrowser** module allows a Python program to open a browser on the user's computer and display links.

Tkinter
The **Tkinter** module allows programmers to create a graphical user interface (GUI) for their code, including elements such as buttons and menus.

Importing and using modules

The process of adding a module to a program so that its functions and definitions can be used is called "importing". In Python, it is possible to import either an entire module or just certain functions of a module. The method used for carrying out the import depends on the requirement of the program. The examples below illustrate the different methods for importing and the required syntax in each case.

import ...

The keyword import followed by the module's name makes all of the module's code available to the program. To access the module's functions, it is necessary to type the imported module's name followed by a dot before the function name in order to call that function.

```
import time

offset = time.timezone

print("Your offset in hours from \
UTC time is: ", offset)
```

Calls the **timezone** function of the **time** module

Prints the value in the variable **offset**

from ... import ...

If a program only needs to use one or two functions from a module it is considered better just to import these, and not the whole module. When functions are imported in this way it is not necessary to include the name of the module before the function name.

```
from random import randint

dice_roll = randint(1,6)

print("You threw a", dice_roll)
```

The **randint()** function produces a random integer between 1 and 6

from ... import ... as ...

If the name of a function in the module is too long or is similar to other names in the code it can be useful to rename it. Just as in "from ... import ...", this allows the programmer to refer to the function simply by its new name, without preceding it with the name of the module.

```
from webbrowser import open as show_me

url = input("enter a URL: ")
show_me(url)
```

Displays the user's choice of web page

PYGAME

The **pygame** library contains a huge number of useful modules for coding games. Since **pygame** is not part of the Standard Library, programmers have to download and install it before they can import it to their code. **pygame** is very powerful, but can be challenging for new programmers. One solution to this is the **Pygame Zero** tool (see pp.176–77), which makes the functions in **pygame** easier to use.

Team allocator

When playing team sports, the first thing you have to do is to pick the teams. One way of doing this is to choose team captains and let them choose the players for their teams. However, it might be fairer to pick people randomly. In this project, you'll automate this process by building a tool in Python that picks teams randomly.

How it works

This project will use Python's **random** module to form teams, with randomly selected players. You will use lists (see p.103) to store the player's names. The **random** module will then shuffle this list into a different order. Loops will be used to iterate through the list and display the players. Finally, an **if** statement (see p.105) checks to see if the user is happy with the selection.

Random allocation
This project will pick two teams and a captain for each team. When you run the program, it will display the chosen teams and captains on the screen.

```
                Python 3.7.0 shell

Welcome to Team Allocator!

Team 1 captain: Rose

Team 1:

Jean

Ada

Sue

Claire

Martin         The list of players
                is displayed in the
Harry           shell window

Alice

Craig

Rose

James
```

YOU WILL LEARN

> How to use the **random** module
> How to use lists
> How to use loops
> How to use branching statements

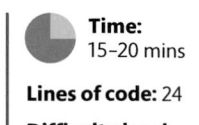

Time: 15–20 mins

Lines of code: 24

Difficulty level
● ● ● ● ●

WHERE THIS IS USED

The code in this project can be reused for tasks that require random allocations. This includes staff shift scheduling, assigning tasks in the workplace, matching people to projects, selecting teams for a quiz, and many more. This can be a quick and fair way of allocating people to teams/tasks.

Program design

The program begins by shuffling the player list. It then allocates the first half as Team 1, randomly selects a captain, and displays the name of the captain along with the names of the rest of the team. The steps are then repeated for the second half of the list – forming Team 2. If you want to pick the teams again, the program repeats the steps, otherwise, the program ends.

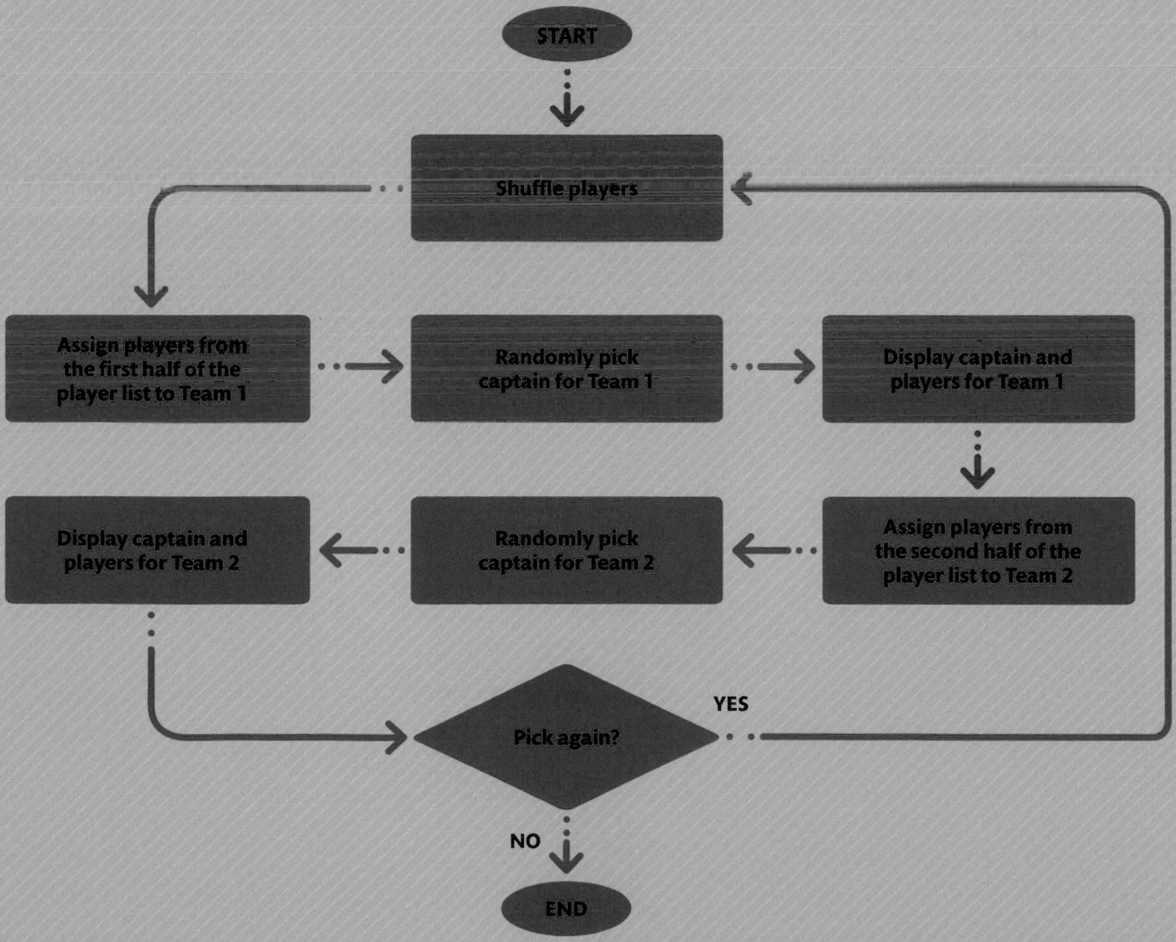

```
              START
                │
        ┌───────▼────────┐
        │ Shuffle players │◄──────────────┐
        └───────┬────────┘                │
    ┌───────────┴──────┐                  │
    ▼                                      │
┌─────────────┐   ┌─────────────┐   ┌─────────────┐
│ Assign      │   │ Randomly    │   │ Display     │
│ players from│──►│ pick        │──►│ captain and │
│ the first   │   │ captain for │   │ players for │
│ half of the │   │ Team 1      │   │ Team 1      │
│ player list │   └─────────────┘   └──────┬──────┘
│ to Team 1   │                            ▼
└─────────────┘                     ┌─────────────┐
┌─────────────┐   ┌─────────────┐   │ Assign      │
│ Display     │   │ Randomly    │   │ players from│
│ captain and │◄──│ pick        │◄──│ the second  │
│ players for │   │ captain for │   │ half of the │
│ Team 2      │   │ Team 2      │   │ player list │
└──────┬──────┘   └─────────────┘   │ to Team 2   │
       │                            └─────────────┘
       ▼
     ◇ Pick again? ◇──── YES ──────────────┘
         │
        NO
         ▼
       END
```

CREATE A TEAM

1 Create a team

This program will simplify the process of picking, or allocating, teams. In this section, you will create the file that will contain the code, import a module, and then make a list of players.

1.1 CREATE A NEW FILE

The first step is to open IDLE. A shell window will appear. Ignore it and click on File in the IDLE menu. Then, choose New File and save the file as "team_selector.py". This will create an empty editor window where you can write your program.

File	Edit	Shell
New File	⌘ N	
Open...	⌘ O	
Open Module...		
Recent Files	▸	
Module Browser	⌘ B	

Click here to create a new file

1.2 ADD THE MODULE

Now, import the **random** module. Type this line at the top of your file, so that you can use the module later. This module contains functions that will allow you to pick players randomly from a list.

```
import random
```

The **random** module can pick random numbers or shuffle a list in a random order

1.3 WELCOME THE USER

Next, create a message to welcome the user to the program. This will show a message to the user when the program executes. Save the file and then run the program to ensure your code works. From the Run menu, choose Run Module. If you have typed in the code successfully the welcome message should appear in the shell window.

```
print("Welcome to Team Allocator!")
```

This phrase will appear as the welcome message in the shell window

SAVE

```
Welcome to Team Allocator!
>>>
```

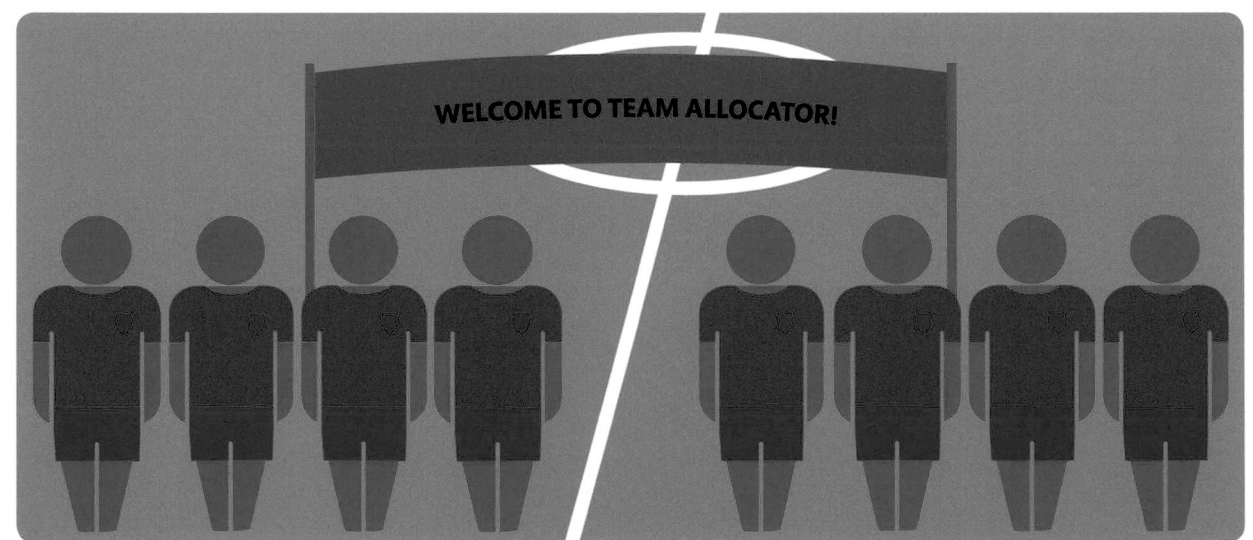

WELCOME TO TEAM ALLOCATOR!

RANDOM NUMBERS

Random numbers can be used to simulate anything that can be random or is meant to be random. For example, rolling a dice, tossing a coin, or picking a card from a deck. Python's **random** module helps add an element of chance to a program. You can read more about how to use this module in the Docs section of IDLE's Help menu.

1.4 MAKE A NAME LIST
You will need names for all the players to generate your teams randomly. In Python, you can keep groups of related items together in a list (see p.103). First, create the variable **players** to store the list by typing this new block of code below the import statement. Put the list contents in square brackets, and separate each item in the list with a comma.

```
import random

players = ["Martin", "Craig", "Sue",
          "Claire", "Dave", "Alice",
          "Sonakshi", "Harry", "Jack",
          "Rose", "Lexi", "Maria",
          "Thomas", "James", "William",
          "Ada", "Grace", "Jean",
          "Marissa", "Alan"]
```

The list is assigned to the variable **players**

You do not need to use a backslash (\) to split a list across two lines. Pressing return or Enter indents the next line in a list

Each item in the list is a string enclosed in quotation marks

This project has 20 players in the list. You can change the number of players if you like (see p. 127)

1.5 SHUFFLE THE PLAYERS
There are a few ways in which the players can be randomly selected. You could randomly keep picking players and assign them to the two teams until you run out of players. This program assumes the number of players is even. However, an even simpler way would be to just shuffle the list of players randomly and assign the first half of the list to "Team 1" and the second half to "Team 2". To do this, the first thing you have to do is to shuffle the players. Use the **shuffle()** function from the **random** module. Type this code below the print command.

```
print("Welcome to Team Allocator!")

random.shuffle(players)
```

This will shuffle the list of players just like you would shuffle a deck of cards

2 Pick teams

Now that the list of players is ready, you can split the players into two teams. You will then assign the team captains. The teams and the names of their captains will be displayed on screen when the program is executed.

SPLITTING LISTS

In Python, when splitting or taking subsets of a list you need to provide two arguments: the start index (position) and the index after the last item in the new list. Remember, indexes start from 0 in Python (see p.103). For example, `players[1:3]` would take the players from index 1 up to index 2. The first index is inclusive (it is included in the new list) and the second index is exclusive (it is included up to the item before it in the new list). If you are splitting the list from the first position up to the last position, then you can leave those indexes blank as Python will understand this. For example, `players[:3]` will take the first three players from the list and `players[4:]` will take the players from index 4 up to the end of the list.

2.1 SELECT THE FIRST TEAM

You now need to split the list into two equal parts. To do this, take the items in the list from position 0 up to the last item in the list and divide it by two. Add the following code at the end of the file for welcoming the user. This will create a new list with the first half of the players list.

```
team1 = players[:len(players)//2]
```
— This new list will be assigned to the variable **team1**

2.2 SELECT TEAM 1 CAPTAIN

Once you have allocated the first team, you need to choose the team captain. To make it a fair selection, this will also be done randomly. A player from **team1** will be picked and assigned to be the team captain. Use the `choice()` function to pick a player randomly from **team1**. Type this code at the end of the file. The captain is randomly selected from the **team1** list using the `choice()` function and appended to the string to be displayed.

```
print("Team 1 captain: " + random.choice(team1))
```
— Prints the message stating who the team captain is

2.3 DISPLAY TEAM 1

After the captain is assigned, you need to display all the players from "Team 1" on screen. Remember you can use a **for** loop (see p.108) to iterate through a list. Type the following code at the end of the file.

Prints a message to tell the user that the players for Team 1 are being displayed

```
print("Team 1:")
for player in team1:
    print(player)
```

This loop iterates through **team1**

Prints the current player's name

SAVE

2.4 TEST THE PROGRAM

This is a good point to test your code. Run the code and look in the shell window to see the result. Does it display the players for Team 1? Does it display the number you expected? Is it randomly selecting a team captain that is actually part of Team 1? Run the code a few times to ensure it is random. If you have any errors, look back over your code carefully to spot any mistakes.

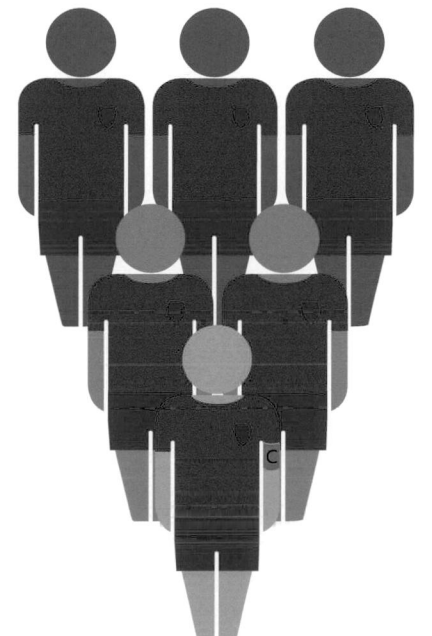

```
Welcome to Team Allocator!
Team 1 captain: Claire
Team 1:
Maria
Jean
William
Alice
Claire
Jack
Lexi
Craig
James
Alan
>>>
```

2.5 SELECT THE SECOND TEAM

Now you can allocate players for the second team by repeating steps 2.1–2.3. Type the following code at the end of the file.

Assigns the second half of the list to the variable **team2**. The players in this list will be part of the second team

```python
team2 = players[len(players)//2:]
print("\nTeam 2 captain: " + random.choice(team2))
print("Team 2:")
for player in team2:
    print(player)
```

"\n" prints the name of the team captain for Team 2 on a new line

This loop iterates through **team2**

SAVE

2.6 **TEST THE PROGRAM**
Run the code to test the program again. Ensure that it is working as expected for both teams. You should be able to see the list of players for both the teams along with the names of their captains.

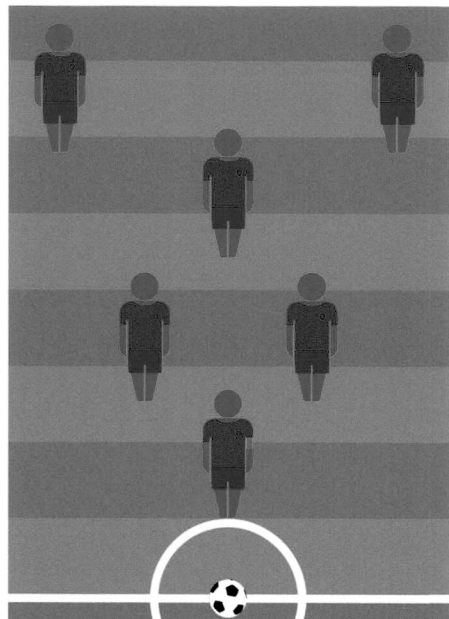

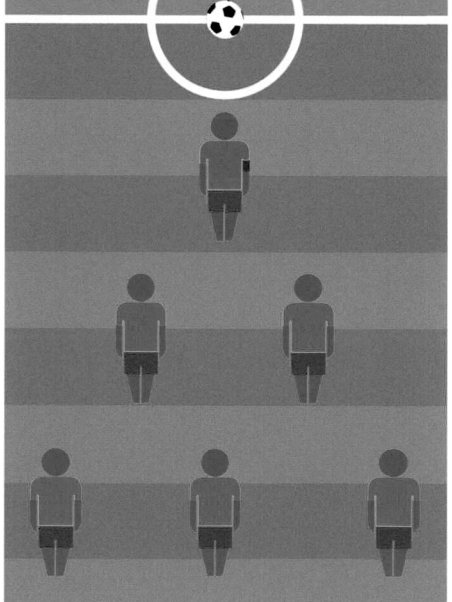

```
Welcome to Team Allocator!
Team 1 captain: Marissa
Team 1:
Harry
Claire
Jack
Sue
Dave
Craig
Marissa
Grace
Alan
Maria

Team 2 captain: James
Team 2:
Martin
Jean
Alice
Ada
William
Rose
Lexi
James
Sonakshi
Thomas
>>>
```

The name of the captain will be displayed before the list of players

3 PICK NEW TEAMS

You can now use a **while** loop to keep selecting teams until you are happy with them. Add a new line of code below the welcome message and remember to add indents for all the lines of code following this new line, as shown below. This will ensure that the existing code is part of the **while** loop.

```python
print("Welcome to Team Selector!")
while True:
    random.shuffle(players)
    team1 = players[:len(players)//2]
    print("Team 1 captain: "+random.choice(team1))
    print("Team 1:")
    for player in team1:
        print(player)
    team2 = players[:len(players)//2:]
    print("\n Team 2 captain: "+random.choice(team2))
    print("Team 2:")
    for player in team2:
        print(player)
```

Adds the loop that allows selecting the teams again

Add indents to these lines of code to make them part of the loop

3.1 REDRAW PLAYERS

Finally, add the following code to ask users if they would like to pick teams again. Store the reply in a variable called **response**. If you choose to redraw the players, the main loop will run again and display the new teams.

Displays a message to ask users if they would like to redraw the players

```python
    response = input("Pick teams again? Type y or n: ")
    if response == "n":
        break
```

Breaks out of the main loop if the response is **n**

SAVE

3.2 RUN THE CODE

The program is now ready. Test the program again. You will see the list of both teams with the team captains, and a message at the end asking if you would like to redraw the players.

```
Welcome to Team Allocator!
Team 1 captain: Rose
Team 1:
Jean
Ada
James
Claire
Martin
Harry
Alice
Craig
Rose
Sonakshi

Team 2 captain: William
Team 2:
Jack
Maria
Sue
Alan
Dave
Grace
Marissa
Lexi
Thomas
William
Pick teams again? Type y or n:
```

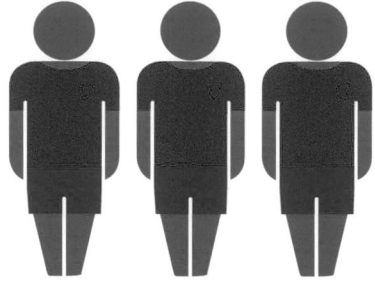

TEAM 1

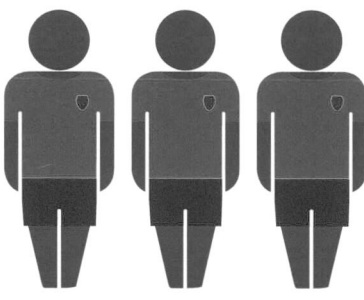

TEAM 2

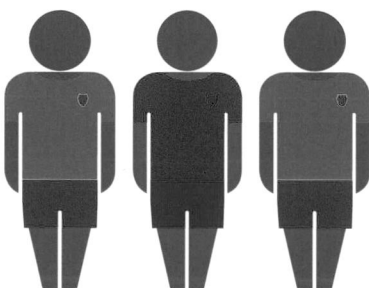

RESHUFFLED TEAM 1

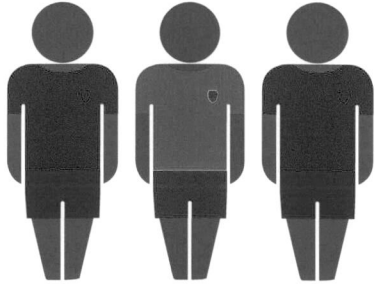

RESHUFFLED TEAM 2

Hacks and tweaks

Add more players

The program has a list of 20 names. To add more players to the team selector, try adding some more names to the list. Keep the total number of players even, so that the teams have equal numbers of players on them.

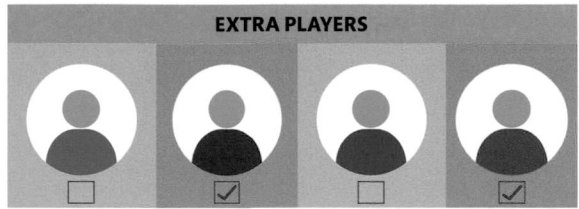

EXTRA PLAYERS

More teams

Different sports have different numbers of players in their teams. The code in this project assumes that there will be two teams. However, if you have a longer list of players, you can even have three or more teams. Update the code in the program to ask the user for the number of players they want in each team. You can then split the number of players into the number of teams they can equally be split into. If a team is short of players, make sure to inform the user of this.

```python
while True:
    random.shuffle(players)
    team1 = players[:len(players)//3]
    print("Team 1 captain: " + random.choice(team1))
    print("Team 1:")
    for player in team1:
        print(player)
    team2 = players[len(players)//3:(len(players)//3)*2]
    print("\nTeam 2 captain: " + random.choice(team2))
    print("Team 2:")
    for player in team2:
        print(player)
    team3 = players[(len(players)//3)*2:]
    print("\nTeam 3 captain: " + random.choice(team3))
    print("Team 3:")
    for player in team3:
        print(player)
```

Splits the number of players into three equal parts and assigns the first part of the players list to **team1**

Assigns the second part of the players list to **team2**

Assigns the third team with its own list of players and the team captain

Team or tournament

Currently the program assumes that the code is for a team sport. If you want to create a program for individual sports, change the code as shown below. This will ask the user if the players need to be split for an individual or team sport. If you pick team, the code should run as you have already tested. However, if you pick "individual", the code will split the players into random pairs to play against each other.

```
print("Welcome to Team/Player Allocator!")
while True:
    random.shuffle(players)
    response = input("Is it a team or individual sport? \
                    \nType team or individual: ")
    if response == "team":
        team1 = players[:len(players)//2]
```

Displays a message to ask the user if it is a team or an individual sport

Checks for the user's response

```
    for player in team2:
        print(player)
    else:
        for i in range(0, 20, 2):
            print(players[i] + " vs " + players[i+1])
```

Range will take the value 0-19 and will increment by 2 each time. This is so we go through the list two players at a time to put them in pairs

Prints the name of players that will play against each other

Who starts?

For both team and individual sports there is usually a method to determine who will go first. Add this extra code to the program from the previous hack to do this for individual sports.

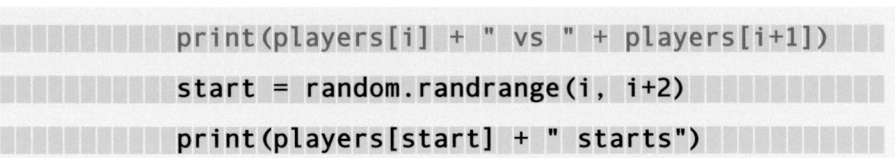

```
        print(players[i] + " vs " + players[i+1])
        start = random.randrange(i, i+2)
        print(players[start] + " starts")
```

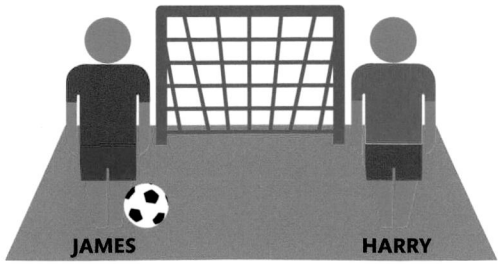

JAMES   HARRY

```
Welcome to Team/Player Selector!
Is it a team or individual sport?
Type team or individual: individual
James vs Harry
James starts
```

The shell window displays who starts

Change to list of numbers

The current program is only a good solution if you always play with the same people. However, if this is not the case, you can replace the player names with numbers to make it a more general solution. Remember to assign the numbers to the players before you use it.

```python
import random


players = [1, 2, 3, 4, 5, 6, 7, 8, 9, 10,
          11, 12, 13, 14, 15, 16, 17, 18,
          19, 20]


print("Welcome to Team Allocator!")
```

Update the code to replace the names with numbers

Number of players

Instead of having to change the size of the list each time you have more or fewer players, you can update the code to ask the user for the total number of players. This will create the number list, as well as create two equal teams. Update the program as shown here.

```python
import random
players = []
print("Welcome to Team Allocator!")
number_of_players = int(input("How many players \
are there? "))
for i in range(1, number_of_players + 1):
    players.append(i)
```

Displays a message for the user to enter the number of players

```python
    team1 = players[:len(players)//2]
    print("Team 1 captain: " + str(random.choice(team1)))
    print("Team 1:")
```

Updates code for **team1**

```python
    team2 = players[len(players)//2:]
    print("\nTeam 2 captain: " + str(random.choice(team2)))
    print("Team 2:")
```

Updates code for **team2**

Debugging

The process of finding and fixing errors in a program is called debugging. Also known as bugs, errors can range from simple mistakes in spellings to problems with the logic of the code. Python has various tools that highlight and help fix these errors.

Syntax errors

Syntax is the term used to describe the arrangement and spelling of words and symbols that make up the code. Syntax errors are the most common and easily fixed errors. They are equivalent to the sort of spelling and grammar mistakes that most word-processing programs highlight. IDLE displays syntax errors in code in a pop-up window.

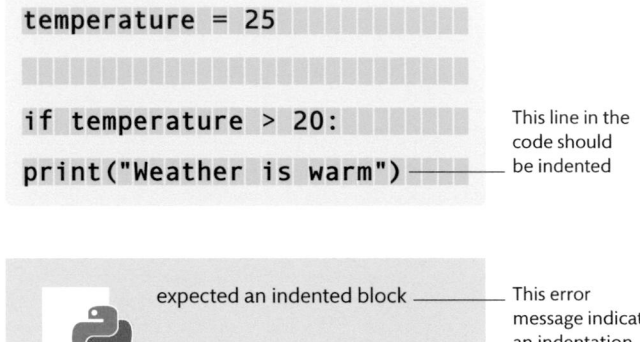

This line in the code should be indented

Indentation errors

Indentation is a way of making a program more readable by using space to reflect its structure. The body of a function, loop, or conditional statement should be placed four spaces to the right of the line introducing it. Python makes indentation compulsory in the code.

expected an indented block ——— This error message indicates an indentation error in the code

OK

Runtime errors

These errors affect the fundamental features of a program. They can include accessing a nonexistent file, using an identifier that has not been defined, or performing an operation on incompatible types of values. Runtime errors cannot be found by checking a program's syntax. The Python interpreter discovers them while running the code and displays an error message called a "traceback" in the shell window.

Type errors

These errors occur when a function or operator is used with the wrong type of value. The "+" operator can either concatenate two strings, or add two numbers. It cannot, however, concatenate a string and a number, which is what causes the error in this example.

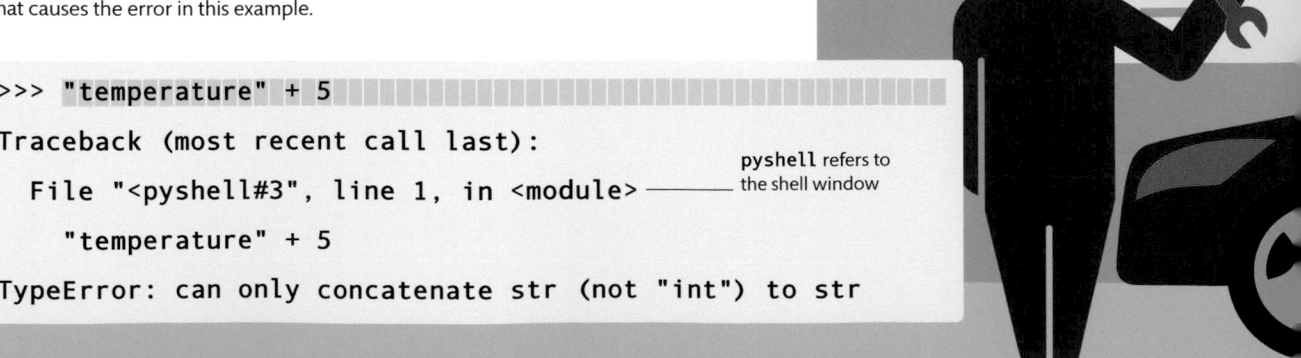

```
>>> "temperature" + 5
Traceback (most recent call last):
  File "<pyshell#3", line 1, in <module>
    "temperature" + 5
TypeError: can only concatenate str (not "int") to str
```

pyshell refers to the shell window

CHECK MODULE

IDLE's "Check Module" command can be found in the Run menu. It checks a program file for syntax errors, allowing programmers to identify and eliminate them before the program is run. This tool does not display any message unless it finds an error.

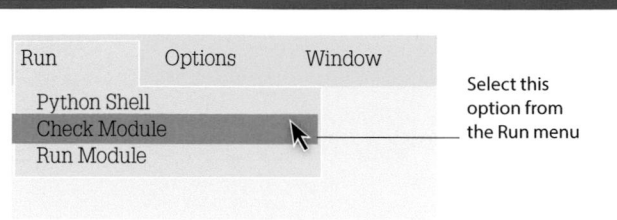

Select this option from the Run menu

Name errors

Misspelling the name of a variable or function can cause a name error. It can also be a result of using a variable before a value is assigned to it, or calling a function before it is defined. In this example, the typographical error is only found at run time, so the message is displayed in the shell window.

Details of where and what the error is

Location of the error in the file

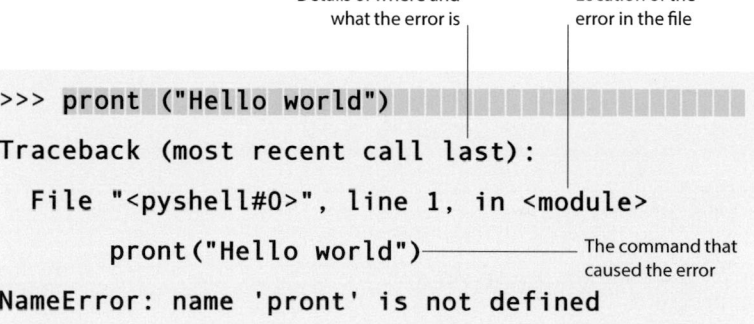

```
>>> pront ("Hello world")
Traceback (most recent call last):
  File "<pyshell#0>", line 1, in <module>
      pront("Hello world")
NameError: name 'pront' is not defined
```

The command that caused the error

Logic errors

Logic errors are usually the trickiest to spot. The program may run without crashing, but it produces an unexpected result. These errors can be caused by a number of issues, including the use of the wrong variable in an expression.

Infinite results

In this example an infinite loop prints the word "counting" indefinitely. Since the value in the variable count is never updated, the loop condition will never be False.

```
count = 1
while count < 5:
    print("counting")
print("finished")
```

The variable count is set to the value 1

This statement will never be reached

Error messages

While they are the most obvious tools to help programmers with debugging, Python's error messages tend to be slightly cryptic, and can appear to add to the mystery of debugging rather than clearing it up. This table lists some of the most common error messages along with their meaning. Programmers tend to become familiar with these errors and their solutions quickly.

ERROR MESSAGES	
Error message	**Meaning**
EOL found while scanning string literal	Closing quotation mark missing for a string on that line
unsupported operand type(s) for +: 'int' and 'str'	The + operator expects the values on either side of it to be of the same type
Expected an indented block	The body of a loop or conditional is not indented
Unexpected indent	This line is indented too much
Unexpected EOF while parsing	Missing bracket just before the end of the program
Name [name of variable or function] is not defined	Usually caused by misspelling the name of the variable or function

Text colouring

Like most other IDEs (see pp.208–209) and dedicated code editing programs, IDLE colours the text of a Python program. This makes it easier to spot errors. For example, keywords such as "for", "while", and "if" are orange and strings are green (see p.98). A part of the code not appearing in the correct colour can be a sign that there is a syntax error. And several lines of code suddenly being coloured green is usually the sign of a missing closing quotation mark on a string.

Wrong colour
There are four errors in this example. The missing quotation marks and misspelling of the keyword "while" mean that the code will not be coloured correctly.

The keyword "while" has been spelled incorrectly

Misspelling of keyword and missing quote mark

Missing a quotation mark at the start

```
answer = input(Pick a number")
whle answer != 7:
    pritn(Not the right number")
    answer = input("Pick a number")
```

CHECK THE ERROR

A common issue when debugging is that the actual error may be located just before the place indicated by the error message. It is therefore worth checking for the error earlier in the indicated line, or on the line above it.

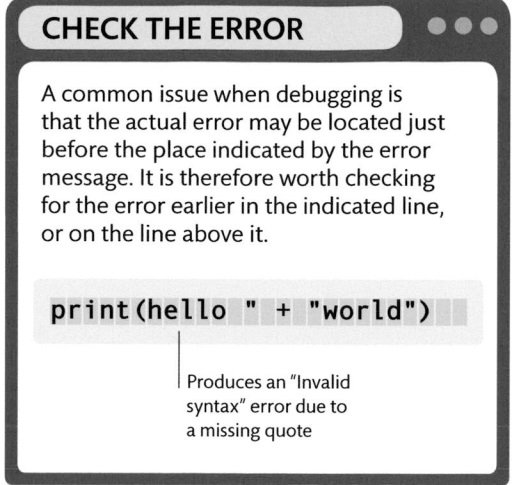

```
print(hello " + "world")
```

Produces an "Invalid syntax" error due to a missing quote

Debugging checklist

When an error appears but its cause is not immediately clear, there are a few things that can be checked. This might not solve every problem, but many errors are caused by trivial mistakes that can be easily fixed. Here is a list of things to look out for:

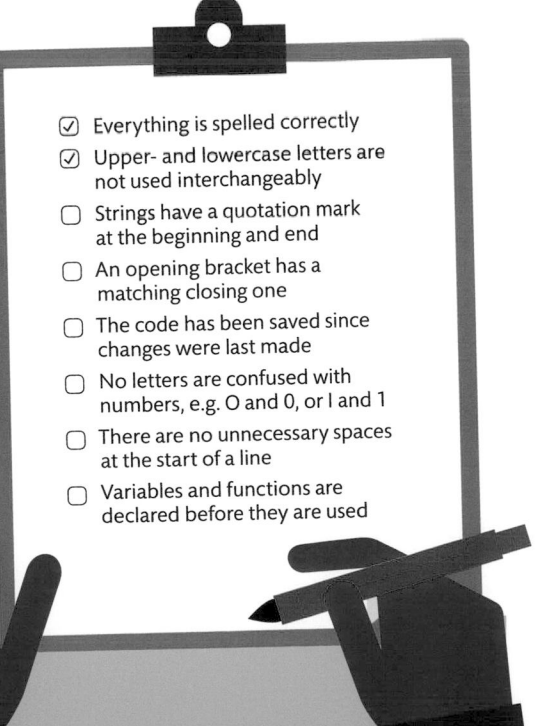

- ☑ Everything is spelled correctly
- ☑ Upper- and lowercase letters are not used interchangeably
- ☐ Strings have a quotation mark at the beginning and end
- ☐ An opening bracket has a matching closing one
- ☐ The code has been saved since changes were last made
- ☐ No letters are confused with numbers, e.g. O and 0, or I and 1
- ☐ There are no unnecessary spaces at the start of a line
- ☐ Variables and functions are declared before they are used

Debugger

IDLE also contains a tool called a debugger. This allows programmers to "step through" the execution of their program, running one line at a time. It also shows the contents of variables at each step in the program. The debugger can be started from the shell window, which includes a Debug menu. Selecting Debugger from this menu will start the debugging process the next time a program is run. Choosing it again will turn it off.

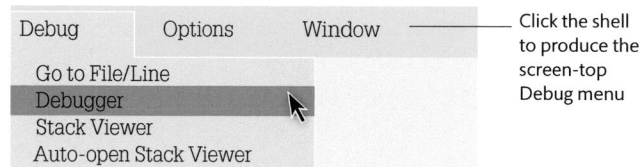

Click the shell to produce the screen-top Debug menu

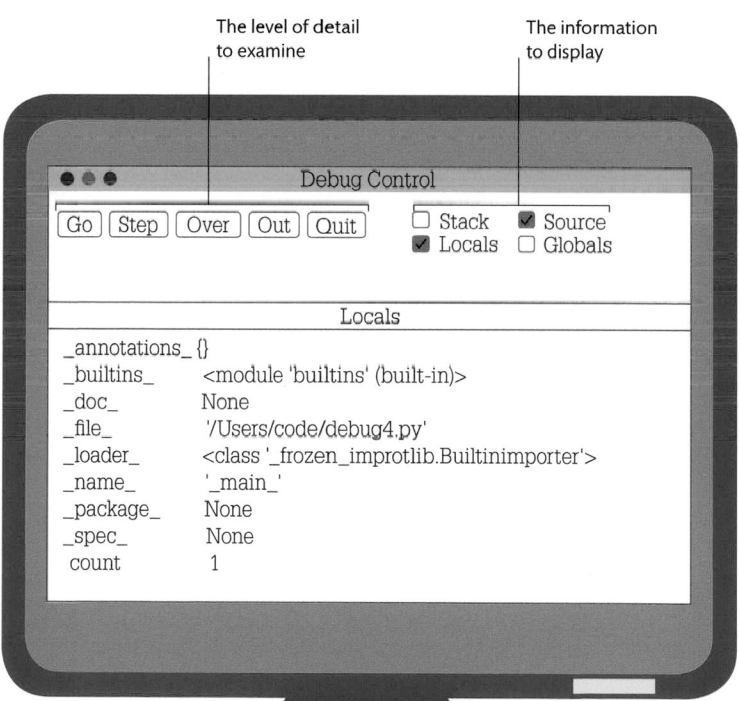

The level of detail to examine

The information to display

IDLE debugger
When a program is run, the debugger will display information about it, including current values of variables. Clicking on the option "Step" will expose the code running behind the scenes, which is normally hidden from programmers.

Project planner

Time management tools can be very useful, both at home and at work. There are several applications that help in tracking the progress of daily chores and activities. This project will use Python's tuples, sets, and graphical modules to create a planner for developing a small gaming app.

How it works

This planner will create a schedule to help users plan their work. The program will display a window with a button that a user can press to choose a project file. It will then read a list of tasks from the file and sort them in the order of their starting time, based on certain prerequisites. The resulting data will be converted into a chart that will display when each task starts and ends.

Gantt chart
A Gantt chart is a type of bar chart that is used to illustrate the schedule of a project. The tasks to be performed are listed on the y axis and the time periods are listed on the x axis. Horizontal bars on the graph display the duration of each activity.

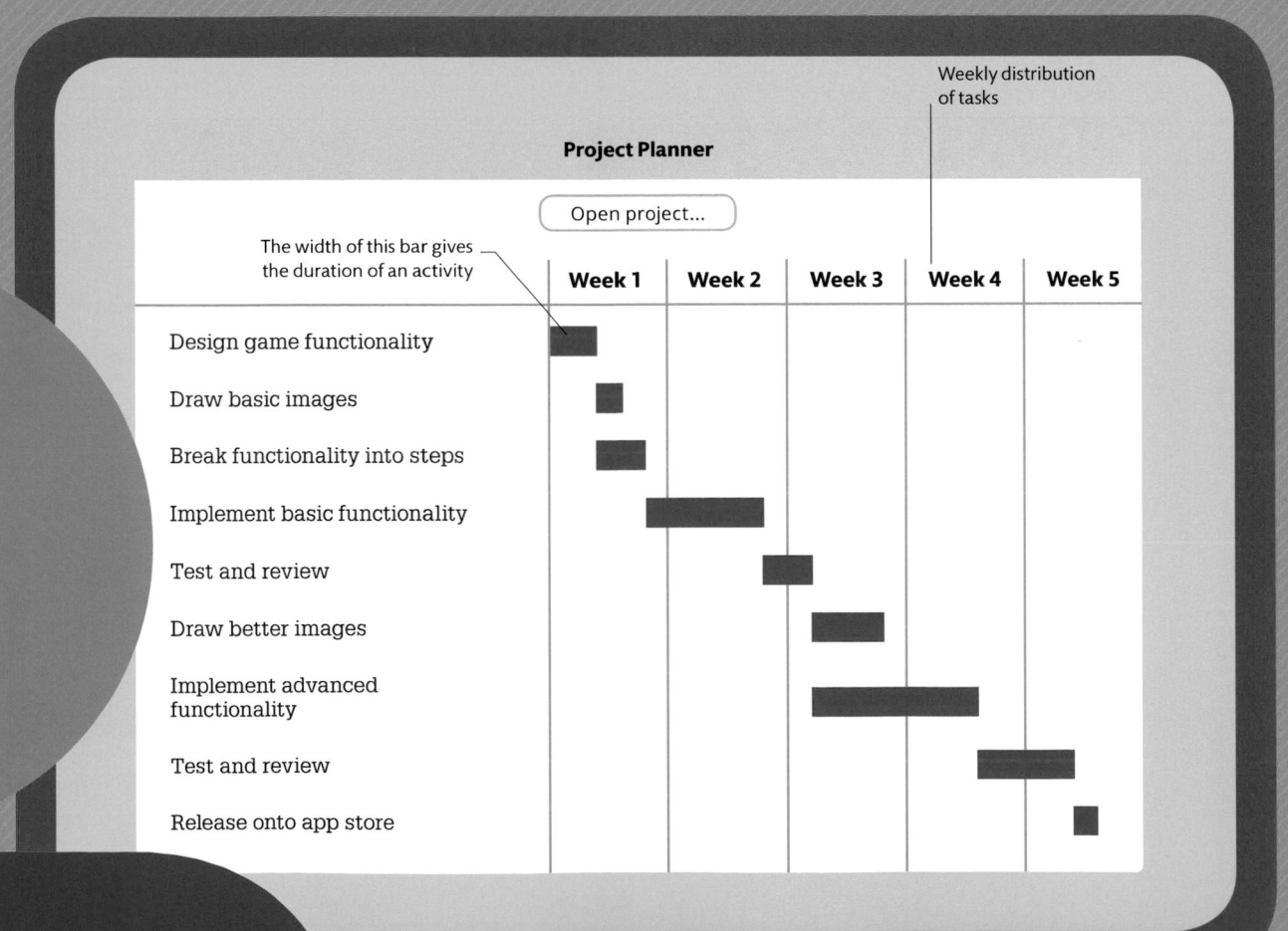

Weekly distribution of tasks

Project Planner

Open project...

The width of this bar gives the duration of an activity

	Week 1	Week 2	Week 3	Week 4	Week 5
Design game functionality					
Draw basic images					
Break functionality into steps					
Implement basic functionality					
Test and review					
Draw better images					
Implement advanced functionality					
Test and review					
Release onto app store					

YOU WILL LEARN

❯ How to extract data from a file
❯ How to use Python sets
❯ How to use **namedtuples**
❯ How to create a simple **Tk UI** app
❯ How to draw using **Tk Canvas**

Time: 1.5 hours

Lines of code: 76

Difficulty level
● ● ● ● ●

WHERE THIS IS USED

Reading data from files and processing it is common to almost all programs, even the ones that do not use documents in an obvious manner: for example, games. The basic tasks of opening windows, laying out buttons, and drawing custom elements are the building blocks of any desktop application.

Program design

This project uses one continuous loop to check if users have pressed the Open project... button. If they have, the program opens a CSV file to read and order its contents before they are displayed as a chart. The chart will display the amount of work to be done in the allotted time.

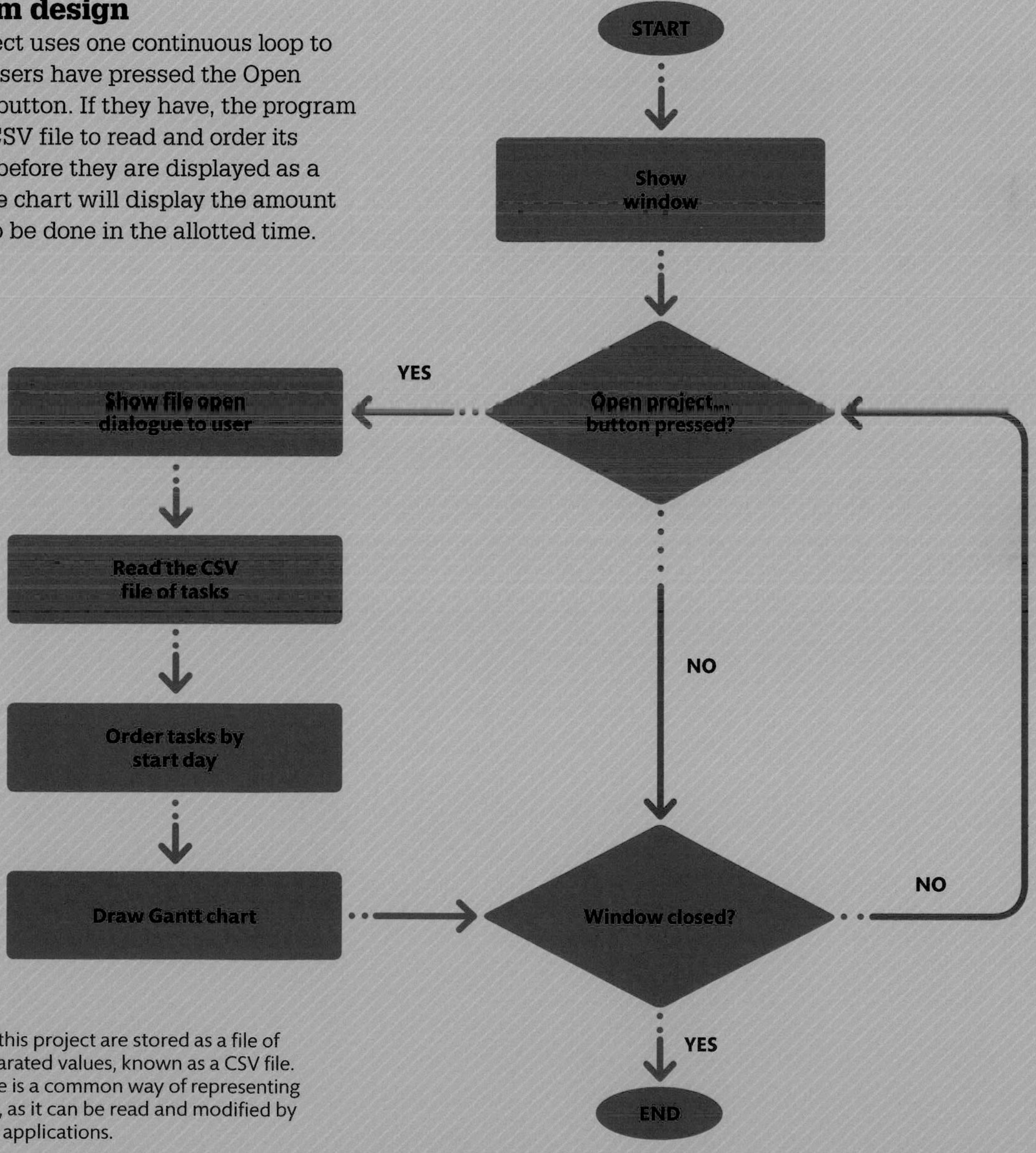

START

↓

Show window

↓

YES ← Open project... button pressed?

Show file open dialogue to user

↓

Read the CSV file of tasks

↓

Order tasks by start day

↓

Draw Gantt chart ····→ Window closed?

NO ↓ (from Open project... button pressed?)

Window closed? → **NO**

↓ **YES**

END

CSV file
The tasks in this project are stored as a file of comma-separated values, known as a CSV file. Using this file is a common way of representing tabular data, as it can be read and modified by spreadsheet applications.

1 Creating and reading the CSV file

To draw the planner in your app, you need to create a CSV file that lists all the tasks that have to be completed. Then, you will write the code in a Python file to read the CSV file.

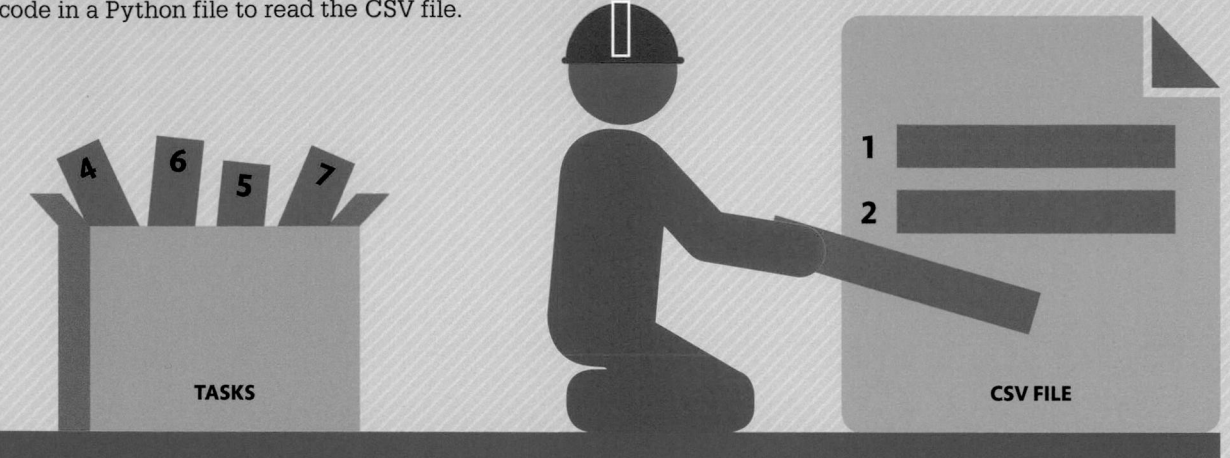

TASKS

CSV FILE

1.1 CREATE A NEW FILE

The first step is to create a new file for the Python code. Create a folder called "ProjectPlanner" on your computer. Then, open IDLE and select New File from the File menu. Choose Save As from the same menu and save the file as "planner.py" inside the ProjectPlanner folder.

File	Edit	Shell
New File	⌘N	
Open...	⌘O	
Open Module...		
Recent Files	▶	
Module Browser	⌘B	

Select this option to create a new file

1.2 CREATE A CSV FILE

Python has a library called **csv** that makes it easy to read and write CSV files. Now add a line of code at the top of your Python file to read the new CSV file. However, before you can read a CSV file, you will need to create one. This can be done with a spreadsheet application, but since a CSV file is a simple text file you can create it in IDLE. Select New File from the File menu, choose Save As and save the file in the ProjectPlanner folder. Name this file "project.csv". You may get a warning message when you do this, as ".csv" is not a standard Python extension, but you should use it anyway.

```
import csv
```

Type this line in the "planner.py" file

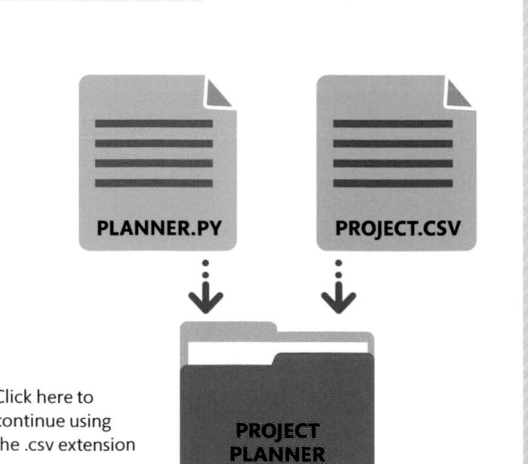

PLANNER.PY

PROJECT.CSV

PROJECT PLANNER

You have used the extension ".csv" at the end of the name. The standard extension is ".py".

You can choose to use the standard extension instead.

(Use .py)   (Cancel)   (Use .csv)

Click here to continue using the .csv extension

WARNING MESSAGE

1.3 WRITE A SIMPLE PROJECT

Now you can write a simple plan for a project to develop a small gaming app. Type the following lines into the CSV file with a list of tasks to be completed to create the gaming app. There should be no blank lines at the beginning or end of the file. Each

line of text in the file will represent one row of the table and each element in the row will represent one column value. For example, the second row has four column values. Save and close the file once you have typed in the tasks correctly.

The first column value represents the task number

The second column value gives a title to the task

The third column value gives the number of days the task is expected to take

The values in each column are separated by commas

```
1,Design game functionality,2,
2,Draw basic images,1,1
3,Break functionality into steps,2,1
4,Implement basic functionality,5,2 3
5,Test and review,2,4
6,Draw better images,3,5
7,Implement advanced functionality,7,5
8,Test and review,4,6 7
9,Release onto app store,1,8
```

Each line represents one row of the table

The fourth column value gives the prerequisites of the task as task numbers with spaces in between

This row is task **8** with the title **Test and review**. It is expected to finish in **4** days and requires tasks **6** and **7** to be completed before it can start

PYTHON TUPLE

A tuple is a data structure like a list, but its length cannot be changed after it has been created and the items inside it cannot be updated. Lists are mostly used to store a sequence of values of the same kind, such as a list of numbers representing the height of a group of people. Tuples, on the other hand, are used when the values are related, but of different kinds, such as one person's name, age, and height.

```
>>> numbers = (1, 2, 3, 4, 5)
>>> print(numbers[3])
4
```

numbers is a tuple with five values

The value at index position 3 in the tuple

Index numbers are enclosed within square brackets

```
>>> numbers[0] = 4
Traceback (most recent call last):
  File "<pyshell>", line 1, in <module>
    numbers[0] = 4
TypeError: 'tuple' object does not support item assignment
```

Try changing the value at index position 0 in the tuple

Returns an error since the values inside a tuple cannot be updated

1.4 READ DATA FROM THE FILE

The functionality in Python's **csv** library makes it easy to read data from the CSV file. Once the data is read, the values are stored in a Python tuple. The tuple is then stored into a "dictionary" (a data structure, where each item has two parts – a key and a value), using the task number (the value from the first column) as the key (see p.160). This will allow you to look up a particular task quickly by its number. Now, add this code to your .py file after the import statement from step 1.2. It will open the CSV file, read the rows of data from it, and place the results into a dictionary.

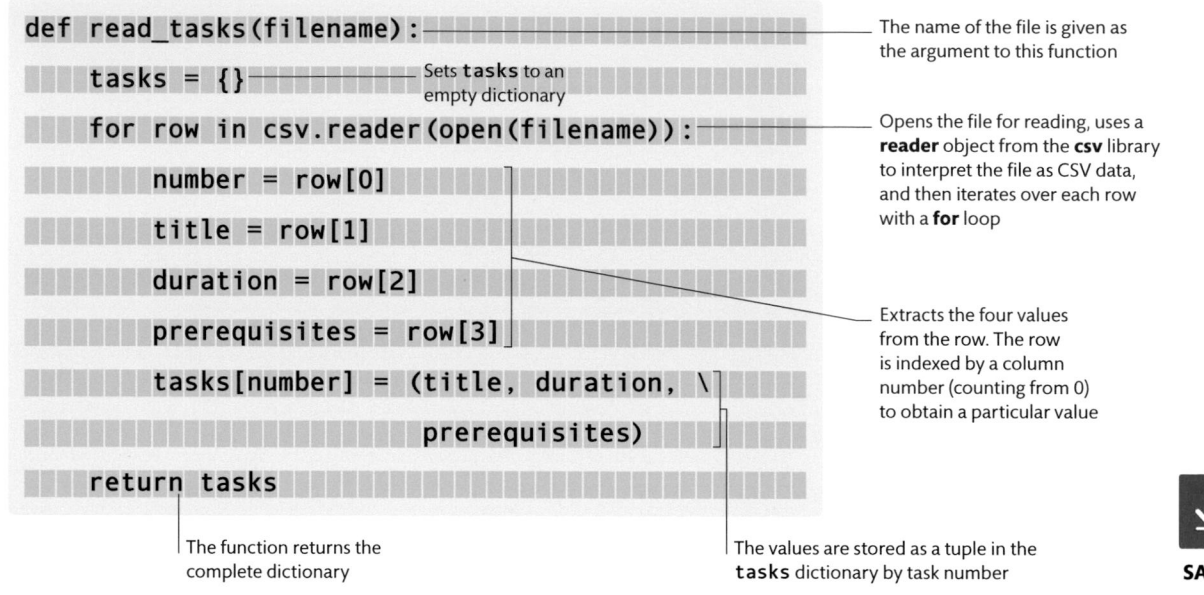

```python
def read_tasks(filename):
    tasks = {}
    for row in csv.reader(open(filename)):
        number = row[0]
        title = row[1]
        duration = row[2]
        prerequisites = row[3]
        tasks[number] = (title, duration, \
                         prerequisites)
    return tasks
```

The name of the file is given as the argument to this function

Sets **tasks** to an empty dictionary

Opens the file for reading, uses a **reader** object from the **csv** library to interpret the file as CSV data, and then iterates over each row with a **for** loop

Extracts the four values from the row. The row is indexed by a column number (counting from 0) to obtain a particular value

The function returns the complete dictionary

The values are stored as a tuple in the **tasks** dictionary by task number

SAVE

1.5 TEST THE CODE

Now test the code to make sure you have typed in the instructions correctly. Choose Run Module from the Run menu and switch to the shell window. Type the code below to call the function with the name of the CSV file you created in step 1.2. The function will return a dictionary containing the information from the file. However, all of the values will be read as Python strings as the **csv.reader** object does not know how to interpret the data that it is reading from a file.

Type this line at the prompt

Reads the data in this CSV file

```
>>> read_tasks("project.csv")
{'1': ('Design game functionality', '2', ''), '2': ('Draw
basic images', '1', '1'), '3': ('Break functionality into
steps', '2', '1'), '4': ('Implement basic functionality',
'5', '2 3'), '5': ('Test and review', '2', '4'), '6': ('Draw
better images', '3', '5'), '7': ('Implement advanced
functionality', '7', '5'), '8': ('Test and review', '4',
'6 7'), '9': ('Release onto app store', '1', '8')}
```

Numbers are also read as strings

1.6 **CONVERT TO OTHER DATA TYPES**

The "task number" and "task duration" values are numbers in the CSV file. Since these are currently read as strings, it will be better if they can be converted into Python number values instead. Update the **read_tasks()** function as shown below. The task number will always be an integer (whole) number, but the task duration will be a float (decimal) value as it can take a non-whole number (like 2.5) of days to finish a task. Save the file and then run the module again to test this.

```python
def read_tasks(filename):
    tasks = {}
    for row in csv.reader(open(filename)):
        number = int(row[0])
        title = row[1]
        duration = float(row[2])
        prerequisites = row[3]
```

— Converts the task number from a string into an integer number

— Converts the task duration from a string into a floating point number

SAVE

```python
>>> read_tasks("project.csv")
{1: ('Design game functionality', 2.0, ''), 2: ('Draw basic
images', 1.0, '1'), 3: ('Break functionality into steps', 2.0,
'1'), 4: ('Implement basic functionality', 5.0, '2 3'), 5:
('Test and review', 2.0, '4'), 6: ('Draw better images', 3.0,
'5'), 7: ('Implement advanced functionality', 7.0, '5'), 8:
('Test and review', 4.0, '6 7'), 9: ('Release onto app store',
1.0, '8')}
```

— Task numbers are read as integer values

— Task duration is read as a floating point value

Converting data types

In Python's **csv** library, it is the standard behaviour of the **csv.reader** object to read every value as a string. You need to specify which values are "numbers" manually to ensure they are read as integers or floating point numbers.

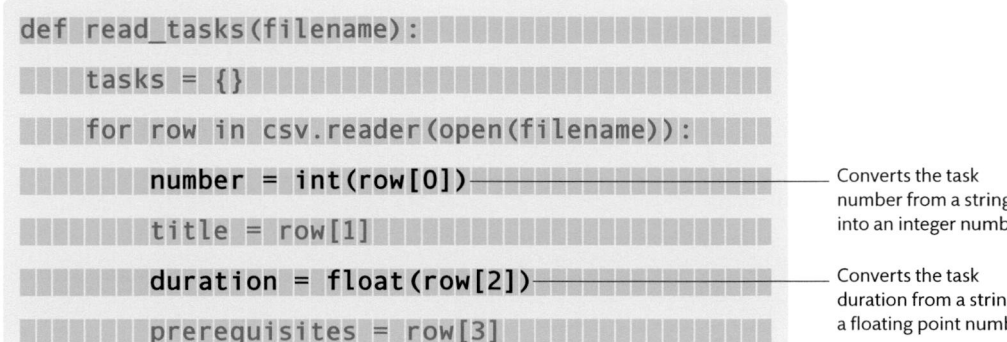

PYTHON SETS

A Python set is another data type that is similar to a list, but it can only contain unique values. This makes it similar to the keys of a dictionary. The syntax for writing a set is similar to that of a dictionary. A set can be assigned to a variable in several ways. Try these examples in the shell window.

Just like a dictionary, Python sets are also written inside curly brackets

```
>>> numbers = {1, 2, 3}
```

Defining a set
The variable **numbers** is defined as a set containing the numbers 1, 2, and 3. You should never write an empty set as "numbers = {}", as Python will read it as an empty dictionary. To avoid this, create an empty set by calling the **set()** constructor function.

Adds the number "4" to the set

```
>>> numbers.add(4)
>>> numbers
{1, 2, 3, 4}
>>> numbers.add(3)
>>> numbers
{1, 2, 3, 4}
```

The number "3" is already in the set, so the value inside it does not change

Adding values to a set
You can add values to a set with the **add** method. Since a set only contains unique values, adding a value that is already in the set will do nothing.

Removes the value "3" from the set

```
>>> numbers.remove(3)
>>> numbers
{1, 2, 4}
```

Removing values from a set
Similarly, you can also remove items from a set using the **remove** method.

1.7 PREREQUISITES AS SETS OF NUMBERS

So far, you have converted the task number and task duration into integers, but the prerequisites are still a string ("1" or "2 3"). To read the prerequisites as a collection of task numbers, first split the string into individual values using Python's built-in **split** method. Then use the **int()** and **map()** functions, as shown here, to turn the string values into a set.

```
>>> value = "2 3"
```
Items separated by spaces will be split into separate values

```
>>> value.split()
['2', '3']
```
The **split** method takes one string and turns it into a list of strings

map() calls the **int()** function on every string in the list

```
>>> set(map(int, value.split()))
{2, 3}
```

int() converts a string value into an integer

Converts the values returned by map() into a (set) data structure

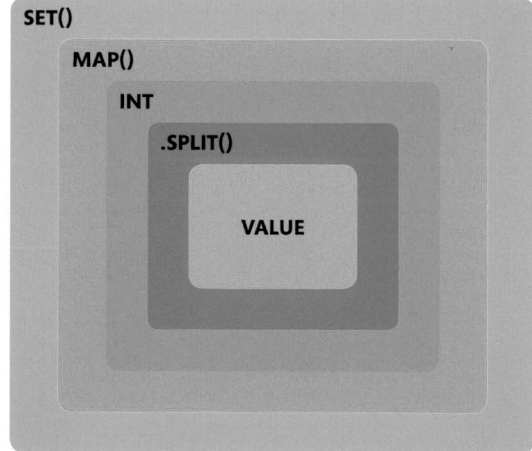

Combining functions
This illustration demonstrates how to combine simple functions to create complex logic. It starts with the original string value and splits it into string parts. The **int()** function is then called on each of these parts using the **map()** function. **set()** turns the result into a Python set.

1.8 **MAKE THE PREREQUISITE CHANGES**
Now incorporate the code from the previous step
into the **read_tasks()** function as shown below. Run the
module again and switch to the shell window to test it.

Converts the prerequisite
values from strings into
sets of integers

```python
import csv
def read_tasks(filename):
    tasks = {}
    for row in csv.reader(open(filename)):
        number = int(row[0])
        title = row[1]
        duration = float(row[2])
        prerequisites = set(map(int, row[3].split()))
        tasks[number] = (title, duration, prerequisites)
    return tasks
```

SAVE

```
>>> read_tasks("project.csv")
{1: ('Design game functionality', 2.0, set()),
2: ('Draw basic images', 1.0, {1}), 3: ('Break
functionality into steps', 2.0, {1}), 4:
('Implement basic functionality', 5.0, {2, 3}),
5: ('Test and review', 2.0, {4}), 6: ('Draw
better images', 3.0, {5}), 7: ('Implement
advanced functionality', 7.0, {5}), 8: ('Test
and review', 4.0, {6, 7}), 9: ('Release onto app
store', 1.0, {8})}
```

All numeric values are
now converted into
the correct data type

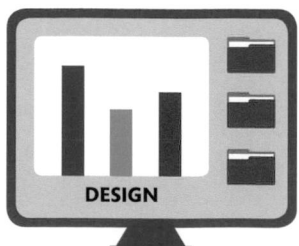

DESIGN

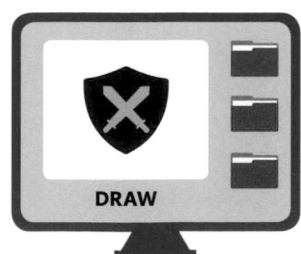

DRAW

TEST

1.9 TEST THE PROGRAM

The data is now ready and you can try to pull out some specific bits to test it. Run the module again and switch to the shell window. Then type the lines of code shown below. This time you will store the resulting dictionary in a temporary variable so that it can be manipulated.

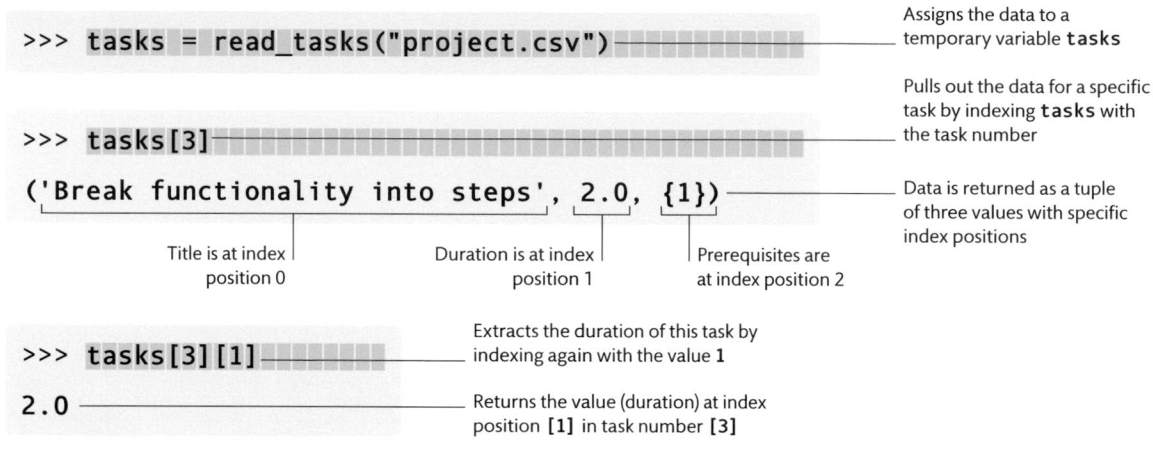

```
>>> tasks = read_tasks("project.csv")
```
Assigns the data to a temporary variable **tasks**

```
>>> tasks[3]
```
Pulls out the data for a specific task by indexing **tasks** with the task number

```
('Break functionality into steps', 2.0, {1})
```
Data is returned as a tuple of three values with specific index positions

Title is at index position 0

Duration is at index position 1

Prerequisites are at index position 2

```
>>> tasks[3][1]
```
Extracts the duration of this task by indexing again with the value **1**

```
2.0
```
Returns the value (duration) at index position **[1]** in task number **[3]**

1.10 USE NAMED TUPLES

Getting task values by their index positions is not an ideal way to extract them. It will be better if they can be referred to by a proper name, such as "title" or "duration". Python provides a standard way of doing this. You can create named tuples that will allow you to extract the values within them by name instead of position. Add this code at the top of your file to create a named tuple type and store it in a variable.

```
import csv
from collections import namedtuple
Task = namedtuple("Task", ["title", "duration", "prerequisites"])
def read_tasks(filename):
```

Imports the **namedtuple()** function from the **collections** module

Defines a named tuple called **Task**

The value names are given as a list of strings

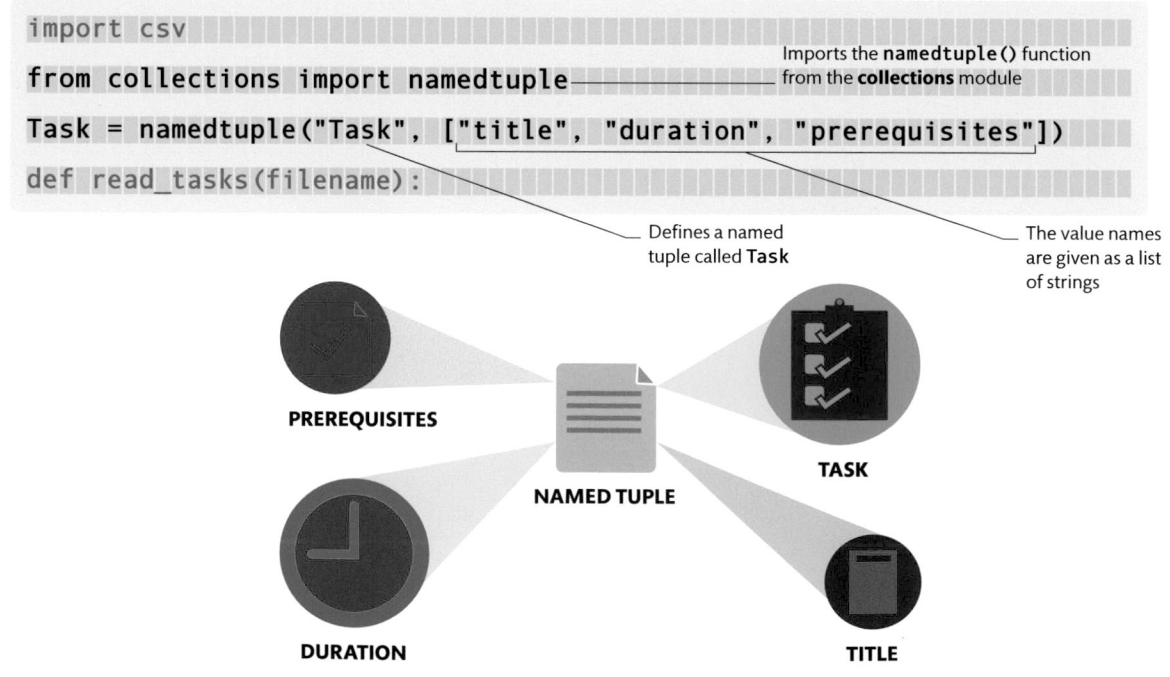

PREREQUISITES

DURATION

NAMED TUPLE

TASK

TITLE

1.11 **CALL THE NAMED TUPLE TYPE**
The named tuple type created in the previous step is stored in the variable **Task**. You can create new values of this type by calling **Task** like a function. Update the **read_task()** function in your code to call **Task** instead of creating a tuple in the normal way. Then, run the module and switch to the shell window to test the code. First, you will display the values in the shell (output 1), and then you will try to extract one of these values by using its name (output 2).

The named tuple **Task** is stored in the **tasks** dictionary

```python
def read_tasks(filename):
    tasks = {}
    for row in csv.reader(open(filename)):
        number = int(row[0])
        title = row[1]
        duration = float(row[2])
        prerequisites = set(map(int, row[3].split()))
        tasks[number] = Task(title, duration, prerequisites)
    return tasks
```

SAVE

```
>>> tasks = read_tasks("project.csv")
>>> tasks[3]
Task(title="Break functionality into steps", duration=2.0,
prerequisites={1})
```

Names are displayed in the shell for each of the values in the named tuple

OUTPUT 1

```
>>> tasks[1].title
"Design game functionality"
>>> tasks[3].duration
2.0
>>> tasks[4].prerequisites
{2, 3}
```

Extracts the title of **task[1]** by name

Extracts the duration of **task[3]** by name

OUTPUT 2

Extracts the prerequisites of **task[4]** by name

2 Ordering the tasks

Now that the tasks have been read in and converted into a useful format, you need to consider how to order them and determine when each task can begin after the project starts. You will do this by creating a function that computes the starting point of a task based on the status of its prerequisites.

START

Mark all tasks
as incomplete

Are there any
incomplete tasks left? — **NO** → END

YES

Look at the first/next
incomplete task

Are all of the task's
prerequisites
complete?

NO

YES

Set task's start day to the latest day
of completion (start day + duration)
of the prerequisite tasks

Mark task as complete

Flowchart for task ordering logic
A task cannot start until its prerequisite tasks have been completed. The program repeatedly loops over all the tasks that are still to be completed, picks an incomplete one, and then calculates when this task can start by computing the starting points and durations of each of its prerequisite tasks.

2.1 IMPLEMENT THE LOGIC

You can now implement the logic for ordering the tasks. Add the following function at the end of the file. This will return a dictionary that will map each task number to a start day, expressed as a number of days from the start of the entire project. So the first task(s) will begin at 0 days.

```python
    return tasks

def order_tasks(tasks):
    incomplete = set(tasks)
    completed = set()
    start_days = {}
    while incomplete:
        for task_number in incomplete:
            task = tasks[task_number]
            if task.prerequisites.issubset(completed):
                earliest_start_day = 0
                for prereq_number in task.prerequisites:
                    prereq_end_day = start_days[prereq_number] + \
                                     tasks[prereq_number].duration
                    if prereq_end_day > earliest_start_day:
                        earliest_start_day = prereq_end_day
                start_days[task_number] = earliest_start_day
                incomplete.remove(task_number)
                completed.add(task_number)
                break
    return start_days
```

Starts with all the tasks incomplete and no start days

Gets the task and checks if its prerequisites have been completed

Loops over the incomplete task numbers while there are still any left

Computes the earliest this task can start based on the end days of its prerequisites

Breaks out of the **for** loop. The loop will start again if there are still some incomplete tasks left

Stores the start date and remembers that this task has been completed

Returns the computed dictionary

ISSUBSET SET METHOD

• • •

The **issubset** set method checks whether one set is contained within another set. An empty set is a subset of any set, including another empty set. This means that **task.prerequisites.issubset(completed)** will be true for a task with no prerequisites and will begin immediately, even when no tasks have been completed yet. The **earliest_start_day** is set to 0 before looping over a task's prerequisites. If there are no prerequisites, then this task will use 0 as its start day. Once this task is added to the completed set, it will allow the tasks that depend on it to begin.

2.2 TEST THE CODE

Save the code and run the module to test the `order_tasks()` function at the prompt. You will see that task 1 can begin immediately (after 0 days) and task 9 is the last task to start, 22 days after the project begins. Tasks 2 and 3 will both start at the same time, as will tasks 6 and 7. It is assumed that the user will be able to do both tasks at the same time.

These tasks start at the same time because they have the same prerequisites

```
>>> tasks = read_tasks("project.csv")
>>> order_tasks(tasks)
{1: 0, 2: 2.0, 3: 2.0, 4: 4.0, 5: 9.0, 6: 11.0, 7: 11.0,
8: 18.0, 9: 22.0}
```

3 Drawing the chart

Now that you have read the CSV file and ordered the tasks inside it, it is time to draw a chart for the project. Python has a built-in, cross-platform toolkit for graphical applications called **Tk**. You will use this to open a window and draw inside it.

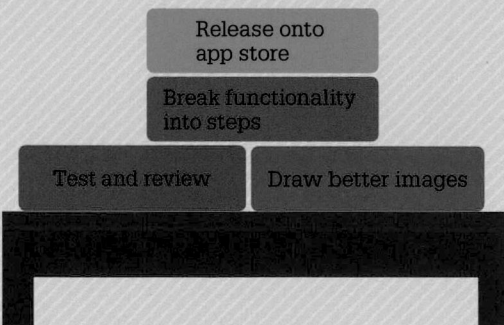

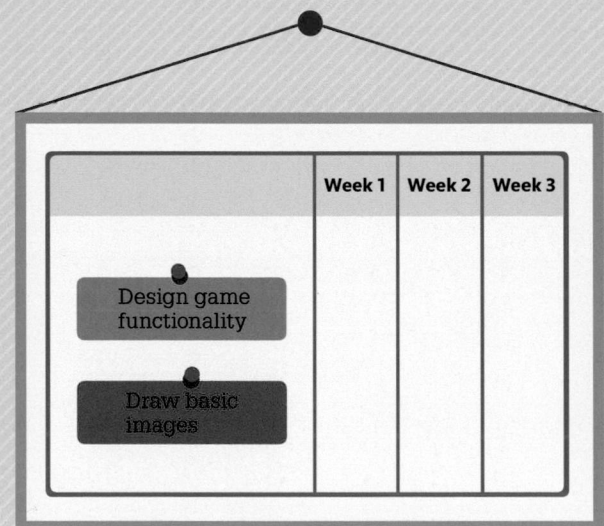

3.1 IMPORT THE TOOLKIT

Start by importing the **Tk** functionality into your program. It is found in Python's standard library called **tkinter** – short for Tk Interface. Add this code at the top of the .py file. By convention, the **import** statements are ordered alphabetically at the top of the file, but it does not matter if they are arranged in a different order.

```
import csv
import tkinter
```

Imports the **Tk** functionality

THE Tk GUI

Visual elements in **Tk** are called "widgets". Widgets are placed inside one another to create a hierarchy of graphical elements. The "root" (first) widget created in this hierarchy is the top-level window widget. Widgets are created by calling their **Tk** constructors with the parent widget as the first argument, followed by a set of keyword arguments specifying different attributes of the widget, such as its size and colour. Widgets are visually packed within their parent widgets. **Tk** module's `mainloop()` function draws the widgets on screen and handles events such as mouse clicks and key presses. This function does not return while the window is open. If you want to do anything after the window opens, you will have to define functions that will be called by `mainloop()` when specific events happen, such as a button being pressed.

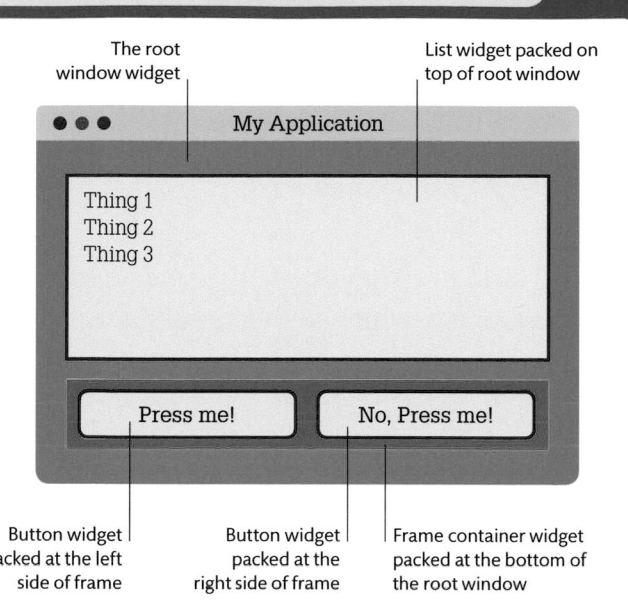

The root window widget

List widget packed on top of root window

Button widget packed at the left side of frame

Button widget packed at the right side of frame

Frame container widget packed at the bottom of the root window

---

3.2 CREATE A WINDOW

Next, add this code at the end of the .py file to create a window. It will contain a button and a canvas widget. The button will display some text as a label, and the canvas widget will define an area that you can draw into. You need to specify the size and background colour of the canvas widget.

Creates a **Tk** top-level window widget (see box, above)

Creates a button widget and places it at the top edge of the window

```
    return start_days

root = tkinter.Tk()

root.title("Project Planner")

open_button = tkinter.Button(root, text="Open project...", \
                        command=open_project)

open_button.pack(side="top")

canvas = tkinter.Canvas(root, width=800, \
                    height=400, bg="white")

canvas.pack(side="bottom")

tkinter.mainloop()
```

Gives the window a title

Creates a canvas widget and places it at the bottom edge of the window

Runs the **Tk** main event-handling function

SAVE

3.3 RUN THE CODE

If you run the code at this point, you will see a blank white window with no button inside it. You will also get an error message in the shell window. This is because the **open_project()** function has not been defined as yet. You will need to close this window to continue.

```
====== RESTART: /Users/tina/ProjectPlanner/planner.py ======
Traceback (most recent call last):
  File "/Users/tina/ProjectPlanner/planner.py", line 35, in <module>
    open_button = tkinter.Button(root, text="Open project...",
command=open_project)
NameError: name 'open_project' is not defined
>>>
```

The program will crash and display this error in the shell window

3.4 ACTIVATE THE BUTTON

The button you created in step 3.2 should allow you to select a .csv project file that will then be drawn into a chart. To do this, use a **Tk** file dialogue found in a sub-module of **tkinter**. Add the import statement at the top of your file as shown. Then add a new **open_project()** function just below the **order_tasks()** function from step 2.1. If you run the program now you will get another error message as the **draw_chart()** function has not been defined yet.

```
import tkinter
from tkinter.filedialog import askopenfilename
```

Imports a single function from **tkinter.filedialog** rather than importing the entire module

Calls the function to open a file dialogue for choosing a CSV file

Specifies the dialogue title

"." is a special directory name for the "current" directory

```
    return start_days
def open_project():
    filename = askopenfilename(title="Open Project", initialdir=".", \
                        filetypes=[("CSV Document", "*.csv")])
    tasks = read_tasks(filename)
    draw_chart(tasks, canvas)
```

Draws a chart of the tasks in the canvas widget

Reads the tasks from the .csv file returned by the dialogue

Specifies the acceptable file format

3.5 **DRAW THE CHART**
It is time to draw the project as a Gantt chart. Before drawing the chart, you will first need to decide what you want it to look like and what visual elements you need to draw it. Add this code below the code from step 2.1 (above the `open_project()` function) to draw the headers and dividers of the chart. This will define a `draw_chart()`

function and gives default values to some of its arguments. Only the first two arguments (`tasks` and `canvas`) are actually required to call the function. The arguments with default values are optional and will take the values that you have specified, creating some local "constants" in the function.

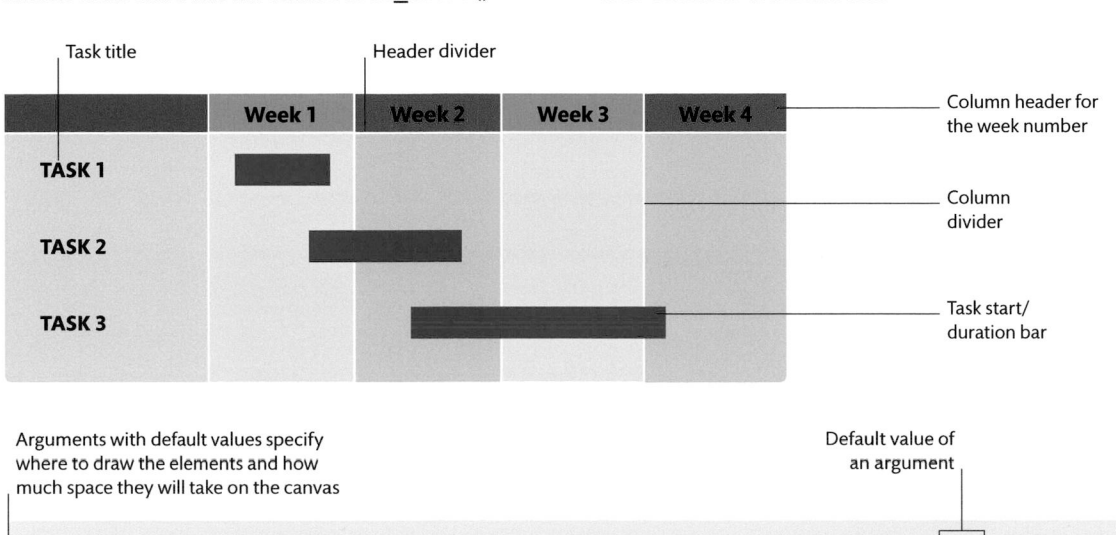

Task title

Header divider

Column header for the week number

Column divider

Task start/ duration bar

Arguments with default values specify where to draw the elements and how much space they will take on the canvas

Default value of an argument

```python
def draw_chart(tasks, canvas, row_height=40, title_width=300, \
               line_height=40, day_width=20, bar_height=20, \
               title_indent=20, font_size=-16):
    height = canvas["height"]
    width = canvas["width"]
    week_width = 5 * day_width
    canvas.create_line(0, row_height, width, line_height, \
                       fill="grey")
    for week_number in range(5):
        x = title_width + week_number * week_width
        canvas.create_line(x, 0, x, height, fill="grey")
        canvas.create_text(x + week_width / 2, row_height / 2, \
                           text=f"Week {week_number+1}", \
                           font=("Helvetica", font_size, "bold"))

def open_project():
```

Defines the height and width of the canvas as local variables

Draws a horizontal line for the header, one row down and across the entire width of the chart

Loops through the number of weeks from 0 to 4

Sets **x** to the width of the title plus the week width times the number of the week

Draws a vertical line at **x** down the entire height of the chart

Draws a text string at a point half a week width past **x** and half a row down

3.6 **RUN THE CODE**
Your Gantt chart is now ready. Save the file and run the code. You will now be able to click on the button, choose a CSV file, and see the headers and dividers being drawn.

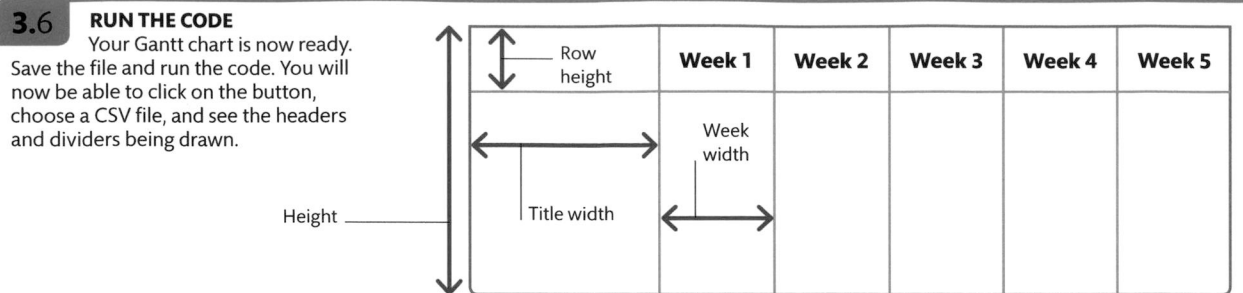

THE Tk CANVAS WIDGET

The Canvas widget provides a space on screen inside which you can add elements, such as lines, rectangles, and text. You need to call methods on the canvas object to create the elements. These methods take one or more coordinates as arguments, followed by a number of optional keyword arguments that allow the user to specify styling information, such as colours, line thicknesses, or fonts (see tables, below). Canvas coordinates are specified in pixels from the top-left corner of the drawing area. Colours can be specified either by their names, such as "red" or "yellow", or by their hex code, such as "#FF0000". Text is drawn centred on the given coordinates by default. The anchor keyword argument can be set to a "compass point" constant (**tkinter.N**, **tkinter.NE** and **tkinter.E**) to draw the text with a corner or edge at the coordinates instead.

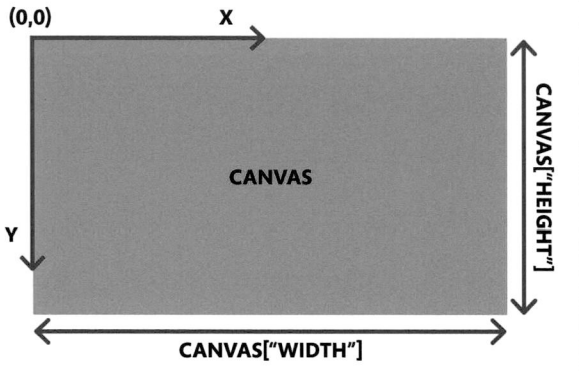

BASIC METHODS	
Method	**Description**
create_line(x1, y1, x2, y2, ...)	Adds a line from **(x1, y1)** to **(x2, y2)**
create_rectangle(x1, y1, x2, y2, ...)	Adds a rectangle from **(x1, y1)** to **(x2, y2)**
create_oval(x1, y1, x2, y2, ...)	Adds an oval with a bounding box from **(x1, y1)** to **(x2, y2)**
create_text(x1, y1, text=t, ...)	Adds a text label anchored at **(x1, y1)** showing string **t**

ADDITIONAL STYLING ARGUMENTS	
Argument	**Description**
width	Line width
fill	Fill colour of a shape or the colour of lines and text
outline	Outline colour of shapes
font	Font used for text, either a tuple of (name, size) or (name, size, style)
anchor	Anchor point of the text used when drawing at the specified coordinates

3.7 DRAWING THE TASKS

Finally, add this code to draw the task title and the task duration bar for each task. Type these lines at the end of the `draw_chart()` function. Then, save the file and run the code to see the complete Gantt chart when you open the "project.csv" file.

> Draws the task title anchored at the centre-left of the text, half a row below **y** and `title_indent` in from the left

```
...canvas.create_text(x + week_width / 2, row_height / 2, \
                      text=f"Week {week_number+1}", \
                      font=("Helvetica", font_size, "bold"))
start_days = order_tasks(tasks)
    y = row_height
    for task_number in start_days:
        task = tasks[task_number]
        canvas.create_text(title_indent, y + row_height / 2, \
                          text=task.title, anchor=tkinter.W, \
                          font=("Helvetica", font_size))
        bar_x = title_width + start_days[task_number] \
                * day_width
        bar_y = y + (row_height - bar_height) / 2
        bar_width = task.duration * day_width
        canvas.create_rectangle(bar_x, bar_y, bar_x + \
                              bar_width, bar_y + \
                              bar_height, fill="red")
    y += row_height
```

> Orders the tasks to get the start days

> Begins with **y**, one row down from the top of the canvas

> Loops over the task numbers in the order that they occur in the **start_days** dictionary

> Calculates the coordinates of the top-left corner of the bar and its width

> Adds a vertical space of `row_height` into the original **y**

> Draws a red-coloured bar using these values

		Week 1	Week 2	Week 3	Week 4	Week 5
	Design game functionality	▇				
Implement basic functionality	Draw basic images		▇			

Hacks and tweaks

Stop the window from resizing
At the moment the user can manually resize the window of the Gantt chart.
However, this causes the contents to move around or be cut off. Drawing the
window properly when it is resized is quite complicated, but you can stop it from
being resized instead. Add this line of code to the program to make this change.

Prevents the root
window from resizing
in any direction

```
root.title("Project Planner")
root.resizable(width=False, height=False)
open_button = tkinter.Button(root, text="Open project...", \
                             command=open_project)
```

You will not be able to
resize the window anymore

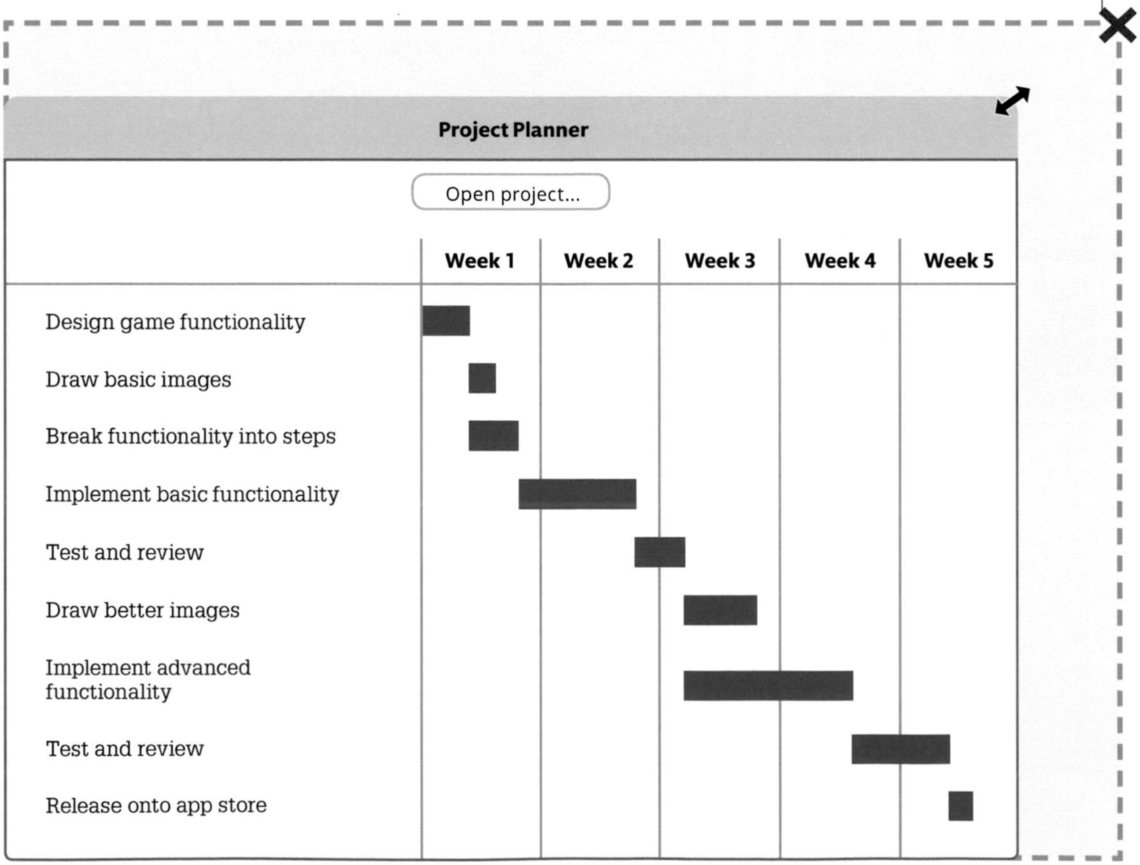

✕

Project Planner					
	Open project...				
	Week 1	**Week 2**	**Week 3**	**Week 4**	**Week 5**
Design game functionality	▄				
Draw basic images	▪				
Break functionality into steps	▪				
Implement basic functionality		▄			
Test and review			▪		
Draw better images			▄		
Implement advanced functionality			▄▄		
Test and review				▄	
Release onto app store					▪

Use a frame to layout the button

You can use a **Tk Frame** widget to change the position of the
Open Project... button. Currently it is stuck in the middle of the
window at the top. You can place it in the top-left corner and add
a bit of space around it. Add the following lines of code at the
bottom of the .py file to create the **button_frame** and then
update the **open_button** so it sits inside this widget.

Creates a frame at the root
of the window, with a small
amount of **x** and **y** padding

```python
root = tkinter.Tk()

root.title("Project Planner")

root.resizable(width=False, height=False)

button_frame = tkinter.Frame(root, padx=5, pady=5)

button_frame.pack(side="top", fill="x")

open_button = tkinter.Button(button_frame, text="Open project...", \

                             command=open_project)

open_button.pack(side="left")

canvas = tkinter.Canvas(root, width=800, height=400, bg="white")
```

Places the frame at the
top of the window, filling
the entire width of **x**

Places the button at
the left of the frame

Creates the **open_button** inside the
button_frame instead of the root

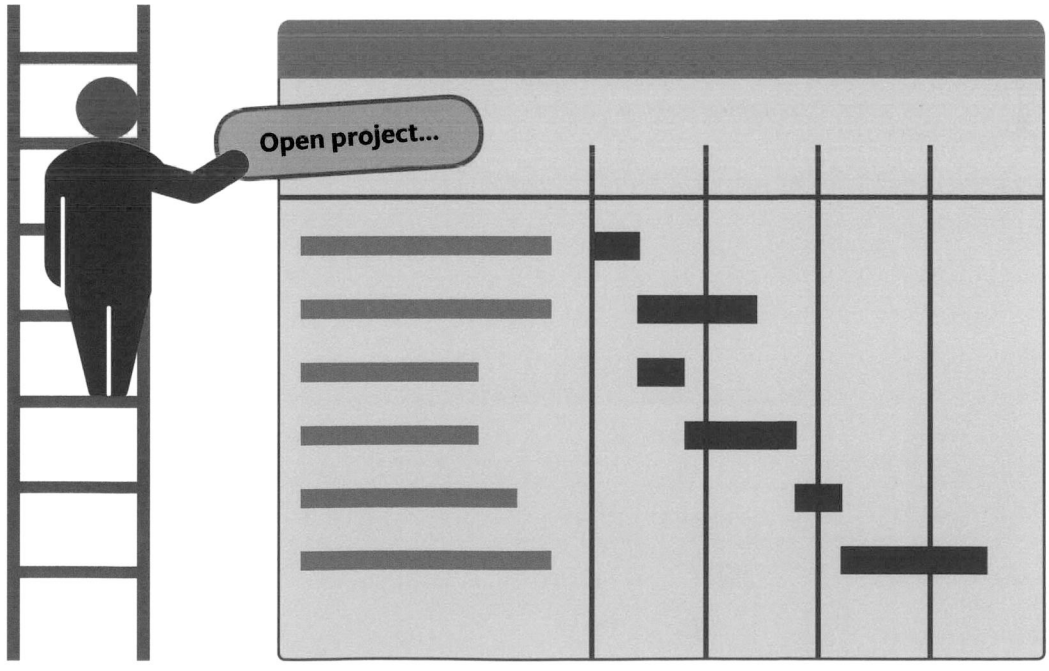

Objects and classes

One of Python's most important features is that it is an object-oriented language (see p.25). This means that data in Python can be arranged in terms of classes and objects, which allows users to have one blueprint from which multiple objects can be created.

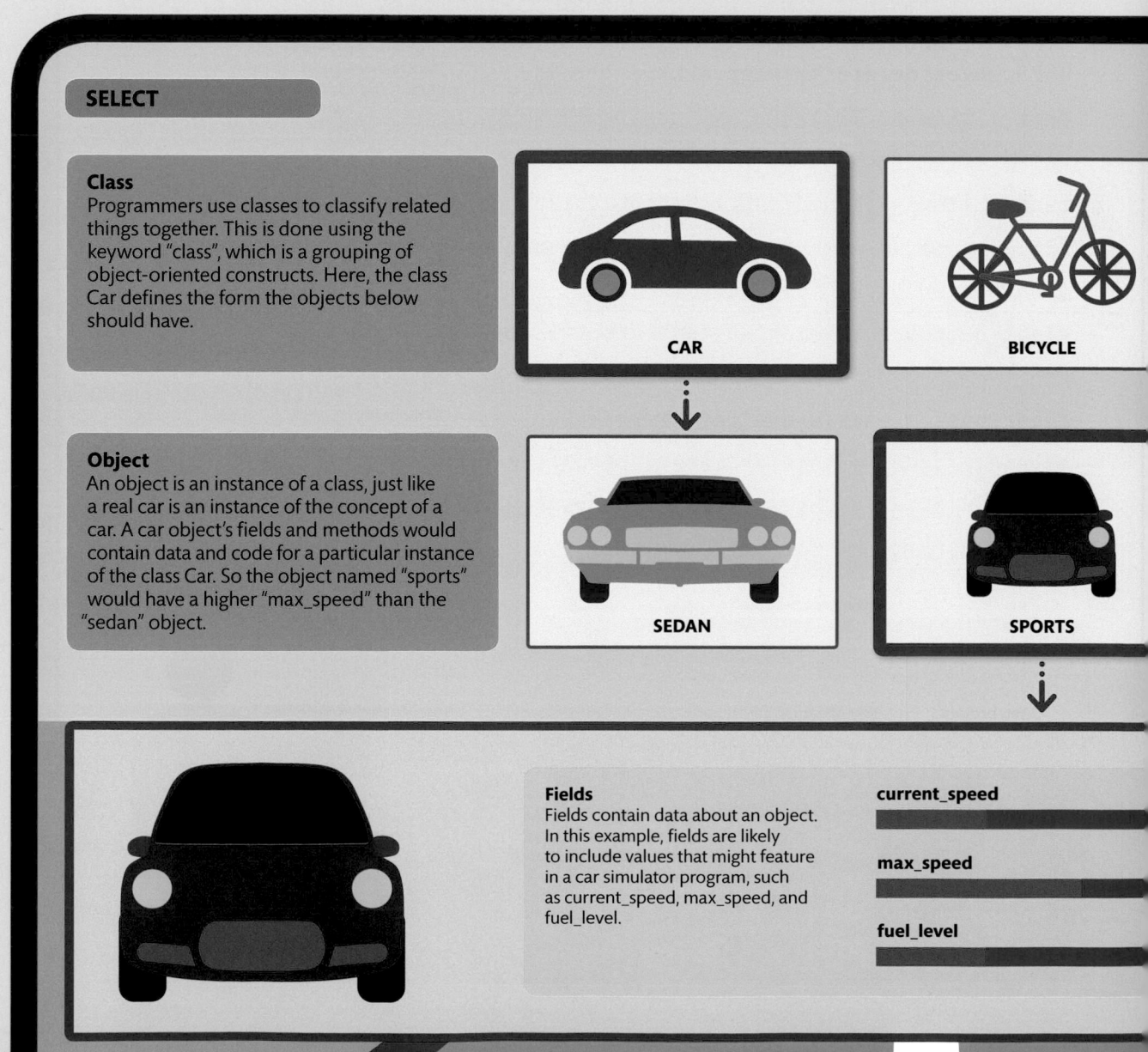

SELECT

Class
Programmers use classes to classify related things together. This is done using the keyword "class", which is a grouping of object-oriented constructs. Here, the class Car defines the form the objects below should have.

CAR

BICYCLE

Object
An object is an instance of a class, just like a real car is an instance of the concept of a car. A car object's fields and methods would contain data and code for a particular instance of the class Car. So the object named "sports" would have a higher "max_speed" than the "sedan" object.

SEDAN

SPORTS

Fields
Fields contain data about an object. In this example, fields are likely to include values that might feature in a car simulator program, such as current_speed, max_speed, and fuel_level.

current_speed

max_speed

fuel_level

What are objects and classes?

An object is a data type that is modelled after a real-world item, such as a car, allowing programmers to create a computer representation of it. Objects usually consists of two parts: fields, containing data, and methods, containing code. A class, on the other hand, defines the form a particular object should have. It is like the "idea" of an object and lays out the types of field that object would have, and what its methods would do.

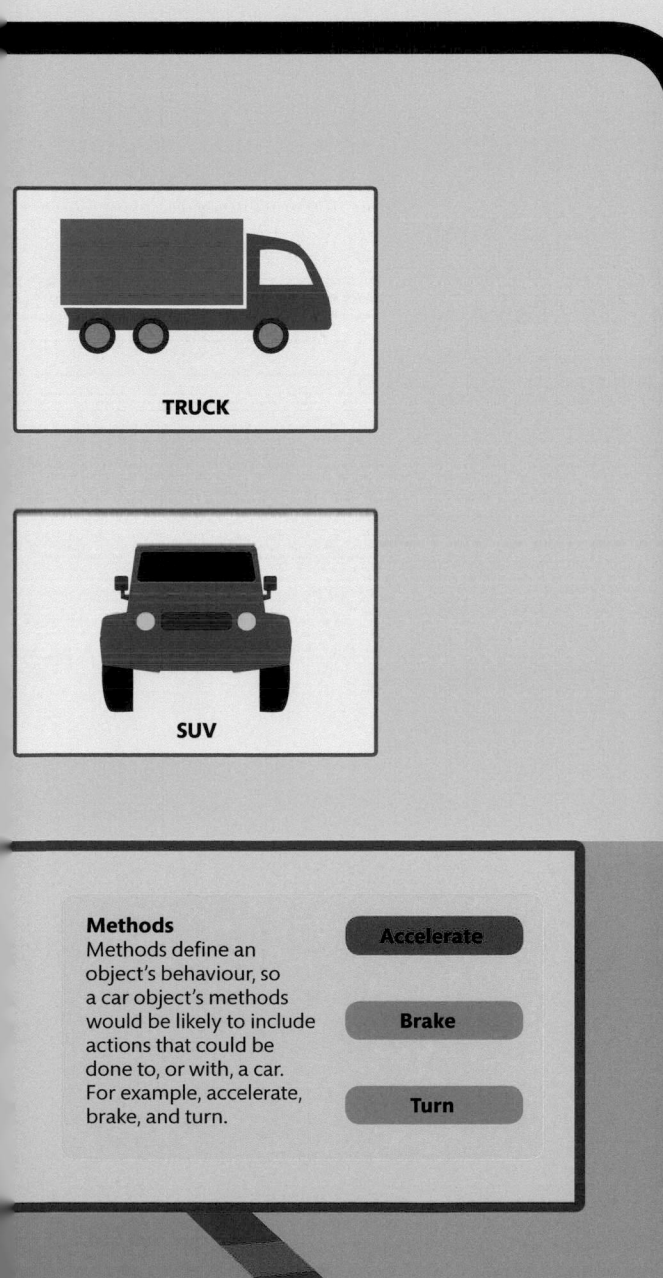

TRUCK

SUV

Methods
Methods define an object's behaviour, so a car object's methods would be likely to include actions that could be done to, or with, a car. For example, accelerate, brake, and turn.

Accelerate

Brake

Turn

Describes the attributes common to any car

Fields of the class Car

```python
class Car:
    current_speed = 0
    max_speed = 0
    fuel_level = 0
    def accelerate(self):
        print("speeding up")
    def break(self):
        print("slowing down")

my_car = Car()
my_car.current_speed = 4.5
my_car.max_speed = 8.5
my_car.fuel_level = 4.5
```

Methods of the class Car

Sets the fields of the **my_car** object to specific values

Instantiating a class
A program that allows users to model the functioning of a car might include the class Car, with attributes common to all cars. A user's car (here, a sports model) would then be an object, with fields containing values related to that particular car, and methods defining the actions done with the car.

Budget manager

Managing money can be a tedious task, which can be made easier with a computer. There are various apps for tracking what you spend, based on setting budgets for different kinds of expenses. This project will create a simple budget manager using Python dictionaries and classes.

What the program does

This budget manager will allow users to keep track of their expenditure against an overall budget of **2500**. To start, a budget is allocated for different kinds of expenditure, such as groceries and household bills. The expenses can then be compared against their allocated budget. A summary is displayed to get a quick overview of the finances.

Budget planner
Rather than directly creating a program, this project will create a set of functions that can be called from the Python shell. These functions can also be imported and used in other programs.

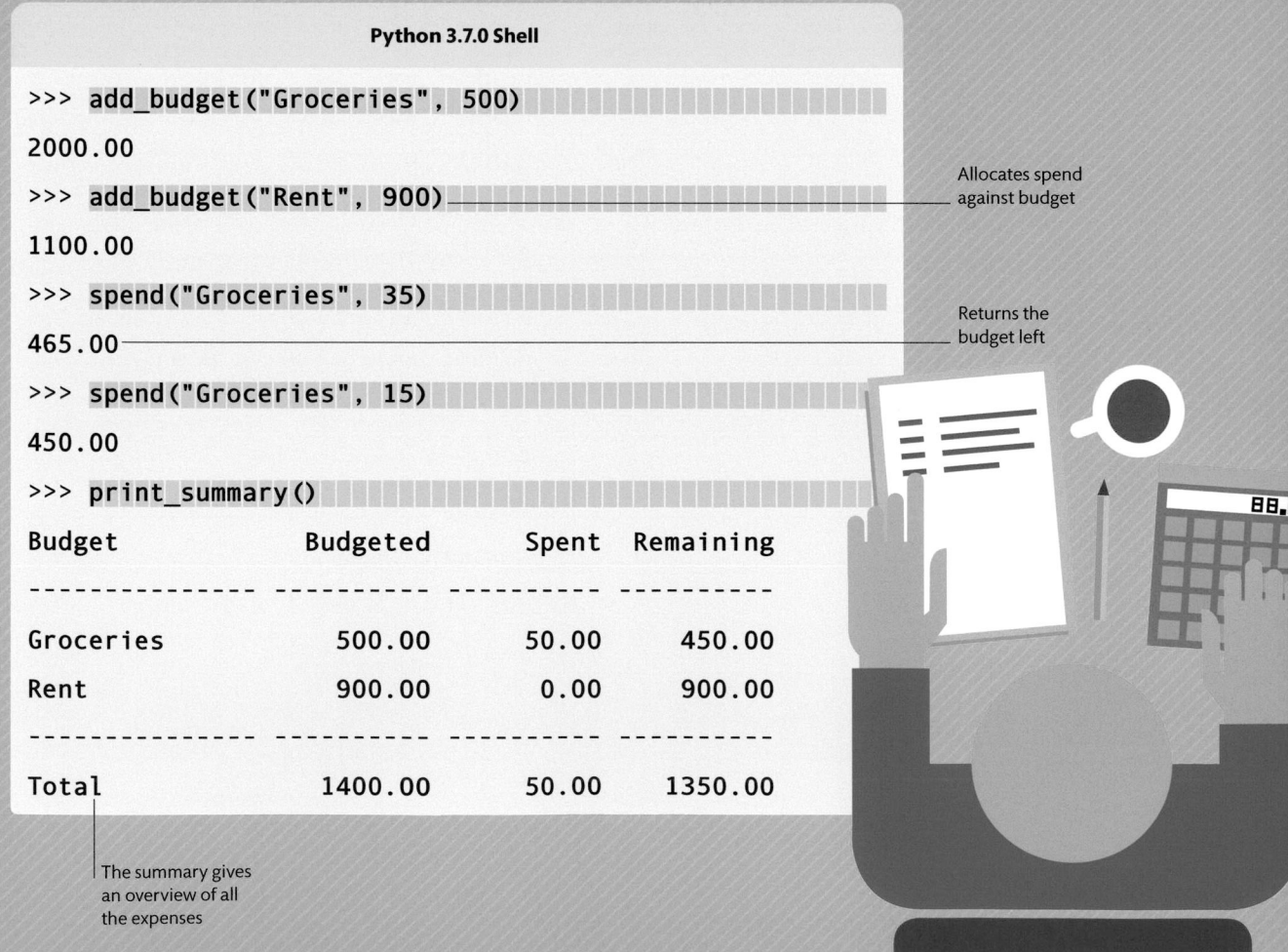

```
                    Python 3.7.0 Shell

>>> add_budget("Groceries", 500)
2000.00
>>> add_budget("Rent", 900)
1100.00
>>> spend("Groceries", 35)
465.00
>>> spend("Groceries", 15)
450.00
>>> print_summary()
Budget          Budgeted       Spent    Remaining
---------------  -----------  ---------  ----------
Groceries          500.00       50.00      450.00
Rent               900.00        0.00      900.00
---------------  -----------  ---------  ----------
Total             1400.00       50.00     1350.00
```

Allocates spend against budget

Returns the budget left

The summary gives an overview of all the expenses

YOU WILL LEARN

› How to use Python dictionaries
› How to raise exceptions for errors
› How to format strings for output
› How to create a Python class

Time:
1 hour

Lines of code: 43

Difficulty level
● ● ● ○ ○

WHERE THIS IS USED

The library developed in this project, with the addition of a user interface, can be used in a simple financial-planning application. Splitting up a program into multiple modules and encapsulating code and data in classes are both techniques that are used extensively in programming.

Function calls

The functions written in this program will allow you to allocate an amount of income to different named budgets. The functions will then track spending against these budgets to see the total amount spent compared to the amount that was budgeted. The diagram below shows an example of making a series of function calls.

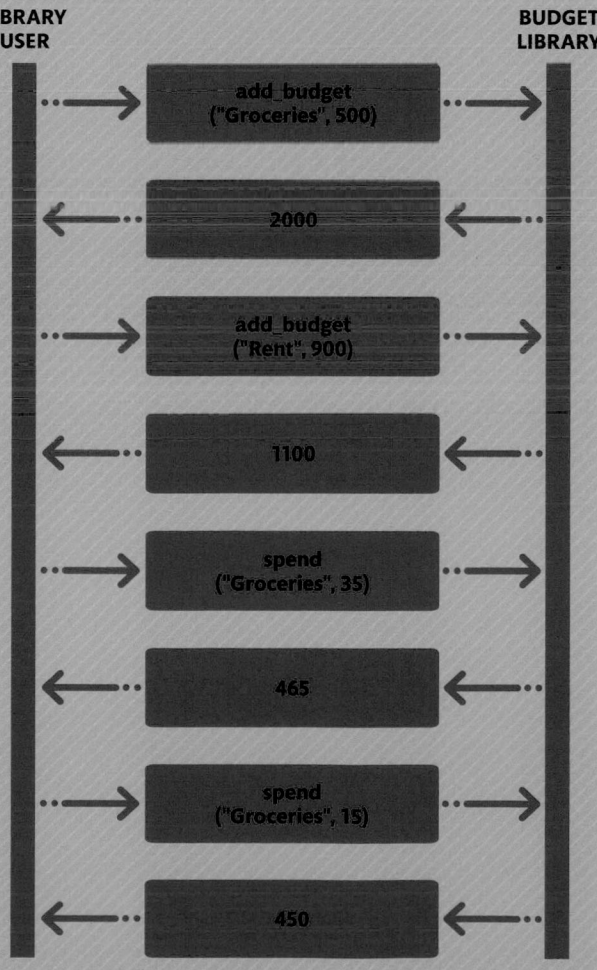

Program design

In this project, functions are added sequentially to create the budget library. Then, a summary of all the expenses is printed. In the end, all the code is converted into a Python class to make it more useful.

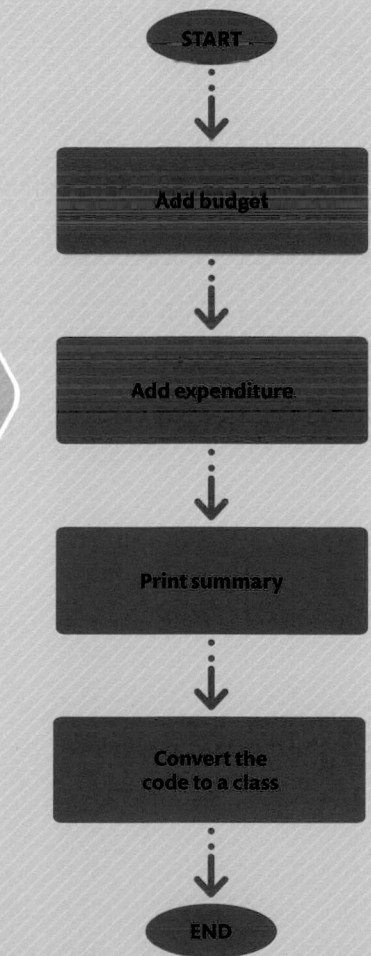

1 Setting up

To create this budget manager, you will need a new Python file. You can then add some basic code to the file and build on it later. The use of Python dictionaries will allow you to save the amount budgeted and spent.

1.1 CREATE A NEW FILE

The first step is to create a new file that will contain the code for this project. Open IDLE and select New File from the File menu. Create a new folder on your desktop called BudgetManager, and save this empty file inside it. Name the file "budget.py".

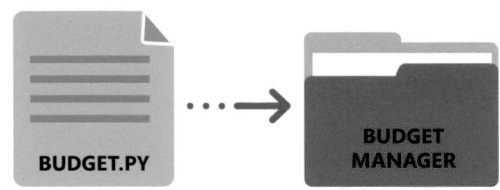

BUDGET.PY

BUDGET MANAGER

1.2 SET UP THE VARIABLES

Now create some global variables that will track the amount of money available, the amount you have budgeted, and the amount spent. You will use Python dictionaries (see box, below) for the budgets and expenditure that will map from a name, such as "Groceries", to an amount of money. Type this code into the new file.

```
available = 2500.00
budgets = {}
expenditure = {}
```

Sets the variable **available** to an example starting amount

Curly brackets are used to create a dictionary – an empty dictionary in this instance

DICTIONARIES

When deciding what Python data structure to use, think about how you would write the information to be stored. Often, the obvious way to write something down is similar to the table shown below. If the information in the first column is unique (the items in it are not repeated), then using Python dictionaries might be the answer. A dictionary is a data structure that consists of multiple key:value pairs. It maps one value, such as a name, to another, such as an amount of money. In the table below, the first column contains the keys of the dictionary and the second contains the values. If the table has multiple value columns, then these can be stored in separate dictionaries using the same keys. You can, therefore, have one dictionary for budgets and another for expenditure.

DICTIONARY FORMAT	
Budget name	**Budget amount**
Groceries	500
Bills	200
Entertainment	50

```
{"Groceries": 500, "Bills": 200, "Entertainment": 50}
```

The table information above as a Python dictionary

2 Adding a budget

In this section, you will create budgets for the various expenses. First, you will add code to enable the user to add these budgets, and then ensure that the code prevents users from making some common budgeting errors.

CLOTHES RENT GROCERIES

2.1 ADD A BUDGET FUNCTION

Write a function to add a budget. The function will take the name of the budget and the amount of money to be budgeted. It will then store these in the budgets dictionary and deduct the amount from the amount available. The function then returns the new available amount to show how much is still left to budget. Add this code below the global variables.

```python
def add_budget(name, amount):
    global available
    budgets[name] = amount
    available -= amount
    expenditure[name] = 0
    return available
```

available will be global when set in this function

Stores the budgeted amount in the **budgets** dictionary

Deducts the budgeted amount from the available amount

Returns the new available amount

Sets the spent amount for this budget to **0**

SAVE

2.2 RUN FILE

Save and then run the file by selecting Run Module from the Run menu. This will open the IDLE Python shell window. You can test the function by typing an example call in the shell. You will see >>> in the window, which is the Python shell prompt. You can type small pieces of Python code next to this and they will be executed when you press Enter or return.

```python
>>> add_budget("Groceries", 500)
2000.0
>>> budgets
{'Groceries': 500}
>>> expenditure
{'Groceries': 0}
```

Type this line and press Enter

Returned value of the function call

Typing the name of variables at the prompt will show their values

2.3 ERROR CHECKING

To see what happens if you add a budget twice, type this code in the shell window. You will notice that the budgets dictionary will be updated with the new value, but the **available** amount is reduced by both. To avoid this, you need to add some code to check if the same budget name has been used twice. Add the code shown in the editor window below to make changes to the **add_budget()** function.

```
>>> add_budget("Rent", 900)
1100.0
>>> add_budget("Rent", 400)
700.0                          The available amount
                               is deducted twice
>>> budgets
{'Groceries': 500, 'Rent': 400}
```

```
def add_budget(name, amount):
    global available
    if name in budgets:
        raise ValueError("Budget exists")
    budgets[name] = amount
```

Checks if **name** already exists as a key in the budgets dictionary

Leaves the function immediately with an exception if a budget name appears more than once

EXCEPTIONS

In Python, errors are indicated by raising exceptions. These exceptions interrupt the normal execution of code. Unless the exception is caught, the program will immediately exit and display the exception that has been raised and the line of code it occurred at.

There are a number of standard exception types in Python. Each of these accept a string value giving an error message that can be displayed to the user to explain what has gone wrong. The table below lists a few standard exception types and when they should be used.

TYPES OF EXCEPTIONS	
Name	**Use when**
TypeError	A value is not of the expected type: for example, using a string where a number was expected
ValueError	A value is invalid in some way: for example, too large or too small
RuntimeError	Some other unexpected error has occurred in the program

2.4 RUN THE MODULE

Test the code again to check if the error has now been fixed. When you run the code, the three global variables will be set back to their initial values. Type this code in the shell window. You will now get an error message if you try adding the same budget twice. If you check the variables **budgets** and **available**, you will see that they have not been updated with the wrong values.

```
>>> add_budget("Groceries", 500)
2000.0
>>> add_budget("Rent", 900)
1100.0
>>> add_budget("Rent", 400)
Traceback (most recent call last):
  File "<pyshell>", line 1, in <module>
    add_budget("Rent", 400)
  File "budget.py", line 7, in add_budget
    raise ValueError("Budget exists")
ValueError: Budget exists
```

Error message displayed on screen

```
>>> budgets
{'Groceries': 500, 'Rent': 900}
>>> available
1100.0
```

The variables will not be updated with wrong values

2.5 MORE ERROR CHECKING

Continue in the shell window to see what happens if you budget an amount of money that is more than what is available. This is clearly an error, since you should not be able to over-budget. Add another check into the **add_budget()** function to fix this.

Update the code in the editor window. Then save the file and run the code once again to test if the new error message is displayed, and over-budgeting is prevented.

```
>>> add_budget("Clothes", 2000)
-900.0
```

A negative value indicates over-budgeting

```
    if name in budgets:
        raise ValueError("Budget exists")
    if amount > available:
        raise ValueError("Insufficient funds")
    budgets[name] = amount
```

Checks if the amount being budgeted is more than the amount available

Raises an exception and leaves the function immediately

SAVE

```
>>> add_budget("Groceries", 500)
2000.0
>>> add_budget("Rent", 900)
1100.0
>>> add_budget("Clothes", 2000)
Traceback (most recent call last):
  File "<pyshell>", line 1, in <module>
    add_budget("Clothes", 2000)
  File "budget.py", line 9, in add_budget
    raise ValueError("Insufficient funds")
ValueError: Insufficient funds
```

Error message for over-budgeting is displayed

3 Tracking expenditure

Next, you need to add a way to track all the expenditure. To do this, you will first add a function that allows you to enter the money that has been spent, and then add another function to display the summary. This will indicate the total money spent and the amount remaining.

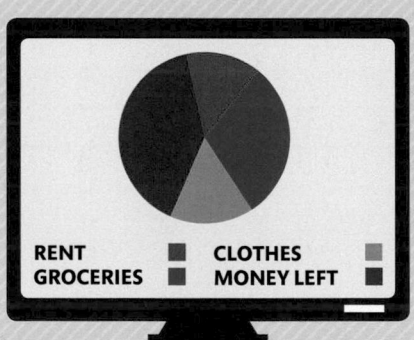

RENT   ■   CLOTHES   ■
GROCERIES   ■   MONEY LEFT   ■

3.1 ADD SPEND FUNCTION

Add a function to note the amount you have spent and the name of the budget that you want to track it against. Add a new **spend()** function below the **add_budget()** function. The Python "+=" operator is used to add an amount to a variable. Save the file and then run the module to try using this new function.

Adds **amount** to the corresponding key in the **expenditure** dictionary

```
        return available                    Raises an exception if the value
                                             of name is not a key in the
def spend(name, amount):                     expenditure dictionary
    if name not in expenditure:
        raise ValueError("No such budget")
    expenditure[name] += amount
```

3.2 RETURNING THE REMAINING AMOUNT

It will also be useful to track the amount left in the budget. Add this code to the end of the **spend()** function you just created, then save and run the file to test the code. You will notice that you can spend more than the budgeted amount. You do not need an exception for this, as you will want to track overspending.

```
                          Gets the budgeted
                          amount for name
    budgeted = budgets[name]

    spent = expenditure[name]

    return budgeted - spent
```
Returns the amount | Gets the total
left in the budget | amount spent

```
>>> add_budget("Groceries", 500)
2000.0
>>> spend("Groceries", 35)
465
>>> spend("Groceries", 15)
450
>>> spend("Groceries", 500)
-50 ─── Negative value indicates that
        spending exceeds the budget
```

3.3 PRINT A SUMMARY

In this step, you will add a function that will display an overview of each budget name, the amount originally budgeted, the amount spent, and the amount left to spend (if any). Add this code at the bottom of the file. Then, save the changes and run the file in the shell window. The summary will display the figures for every category.

```
def print_summary():
    for name in budgets:
        budgeted = budgets[name]
        spent = expenditure[name]
        remaining = budgeted - spent
        print(name, budgeted, spent, remaining)
```

Loops through all the keys — In the **budgets** dictionary

Gets the budgeted amount for the **name** key

Gets the amount spent for the **name** key

Calculates the remaining amount by deducting budgeted from spent

Prints a single line summary for this budget

```
>>> add_budget("Groceries", 500)
2000.0
>>> add_budget("Rent", 900)
1100.0
>>> spend("Groceries", 35)
465
>>> spend("Groceries", 15)
450
>>> print_summary()
Groceries 500 50 450
Rent 900 0 900
```

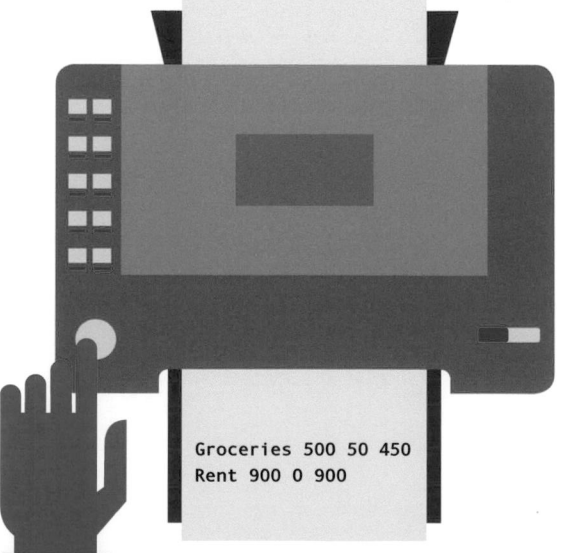

3.4 FORMAT THE SUMMARY

At this stage, the summary will be a bit hard to read with the numbers squeezed together. To fix this, you can line them up in a proper table by using "string formatting" (see box, below). Change the **print** line in

the **print_summary()** function as shown below. This will create a string from the values, formatting each to a specific width and number of decimal places. It will then print that string.

```
        remaining = budgeted - spent
    print(f'{name:15s} {budgeted:10.2f} {spent:10.2f} '
            f'{remaining:10.2f}')
```

The amount will be displayed with two decimal places

```
>>> add_budget("Groceries", 500)
2000
>>> add_budget("Rent", 900)
1100
>>> spend("Groceries", 35)
465
>>> spend("Groceries", 15)
450
>>> print_summary()
Groceries              500.00       50.00      450.00
Rent                   900.00        0.00      900.00
```

The values will have two decimal places and will be lined up in columns, similar to a table

FORMAT STRINGS

In Python, formatted strings can be created from values with special format strings. These are written like normal strings, but have an "f" character before the opening quotation mark. Inside the string, you can place code expressions within curly brackets. These will be executed and replaced with their values. The most common expressions used are variable names, but arithmetic calculations can also be used. Any part of the string outside the brackets is used without change. Detailed formatting instructions can be added after a colon. This includes a letter specifying how to format the value. Placing a number before this letter allows a width to be specified.

EXAMPLES OF FORMAT STRINGS	
Example	Result
f'{greeting} World!'	'Hello World!'
f'{greeting:10s}'	'Hello '
f'{cost:5.2f}'	' 3.47'
f'{cost:5.1f}'	' 3.5'
f'The answer is {a * b}'	'The answer is 42'

3.5 ADD A TABLE HEADER

Now, add a header to the table so that the numbers within each category can be easily distinguished. Add two `print` statements in the `print_summary()` function. It may be easier to type the line with dashes first – 15 dashes followed by three lots of 10 dashes, with spaces in between. You can then line up the titles against the dashes.

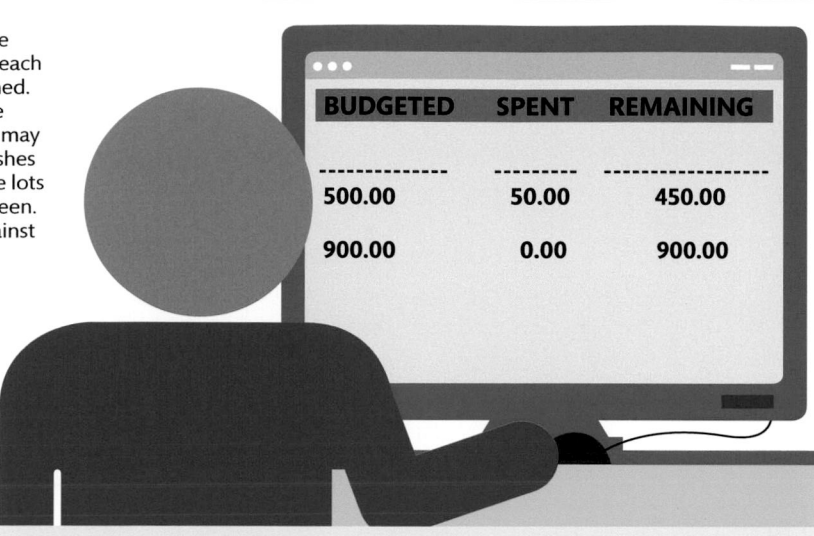

BUDGETED	SPENT	REMAINING
---------------	---------	------------------
500.00	50.00	450.00
900.00	0.00	900.00

```python
def print_summary():
    print("Budget            Budgeted       Spent   Remaining")
    print("--------------- ---------- ---------- ----------")
    for name in budgets:
        budgeted = budgets[name]
        spent = expenditure[name]
```

The titles have been aligned against the dashes

3.6 ADD A TABLE FOOTER

To complete the summary table, you can add a footer to it. This will add up the contents of the various columns and display their total value. Update the `print_summary()` function as shown below. Use the same format instructions for printing the totals that you used for the budget. However, remember to use "Total" instead of the budget name, and `total_budgeted`, `total_spent`, and `total_remaining` for the other variables.

```python
def print_summary():
    print("Budget            Budgeted       Spent   Remaining")
    print("--------------- ---------- ---------- ----------")
    total_budgeted = 0
    total_spent = 0
    total_remaining = 0
    for name in budgets:
```

Sets the total variables to 0

TRACKING EXPENDITURE

```
        budgeted = budgets[name]
        spent = expenditure[name]
        remaining = budgeted - spent
        print(f'{name:15s} {budgeted:10.2f} {spent:10.2f} '
              f'{remaining:10.2f}')
        total_budgeted += budgeted
        total_spent += spent
        total_remaining += remaining
    print("--------------- ---------- ---------- ----------")
    print(f'{"Total":15s} {total_budgeted:10.2f} {total_spent:10.2f} '
          f'{total_budgeted - total_spent:10.2f}')
```

Adds the amount to the totals

Prints another separator line and the summary with the totals below it

```
>>> add_budget("Groceries", 500)
2000.0
>>> add_budget("Rent", 900)
1100.0
>>> spend("Groceries", 35)
465
>>> spend("Groceries", 15)
450
>>> print_summary()
Budget          Budgeted     Spent  Remaining
--------------- ---------- ---------- ----------
Groceries          500.00     50.00     450.00
Rent               900.00      0.00     900.00
--------------- ---------- ---------- ----------
Total             1400.00     50.00    1350.00
```

Final summary table printed with a header and footer

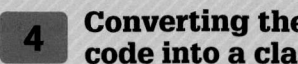

4 Converting the code into a class

In this section, you will take all the code written so far and turn it into a Python class (see pp.156–57). This will allow the user to track multiple budgets simultaneously.

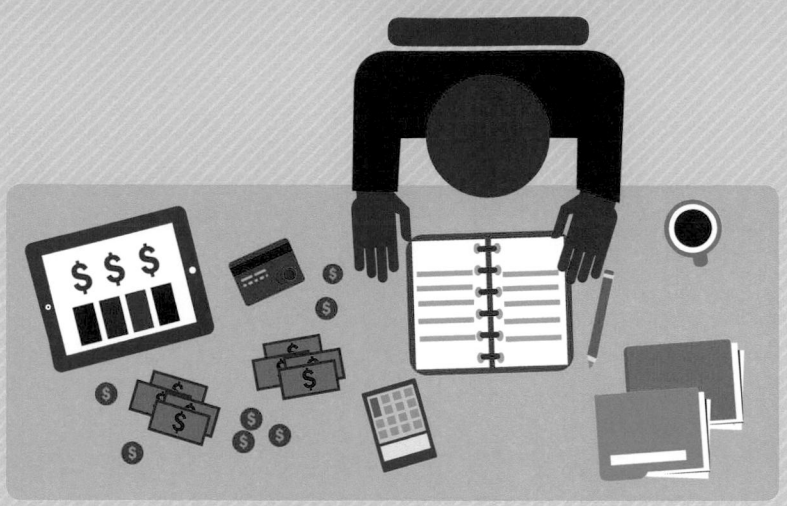

4.1 INDENT THE CODE

Since Python is structured using indentation, you need to indent the entire code to convert it into a class. Select all the code in the file and then choose "Indent Region" from the Format menu. Next, add a new class header at the top of the file, before the variables.

Format	Run	Options
Indent Region		
Dedent Region		
Comment Out Region		

Click here to add indents to the entire file

Defines the new class

The variables will now appear indented

```python
class BudgetManager:
    available = 2500
    budgets = {}
    expenditure = {}
```

4.2 ADD INITIALIZER

Indent the three variables again and add a function header to them. Functions inside a class are known as methods. The __init__ method is called when a new instance of a class is created. This method is called the "initializer" as it sets the initial values for the instance variables. The first argument of the initializer is the new instance, called **self** by convention. You can also add additional arguments that will allow you to provide useful values, such as **amount** here.

```python
class BudgetManager:
    def __init__(self, amount):
        available = 2500
        budgets = {}
        expenditure = {}
```

Arguments within the initializer

CONVERTING THE CODE INTO A CLASS

4.3 CREATE INSTANCE VARIABLES

Next, convert the three variables into instance variables. This is done by adding "**self.**" before each of the variable names. Use the argument **amount** instead of **2500** as the initial value for the available instance variable.

```
class BudgetManager:
    def __init__(self, amount):
        self.available = amount
        self.budgets = {}
        self.expenditure = {}
```

Converts the variables to instance variables

4.4 TURN THE FUNCTIONS INTO METHODS

Now you need to turn all the other functions in the code into methods. Just like with the initializer, you can do this by adding **self** as the first argument of every function, and then adding **self.** before each use of the instance variables. Modify the **add_budget()** function as shown below. Delete the **global available** line from the **add_budget** method, as **available** is now an instance variable.

Remove the line **global available** from between these two lines of code

```
    def add_budget(self, name, amount):
        if name in self.budgets:
            raise ValueError("Budget exists")
        if amount > self.available:
            raise ValueError("Insufficient funds")
        self.budgets[name] = amount
        self.available -= amount
        self.expenditure[name] = 0
        return self.available
    def spend(self, name, amount):
        if name not in self.expenditure:
            raise ValueError("No such budget")
        self.expenditure[name] += amount
        budgeted = self.budgets[name]
        spent = self.expenditure[name]
        return budgeted - spent
    def print_summary(self):
```

Adds an argument to the function

```
        print("Budget              Budgeted     Spent  Remaining")
        print("---------------- ----------- ----------- ----------")
        total_budgeted = 0
        total_spent = 0
        total_remaining = 0
        for name in self.budgets:
            budgeted = self.budgets[name]
            spent = self.expenditure[name]
```

Add **self.** before
each use of the
instance variable

SAVE

4.5 RUN THE MODULE

Save and run the module. Type these lines in the shell window to test the code. This will add a newly created instance of the BudgetManager class. The code inspects the instance variables by putting **outgoings.** before their name. You can call methods in a similar way, by putting the variable name before the function name with a full stop.

Sets the variable **outgoings** to an instance of the BudgetManager class

```
>>> outgoings = BudgetManager(2000)
>>> outgoings.available
2000
>>> outgoings.budgets
{}
>>> outgoings.expenditure
{}
>>> outgoings.add_budget("Rent", 700)
1300
>>> outgoings.add_budget("Groceries", 400)
900
```

```
>>> outgoings.add_budget("Bills", 300)
600
>>> outgoings.add_budget("Entertainment", 100)
500
>>> outgoings.budgets
{'Rent': 700, 'Groceries': 400, 'Bills': 300, 'Entertainment': 100}
>>> outgoings.spend("Groceries", 35)
365
>>> outgoings.print_summary()
Budget              Budgeted       Spent   Remaining
--------------      ----------   ---------- ----------

Rent                   700.00        0.00      700.00
Groceries              400.00       35.00      365.00
Bills                  300.00        0.00      300.00
Entertainment          100.00        0.00      100.00
--------------      ----------   ---------- ----------

Total                 1500.00       35.00     1465.00
```

5 TRACKING MULTIPLE BUDGETS

It is possible to reset the budget by simply creating a new instance of the BudgetManager class, by typing this code in the shell window. You can even have multiple BudgetManager instances for tracking separate budgets. To test this, create a new budget called **holiday**. As the available, budgets, and expenditure variables are stored within each instance, they are distinct from each other and can have different values for the different instances.

Creates a new instance of the BudgetManager class

```
>>> outgoings = BudgetManager(2500)
>>> outgoings.add_budget("Groceries", 500)
2000
>>> outgoings.print_summary()
```

Prints the summary for the new instance

```
Budget              Budgeted        Spent    Remaining
--------------     ----------     ----------   ----------
Groceries            500.00          0.00       500.00
--------------     ----------     ----------   ----------
Total                500.00          0.00       500.00
>>> holiday = BudgetManager(1000)
>>> holiday.add_budget("Flights", 250)
750
>>> holiday.add_budget("Hotel", 300)
450
>>> holiday.spend("Flights", 240)
10
>>> holiday.print_summary()
Budget              Budgeted        Spent    Remaining
--------------     ----------     ----------   ----------
Flights              250.00        240.00        10.00
Hotel                300.00          0.00       300.00
--------------     ----------     ----------   ----------
Total                550.00        240.00       310.00
```

Adds another new instance of BudgetManager

5.1 USING THE CODE

The code written in this project is a module that can be used in other programs. This module can be imported and used like any other Python library (see pp.116–17). Try this out by creating a new module that will import this one. Open a new file and save it in the BudgetManager folder you created earlier. Name this new file "test.py". Now add this code to create an instance of the BudgetManager class that calls methods on it.

```
import budget
outgoings = budget.BudgetManager(2500)
outgoings.add_budget("Groceries", 500)
outgoings.print_summary()
```

Imports the module **budget** into this new one

The BudgetManager class is referenced by adding the **budget** module name before it with a full stop

Pygame Zero

Pygame Zero is a tool that enables programmers to build games using Python. It provides a simplified way to create programs using the powerful functions and data types in the pygame library.

Installing Pygame Zero on Windows

The latest versions of **pygame** and **Pygame Zero** can be installed on a Windows computer by following the steps given below. An active Internet connection is required for this.

START

1 Open the Command Prompt
On a Windows 10 operating system, click Start and open the Command Prompt by typing "Cmd" into the Search field. If you have an older version of Windows, find the Command Prompt in the Systems folder.

The Command Prompt thumbnail looks like this

2 Install a package manager
The easiest way to install or update Python libraries and modules on a system is to use a package manager called "pip". Type the following command in the Command Prompt and press Enter.

```
python -m pip install -U pip
```

Installing Pygame Zero on a Mac

The latest versions of **pygame** and **Pygame Zero** can be installed on a computer with macOS using the "Homebrew package manager". Internet connectivity is essential for this.

2 Install Python 3
Next, use "Homebrew" to check if Python 3 is already installed on the system, and install it if not. Type the following command in the Terminal window and then press Enter.

```
brew install python3
```

START

1 Open the Terminal and install a package manager
Use the Terminal app to install the modules. It can be found in the "Utilities" folder under "Applications". Type the following command and then press Enter to install "Homebrew". The installation process will ask for a user login password to continue, and may take some time to complete.

```
ruby -e "$(curl -fsSL https://raw.
githubusercontent.com/Homebrew/
install/master/install)"
```

UPDATES

Occasionally, programmers may experience problems while running **Pygame Zero** programs after updating to a new version of their operating system. To fix this, the tools added during **Pygame Zero** installation can be uninstalled, then reinstalled using the instructions here.

3 Install Pygame
Once the "pip" package manager is installed, type the command shown below and then press Enter. This will use "pip" to install the **pygame** library.

```
pip install pygame
```

4 Install Pygame Zero
Finally, type the following command and then press Enter. This will install **Pygame Zero**.

```
pip install pgzero
```

FINISH

3 Install extra tools
To install some extra tools that the system requires to run **Pygame Zero**, use "Homebrew" and type this command into the Terminal window followed by Enter.

```
brew install sdl sdl_mixer sdl_sound
sdl_ttf
```

5 Install Pygame Zero
Finally, this last command will install **Pygame Zero**.

```
pip3 install pgzero
```

FINISH

4 Install pygame
Now type this command to install the **pygame** library and press Enter.

```
pip3 install pygame
```

Knight's quest

This fast-paced, two-dimensional game will put your reflexes to the test. It uses coordinates to create a two-dimensional playing area, and Pygame Zero's Actor class to introduce the characters and collectable items in the game. An event loop program makes the game run smoothly.

How to play this game

The aim of this game is to navigate the knight around the dungeon – a two-dimensional playing area – with the arrow keys, but you cannot move through walls or the locked door. Collect the keys by moving over them. However, you need to avoid the guards as they try to move towards the knight. Any contact with the guards ends the game. You win if you can get to the door after picking up all of the keys.

Dungeon crawl

This project is an example of a style of game called dungeon crawl. In such games, the player usually navigates a labyrinthine environment, collecting items and battling or avoiding enemies. This game will use the classic top-down 2D view, where the player appears to be looking down at the play area from above.

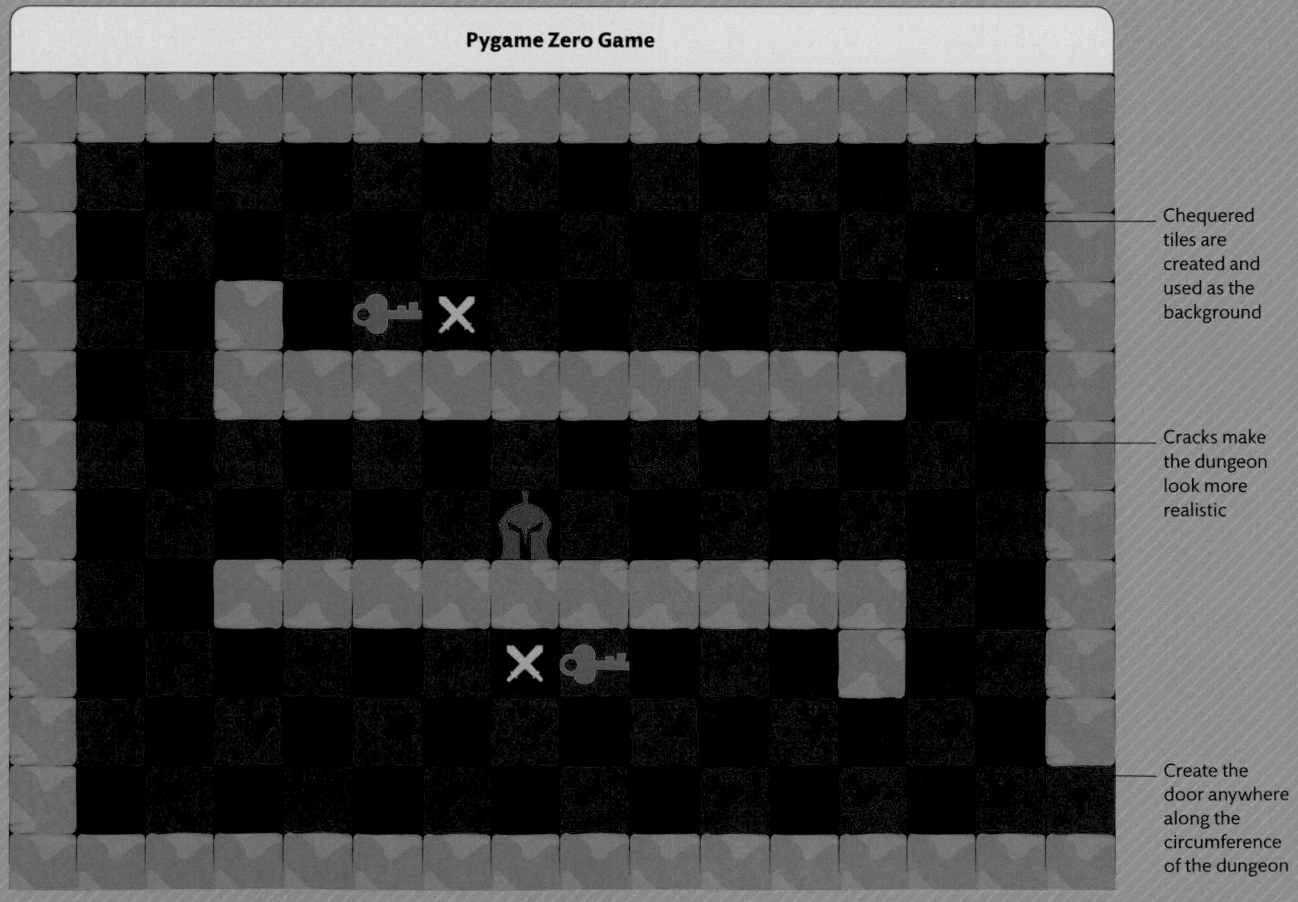

Pygame Zero Game

Chequered tiles are created and used as the background

Cracks make the dungeon look more realistic

Create the door anywhere along the circumference of the dungeon

YOU WILL LEARN

> How to use lists
> How to index strings
> How to use nested loops
> How to use **Pygame Zero** to make a simple game

Time:
2 hours
Lines of code:
151
Difficulty level

WHERE THIS IS USED

The concepts in this project are applicable to all kinds of 2D computer games, especially ones that are played on mobile phones. Apart from in dungeon-crawl games, image tile grids are also used in colour- and shape-matching games. The logic applied in this game could also be adapted to simple robotics projects.

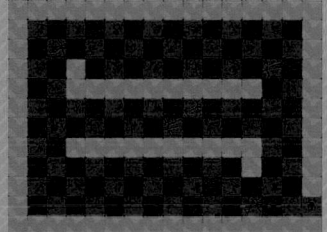

The scenery
The game is based on a simple grid on which square images called "tiles" are placed. The scenery of the game consists of a background of floor tiles, with additional tiles representing the walls and the door.

GUARD

KNIGHT

KEY

The actors
The movable or collectable items in the game are called actors. In this game, the actors are the same size as the tiles so that each is contained within one grid square. They are drawn on top of the scenery so that the background can be seen behind and through them.

The Pygame Zero game loop

A **Pygame Zero** program is an example of an event loop program. An event loop runs continuously, calling other parts of the program when an event occurs so that actions can be taken. The code necessary to manage this loop is part of **Pygame Zero**, so you only need to write the handler functions that deal with these events.

Set up game
Top-level statements in the Python file will be executed first and can be used to initialize the game state and configure **Pygame Zero** itself. **Pygame Zero** will then open a window and repeat the event loop continuously.

Handle input events
Pygame Zero will check for input events, such as key presses, mouse movements, and button presses each time through the loop. It will call the appropriate handler function (see p.185) when one of these events occurs.

Handle clock events
The **Pygame Zero** clock allows users to schedule calls to handler functions in the future. These delayed function calls will be made during this part of the event loop.

Update game state
At this point, **Pygame Zero** allows the user to do any work that they want done on every loop iteration by calling the update handler function. This is an optional function.

Draw interface
Finally, **Pygame Zero** calls the draw handler function, which will redraw the contents of the game window to reflect the current game state.

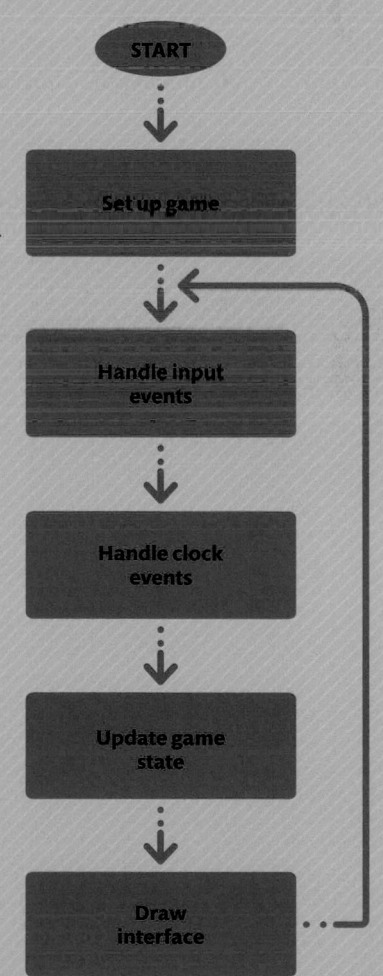

Setting up

1

To get started with this project, you will first need to create the folders to hold all the files. The next step will be to write some code to draw the background and the players on screen.

1.1 CREATE THE GAME FILE

First, create a new folder on your desktop and name it "KnightsQuest". Then, open IDLE and create a new file by choosing the New File option from the File menu. Save this file in the KnightsQuest folder by choosing Save As... from the same menu. Name the file "quest.py".

IDLE

File	Edit	Shell
New File	⌘N	← Select this option to create a new file
Open...	⌘O	
Open Module...		
Recent Files	▶	
Module Browser	⌘B	

1.2 SET UP THE IMAGES FOLDER

You now need a folder to hold the images required for this project. Go to the KnightsQuest folder and create a new folder inside it called "images". Go to *www.dk.com/coding-course* and download the resource pack for this book. Then copy the image files for this project into the new "images" folder.

IMAGES

1.3 INITIALIZE PYGAME ZERO

Go to the "quest.py" file you created earlier and type these lines of code into it to define the dimensions of the game grid. This will create a working **Pygame Zero** program. Save the file, then choose Run Module from the Run menu (or press the F5 key on your keyboard) to execute the code. You will only see a black window at this point. Close this window and continue.

Imports the **Pygame Zero** functionality

```
import pgzrun


GRID_WIDTH = 16

GRID_HEIGHT = 12

GRID_SIZE = 50


WIDTH = GRID_WIDTH * GRID_SIZE

HEIGHT = GRID_HEIGHT * GRID_SIZE


pgzrun.go()
```

These define the width and height of the game grid and the size of each tile

WIDTH and **HEIGHT** are special **Pygame Zero** variable names

These define the size of the game window

Starts **Pygame Zero**

SAVE

AGILE SOFTWARE DEVELOPMENT

Each step in this project will describe a new piece of functionality that makes the program more useful or interesting, and will then show you the code you need to add to implement this. At the end of each step you will have a working program that you can run and try out. This process of evolving a program by iteratively describing, developing, and testing small pieces of new functionality is part of a style of programming called Agile Software Development.

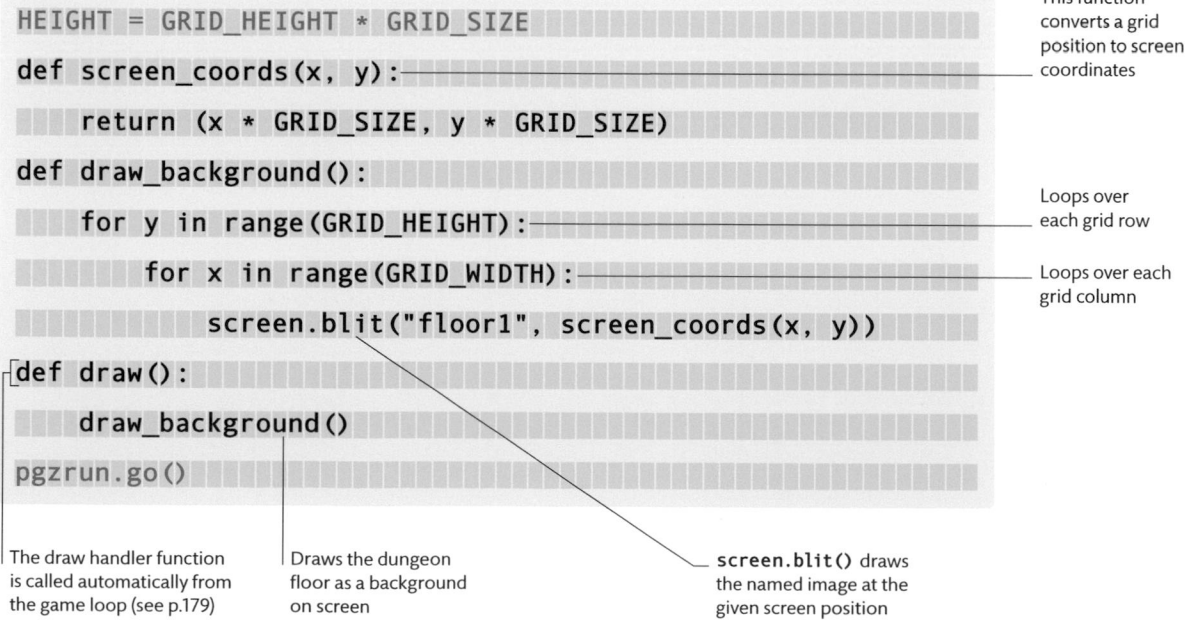

1.4   **DRAW THE BACKGROUND**
In this step, you will draw the floor of the dungeon as a grid of floor tiles filling the game window. Add the following lines of code to your program.

```python
HEIGHT = GRID_HEIGHT * GRID_SIZE
def screen_coords(x, y):
    return (x * GRID_SIZE, y * GRID_SIZE)
def draw_background():
    for y in range(GRID_HEIGHT):
        for x in range(GRID_WIDTH):
            screen.blit("floor1", screen_coords(x, y))
def draw():
    draw_background()
pgzrun.go()
```

This function converts a grid position to screen coordinates

Loops over each grid row

Loops over each grid column

The draw handler function is called automatically from the game loop (see p.179)

Draws the dungeon floor as a background on screen

`screen.blit()` draws the named image at the given screen position

GRID AND SCREEN COORDINATES

The playing area in this project is a grid that is 16 squares wide and 12 squares high. Each of these squares is 50 x 50 pixels. The position of a square is denoted by **x** and **y** coordinates, written as a pair in brackets (x, y). The x coordinate refers to a column number and the y coordinate refers to a row number. In programming, counting starts at the number 0, so the top left grid position for this project is (0, 0) and the bottom right grid position is (15, 11). In Python, **range(n)** iterates over the numbers 0 to n-1, so **range(GRID_HEIGHT)** is 0...11 and **range(GRID_WIDTH)** is 0...15.

Nesting one loop inside another allows the program to iterate across every grid position. Multiplying the grid coordinates by the size of the grid squares gives the coordinate of the top left corner of that grid square relative to the top left corner of the game window. **Pygame Zero** refers to this as the screen.

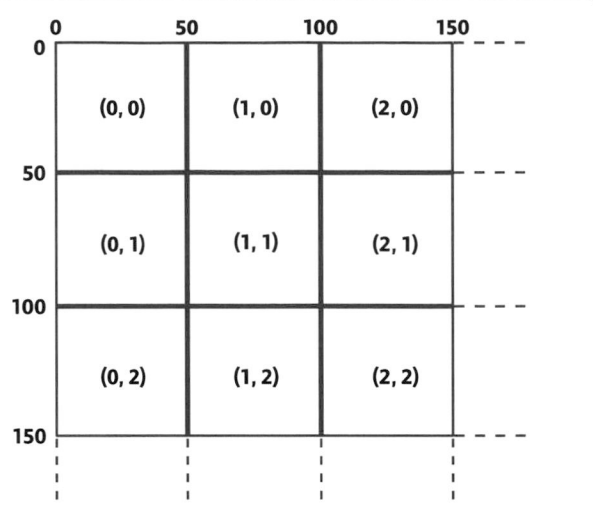

1.5 DEFINE THE SCENERY

You can now draw the walls of the dungeon, add a door, and define the map of the game. Add the following code below the constants in your IDLE file to do this. The map is defined as a list of 12 strings, each representing a row of the grid. Each string is 16 characters wide, with each character describing a single grid square.

K is a key, and G is a guard

The dungeon has 12 rows and 16 columns of wall tiles

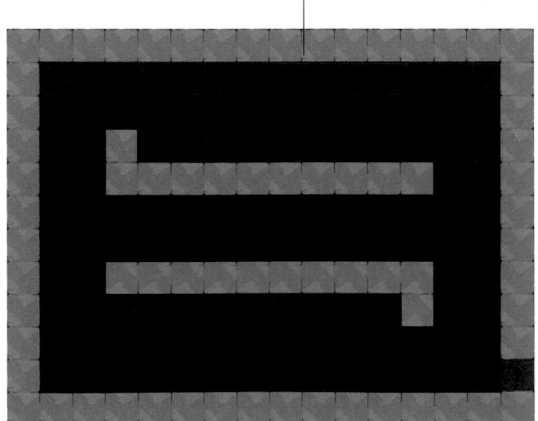

OUTPUT ON THE SCREEN

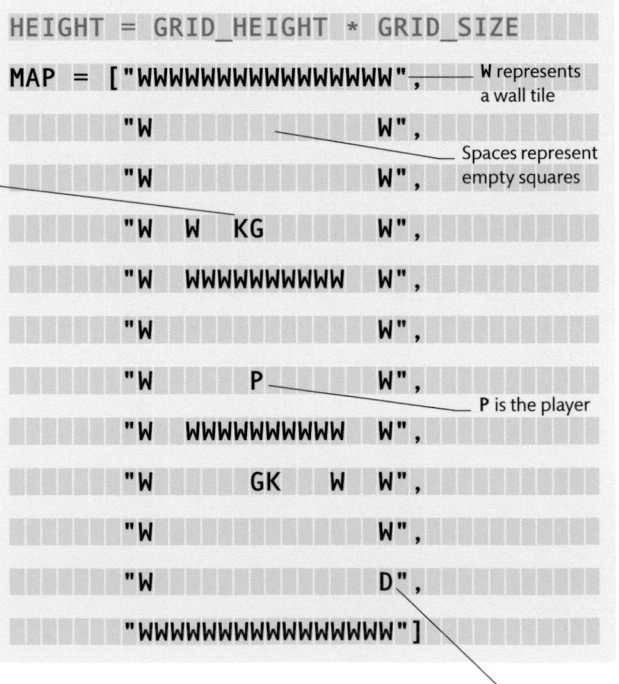

```
HEIGHT = GRID_HEIGHT * GRID_SIZE

MAP = ["WWWWWWWWWWWWWWWW",          W represents
                                    a wall tile
       "W              W",
                                    Spaces represent
       "W              W",          empty squares
       "W  W   KG       W",
       "W   WWWWWWWWW   W",
       "W              W",
       "W        P      W",          P is the player
       "W   WWWWWWWWW   W",
       "W       GK    W W",
       "W              W",
       "W             D",            D is the door
       "WWWWWWWWWWWWWWWW"]
```

1.6 ADD A FUNCTION TO DRAW THE SCENERY

Next, add a new `draw_scenery()` function above the `draw()` function. This will draw the background of each square on the map. Since the map is a list of strings, subscripting it as `MAP[y]` selects the string representing the row of the grid specified by y (counting from 0). Subscripting this string with `[x]` selects the character representing the square in the column specified by x (also counting from 0). The second subscript is written immediately after the first as `MAP[y][x]`.

```python
                screen.blit("floor1", screen_coords(x, y)

def draw_scenery():

    for y in range(GRID_HEIGHT):

        for x in range(GRID_WIDTH):

            square = MAP[y][x]

            if square == "W":

                screen.blit("wall", screen_coords(x, y))

            elif square == "D":

                screen.blit("door", screen_coords(x, y))

def draw():

    draw_background()

    draw_scenery()
```

Loops over each grid position

Extracts the character from the map represented by this grid position

Draws a wall tile at the screen position represented by **W**

Draws a door tile at position **D**

Draws the scenery after (on top of) the background has been drawn

THE ACTOR CLASS

Pygame Zero provides a class called Actor to represent the actors, or the movable items, in games. You can create an Actor object with the name of the image that should be used when drawing it, and then keyword arguments that specify other properties of the object, if required. The most important property is **pos**, which specifies the screen coordinates that the image should be drawn at. The **anchor** property specifies what point on the image the **pos** coordinates refer to. It is a pair of strings where the first gives the x anchor point – "left", "middle", or "right" – and the second gives the y anchor point – "top", "middle", or "bottom". You will anchor the actors' **pos** to the top left of the image, as this matches the coordinates returned by the `screen_coords()` function.

THE ACTORS

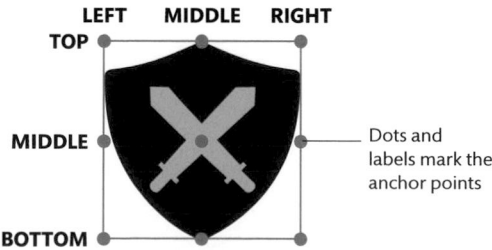

LEFT   MIDDLE   RIGHT
TOP

MIDDLE

BOTTOM

Dots and labels mark the anchor points

1.7 INITIALIZE THE PLAYER

Create an actor for the player and set its starting position on the map. Add a new setup function below the **screen_coords()** function to do this.

```
def screen_coords(x, y):
    return (x * GRID_SIZE, y * GRID_SIZE)
def setup_game():
    global player
    player = Actor("player", anchor=("left", "top"))
    for y in range(GRID_HEIGHT):
        for x in range(GRID_WIDTH):
            square = MAP[y][x]
            if square == "P":
                player.pos = screen_coords(x, y)
```

Defines **player** as a global variable

Creates a new **Actor** object and sets its anchor position

Loops over each grid position

Extracts the character from the map representing this grid position

Checks if this grid position is the player

Sets the position of **player** to the screen coordinates of this grid position

1.8 DRAW THE PLAYER

After initializing the player, you need to draw it on screen. Add a **draw_actors()** function above the **draw()** function in the code. Then, add a call to it at the end of the **draw()** function. Finally, call the **setup_game()** function just before **Pygame Zero** runs.

```
                    screen.blit("door", screen_coords(x, y))
def draw_actors():
    player.draw()
def draw():
    draw_background()
    draw_scenery()
    draw_actors()
setup_game()
pgzrun.go()
```

Draws the player actor on screen at its current position

Draws the actors after (on top of) the background and scenery have been drawn

SAVE

2 Moving the player

Now that you have created the player, it is time to write code to move it on the screen. You will use an event-handler function, which reacts to key presses, to do this.

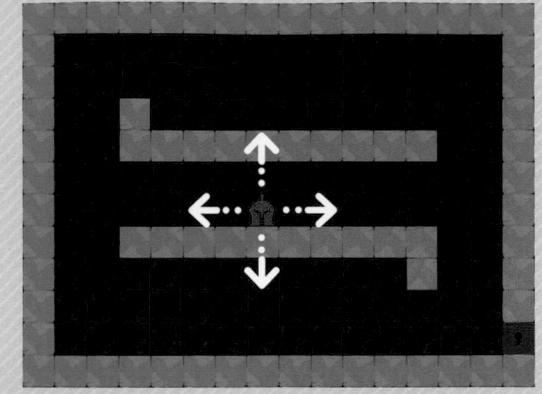

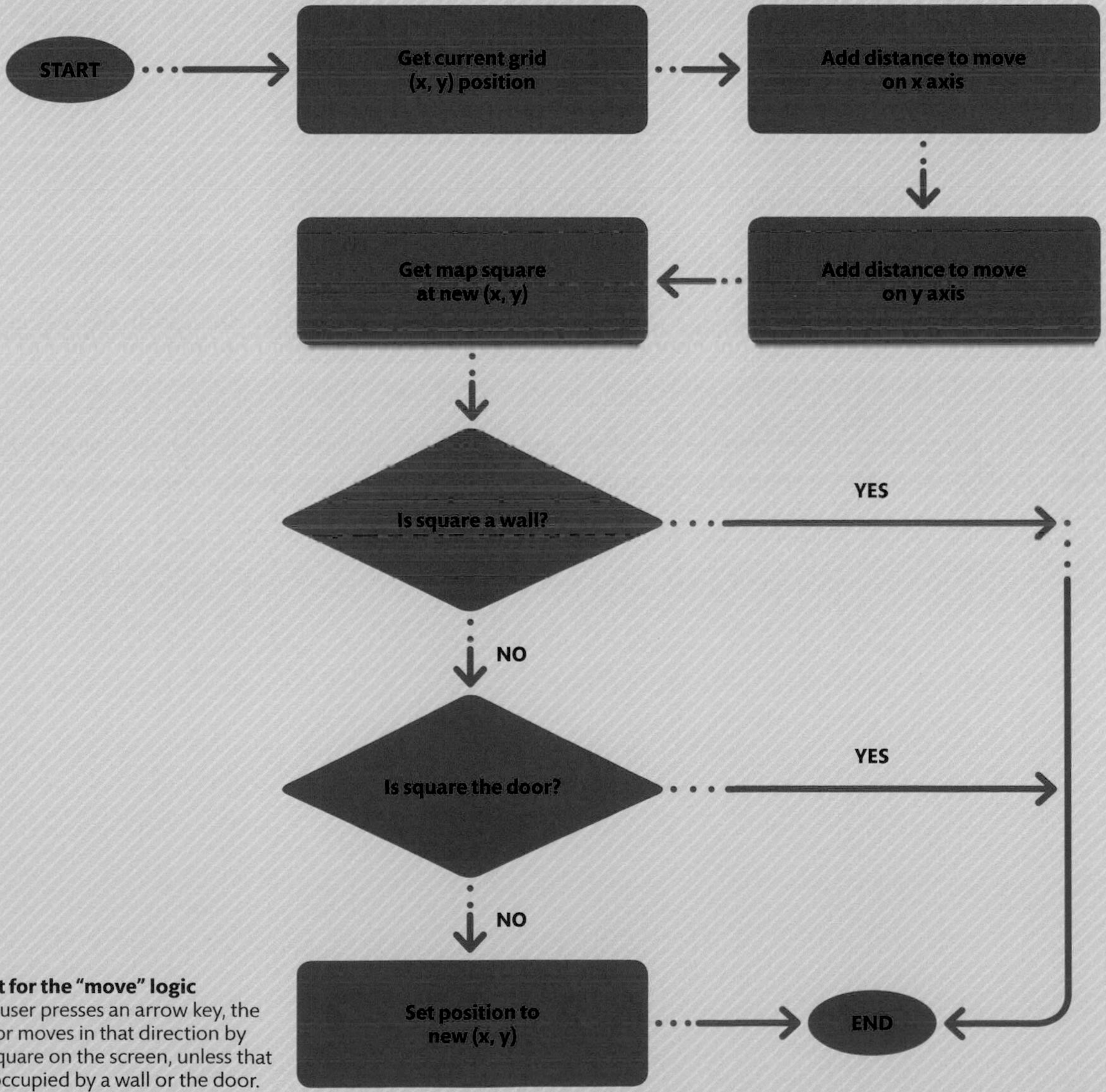

```
START ·····> Get current grid
             (x, y) position    ····> Add distance to move
                                      on x axis

Get map square         <····  Add distance to move
at new (x, y)                 on y axis

Is square a wall?  ·····> YES

        NO

Is square the door?  ·····> YES

        NO

Set position to    ·····> END  <····
new (x, y)
```

Flowchart for the "move" logic
When the user presses an arrow key, the player actor moves in that direction by one grid square on the screen, unless that square is occupied by a wall or the door.

2.1 ADD A UTILITY FUNCTION

First you need to define a function to determine which grid square the actor is in. You can do this by dividing the actor's x and y coordinates by the size of a grid square and then using the built-in **round()** function to make sure that the result is the nearest whole number. Add this function below the existing **screen_coords()** function.

```python
    return (x * GRID_SIZE, y * GRID_SIZE)

def grid_coords(actor):

    return (round(actor.x / GRID_SIZE), round(actor.y / GRID_SIZE))
```

Determines the position of an actor on the grid

2.2 ADD KEY HANDLER

Now add an event handler function that will react when the user presses an arrow key. This function ensures the player moves in the right direction when any of the four arrow keys are pressed. Add this new function below the **draw()** function.

```python
    draw_actors()

def on_key_down(key):

    if key == keys.LEFT:

        move_player(-1, 0)

    elif key == keys.UP:

        move_player(0, -1)

    elif key == keys.RIGHT:

        move_player(1, 0)

    elif key == keys.DOWN:

        move_player(0, 1)
```

Last line of the **draw()** function

Reacts when the user presses down on a key

Player moves left by one grid square

Player moves up by one grid square

Player moves right by one grid square

Player moves down by one grid square

2.3 MOVE THE ACTOR

Next, define the **move_player()** function. This function takes the distance in grid squares that a player moves on the x and y axes, respectively. Add this function immediately after the **on_key_down()** function.

```python
def move_player(dx, dy):

    (x, y) = grid_coords(player)

    x += dx

    y += dy

    square = MAP[y][x]

    if square == "W":

        return

    elif square == "D":

        return

    player.pos = screen_coords(x, y)
```

Gets the current grid position of **player**

Adds the x axis distance to **x**

Adds the y axis distance to **y**

Gives the tile at this position

Stops the execution of the **move_player()** function, if the player touches the wall

Updates position of **player** to the new coordinates

Returns immediately if it is a door

MOVING ON THE GRID

As the grid and screen coordinates start at the top left corner, moving left on the grid represents a negative change on the x axis and moving right represents a positive change. Similarly, moving up is a negative change on the y axis and moving down is a positive change.

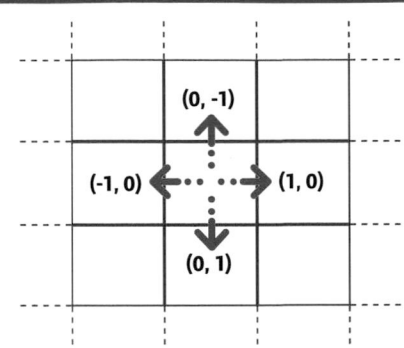

3   ADD THE KEYS

You now need to add more actors to the game. Add some keys for the player to collect. For each key marked on the map, create an actor with the key image and set its position to the screen coordinates of that grid position. Add this code to the **setup_game()** function to create the key actors.

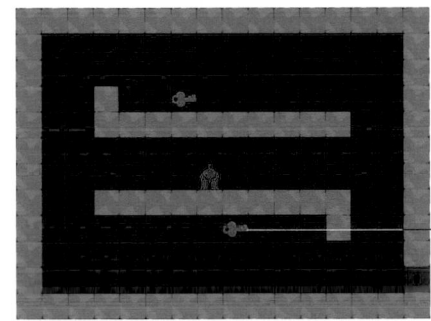

Keys will appear at the coordinates set in the code

Defines **keys_to_collect** as a global variable

```python
def setup_game():
    global player, keys_to_collect
    player = Actor("player", anchor=("left", "top"))
    keys_to_collect = []
    for y in range(GRID_HEIGHT):
        for x in range(GRID_WIDTH):
            square = MAP[y][x]
            if square == "P":
                player.pos = screen_coords(x, y)
            elif square == "K":
                key = Actor("key", anchor=("left", "top"), \
                            pos=screen_coords(x, y))
                keys_to_collect.append(key)
```

Sets **keys_to_collect** to an empty list initially

Creates a key if the square is K

Creates the **key** actor with an image, anchor, and position

Adds this actor to the list of keys created above

SPECIAL NAMES

It would have seemed natural to name the global variable with the list of key actors, **keys**. However, you need to be careful when choosing names for your variables to avoid confusion with either built-in function names or names that are special to **Pygame Zero**. You may remember from the last step that **keys** is a special object with items representing all of the keys on the keyboard.

3.1 DRAW NEW KEY ACTORS

Make the game more interesting by adding multiple keys for the player to collect. Draw the new key actors by adding the following lines to the **draw_actors()** function.

```
def draw_actors():
    player.draw()
    for key in keys_to_collect:
        key.draw()
```

Draws all the actors in the list **keys_to_collect**

3.2 PICK UP THE KEYS

When the player actor moves into a grid square containing a key, the program will remove that key from the list of keys to be collected and stop drawing it on screen. When there are no more keys to be collected, the player actor will be allowed to move into the grid square containing the door. Make the following changes to the **move_player()** function to do this. Then, save the code and try running the program to check if you can move around and pick up the keys. You should be able to go into the door square once you pick up all the keys, but see what happens if you try moving further – we will fix this problem in the next few steps.

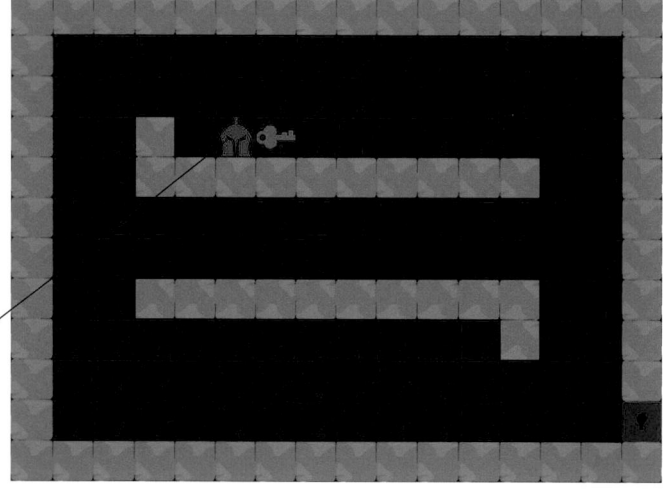

Move the player over the key to pick it up

Checks if the **keys_to_collect** list is not empty

```
    elif square == "D":
        if len(keys_to_collect) > 0:
            return
        for key in keys_to_collect:
            (key_x, key_y) = grid_coords(key)
            if x == key_x and y == key_y:
                keys_to_collect.remove(key)
                break
    player.pos = screen_coords(x, y)
```

Returns immediately if the list is not empty

Loops over each of the key actors in the list

Gets the grid position of a key actor

Checks if the new player position matches the key position

Removes this key from the list if player position matches key position

Breaks out of the **for** loop, as each square can only contain one key

SAVE

3.3 GAME OVER!

If the player actor moves into the grid square that contains the door (after having picked up all of the keys) then the game should come to an end and the player should no longer be allowed to move. To do this, update the **setup_game()** function to define a new global variable that checks whether the game is over or not.

Defines **game_over** as a global variable

```
def setup_game():
    global game_over, player, keys_to_collect
    game_over = False
    player = Actor("player", anchor=("left", "top"))
    keys_to_collect = []
    for y in range(GRID_HEIGHT):
```

Sets the variable to **False** initially

3.4 TRIGGER GAME OVER

Now set the game to be over when the player gets to the door. Make the following changes to the **move_player()** function. Run the program to try it out. You should not be able to move when you get to the door so the program will not crash.

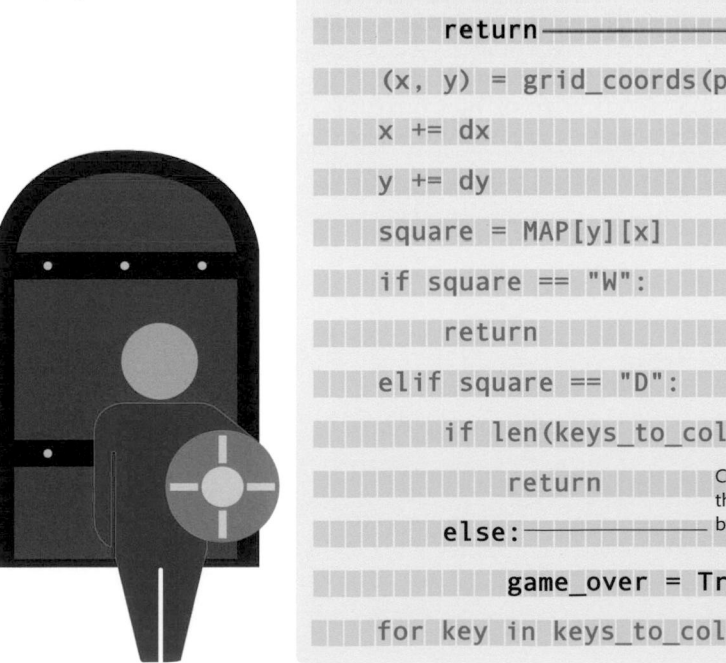

```
def move_player(dx, dy):
    global game_over
    if game_over:
        return
    (x, y) = grid_coords(player)
    x += dx
    y += dy
    square = MAP[y][x]
    if square == "W":
        return
    elif square == "D":
        if len(keys_to_collect) > 0:
            return
        else:
            game_over = True
    for key in keys_to_collect:
```

Checks if **game_over** is set

Returns immediately, without moving

Checks if all the keys have been picked

Sets **game_over** to **True** and continues the move

SAVE

3.5 **GAME OVER MESSAGE**

When the player gets to the door, the program stops, but it is not clear to the user that the game is over. You need to add a **GAME OVER** message to your code that is displayed on screen when the game ends. Define a new function, **draw_game_over()**, to draw a **GAME OVER** overlay on the screen. Add the code above the **draw()** function.

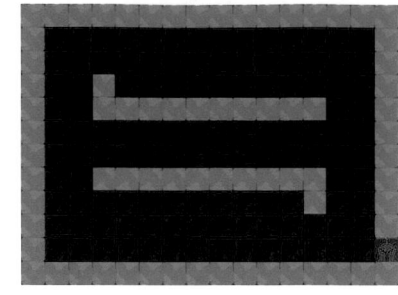

Sets the position of the **GAME OVER** message on screen

Anchors the text by its bottom edge

Draws the text at this location

```
def draw_game_over():
    screen_middle = (WIDTH / 2, HEIGHT / 2)
    screen.draw.text("GAME OVER", midbottom=screen_middle, \
                    fontsize=GRID_SIZE, color="cyan", owidth=1)
def draw():
    draw_background()
    draw_scenery()
    draw_actors()
    if game_over:
        draw_game_over()
```

Draws the text at this location

DRAWING TEXT WITH PYGAME ZERO

The **screen.draw.text()** function allows you to draw a piece of text on screen. This function takes a string with the text to be drawn and then some optional keyword arguments, as shown here. See the **Pygame Zero** online documentation for other keywords.

KEYWORD ARGUMENTS	
Property name	**Description**
fontsize	The font size in pixels
color	A string giving a colour name or an HTML-style "#FF00FF" colour, or an (r, g, b) "tuple" such as (255, 0, 255)
owidth	A number giving a relative width of an outline to draw around each character; defaults to 0 if not specified; 1 represents a reasonable outline width
ocolor	The colour for the outline (in the same format as **color**), defaults to "black" if not specified
topleft, bottomleft, topright, bottomright, midtop, midleft, midbottom, midright, center	Use one of these with a pair of numbers to give the x and y screen coordinates relative to an anchor point

3.6 CREATE THE GUARD ACTORS

The game is pretty easy to win so far. To make it more difficult, add some guards as obstacles. For each guard on the map, create an actor with a guard image and set its position to the screen coordinates of that grid position. Update the **setup_game()** function to do this.

Defines **guards** as a global variable

```
def setup_game():
    global game_over, player, keys_to_collect, guards
    game_over = False
    player = Actor("player", anchor=("left", "top"))
    keys_to_collect = []
    guards = []
    for y in range(GRID_HEIGHT):
        for x in range(GRID_WIDTH):
            square = MAP[y][x]
            if square == "P":
                player.pos = screen_coords(x, y)
            elif square == "K":
                key = Actor("key", anchor=("left", "top"), \
                    pos=screen_coords(x, y))
                keys_to_collect.append(key)
            elif square == "G":
                guard = Actor("guard", anchor=("left", "top"), \
                    pos=screen_coords(x, y))
                guards.append(guard)
```

Sets **guards** to an empty list initially

Creates the **guard** actor

Creates a guard if the square is **G**

Adds this actor to the list of guards created above

3.7 DRAW THE GUARDS

To add another guard to the game, add this code to the **draw_actors()** function. Save the code and then run the program to check if the guards appear on screen.

```
        key.draw()
        for guard in guards:
            guard.draw()
```

Draws all the actors in the list **guards**

SAVE

4 Moving the guards

Once the guards are in place, they will attempt to move one grid square closer to the player along either the x or y axis every half-second, unless they move into a square occupied by a wall. If the move takes the guard into the same grid position as the player, then the game is over. Like the player, the guards should not move if the game is over. Add the code in this section to make the guards move.

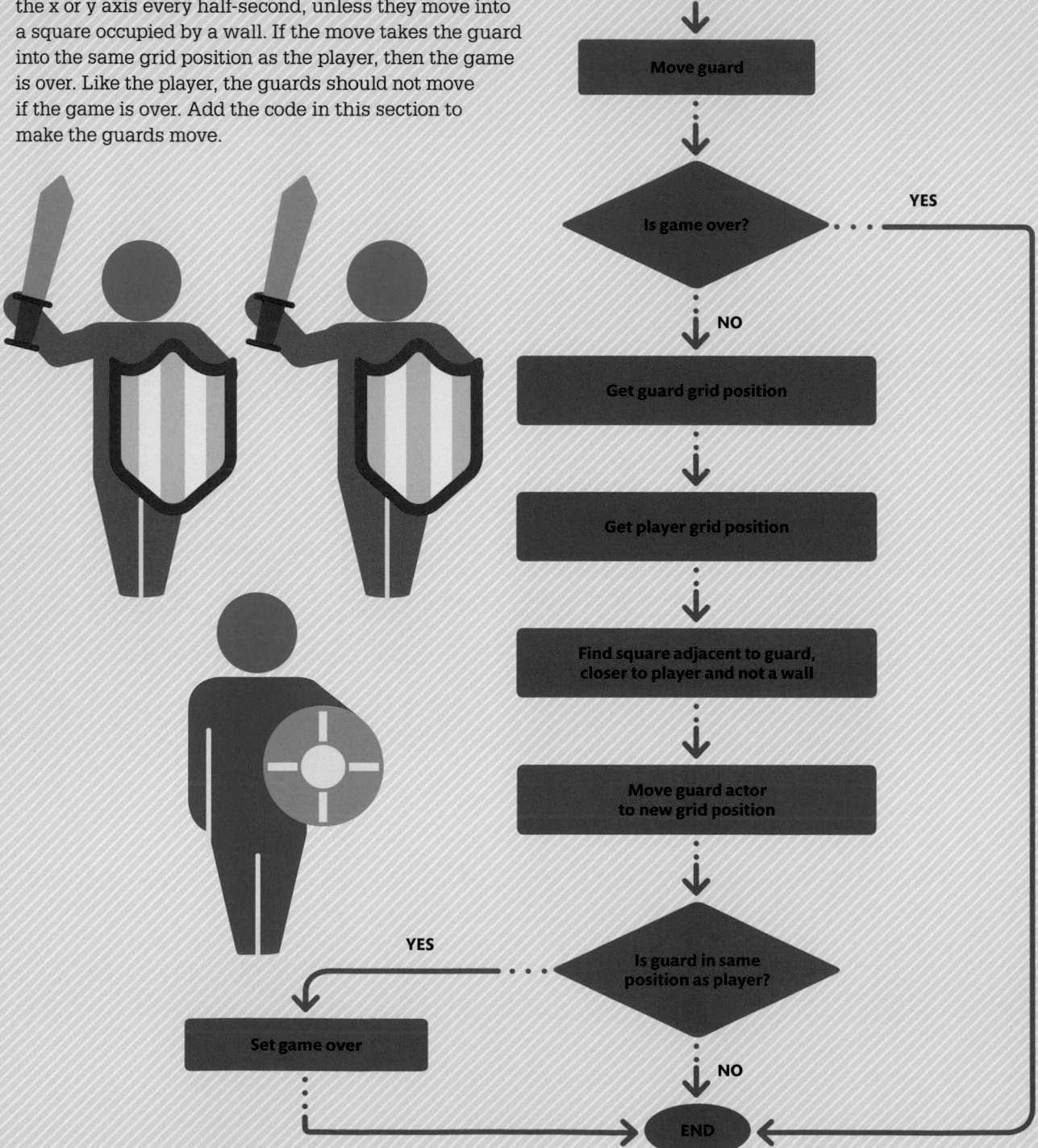

START

Move guard

Is game over? — YES

NO

Get guard grid position

Get player grid position

Find square adjacent to guard, closer to player and not a wall

Move guard actor to new grid position

Is guard in same position as player?

YES

Set game over

NO

END

4.1 ADD A FUNCTION TO MOVE A GUARD

Start by adding a new function, **move_guard()**, to move a single guard. The code will work for any guard actor, so pass an argument for the guard you want to move. Add the following code immediately after the **move_player()** function.

Gets the grid position of the player actor

Checks if the player is to the right of the guard, and whether the square to the right is a wall

```python
        break
    player.pos = screen_coords(x, y)
def move_guard(guard):
    global game_over
    if game_over:
        return
    (player_x, player_y) = grid_coords(player)
    (guard_x, guard_y) = grid_coords(guard)
    if player_x > guard_x and MAP[guard_y][guard_x + 1] != "W":
        guard_x += 1
    elif player_x < guard_x and MAP[guard_y][guard_x - 1] != "W":
        guard_x -= 1
    elif player_y > guard_y and MAP[guard_y + 1][guard_x] != "W":
        guard_y += 1
    elif player_y < guard_y and MAP[guard_y - 1][guard_x] != "W":
        guard_y -= 1
    guard.pos = screen_coords(guard_x, guard_y)
    if guard_x == player_x and guard_y == player_y:
        game_over = True
```

Defines **game_over** as a global variable

Returns immediately, without moving, if the game is over

Gets the grid position of this guard actor

Increases the guard's x grid position by 1 if the above condition is true

Checks if the player is to the left of the guard

Updates the guard actor's position to the screen coordinates of the (possibly updated) grid position

Ends the game if the guard's grid position is the same as the player's grid position

4.2 MOVE ALL THE GUARDS

Next, add a function to move each of the guards in turn. Add this code just below the lines you typed in the previous step.

```python
def move_guards():
    for guard in guards:
        move_guard(guard)
```

Loops through each guard actor in **guards** list

Moves all the guard actors in the list

4.3 CALL THE FUNCTION

Finally, add this code to call the **move_guards()** function every half-second. You need to add a new constant at the top of the file to specify this interval.

```
GRID_SIZE = 50

GUARD_MOVE_INTERVAL = 0.5
```

Sets the time interval for a guard to move on screen

4.4 SCHEDULE THE CALL

To ensure that the guards move smoothly after every half-second, you need to add a timer that calls the **move_guards()** function repeatedly during the course of the program. Add the following code at the bottom of the file. This calls the **move_guards()** function after every

GUARD_MOVE_INTERVAL seconds. Run the program and check if the guards chase the player. You should be able to see the GAME OVER message if a guard catches the player. Try changing the value of GUARD_MOVE_INTERVAL to make the game easier or harder.

```
setup_game()

clock.schedule_interval(move_guards, GUARD_MOVE_INTERVAL)

pgzrun.go()
```

Schedules regular calls to the **move_guards()** function

SAVE

THE CLOCK OBJECT

The clock object has methods for scheduling function calls in a program. Some of them are given here. When calling a function, make sure you use the name of the function without the brackets. This is because you can only schedule calls to functions that take no arguments as there is no way to specify what arguments would be used when the call is made in the future.

METHODS FOR SCHEDULING FUNCTION CALLS	
Method	**Description**
clock.schedule(function, delay)	Call the **function** in **delay** seconds – multiple calls to this will schedule multiple future calls to the **function**, even if the previous ones have not yet happened
clock.schedule_unique(function, delay)	Similar to **clock.schedule()**, except that multiple calls to this will cancel any previously scheduled calls that have not yet happened
clock.schedule_interval(function, interval)	Call the **function** every **interval** seconds
clock.unschedule(function)	Cancel any previously scheduled calls to the **function**

5 TRACK THE RESULT

When the game finishes and the **GAME OVER** message is displayed, you can show an additional message to indicate whether the player unlocked the door and won, or was caught by a guard and lost. Create a new global variable to track whether the player won or lost. Add this code to the **setup_game()** function.

Defines `player_won` as a global variable

```python
def setup_game():
    global game_over, player_won, player, keys_to_collect, guards
    game_over = False
    player_won = False
    player = Actor("player", anchor=("left", "top"))
```

Sets the variable to **False** initially

5.1 SET A VARIABLE

Now set the global variable when the game finishes because the player reached the door with all of the keys. Add this code to the **move_player()** function to do this.

```python
def move_player(dx, dy):
    global game_over, player_won
    if game_over:
        return
    (x, y) = grid_coords(player)
    x += dx
    y += dy
    square = MAP[y][x]
    if square == "W":
        return
    elif square == "D":
        if len(keys_to_collect) > 0:
            return
        else:
            game_over = True
            player_won = True
    for key in keys_to_collect:
```

Sets it to **True** when the player wins the game

5.2 ADD THE MESSAGES

Collecting all of the keys and reaching the door is the only way that the player can win the game, so it is safe to assume that if the game finishes any other way, the player has lost. You need to display an appropriate message in each case. Add the following code to the **draw_game_over()** function. You will be using the **midtop** property to set the location of the new message. This anchors the top edge of the message to the centre of the screen. As the **GAME OVER** message is anchored by its bottom edge, this new message will appear centred below it. Try running the game and deliberately losing. Now close the window and run it again, but try to win this time. It should not be too hard.

```
    screen.draw.text("GAME OVER", midbottom=screen_middle, \
                     fontsize=GRID_SIZE, color="cyan", owidth=1)
    if player_won:
        screen.draw.text("You won!", midtop=screen_middle, \
                         fontsize=GRID_SIZE, color="green", owidth=1)
    else:
        screen.draw.text("You lost!", midtop=screen_middle, \
                         fontsize=GRID_SIZE, color="red", owidth=1)
```

Draws the message on screen

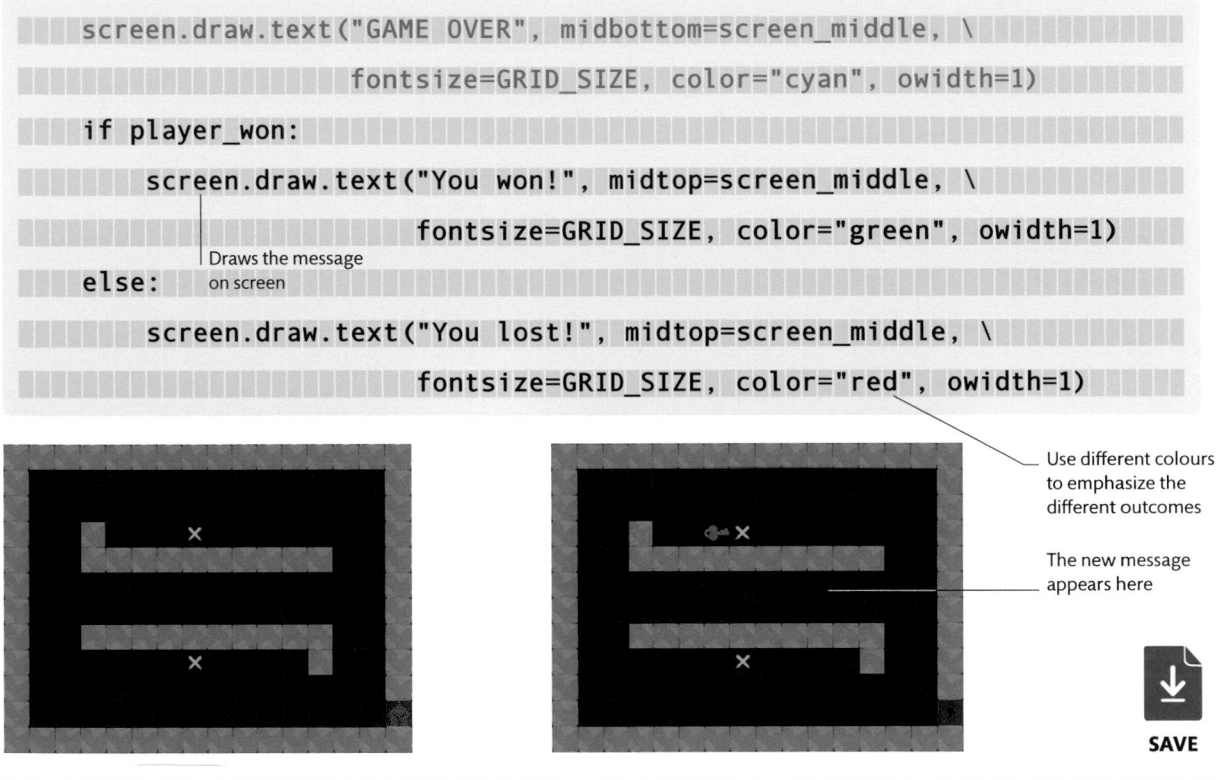

Use different colours to emphasize the different outcomes

The new message appears here

SAVE

5.3 REPLAY THE GAME

At the moment, the only way to have another go at the game is to close the window and run the program again. Add the following code after the **draw()** function to allow the user to press the space-bar when the game ends to play again. To reset the game to the beginning, you just need to call the **setup_game()** function again. It contains all the code that is necessary to initialize the game, and will recreate all of the actors in their starting positions. It will also reset the variables that track game progress.

```
    if game_over:
        draw_game_over()

def on_key_up(key):
    if key == keys.SPACE and game_over:
        setup_game()
```

Checks if the space-bar has been pressed once the game is over

Calls **setup_game()** to reset the game

5.4 ADD ANOTHER MESSAGE

It will be useful to tell the player that they can press the space-bar to restart. To do this, add a new message at the end of the **draw_game_over()** function. You need to use **midtop** anchoring again to position the text **GRID_SIZE** pixels below the centre of the screen. Run the game. You should be able to replay it now.

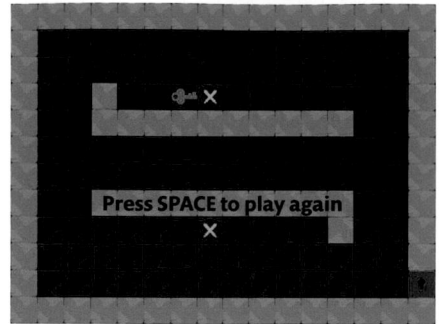

```
    else:
        screen.draw.text("You lost!", midtop=screen_middle, \
                         fontsize=GRID_SIZE, color="red", owidth=1)
    screen.draw.text("Press SPACE to play again", midtop=(WIDTH / 2, \
                     HEIGHT / 2 + GRID_SIZE), fontsize=GRID_SIZE / 2, \
                     color="cyan", owidth=1)
```
Draws the new message on screen

6 Animating the actors

The game feels a little odd at the moment as the actors jump from one square to another in the grid. It would be much better if they looked more like they were moving on the screen. You can make that happen by using **Pygame Zero**'s **animate()** function.

6.1 ANIMATE THE GUARDS

Start by animating the guards. The **animate()** function creates animations that run automatically on each iteration of the game loop to update the properties of actors. Make the following change to the **move_guard()** function to animate the guards. The parameters of the **animate()** function will include the actor to animate (**guard**), the property that you want to change (**pos**), and how long the animation will run (**duration**). If you save and run the code now, you will see the guards moving smoothly across the screen towards the player.

```
    elif player_y < guard_y and MAP[guard_y - 1][guard_x] != "W":
        guard_y -= 1
    animate(guard, pos=screen_coords(guard_x, guard_y), \
            duration=GUARD_MOVE_INTERVAL)
    if guard_x == player_x and guard_y == player_y:
        game_over = True
```
Moves the actor smoothly instead of changing its position suddenly

ANIMATIONS

The **animate()** function can take two other optional keyword arguments – **tween**, which specifies how to animate the in-between values of the property, and **on_finished**, which allows you to specify the name of a function you want to call after the animation is complete. The value of **tween** should be one of the strings mentioned below.

VALUE OF THE TWEEN KEYWORD ARGUMENT	
Value	**Description**
"linear"	Animate evenly from the current property value to the new; this is the default
"accelerate"	Start slowly and speed up
"decelerate"	Start quickly and slow down
"accel_decel"	Speed up and then slow down again
"end_elastic"	Wobble (as if attached to an elastic band) at the end
"start_elastic"	Wobble at the start
"both_elastic"	Wobble at the start and the end
"bounce_end"	Bounce (as a ball would) at the end
"bounce_start"	Bounce at the start
"bounce_start_end"	Bounce at the start and the end

6.2 ANIMATE THE PLAYER

Now it is time to animate the player actor. Unlike the guards, the player does not have a particular rate at which it moves, so you need to define how quickly a move should be completed. Add a new constant at the top of your file to do this. Choose **0.1** seconds as the duration the user will take to tap the movement keys to quickly evade the guards. Update the **move_player()** function as shown below. Try the game again and check if the player actor slides quickly from square to square.

```
GUARD_MOVE_INTERVAL = 0.5

PLAYER_MOVE_INTERVAL = 0.1
```
Time it takes for the player actor to move from one position to another

```
            keys_to_collect.remove(key)
            break
    animate(player, pos=screen_coords(x, y), \
            duration=PLAYER_MOVE_INTERVAL)
```
Updates the player's position after **0.1** seconds

SAVE

7 Make a chequerboard background

Now return to some of the earlier graphical elements and see if you can make the game look a little more interesting. At the moment, the background is just a single tile repeated across the entire floor. Add a chequerboard pattern to break things up a little and make the floor look more "tiled".

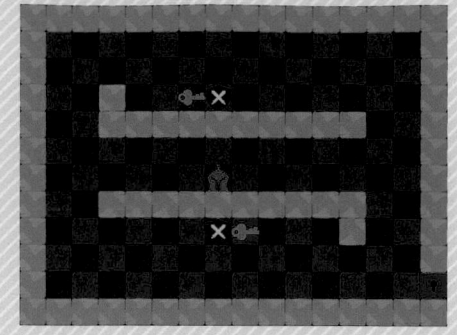

7.1 UPDATE THE BACKGROUND FUNCTION

For a chequerboard pattern, on the first row, all of the odd squares should be one colour and the even squares another; on the second row the colours need to be swapped. The following rows should repeat this pattern. You can do this by using the first colour on either odd columns of odd rows or even columns of even rows, then the second colour for the other squares. You can determine if a number is odd or even by using Python's **modulo** operator (see box below). Make the following changes to the **draw_background()** function to select a different floor tile image for alternate squares.

```
def draw_background():
    for y in range(GRID_HEIGHT):
        for x in range(GRID_WIDTH):
            if x % 2 == y % 2:
                screen.blit("floor1", screen_coords(x, y))
            else:
                screen.blit("floor2", screen_coords(x, y))
```

Checks if the **x** and **y** values are either both odd or both even

Draws the **floor1** tile at this position if the above condition is true

Draws the **floor2** tile if either of the **x** and **y** values are odd and even

THE MODULO (REMAINDER) OPERATOR

An odd or even number can be determined by dividing the number by two and then looking to see if there is a remainder or not. Python has an arithmetic operator, called the **modulo** operator, that returns the remainder from a division. It is written as **a % b**, which gives the remainder of dividing a by b. Take a look at the remainders after dividing the x and y coordinates by two. If the remainders are the same, then either the row and column are both odd or they are both even. Shown here are some examples of how the modulo operator works.

N	N % 2	N % 3	N % 4	N % 5
0	0	0	0	0
1	1	1	1	1
2	0	2	2	2
3	1	0	3	3
4	0	1	0	4
5	1	2	1	0
6	0	0	2	1
7	1	1	3	2
8	0	2	0	3
9	1	0	1	4

MAKE A CHEQUERBOARD BACKGROUND

7.2 CRACKING UP!

Finally, make the dungeon look more realistic by adding some cracks in the floor tiles. You can do this by drawing the cracks on top of the floor tile images. Make sure to add cracks on only a few tiles; you can choose these tiles at random. Start by importing Python's **random** module and add it to the top of your file. You need to use the `randint(a, b)` function from this module, which returns a random whole number between **a** and **b** (see box, right). You will choose random numbers in the `draw_background()` function and decide when to draw a crack based on them. Since the same squares need to be picked for the cracks every time the `draw_background()` function is called, set the "seed value" (see box, right) to a specific number at the start of the function.

```
import pgzrun

import random
```

Makes the functionality in the **random** module available

```
PLAYER_MOVE_INTERVAL = 0.1

BACKGROUND_SEED = 123456
```

Adds a new constant for the seed value at the top of the file

Tells the program to pick random numbers starting from **BACKGROUND_SEED**

```
def draw_background():
    random.seed(BACKGROUND_SEED)
    for y in range(GRID_HEIGHT):
        for x in range(GRID_WIDTH):
            if x % 2 == y % 2:
                screen.blit("floor1", screen_coords(x, y))
            else:
                screen.blit("floor2", screen_coords(x, y))
            n = random.randint(0, 99)
            if n < 5:
                screen.blit("crack1", screen_coords(x, y))
            elif n < 10:
                screen.blit("crack2", screen_coords(x, y))
```

Picks a random number between **0** and **99**

Checks if **n** is less than 5

Draws **crack1** on top of the floor tile at this position if **n** is less than **5**

Checks if **n** is less than **10**

Draws **crack2** on top of the floor tile at this position if **n** is less than **10**, but not less than **5**

RANDOM NUMBERS AND PROBABILITY

The `randint()` function returns a number in a specific range. Repeated calls will return numbers that are roughly distributed across this range. To be more precise, this function actually returns a pseudo-random number. These are numbers that appear random – in that the numbers are evenly distributed across the range and the sequence does not look obviously predictable – but are actually generated by an algorithm that will always generate the same sequence of numbers from a given starting point. You can call the starting point for a pseudo-random sequence the "seed". If you repeatedly pick random numbers between 0 and 99, then you should get the numbers 0 to 4 about 5% of the time. If you look at the example below, you will see that if **n** is a number between 0 and 4, `crack1` image will be drawn. So you can expect this to happen for about five per cent of the floor tiles. If **n** is greater than 5 and lies between 5 and 9, `crack2` image will be drawn, which should also happen for about five per cent of the tiles. If you look carefully at the map, you will be able to count 118 exposed floor tiles, so you should expect to see about six of each types of cracks (five per cent of 118).

```python
n = random.randint(0, 99)
if n < 5:
    screen.blit("crack1", screen_coords(x, y))
elif n < 10:
    screen.blit("crack2", screen_coords(x, y))
```

Tells the code to pick a random number between 0 and 99

Draws **crack1** if **n** is between 0 and 4

Draws **crack2** if **n** is between 5 and 9

7.3 TIME TO PLAY

The game should now be ready to play. Run the program to make sure it is working properly. If there is a problem, carefully check your code for bugs (see pp.130–33) and run it again.

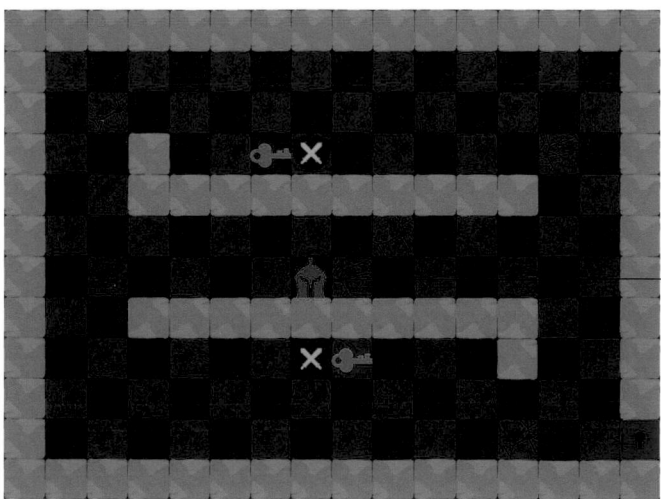

Move the player quickly to collect all the keys. Watch out for the guards

SAVE

Hacks and tweaks

Opening the door

While users may immediately realize that they need to collect the keys, it may not be obvious when they can leave the dungeon. If you can visually open the door when the last key has been collected, it will be obvious what to do. The easiest way to do this is to only draw the door when there are no keys left to be collected. In the **draw_scenery()** function, change the logic for deciding when to draw the door as shown here.

```
                    screen.blit("wall", screen_coords(x, y))
            elif square == "D" and len(keys_to_collect) > 0:
                    screen.blit("door", screen_coords(x, y))
```

Checks if there are any keys left to be collected

Keep moving

It would help if the player could move continuously in one direction by holding down an arrow key instead of repeatedly pressing it. To do this, you can use the **on_finished** argument of **animate()** function. This allows the user to specify a function to be called when the actor has finished moving. Make a change in the **move_player()** function, as shown here. Then add a new **repeat_player_move()** function below the **move_player()** function. It uses members of **Pygame Zero**'s **keyboard** object to check if a particular key is pressed. You might find that the game is now too easy. You can change the **PLAYER_MOVE_INTERVAL** constant at the top of the file to slow the player down and make the game more challenging.

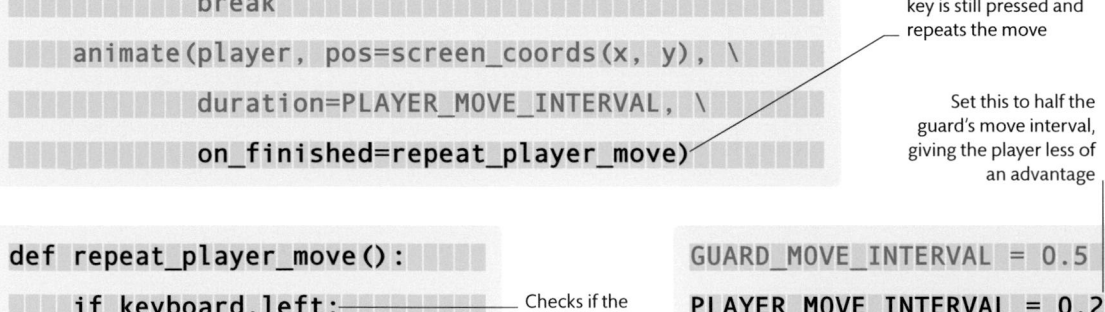

```
                    break
            animate(player, pos=screen_coords(x, y), \
                    duration=PLAYER_MOVE_INTERVAL, \
                    on_finished=repeat_player_move)
```

Checks if the arrow key is still pressed and repeats the move

Set this to half the guard's move interval, giving the player less of an advantage

```
def repeat_player_move():
    if keyboard.left:
        move_player(-1, 0)
    elif keyboard.up:
        move_player(0, -1)
    elif keyboard.right:
        move_player(1, 0)
    elif keyboard.down:
        move_player(0, 1)
```

Checks if the left arrow key is still pressed

Calls **move_player()** again to repeat the move

```
GUARD_MOVE_INTERVAL = 0.5
PLAYER_MOVE_INTERVAL = 0.25
```

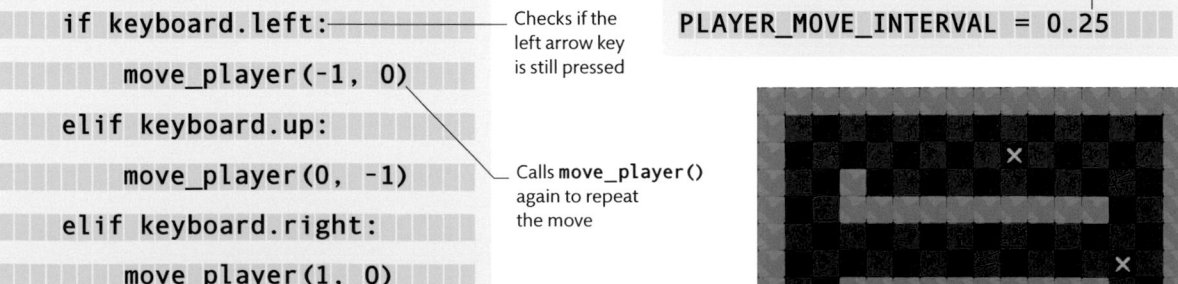

The player will now move continuously in the chosen direction

Make a bit more room

You can make the game more interesting by designing a larger, more complicated map. You can design your own, but try this one to get the idea. First, change the size of the grid by editing the values of the constants at the top of the file. Then carefully edit the **MAP** constant as shown here. You can add as many guards or keys as you want because of the way you have written the code.

```
GRID_WIDTH = 20

GRID_HEIGHT = 15
```

Increase the value of these variables

This dungeon has 20 columns, so there should be 20 W characters in this line

Remember to add the door in this line

```
MAP = ["WWWWWWWWWWWWWWWWWWWW",
       "W             W        W",
       "W             W        W",
       "W   W              W   D",
       "W   W G K          W   W",
       "W   WWWWWWWWWWW        W",
       "W                      W",
       "W                      W",
       "W   WWWWW    WWWWW     W",
       "W   W        W  KW     W",
       "W   W P      WG  W     W",
       "W   WWWWWWW      W     W",
       "W      G              W",
       "W      K               W",
       "WWWWWWWWWWWWWWWWWWWW"]
```

This dungeon has 15 rows, so there should be 15 lines in total

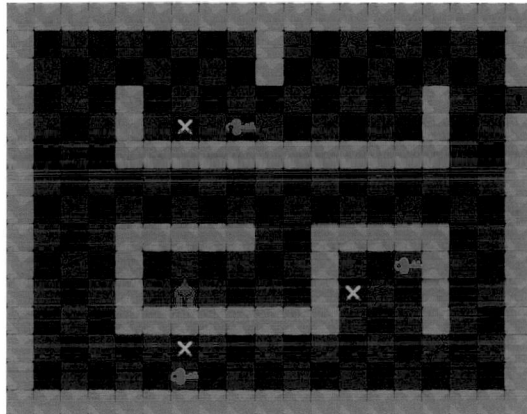

LARGE PLAYING AREA

Upload new characters

You can upload your own images to add different characters to the game, or set it up in a completely new background. Copy the new images into the "images" folder you created earlier. Then, update the code so that the actor image names match the new file names.

ENEMY

PLAYER

ITEM

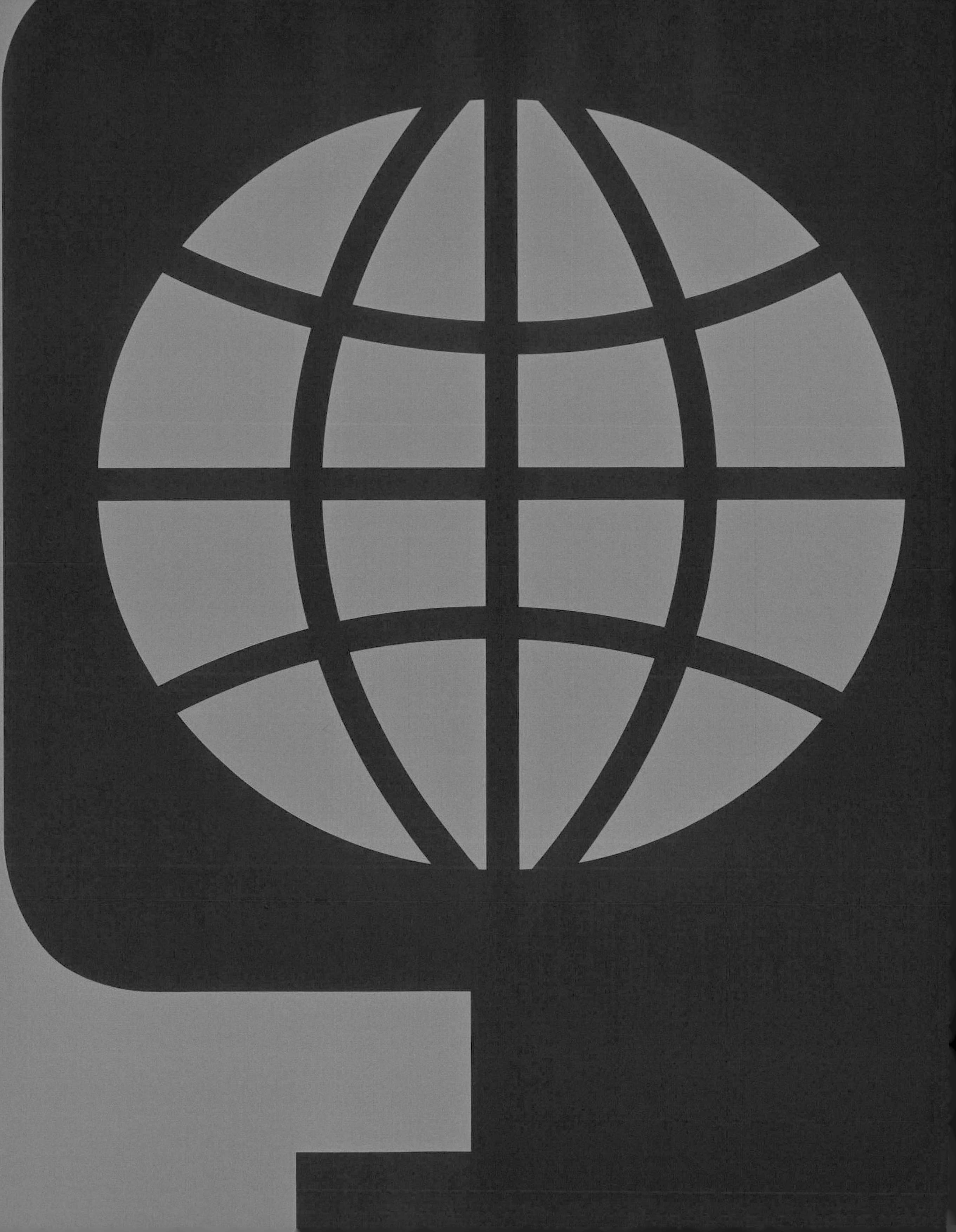

WEB TECHNOLOGIES

How the Web works

The World Wide Web is a set of technologies that work together to allow information to be shared between computers via the Internet. The Web is characterized by its combination of text, images, video, and audio to deliver an interactive multimedia experience.

Connecting to a website

The Web is based on a client/server model. A browser is a client that requests a web page from a server. The server then responds to the request by sending an HTML file. The content of each request is determined by the communication protocol being used. Hypertext Transfer Protocol (HTTP) is the most common protocol used over the Internet – a global network created from connections between billions of devices.

1 Enter web page URL
The process begins when a user enters a Uniform Resource Locator (URL) into the address bar of an Internet browser. This url contains the address of the requested web page and can be used to locate the web server that hosts the website.

2 Request
The web browser sends a request message to a router, which sends the message to the destination web server via the Internet. The web server will then send a response message back to the computer that requested the url.

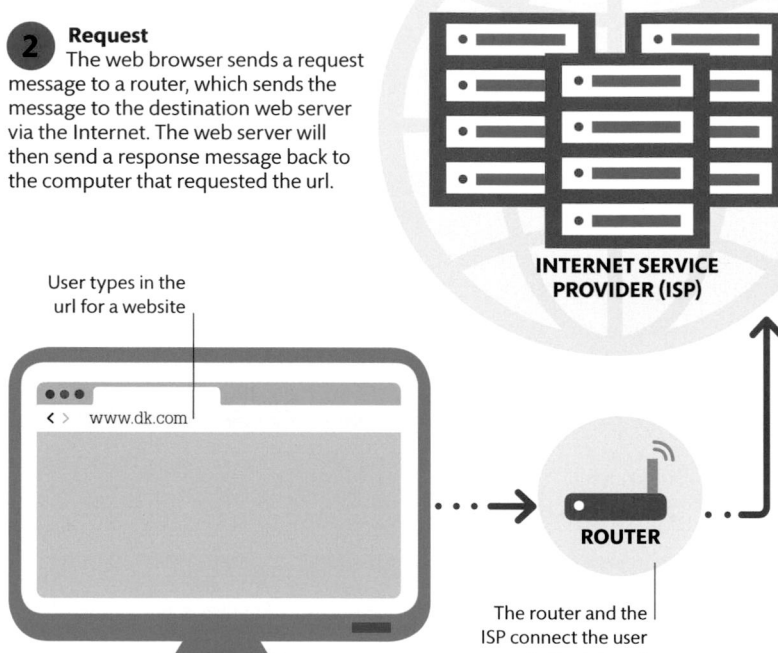

User types in the url for a website

www.dk.com

INTERNET SERVICE PROVIDER (ISP)

ROUTER

The router and the ISP connect the user to the Internet

Packets and IP routing

All communication over the Web is done by dividing the request into smaller segments of data called packets. These packets are routed from the source to the destination, where they are reassembled into the original message. The networks that convey data in packets are called "packet switched networks". Packets consist of two parts: information and data. Information defines where and how to send the data, while data is the content that the packet is trying to deliver.

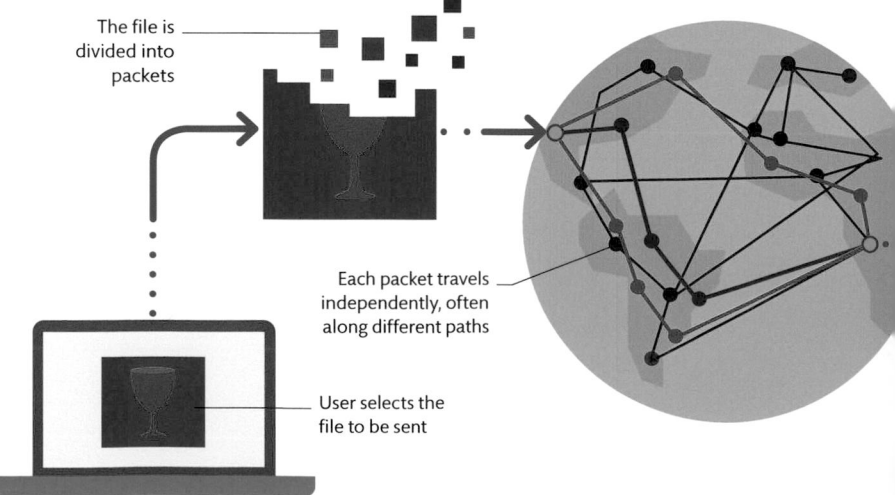

The file is divided into packets

Each packet travels independently, often along different paths

User selects the file to be sent

Protocols

A protocol is a set of rules that governs the communication between two entities. Protocols on the Web exist to manage the communication between the client browser and the web server. Network protocols are structured as a series of layers. Each layer is designed for a specific purpose, and exists on both the sending and receiving hosts.

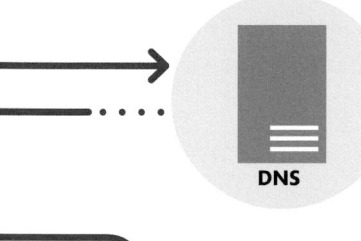

DNS

3 Finding the website

The Domain Name Systems (DNS) protocol allows the browser to convert the human-friendly text into an IP address. This address is then used by the routers to find a path to the web server. The request may be passed along many routers before it arrives at the destination web server.

The website is displayed on the user's hardware

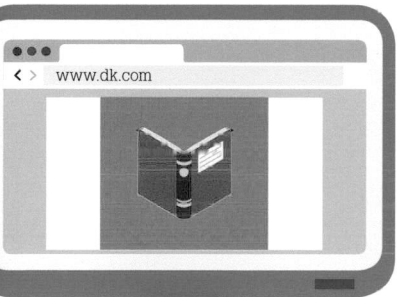

www.dk.com

4 View the page

The web server receives the request and returns an HTML file as a response to the browser. The browser reads the contents of the HTML document and renders the text, images, and data on screen.

Application layer protocol
Defines how an application must format its data so that it can communicate with other applications. For example, HTTP and File Transfer Protocol (FTP) define how a web browser can communicate with a web server.

Link layer protocol
Defines how data can be sent from one network to another by using routers to find the destination computer and deliver the message.

Transport layer protocol
Defines how to manage communications by maintaining sessions between the source and destination computers and combining the received packets back into the correct order.

Web protocols
Transmission Control Protocol (TCP) manages the sessions and ordering of the packets received by the browser. Internet Protocol (IP) handles routing of data between the client and the server. HTTP/FTP/UDP (User Datagram Protocol) defines the messages being sent between the browser and the server.

Why packets?

To allow communication channels to be used more efficiently, images, text, and even basic HTTP requests are broken down and transferred piece by piece. Each piece of data has a packet sequence, which tells the receiving server how to reassemble the information.

The reassembled file can be viewed by the receiver

The file is reassembled in the right order

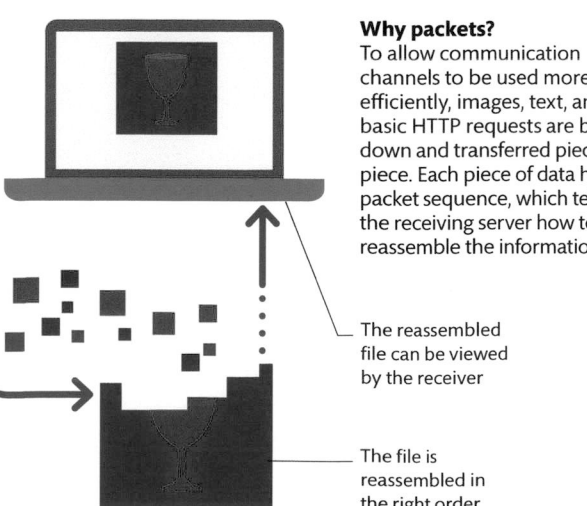

HTTP ●●●

HTTP is an application level protocol that describes how a client can format and send a request message to a server, and how the server can format and reply with a response message.
- The GET method retrieves data
- The POST method updates data
- The PUT method creates data
- The DELETE method removes data

Code editors

One of the most important tools for programmers, code editors are specifically designed for editing the source code of computer programs. They can be stand-alone applications or part of any IDE (see p.23) or web browser. A number of code editors are available online, all customized to fit specific work situations or programming languages.

Code editor tools

Simple text editors, such as Notepad, can be used to write code, but they cannot enhance or ease the process of code editing. The code editors available online have specialized functionalities, or certain built-in features, that simplify and accelerate the process of editing. These elements automate common repetitive tasks and assist the programmer to write better software by identifying problems and debugging code. Some of the most useful code editor tools are listed here.

Syntax highlighting
Displays different parts of the code in different colours, making the code easier to read. For example, HTML tags are highlighted in one colour and comments are highlighted in another colour.

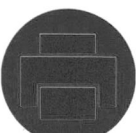

Printing
Enables the programmer to print a hard copy of the code. The output can then be shared and used as a tool to facilitate communication and problem solving.

Multiview
Allows the programmer to view multiple files side by side. Some code editors even allow two instances of the same file to be viewed alongside each other.

Preview window
Allows the programmer to see a quick representation of how the HTML code will render without having to start a web server to execute the code.

Types of code editors

There are two types of code editors most commonly used by programmers – lightweight editors and IDEs. The choice of editor to be used depends on the programming language and the type of program to be edited.

Lightweight editors
These editors are used to open and edit a file instantly. They have basic features and are fast and simple to use. Lightweight editors can only be used when working on a single file. This table lists some of the most commonly used lightweight editors.

LIGHTWEIGHT EDITORS	
Code editors	**Features**
Brackets	An open source code editor that focuses on web development languages, such as HTML, CSS, and JavaScript. It has lots of useful extensions and plugins. (*http://brackets.io/*)
Atom	A hackable open source code editor that supports many languages and is designed primarily for web development. Atom is well integrated with Git (a free system for tracking changes in source code) and has lots of custom plugins. (*https://atom.io/*)
Sublime Text	A small but powerful code editor that works with several languages and has many tools and shortcuts to aid coding. (*https://www.sublimetext.com/*)
Visual Studio Code	Smaller and simpler than the Community edition (see right), Code is a very popular editor that can work with many languages and has advanced features. (*https://visualstudio.microsoft.com/*)

CLIENT-SIDE AND SERVER-SIDE SCRIPTING

In client-side scripting, processing takes place in a web browser. The code is transferred from a web server to the user's browser over the Internet.

In server-side scripting, processing takes place on a web server. The user sends a request to the web server over the Internet, which is fulfilled when the server generates dynamic HTML pages in response and sends them to the user's browser through the same channel.

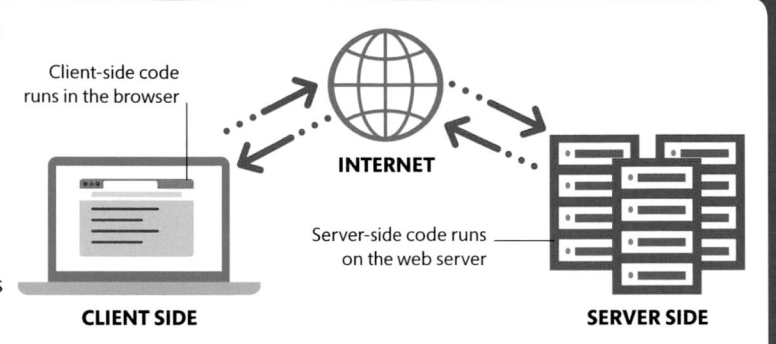

Client-side code runs in the browser

INTERNET

Server-side code runs on the web server

CLIENT SIDE

SERVER SIDE

Tabs
Tabs provide an easy way to arrange and manage multiple open files in a code editor. Each tab displays the name of a file, and clicking the name displays the file in a code window.

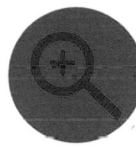

Zoom
Zooming in makes a part of the text larger and easier to read, while zooming out offers a quick way to view the entire document on the screen in one go.

Plugins
Many code editors allow programmers to write plugins to extend the features of a code editor. For example, adding a spell checker or a plugin to format HTML.

Error and warning marks
These indicate the presence of a spelling mistake or a syntax error that could cause the program to stop executing or behave unexpectedly.

INTEGRATED DEVELOPMENT ENVIRONMENT	
Code editors	**Features**
WebStorm	A fully featured IDE for web development that uses client-side JavaScript frameworks (see pp.284–85), such as Angular, TypeScript, Vue, and React, and server-side development applications, such as Node.js. (*https://www.jetbrains.com/webstorm/*)
NetBeans	Can be used for developing web and desktop applications using open source languages, such as Java and PHP, and web development languages, such as HTML, CSS, and JavaScript. (*https://netbeans.org/*)
CodePen	An online code editor that can be used for testing and sharing HTML, CSS, and JavaScript code snippets. It is very useful for finding important components to use on websites. (*https://codepen.io/*)
Visual Studio Community	Used to create web and desktop applications for Microsoft, Apple, and Linux environments. It helps programmers build large-scale systems using multiple languages and frameworks. (*https://visualstudio.microsoft.com/*)

IDEs
IDEs are powerful editors that work with many languages and have advanced features that enable a programmer to integrate several languages into a single solution. IDEs are used when working on the entire project. This table lists a few commonly used IDEs.

Exploring basic HTML

HTML is the most basic building block of the Web. An HTML file contains all the text, images, and data that is displayed on the browser. It also includes a list of any other files, such as fonts, styles, and scripts that are required to render the HTML elements correctly.

HTML tags

An HTML tag is a keyword, or a set of characters, that defines the format of a web page and determines how its content is displayed on screen. The combination and order of the HTML tags determine the structure and design of the HTML document. A client browser uses the information in each tag to understand the nature of the tags' content and how to display them correctly. The combination of a tag and its content is known as an element. Some tags, called parent tags, can contain other tags, called children tags. Most tags must have an opening and closing tag, like a set of brackets, but some tags do not require a closing tag and include a closing slash to indicate that they are single tags.

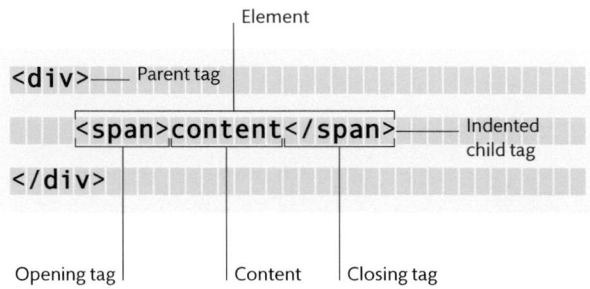

```
<div>——— Parent tag
    <span>content</span>——— Indented child tag
</div>
```

Element

Opening tag | Content | Closing tag

\<body\>\</body\>
The \<body\> tag contains all the text, data, and images that are displayed when the HTML document is opened in a browser.

\<p\>\</p\>
This tag contains the text that should appear as a paragraph on screen. The browser starts a new line and adds margins for spacing around the paragraph.

\<div\>\</div\>
The \<div\> tag is a container for all the HTML elements that can be styled and positioned as a group. This tag displays elements on a new line.

\<img/\>
The \<img/\> tag is used to describe an image on the page. Its "src" attribute contains the url that points to the location of the image file.

\<a\>\</a\>
The \<a\> (anchor) tag describes a hyperlink, which is used to link one page to another. This tag contains the "href" attribute (see p.211), which holds the link's destination.

\<html\>\</html\>
These are outer tags that apply to the entire HTML document. The first \<html\> tag indicates the markup language used for the document, and the \</html\> tag marks the end of the web page.

\<h1\>\</h1\>
The \<h1/h2/h3/h4/h5/h6\> tags indicate that the text is a header. \<h1\> is usually used for the title of the page, while the others are used to style smaller headings on the document.

\<br/\>
The \<br/\> tag tells the browser to start a new line. It is a single tag, with the closing slash included before the closing greater-than sign.

INDENTING TAGS

Good programming includes using visual aids to make code more readable. One of the easiest ways to improve the readability of code is to indent child tags inside their parent tags. To help with the indentation, a "Tidy HTML" or "Format HTML" tool can be used to format the code and indent the children tags.

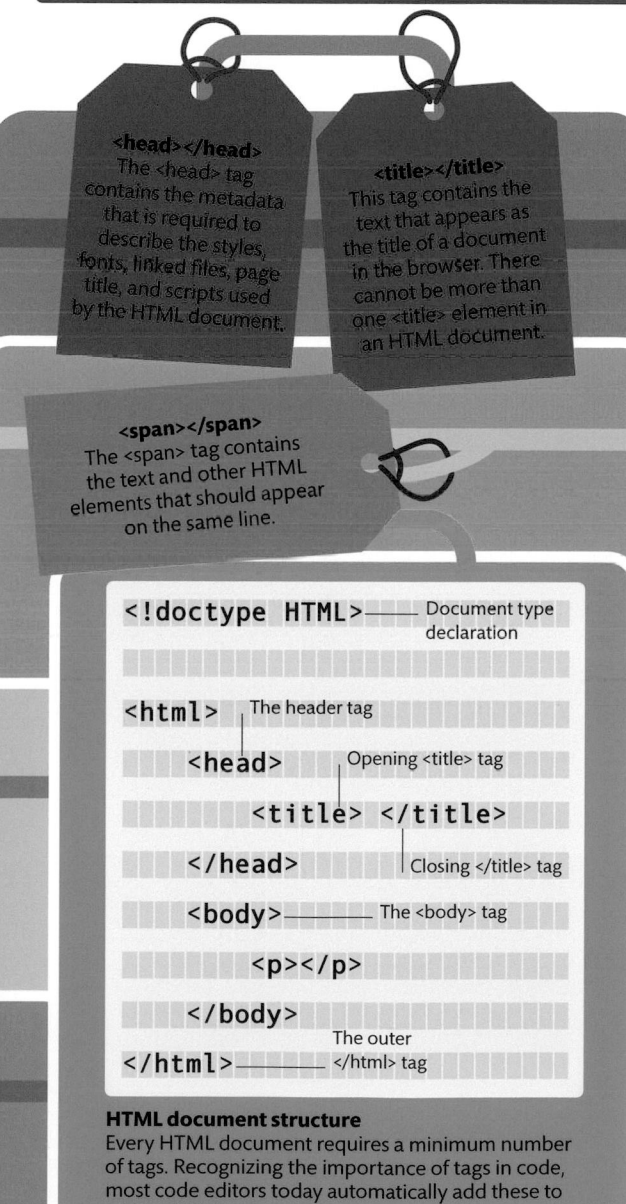

<head></head>
The <head> tag contains the metadata that is required to describe the styles, fonts, linked files, page title, and scripts used by the HTML document.

<title></title>
This tag contains the text that appears as the title of a document in the browser. There cannot be more than one <title> element in an HTML document.

<span></span>
The <span> tag contains the text and other HTML elements that should appear on the same line.

```
<!doctype HTML>———— Document type
                      declaration

<html>   The header tag

    <head>       Opening <title> tag

        <title> </title>

    </head>          Closing </title> tag

    <body>———— The <body> tag

        <p></p>

    </body>
                The outer
</html>———— </html> tag
```

HTML document structure
Every HTML document requires a minimum number of tags. Recognizing the importance of tags in code, most code editors today automatically add these to a blank HTML document.

Attributes

Most HTML tags have attributes that provide additional information about the HTML element. An attribute describes a property or characteristic of the element. It always appears inside the element's opening tag in a key="value" format. Some attributes may be required by the tag type to render correctly, while other attributes may be optional.

<img/> tag attributes
Apart from "src", the "width" and "height" attributes define the dimensions of an image, and the "alt" attribute provides an alternative text description for images that cannot be displayed.

<a> tag attributes
The "href" attribute contains a url that points to the hyperlink's destination, and the "target" attribute instructs the browser to open the hyperlink in a new browser tab or the same tab.

"id" attribute
The "id" attribute describes the identity of an element. It can be added to any kind of tag and is specific to it. This attribute can also be used to select the element in CSS and JavaScript.

"name" attribute
This attribute is used by input elements to define the name of the property, or characteristic of the element, that is sent to the server. This attribute must be unique to each element in a form.

"class" attribute
The "class" attribute describes the name of a group that the element is a part of. Many elements on the same page can be members of the same class.

"style" attribute
The "style" attribute describes the visual characteristics of an element. It defines a list of key-value pairs. Each key-value style definition is separated by a semicolon (see p.234).

HTML forms and hyperlinks

Web pages are connected by hyperlinks and forms. While hyperlinks send requests for a specific url, forms send a request that includes data from the current web page. This data is then used by the server to process the request.

HTML forms

An HTML <form> tag contains input elements that allow the user to enter data to be sent to the server. When a user clicks the submit button, the browser will send the values of all the input fields in the form to the server. Every input field must have a "name" attribute. This identifier is used as the key for the data value. A form can include various elements for inputting data, including text fields, text areas, labels, checkboxes, radio buttons, select drop-down lists, and hidden fields.

Labels
The <label> tag adds a text label to an input control. When the label is clicked, the cursor jumps to the input control. The "for" attribute in the <label> tag must point to the "id" attribute (see p.211) of the input control.

```
<label for="Name">Name:</label>
<input type="text" id="Name" name="Name"
placeholder="Enter name" />
```

Checkboxes
This is used for indicating a true or false value. If the checkbox is ticked, the browser submits the value in the "value" attribute.

```
<input type="checkbox" name="hasDrivingLicense"
value="true"> Do you have a driving license?
```

Select drop-down lists
Select elements allow the user to choose an input from a list of possible values. This selected value is included in the form data sent to the server.

```
<select name="city">
        <option value="delhi">Delhi</option>
        <option value="cairo">Cairo</option>
</select>
```

Radio buttons
Radio buttons are used to select one of a group of possible values. Each radio button's "name" attribute will contain the same value. This indicates that they are possible answers for the same field.

```
<input type="radio" name"gender" value="male"
checked/> Male<br/>
<input type="radio" name"gender" value="female"
/> Female
```

Hyperlinks and URLs

Hyperlinks are text hotspots that, when clicked, navigate the browser to a new HTML document. They can also refer to another element on the same web page, in which case the browser will simply scroll to the required area. In HTML, hyperlinks are indicated by an anchor <a> tag. This tag contains an "href" attribute (see p.211) that stores a url. This url is the address to the new HTML document.

External hyperlink
These are hyperlinks to an HTML document on another website. It requires a complete url to navigate.

```
<a href="http://www.dk.com/otherPage.html">link</a>
```

External hyperlinks begin with the "http://" prefix

Text field
Text fields are used to enter an alphanumeric value. It is placed on a web page using the <input> tag. The "placeholder" attribute adds a hint to the input text field.

```
<input type="text" name="name"
placeholder="Enter name"/>
```

Input validation
Modern browsers use the "type" attribute to help ensure that the correct data is entered in a text input field. Since users can easily enter an invalid value in the browser, input validation must be applied at the server level. Here, the browser will not accept an input unless it is in fact an email address.

```
<label for="email">Email</label>
<input name="emailaddress"
type="email" />
```

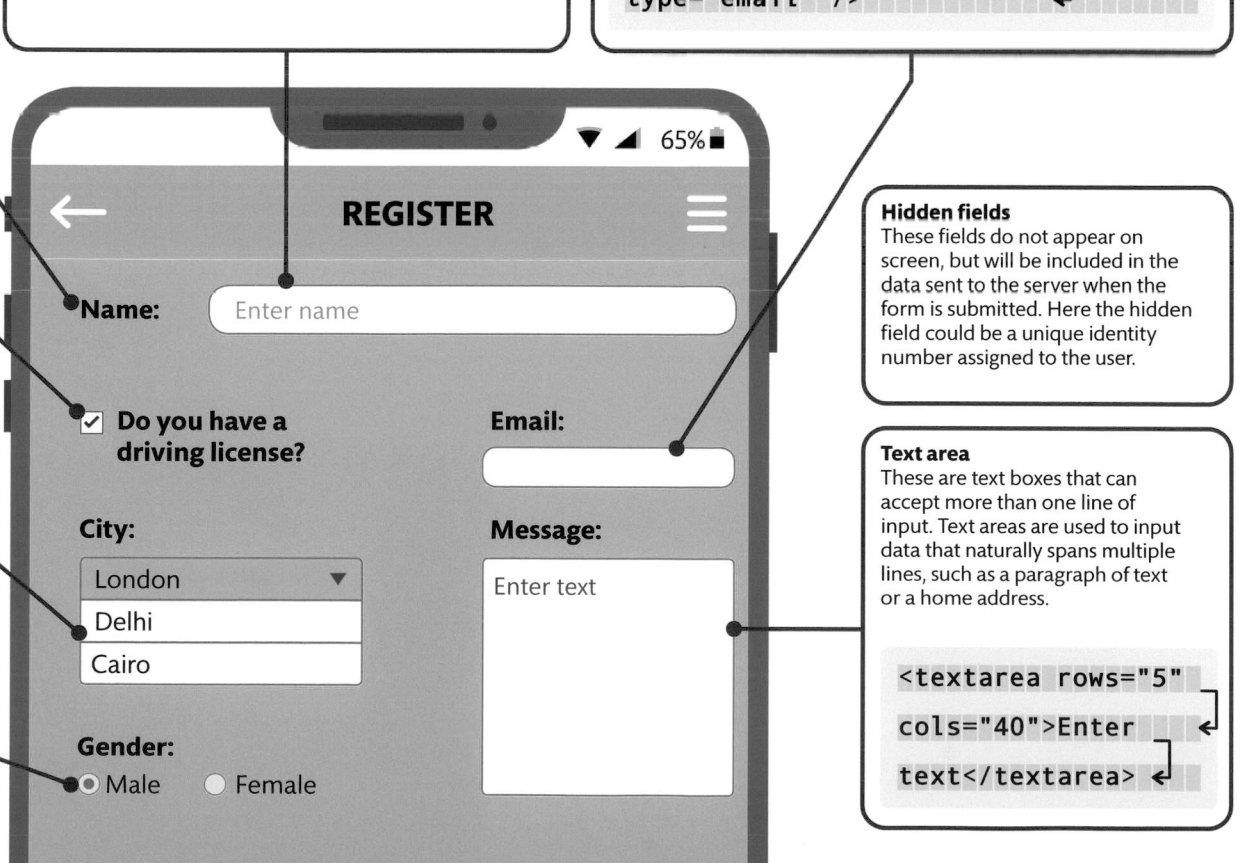

Hidden fields
These fields do not appear on screen, but will be included in the data sent to the server when the form is submitted. Here the hidden field could be a unique identity number assigned to the user.

Text area
These are text boxes that can accept more than one line of input. Text areas are used to input data that naturally spans multiple lines, such as a paragraph of text or a home address.

```
<textarea rows="5"
cols="40">Enter
text</textarea>
```

Build a better website

A well-built website should be easy to read and navigate through. It should be programmed to allow the largest-possible number of clients to view it, and should be thoroughly indexed by search engines to draw traffic to the site.

Accessibility

Not all clients are web browsers. An HTML document might also be read on a device that converts text into braille for the blind, or reads the text out loud for people with a hearing disability. An HTML document can be programmed to ensure that it is correctly rendered by these alternative clients. This requires including additional attributes in the HTML tags (see pp.210–11) and adding alternative methods of navigating the site to ensure that it can be accessed by users with special needs. Programmers should think about the topics mentioned below to improve the accessibility of their website.

Readable content
Ensure there is enough contrast between the background and the text colour to make the content easy to read. A dark coloured font will be easier to read on a light background, and vice versa.

HELLO WORLD!

Content organization
The content of a website should be arranged in a logical and intuitive way. There should be buttons and hyperlinks to suggest the next page the user should visit on their journey through the site. Breadcrumb links show the user where they are in the context of the site and allow them to go back to a previous page if necessary.

Keyboard alternatives
Some users may prefer using a keyboard rather than a mouse, so websites should provide for keyboard alternatives for actions, such as scrolling, that usually rely on a mouse.

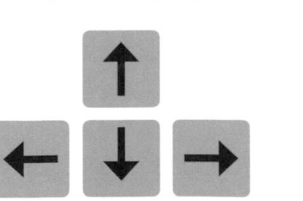

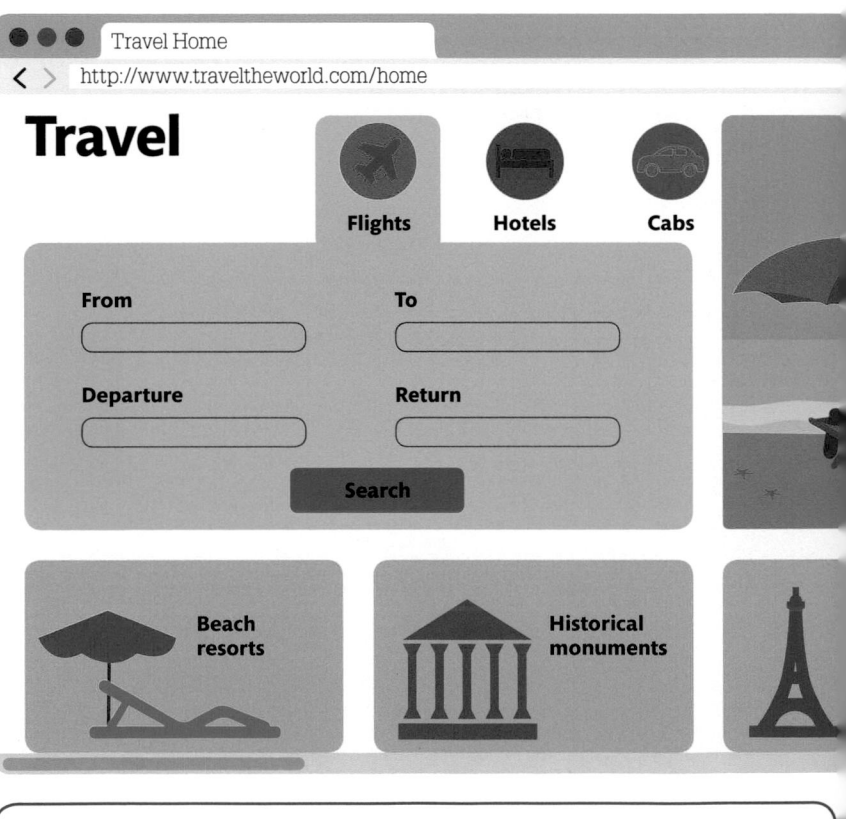

Text alternatives
Non-browser clients require text alternatives for non-text items. Include an "alt" attribute in an <img/> tag to ensure that such clients can display a text value if they cannot display images.

Describes the image in text

```
<img src="image.jpg" alt="Eiffel Tower"/>
```

Semantics

One of the key concepts in HTML is that the tags, or semantic elements, should express the meaning of the text, data, and images contained within them. For example, it is expected that an <h1> tag contains the main page header, a <p> tag contains text that should appear in a paragraph style, and a <ul> tag contains items that are all part of a list. Using the correct tag and tag attributes allows browsers and other types of web clients to understand the programmer's intention and correctly render the content in the output format for that client, be it as a web page on a screen or a ticker tape on a braille terminal.

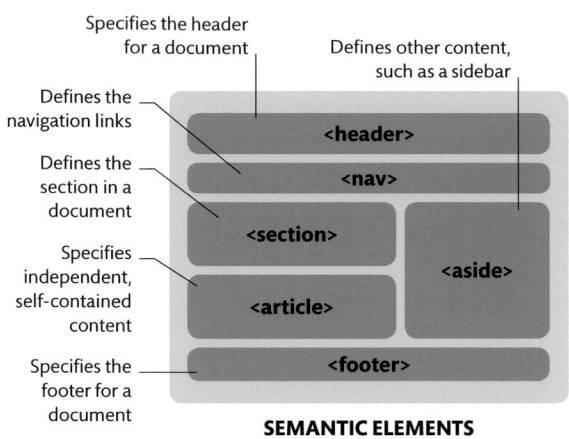

Specifies the header for a document

Defines other content, such as a sidebar

Defines the navigation links

Defines the section in a document

Specifies independent, self-contained content

Specifies the footer for a document

SEMANTIC ELEMENTS

Responsive layout

In the past, when the Web was primarily viewed in a browser running on a desktop, the width of HTML documents was commonly defined by a fixed number of pixels. Since many users today view websites on a range of devices, such as smartphones and tablets, it is necessary to code the HTML so that the website can fit on any size screen. The ability to stretch and shape the HTML to fit different screens is known as being "responsive".

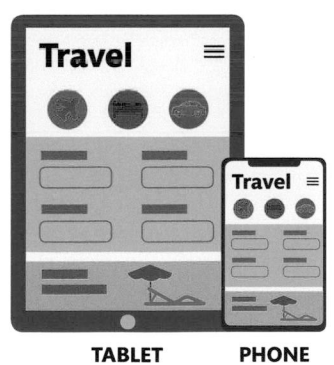

Tourist spots

TABLET   **PHONE**

Compliance with guidelines

All the code should comply with the Web Content Accessibility Guidelines to ensure that users with disabilities are able to enjoy the website. More information can be found at *https://www.w3.org/WAI/standards-guidelines/wcag/*

Hosting considerations

Web hosting is a service that makes websites accessible over the World Wide Web. Although it is possible to host a website from a personal computer, it is better to do so from a server that is designed to be online 24/7 and can provide backup and security to protect the site.

Shared hosting
In shared hosting, the web server hosts many different websites and databases. Each user can rent enough disk space, bandwidth, and database access to provide hosting for a single website.

Virtual Private Server (VPS) hosting
This involves a single server being divided into multiple virtual machines. Each website being hosted rents a machine, which is managed as a standalone server, but actually shares resources with all other virtual machines on that server.

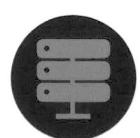

Dedicated server
A single server is used to host the website, and there is no sharing of resources. The user is responsible for installing and configuring all software and security on the server.

Elastic cloud computing
This system can adapt so that the needs of the system match the resources available to it. It provides the most functionality and flexibility, but comes at a higher cost than other hosting options.

Build a web page

A modern website is built using more than one programming language. In this project you will learn to create a basic web page, in this instance a pet store. You will need to combine HTML, CSS, and JavaScript, but the project is made up of three parts. First you will learn how to build an HTML framework.

How it works

The use of elements from HTML, CSS, and JavaScript will make the website structured, intuitive to navigate, and interactive.

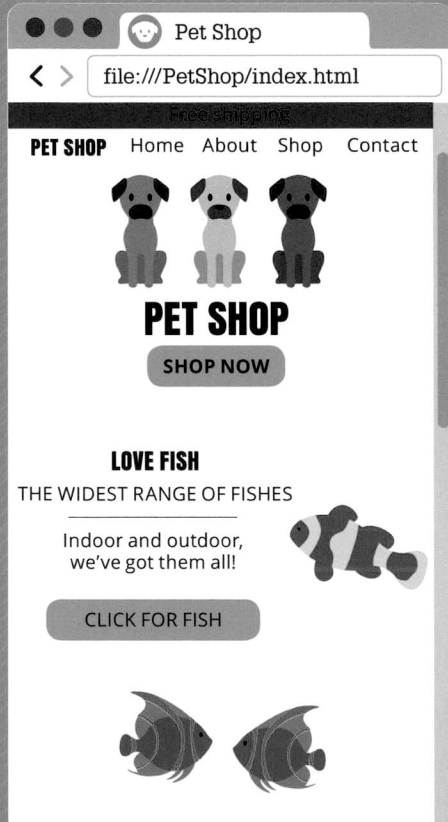

Final website
The website will be the home page of a pet supplies retail store. CSS (see pp.242–63) will add the visual styles and layout definitions, while JavaScript (see pp.288–303) will add interactive behaviours to enrich user experience on the page.

The HTML stage

You will create all the HTML elements of the web page in the first part of this project. This will include all the text, information, and data that need to appear on the website.

START

Create the HTML document, which will include all text, images, and data

Web page will display unformatted elements without any styles

END

PROGRAM DESIGN

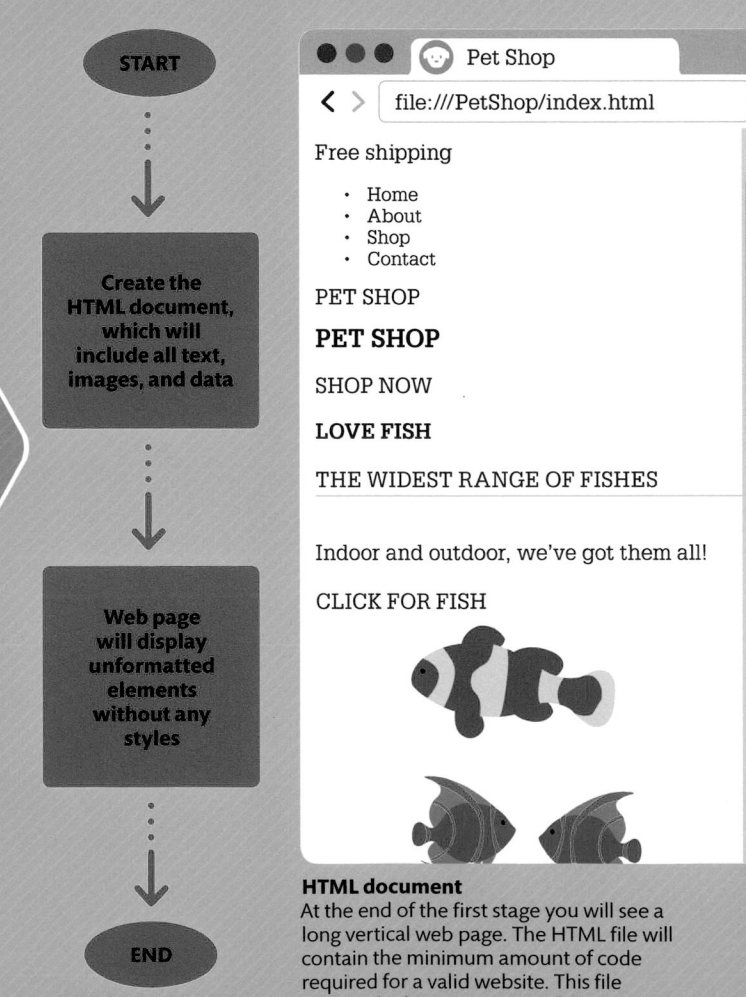

HTML document
At the end of the first stage you will see a long vertical web page. The HTML file will contain the minimum amount of code required for a valid website. This file defines the basic structure of the website.

YOU WILL LEARN

> How to structure a page
> How to create feature boxes
> How to use HTML tags and attributes

Time:
2–3 hours
Lines of code:
182
Difficulty level
● ● ● ● ●

WHERE THIS IS USED

HTML is the backbone of all websites, even the most complicated ones. The HTML code used in this project can be reused to create different types of web pages. Any web browsers can be used to read the HTML document as a web page, including Google Chrome, Internet Explorer, and Safari.

Program requirements

You will need a few programming elements to build this website. You may also have to download and install certain components before you can start writing the code.

Development environment
The IDE (see pp.208–209) "Microsoft Visual Studio Community 2019" will be used in this project. It is a free software available for both Windows and macOS, and supports various programming languages.

Browser
This project uses the Google Chrome browser to run and debug the code. You are welcome to use a different browser if you are more comfortable with it.

Images
You will need to download the images folder from *www.dk.com/coding-course*. A copy of this folder is required to create the home page of the website. You can also use your own images if you like.

Installing an IDE

1 To write the code for the website you will first need a development environment. Follow the steps given below to install "Microsoft Visual Studio Community 2019" on your computer.

1.1 **DOWNLOAD VISUAL STUDIO**
Open a browser, go to the website mentioned below and download the Community edition of Visual Studio. The browser will download a .dmg file to the Downloads folder on a Mac. If it does not run automatically, go to the folder and double-click the file to run it. On a Windows computer, save the installation .exe file to your hard drive and then run it.

www.visualstudio.com/downloads

1.2 **INSTALL COMPONENTS**
The Visual Studio Installer will display a list of languages you can program in. This project only requires languages for web development, so make sure to select the component **.Net Core** or **ASP.net and web development**. The installer will then download and install the necessary components.

Visual Studio for Mac 8.1
Create apps andgames across web, and desktop with .NET. Unity, Azure, and Docker support is included by default.

☑ **.NET Core** 2.1
The open source, cross-platform .NET framework and runtime.

MAC

ASP.NET and web development ☑
Build web applications using ASP.NET, ASP.NET Core, HTML/JavaScript, and Containers including Docker support

WINDOWS

1.3 OPEN VISUAL STUDIO
Allow any updates and then open Visual Studio. On a Mac, you can open Visual Studio by clicking its icon in the Applications folder, taskbar, or the desktop. To open it in Windows, click the icon on the startup menu, taskbar, or desktop.

VISUAL STUDIO

REMEMBER

HTML, JavaScript, and CSS files are just text files. Their code can be written in a simple text editor, such as Notepad or TextEdit. However, a dedicated development environment, such as Visual Studio, offers tools to improve the coding experience.

2 Getting started

After installing an IDE, it is important to get the basic elements required for coding the website. The next few steps will teach you how to create the root folder for the website, as well as the solution and index file required for writing the HTML code.

2.1 CREATE ROOT FOLDER
You will need a folder to hold all the files for the website. Use Finder to navigate to the "Users/[user account name]" folder on a Mac, or use File explorer to navigate to the "C" drive on a Windows computer. Then right-click and choose New Folder to create the website folder. Name it "PetShop".

PETSHOP

2.2 GET THE IMAGES FOLDER
Paste the previously downloaded "images" folder (see p.217) into the root folder of the website. This contains all the images required to create the home page. The full path to the folder on a Mac should be "Users/[user account name]/PetShop/images", and in Windows it should be "C:/PetShop/images".

IMAGES

Images in the website folder will appear on the web page

IMAGE

PETSHOP

PROJECT

2.3 OPEN A NEW PROJECT

The next step is to open a website project in Visual Studio. On a Mac, open Visual Studio, go to the File menu, and select New Solution. In the Other section, select Miscellaneous and then Blank Solution. In Windows, open the File menu, select Open, and then select Web Site. Choose the PetShop folder that was created in the previous step.

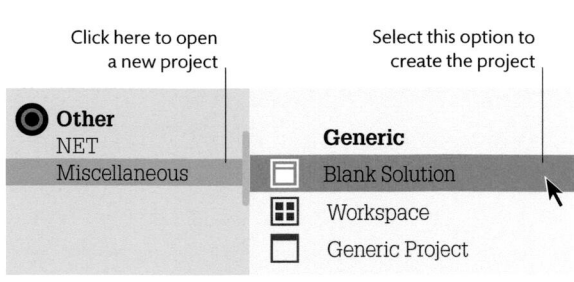

Click here to open
a new project

Select this option to
create the project

MAC

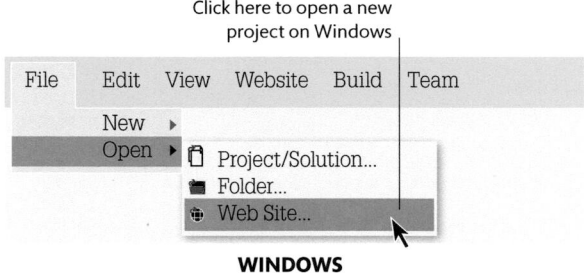

Click here to open a new
project on Windows

WINDOWS

2.4 CREATE A SOLUTION FILE

You now need a solution file to keep track of the project preferences. On a Mac, enter the solution name "PetShop" in the "Configure your new solution" window, and then enter the location of the website folder. Click Create to save a file called "PetShop.sln" to this folder. In Windows, save the project to create a .sln file. Click the File menu and choose Save All. This will open a dialogue box to save a file called "PetShop.sln". Save this file in the website folder.

2.5 ADD AN INDEX FILE

Next, add an "index.html" file to the root folder of the website. In the Solution Explorer, right-click on the project name "PetShop" and select Add, then select New File on a Mac or Add New Item in Windows. Now choose HTML Page, and name it "index.html". Visual Studio will add a file called "index.html" to the website folder.

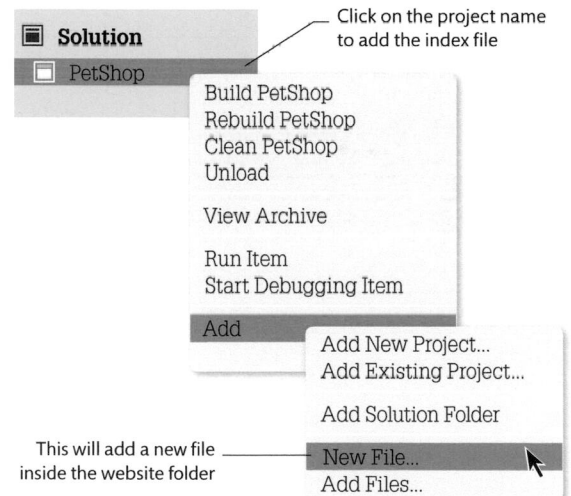

Click on the project name
to add the index file

This will add a new file
inside the website folder

**LOOK FOR THE
"VIEW" MENU
TO DISPLAY THE
"SOLUTION EXPLORER" IF IT
IS NOT VISIBLE**

SOLUTIONS

The solution file
tracks the project's
preferences

2.6 HTML PAGE

Visual Studio will create the "index.html" file with the minimum code required for a valid HTML page. If you are using another development environment, type the code shown here into the new index file.

```
<!DOCTYPE html>                    ——— Document type
                                         declaration
<html>

<head>

        <meta charset="utf-8" />

        <title></title>

</head>

<body>

</body>

</html>
```

The "charset" attribute specifies the character encoding for the HTML document. A character encoding tells the computer how to interpret binary data into real characters

This tag is a container for the text that will appear as the page title in the browser

This tag contains all the text, data, and images visible on the web page

Outer tag for the HTML document

3 Structure the home page

In HTML, the home page will be a series of horizontal layers one above the other. The first layer will contain an animated line of promotional messages. This will be followed by the "Top Menu", a banner with a large picture, company logo, and a call-to-action button. The next element will be a feature box and then a large image. More layers repeating this pattern of alternating feature boxes and large images will be included. The layers at the bottom will contain contact details, a subscription link, hyperlinks, and a copyright notice. We will also add a "Scroll to top" button to help the user navigate back to the top of the page easily.

Pet Shop

file:///PetShop/index.html

PROMOTIONAL MESSAGES

TOP MENU

BANNER

FEATURE BOX 1

IMAGE 1

CONTACT US

SUBSCRIBE

FOOTER

COPYRIGHT

SCROLL TO TOP BUTTON

This is a line of menu items with hyperlinks to other pages in the site

Feature boxes have a short description, a picture, and a call-to-action link

This button will help the user navigate

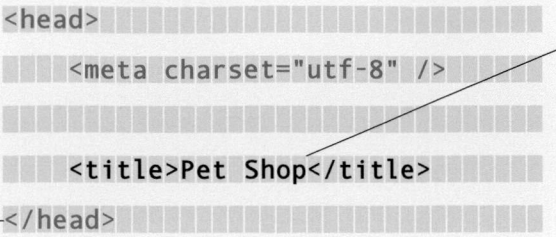

3.1 ADD THE WEBSITE NAME

Before adding the text, images, and data to the page, add the website name into the <head> tag by adding the page title definition into the <title> tag.

The <head> tag loads the metadata before the page is displayed

```
<head>
    <meta charset="utf-8" />

    <title>Pet Shop</title>
</head>
```

This text will appear as the tab title in the browser

3.2 ADD THE FAVICON DEFINITION

Next, add the favicon <link> tag below the <title> tag to add the icon for the website. The "href" attribute points to the icon file in the images folder of the website.

```
<title>Pet Shop</title>

<link rel="icon" type="image/png"

href="images/favicon.png">
```

This icon has been used in the book to split code across two lines

FAVICON

The favicon is a small image that appears in the browser tab next to the page title. It is a square image that makes it easier for a user to find the tab for the web page in a browser. The favicon can have a solid or a transparent background, and must have a .png or .ico file format.

Pet Shop

3.3 ADDING TEXT

You can now start adding the text, data, and images inside the <body> tag. This will make these elements visible when the HTML document opens in the browser. To add the promotional messages, add an outer <div> tag, followed by the child tags to contain the messages. All the message divs, except the first, must have a style attribute instructing the browser not to display them. For now we will only show a single promotional message. JavaScript will be added later to the project to cycle through the promotional messages.

This tag will contain the elements that can be styled as a group

Child tags are indented under the parent "promo" <div> tag

The promotional messages

```
<body>
    <div id="promo" >
        <div>Free shipping</div>
        <div style="display:none;">New toys for puppies</div>
        <div style="display:none;">Buy 5 toys and save 30%</div>
        <div style="display:none;">Same day dispatch</div>
    </div>
</body>
```

3.4 VIEW THE PAGE

You can now view this HTML page inside a browser. Save the HTML file, then in the Solution Explorer window, right-click on "index.html" and select "View in Browser". You can also open a web browser and type the url into the address bar. On a Windows computer, the url will be "file:///C:/PetShop/index.html". On Mac, the url will be "file:///Users/[user account name]/PetShop/index.html". You will now be able to view the page title in the tab name, the url in the address bar, and the text "Free shipping" in the browser window.

url to the website

GOOGLE CHROME BROWSER

DEVELOPER TOOLS

To see what is happening on an HTML page inside the browser, open its Developer tools. The Developer tools allow you to select individual HTML elements and see what CSS styles are being applied to them.

KEYBOARD SHORTCUT TO OPEN DEVELOPER TOOLS		
Browser	**Keyboard shortcut macOS**	**Keyboard shortcut Windows**
Chrome	Cmd+Option+J	Ctrl+Shift+J
Opera	Cmd+Option+I	Ctrl+Shift+I
Safari	Cmd+Option+C	n/a
Internet Explorer	n/a	F12
Edge	n/a	F12

3.5 ADD THE TOP MENU SECTION

Next, it is time to add the Top Menu section. Under the "promo" div, add a new div with id ="topMenu". To make the Top Menu run across the full screen with the text inside centred on the page, surround it with a "wrap" div. This "wrap" class will be defined later in the CSS project "Styling the website" to instruct the browser to display the Top Menu in the centre of the page. Inside the "topMenu" div, add a div with class="wrap", and then inside the "wrap" div, add another div with id="topLinks". This div will contain the list of hyperlinks in the Top Menu.

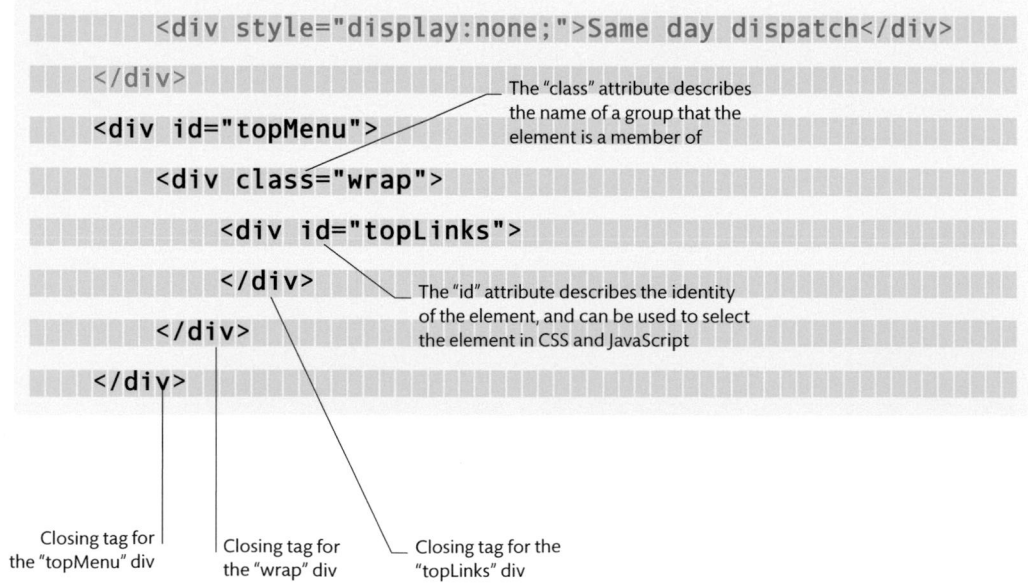

```
            <div style="display:none;">Same day dispatch</div>
      </div>
    <div id="topMenu">
        <div class="wrap">
            <div id="topLinks">
            </div>
        </div>
    </div>
```

The "class" attribute describes the name of a group that the element is a member of

The "id" attribute describes the identity of the element, and can be used to select the element in CSS and JavaScript

Closing tag for the "topMenu" div

Closing tag for the "wrap" div

Closing tag for the "topLinks" div

3.6 **ADD THE HYPERLINK LIST**

Inside the "topLinks" div, add an unordered list that will contain the actual hyperlinks in the Top Menu for the HTML pages: Home, About, Shop, and Contact. Then add a small link, which appears as the company name, back to the home page. Just below the "topLinks" div, add another anchor tag to contain the name of the website. This will hyperlink to the home page.

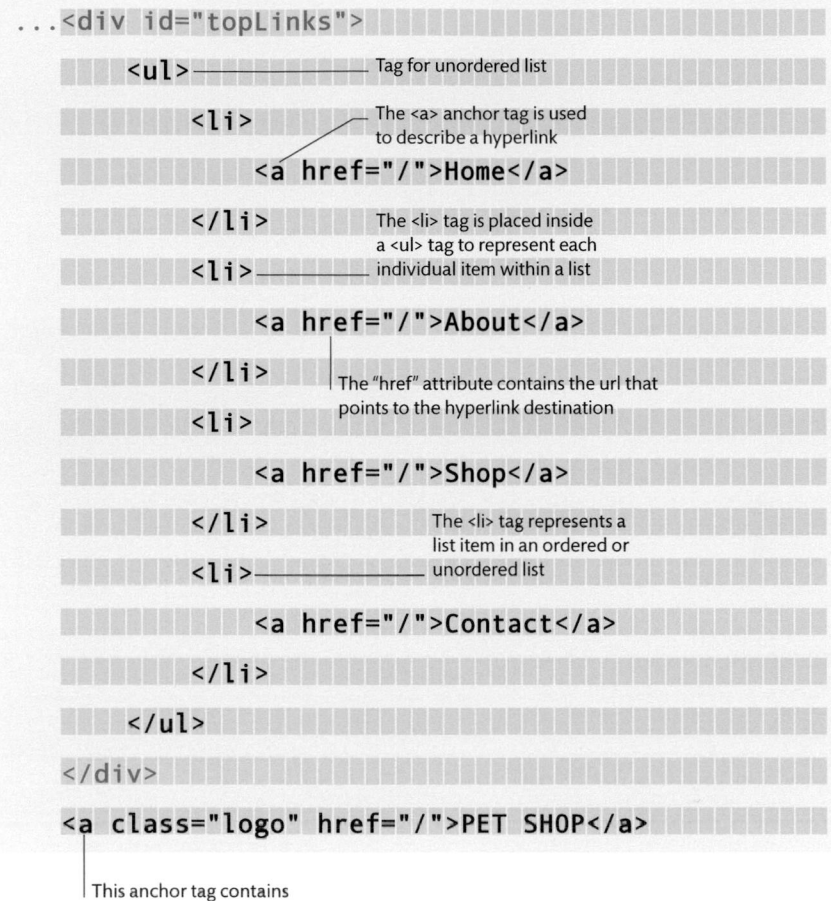

```
...<div id="topLinks">
        <ul>                          Tag for unordered list
            <li>                      The <a> anchor tag is used
                                      to describe a hyperlink
                <a href="/">Home</a>
            </li>                     The <li> tag is placed inside
                                      a <ul> tag to represent each
            <li>                      individual item within a list
                <a href="/">About</a>
            </li>                     The "href" attribute contains the url that
                                      points to the hyperlink destination
            <li>
                <a href="/">Shop</a>
            </li>                     The <li> tag represents a
                                      list item in an ordered or
            <li>                      unordered list
                <a href="/">Contact</a>
            </li>
        </ul>
</div>
<a class="logo" href="/">PET SHOP</a>
```

This anchor tag contains the name of the website

The Top Menu list appears as hyperlinks

View the website

Save the HTML file and then refresh the page in the browser. You will see the promotional message on top, with the Top Menu list below it, followed by the hyperlink to the home page with the company logo.

3.7 ADD THE BANNER

Next, add the banner section that will contain a large company logo and a call-to-action button to visit the shopping page. This banner image and heading should appear centred in the page, so it needs to be surrounded by a div with class="wrap".

The "topMenu" div closing tag

Add a div with id="banner" inside the <div> tag with class="wrap"

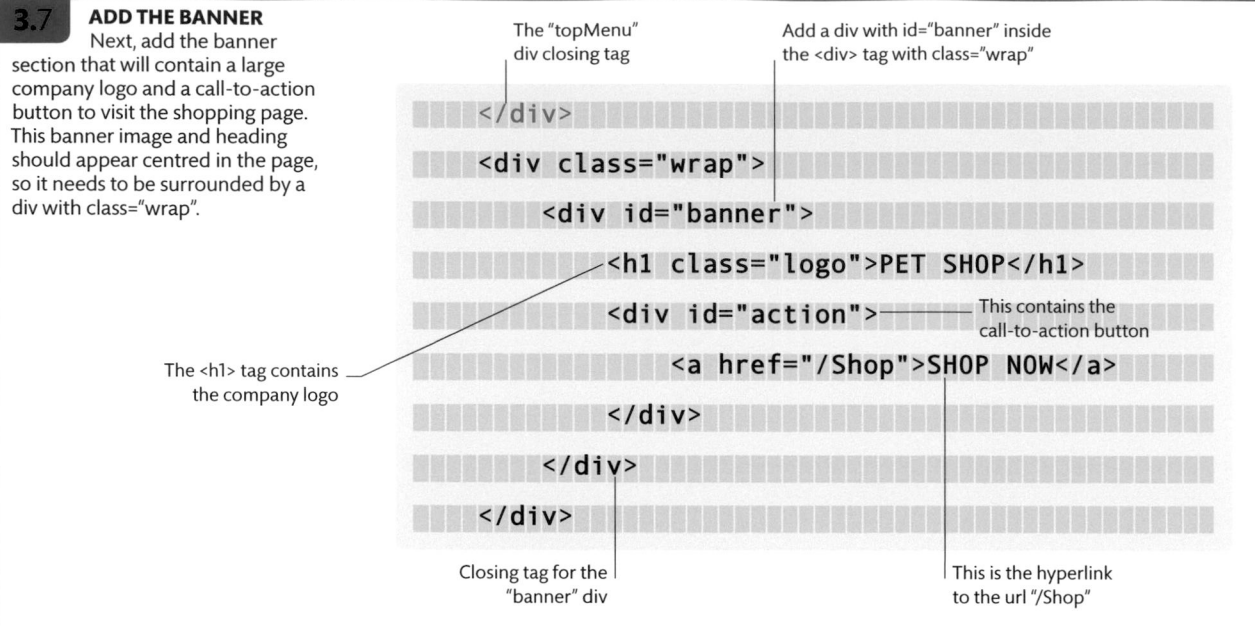

```
    </div>
  <div class="wrap">
      <div id="banner">
        <h1 class="logo">PET SHOP</h1>
        <div id="action">
          <a href="/Shop">SHOP NOW</a>
        </div>
      </div>
  </div>
```

The <h1> tag contains the company logo

This contains the call-to-action button

Closing tag for the "banner" div

This is the hyperlink to the url "/Shop"

3.8 ADD VERTICAL SPACE

Below the "banner" div, add another div with class="spacer clear v80". The "spacer v80" classes will be used in Styling the web page (see pp.242–63) to define a standard vertical spacer between the elements. The "clear" class will be used later to instruct the browser to add the next element on a new line.

```
  </div>
    <div class="clear spacer v80"></div>
  </div>
```

4 Feature box control

The next step is to add a feature box control to advertise the fish department. This feature box control can be reused a few more times on the page, each time alternating the side of the page that has the image and text.

Feature box structure
The left half of the feature box will contain a heading, subheading, a text description, and a link to the category on the website. The right half will hold an image.

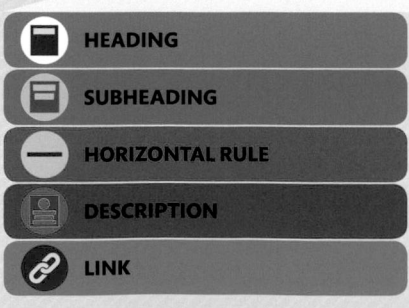

- HEADING
- SUBHEADING
- HORIZONTAL RULE
- DESCRIPTION
- LINK

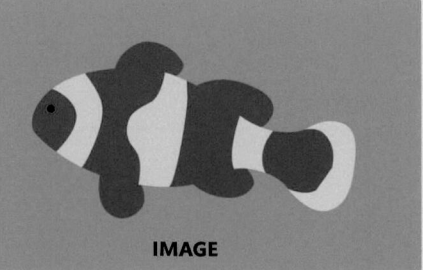

IMAGE

4.1 USING THE CLASS ATTRIBUTE

Add this code below the "spacer" div to define the left and right columns of the feature box for the fish department. The "class" attribute is used instead of the "id" attribute to style the HTML tag because the feature box will be used multiple times on the same page.

```
<div id="fishFeature" class="feature">
    <div class="leftColumn">
    </div>
    <div class="rightColumn">
    </div>
</div>
```

This will contain elements for the left column

This will contain elements for the right column

4.2 DEFINE THE LEFT COLUMN ELEMENTS

Inside the "leftColumn" div, add a div class="text" to contain the text elements. This code will add the heading, the subheading, a horizontal rule, and a description of the feature box in the left column. Add a div class="spacer" to define the vertical space between the elements, and then add an anchor tag to hyperlink to the page.

This text will appear as the subheading of the feature box

This icon has been used to split code over two lines

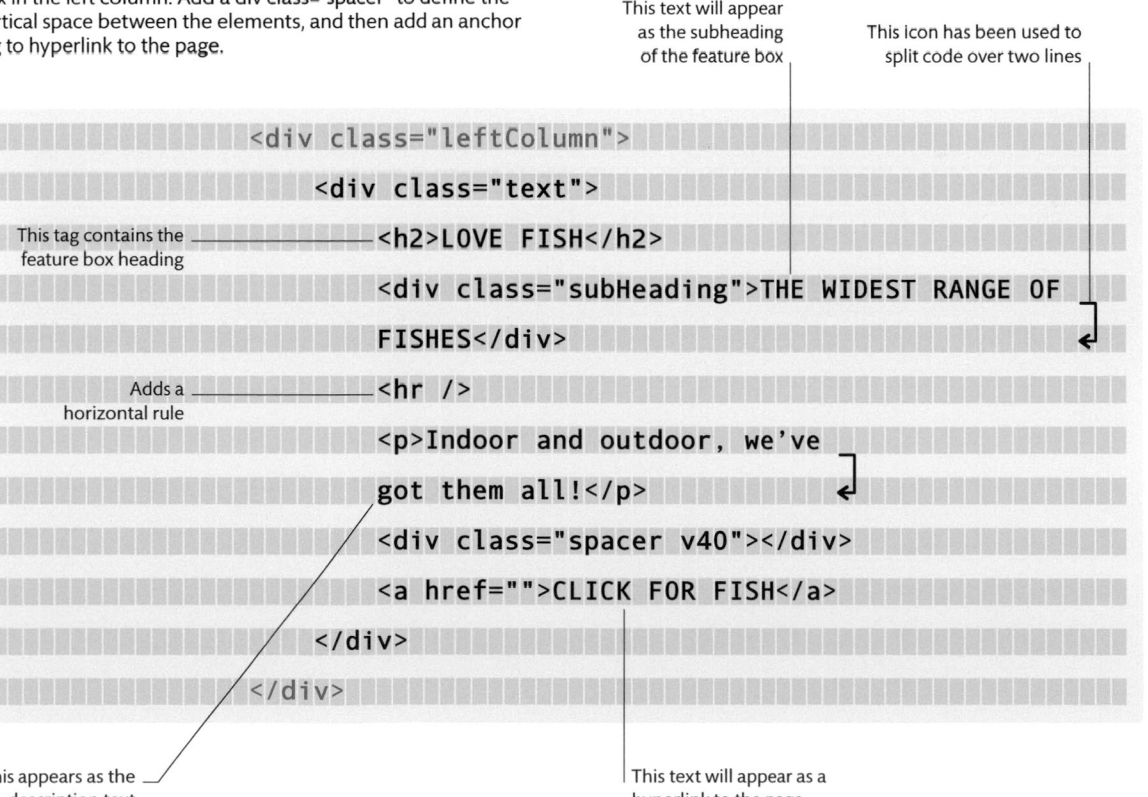

```
<div class="leftColumn">
    <div class="text">
        <h2>LOVE FISH</h2>
        <div class="subHeading">THE WIDEST RANGE OF
        FISHES</div>
        <hr />
        <p>Indoor and outdoor, we've
        got them all!</p>
        <div class="spacer v40"></div>
        <a href="">CLICK FOR FISH</a>
    </div>
</div>
```

This tag contains the feature box heading

Adds a horizontal rule

This appears as the description text

This text will appear as a hyperlink to the page

4.3 RIGHT COLUMN ELEMENTS

Now add this code to define the elements for the right column. In the "rightColumn" div, add an anchor tag and inside the <a> tag add an <img/> with the picture for the fish department. Then, add a vertical spacer that can be reused throughout the website to give consistent vertical height between elements.

```
<div class="rightColumn">
    <a class="featureImage" src="/Fish">
        <img src="images/fish_feature_1.jpg" />
    </a>
</div>
</div>
<div class="clear spacer v20"></div>
```

The <a> tag describes a hyperlink

The "src" attribute contains the url to the image file

Closing tag for the "fishFeature" div

This is the name of the picture in the images folder

Adds a vertical space between elements

4.4 ADD A NEW DIV

Below the "spacer" div, add a new div with id="fishImage" and class="middleImage". This will contain the second image for the fish department, and will appear under the main fish feature box. These "middleImage" containers will be used again later in this page.

Defines the middle image for the fish department

```
<div id="fishImage" class="middleImage">
    <img src="images/fish_feature_2.jpg" />
</div>
<div class="spacer v80"></div>
</div>
```

This points to the image file location

Adds another vertical space after the middle image

Closing tag for the "wrap" div

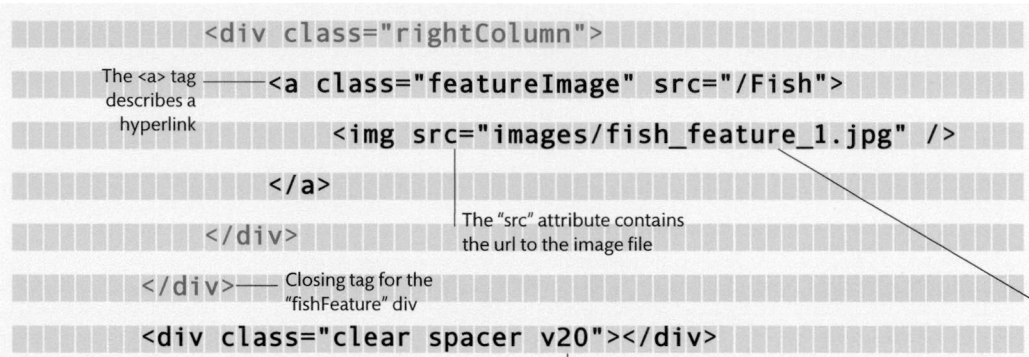

$15

$10

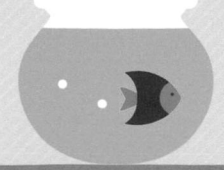
$10

$4

$4

ON SALE

5 Advertising the dog category

It is now time to add a second category to the website to advertise the dog department. This feature box will appear below the fish department, and will have the image on the left and all the text elements on the right.

5.1 DOG FEATURE

To create the dog feature control box, add a div beneath the "spacer" div. Inside this new "dogFeature" div, add the "leftColumn" and "rightColumn" divs with all the text and image elements required for the dog department.

File name of the dog image in the images folder

```html
<div id="dogFeature" class="feature">
    <div class="leftColumn">
        <a class="featureImage">
            <img src="images/dog_feature_1.jpg" />
        </a>
    </div>
    <div class="rightColumn">
        <div class="text">
            <h2>HAPPY DOGS</h2>
            <div class="subHeading">EVERYTHING YOUR DOG
            NEEDS</div>
            <hr />
            <p>Make sure your pooch eats well and feels good
            with our range of doggie treats.</p>
            <div class="spacer v40"></div>
            <a href="">CLICK FOR DOGS</a>
        </div>
    </div>
</div>
```

Heading for the dog feature box

This text will appear as the subheading

The "href" attribute contains the url that points to the hyperlink's destination

This text will appear as a hyperlink for the dog department

Description text for the dog department

5.2 **MIDDLE IMAGE**
Below the "dogFeature" div, add another div with class="clear" to start a new line. Then add the second image for the dog feature box. Next, add another vertical spacer under the image.

```
<div class="clear"></div>
<div id="dogImage" class="middleImage">
    <img src="images/dog_feature_2.jpg" />
</div>
<div class="spacer v80"></div>
```

Adds a vertical space below the middle image

File name for the middle image

6 Advertising the bird category

The next feature box to be included is for the bird department. Similar to the fish feature box, this department will have the text elements on the left and the image on the right. The bird category will appear below the dog category on the website.

6.1 **BIRD FEATURE**
Type the following lines of code below the "spacer" div to add another feature box to advertise the bird department. This will include the "leftColumn" and "rightColumn" text and image elements for this category.

Defines the feature box control for the bird department

Subheading for the bird department

This is the heading for the bird department

```
<div id="birdFeature" class="feature">
    <div class="leftColumn">
        <div class="text">
            <h2>BIRDY NUM NUM</h2>
            <div class="subHeading">KEEP YOUR BIRDS
            CHIPPER</div>
            <hr />
```

Description for the bird department ────────

```
<p>Yummy snacks and feeders for
    every kind of bird.</p>
<div class="spacer v40"></div>
<a href="">CLICK FOR BIRDS</a>
</div>
</div>
<div class="rightColumn">
<a class="featureImage" src="/Bird">
<img src="images/bird_feature.jpg" />
</a>
</div>
</div>
```

Hyperlink for the bird department

Closing tag for the right column

File name for the bird image in the feature box

6.2 ADD ANOTHER IMAGE

Now add another "clear" div to start on a new line. Next, add the middle image for the bird department. Inside the "birdImage" div, add the <img/> tag with the url to the image.

Closing tag for the "birdFeature" div

```
</div>
<div class="clear"></div>
<div id="birdImage" class="middleImage">
    <img src="images/bird_feeder.jpg" />
</div>
```

File name of the middle image

The bird image is picked up from the main images folder and added to the website

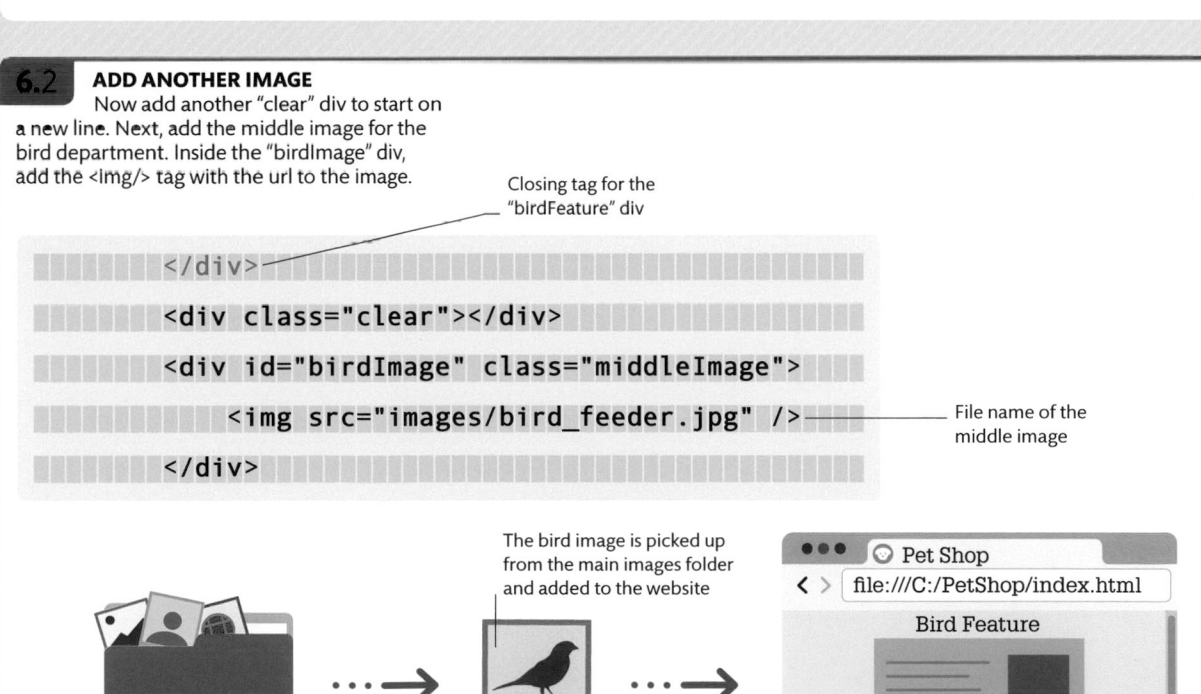

IMAGES

● ● ● ◉ Pet Shop
< > file:///C:/PetShop/index.html
Bird Feature

7 SCROLL TO THE TOP

Add a button to allow the user to scroll back to the top of the page. Create a "scrollToTop" div and then add a <span> tag inside it with an HTML entity (see p.233) indicating the upwards arrow. The "title" attribute adds a "tooltip" to the button so that when a user hovers their mouse over the button, a label will appear on top saying "Scroll to top". Another vertical spacer is added below the button.

```
</div>————— Closing tag for the "birdImage" div

<div id="scrollToTop" title="Scroll to top">————— Defines the Scroll to top button

    <span>&uarr;</span>————————— The <span> tag contains the HTML entity indicating the upwards arrow

</div>

<div class="clear spacer v40"></div>————————— Adds a vertical space below the Scroll to top button
```

8 ADD A CONTACT SECTION

Add the contact section for the website immediately below the "spacer" div from the previous step. You can reuse the feature box controls that were used to split the page into a left and right column. In the left column, you will add the address and other contact details.

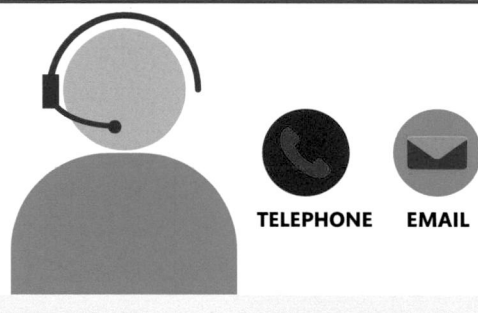

TELEPHONE   EMAIL   ADDRESS

Defines the contact section

```
<div id="contactUs" class="feature">

    <div class="leftColumn">————————— Defines the elements in the left column of the feature box

        <div class="text">

            <h2>CONTACT US</h2>————————— Header for the section

            <hr />

            <p>

                TEL : 012-345-6789

            </p>

            <p>

                EMAIL : <a href="mailto:INFO@PETSHOP.COM"

                class="emailLink">INFO@PETSHOP.COM</a>

            </p>
```

The <p> tag makes the information appear as a paragraph

This will appear as the email link to the website

```
                        <p>
                    PET SHOP<br />
                    80 Strand<br />
                    London<br />
                    WC2R 0RL
                        </p>
                    </div>
                </div>
                <div class="rightColumn">
                </div>
            </div>
```

The <br /> tag tells the browser to start a new line

This text will appear as the address of the Pet Shop

Defines the right column of the feature box

8.1 ADD A MAP TO THE CONTACT SECTION

In the right column, you can now embed a map to show the location of the Pet Shop. Inside the "rightColumn" div, add an <iframe> tag with the "src" attribute set to the url of the map on Google Maps. The <iframe> tag is used to insert content from another web page onto your page.

Link to the map in Google Maps

```
            <div class="rightColumn">
                <iframe src="https://www.google.com/maps/embed?p
b=!1m18!1m12!1m3!1d2483.1688989591494!2d-0.12403078438577886!3d51.510
117279635615!2m3!1f0!2f0!3f0!3m2!1i1024!2i768!4f13.1!3m3!1m2!1s0x4876
04c97bf47a1d%3A0xaf65b3d1a31e2229!2s80+Strand%2C+London+WC2R+0BP%2C+U
K!5e0!3m2!1sen!2sza!4v1539340576969" frameborder="0" style="border:0"
allowfullscreen class="contactMap"></iframe>
            </div>
        </div>
    </div>
    <div class="clear spacer v80"></div>
```

Closing tag for the "contactUs" div

Closing tag for the "wrap" div

Add this line to include a vertical space after the map

9 ADD THE SUBSCRIBE SECTION

Next, add the "Subscribe" section for the website. Below the "spacer" div add the "subscribe" div to make this section run across the full screen. Inside the "subscribe" div, add a header, a form with action="/subscribe" and method="post". The "action" and "method" attributes define where the form gets sent when the user clicks the "submit" button. Then inside the <form> tag, add a text input field to allow the user to enter an email address, and a button which says "Join Now"

```
<div id="subscribe">
    <h2>SUBSCRIBE TO OUR MAILING LIST</h2>
    <form action="/subscribe" method="post">
        <input name="email" type="text" placeholder="Enter
        your email address" />
        <input type="submit" value="Join Now" />
    </form>
</div>
```

Header for the Subscribe section

Text for the button

10 ADD THE FOOTER

Let us now add the "footer" section after the "subscribe" </div> closing tag. This will contain the unordered list of footer hyperlinks for the website.

The "href" attribute describes the url of the page to link to

This will appear as the first footer hyperlink

```
<div id="footer">
    <ul>
        <li>
            <a href="/storeFinder">Store Finder</a>
        </li>
        <li>
            <a href="/shipping">Shipping</a>
        </li>
        <li>
            <a href="/FAQ">FAQ</a>
        </li>
    </ul>
</div>
```

The second hyperlink

The <ul> tag is a block element used to designate an unordered list

11 ADD THE COPYRIGHT NOTICE

Then add a copyright notice at the bottom of the page. This will contain the copyright message and the company logo. Notice that in the code below, the company logo is contained in a <span> tag so that it can be styled later in Styling the web page (see pp.242–63). An HTML entity has also been used for the copyright symbol. You have now created the basic framework for your web page. Additional pages can also be created to build a fully functioning website (see p.303).

© 2020 PET SHOP

Text for the copyright message

```
<div id="copyright">
    <div>&copy; 2020 <span class="logo">PET SHOP</span>
    </div>
</div>
</body>
```

HTML entity for the copyright symbol

The company logo

ENTITIES

Some characters are not allowed in HTML because they are reserved by HTML, CSS, or JavaScript. So when you want these restricted characters to appear on screen, they must be coded with an HTML entity so that they will render correctly in the browser.

This HTML entity will display a © symbol

```
<p>
        &copy; DK Books 2020
</p>
```

Common entities
Here is a list of some of the most commonly used HTML entities. See *https://dev.w3.org/html5/html-author/charref* for a full list.

COMMON ENTITIES		
Symbol	**Meaning**	**HTML entity**
"	Quotation Marks	&quot;
●	Whitespace/spacebar	
&	Ampersand	&amp;
%	Percent	&percent;
$	Dollar	&dollar;
©	Copyright	&copy;
'	Apostrophe	&apos;

Cascading Style Sheets

Cascading Style Sheets (CSS) define how the contents of an HTML file should appear in a web browser. It allows for the design of a website to be easily updated by making changes to the CSS style definitions.

Why CSS?

Website styling, until 1996, was done inside individual HTML tags, making code extremely long and cluttered. CSS simplified this by separating style from content. A CSS file contains a list of rules that provide an easy way to define the style of single elements, and to share the same styles across multiple elements in an HTML document. The client web browser reads the CSS files and applies the style definition to each element in the HTML document.

Adding CSS styles to an HTML document

A CSS style can be defined in three places in an HTML document: in an external CSS file, in a <style> tag inside the HTML file, and in a "style" attribute inside an HTML tag.

External CSS file

When CSS style definitions are contained in a separate CSS file, the style definitions can be shared by all the pages in a website. Use a <link> tag to reference the sheet in an HTML document.

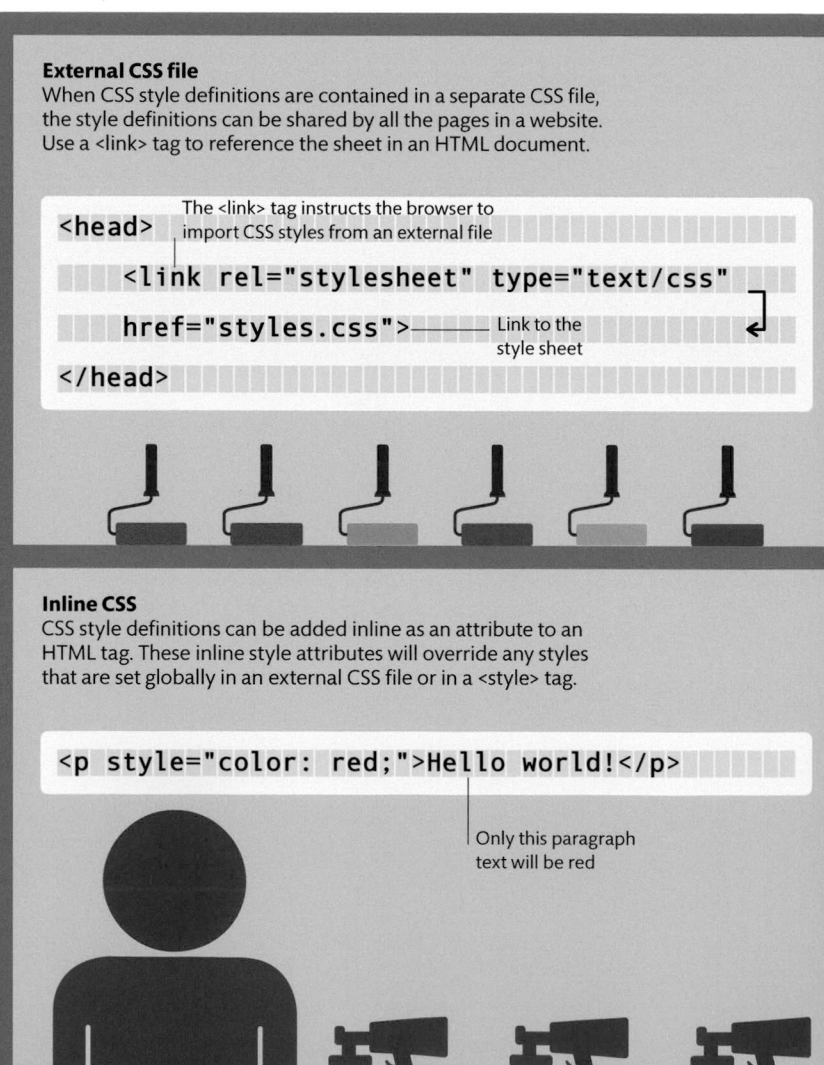

The <link> tag instructs the browser to import CSS styles from an external file

```
<head>
    <link rel="stylesheet" type="text/css"
    href="styles.css">
</head>
```

Link to the style sheet

In a <style> tag

An HTML file can contain CSS definitions inside a <style> tag, which is usually placed inside the <head> section. These CSS definitions do not apply to other pages on the website.

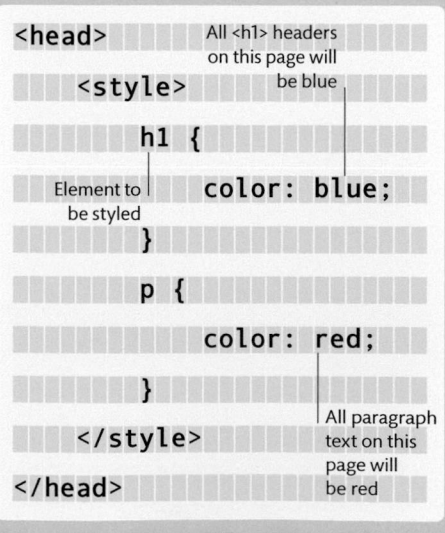

```
<head>
    <style>
        h1 {
            color: blue;
        }
        p {
            color: red;
        }
    </style>
</head>
```

All <h1> headers on this page will be blue

Element to be styled

All paragraph text on this page will be red

Inline CSS

CSS style definitions can be added inline as an attribute to an HTML tag. These inline style attributes will override any styles that are set globally in an external CSS file or in a <style> tag.

```
<p style="color: red;">Hello world!</p>
```

Only this paragraph text will be red

Style options

CSS can define various aspects of an element's appearance on screen, including its placement, font, colour, border style, and special effects such as animation. CSS contains instructions that tell the browser how to render an HTML element on screen. In order to work on all browsers CSS expects precise names for the properties and values. For example, to make an HTML element invisible the "display" property will have the value "none".

CSS STYLE OPTIONS	
CSS code	**Output**
`display:block;`	The element will appear as a block element
`display:inline;`	The element will appear as an inline element
`display:none;`	The element will not appear on the screen

`font-family: "Times New Roman", serif;`
`font-weight: bold;`
`color: red;`
	Specifies the font settings and font colour

`padding: 10px 12px 15px 30px;` `margin 40px;`	Specifies the spacing settings (see p.245)
`background-color: white;`	Sets the background colour

How CSS works

CSS works by selecting a set of HTML elements, and then adding styles to all the elements in the set. Every CSS instruction consists of two parts: the selector and the style definition. The selector tells the browser which elements are to be included in the instruction, while the style definition specifies how to display the elements included in the selector.

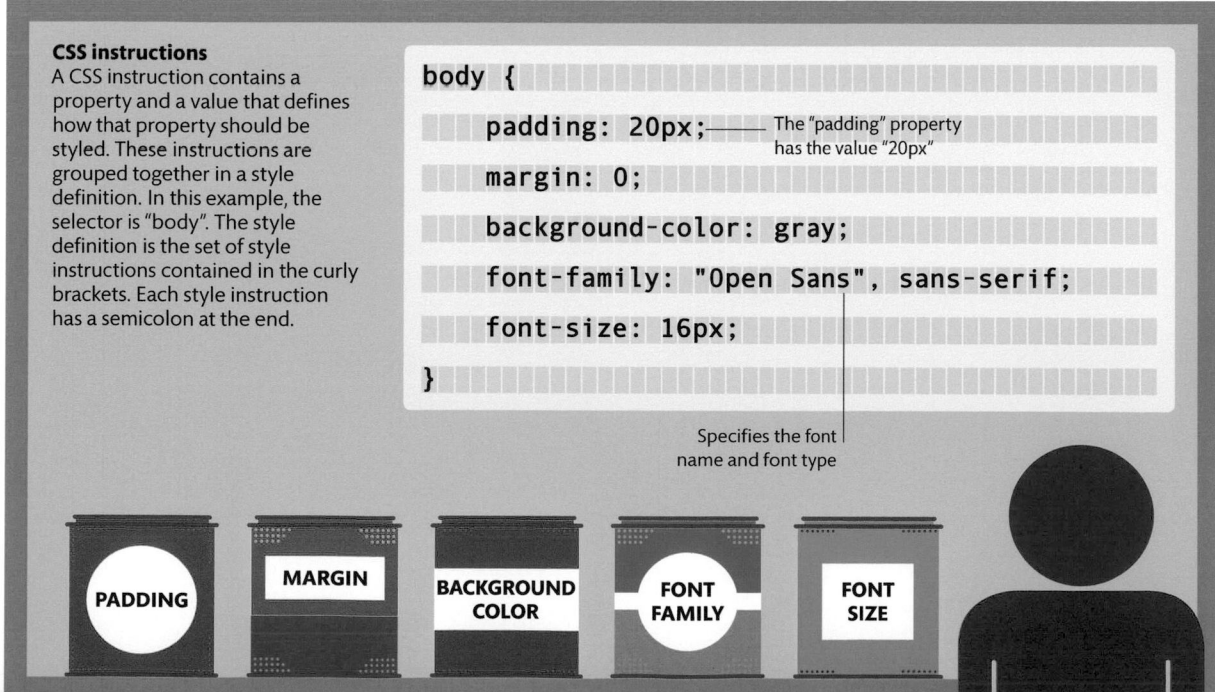

CSS instructions
A CSS instruction contains a property and a value that defines how that property should be styled. These instructions are grouped together in a style definition. In this example, the selector is "body". The style definition is the set of style instructions contained in the curly brackets. Each style instruction has a semicolon at the end.

```
body {
    padding: 20px;        The "padding" property
                          has the value "20px"
    margin: 0;

    background-color: gray;

    font-family: "Open Sans", sans-serif;

    font-size: 16px;
}
```

Specifies the font name and font type

PADDING
MARGIN
BACKGROUND COLOR
FONT FAMILY
FONT SIZE

CSS selectors

A CSS selector tells the browser which HTML elements are to be styled. An element must satisfy the selection criteria in order to have the style applied to it. Selectors can target either a single element or a group of elements.

Basic selectors

A CSS selector is a pattern used to identify which HTML elements qualify to have the style applied to them. CSS selectors allow programmers to target specific HTML elements with style sheets. There are three basic selectors in CSS: the element selector, id selector, and class selector.

GROUPING SELECTORS MINIMIZES CODE IN A STYLE SHEET

Element selector
This is used to target all the HTML elements of a certain type. For example, all elements inside the <p> tag will be coloured red.

```
<p>This text to be in red</p>
```
HTML

This text will implement the style definition applied to the <p> tag

```
p {
    color: red;
}
```
Selects all paragraph elements

CSS

Class selector
The dot (.) prefix indicates a class selector. Multiple elements in an HTML document can share the same class. A class selector is used to target a group of HTML elements that all have a certain "class" attribute value. For example, all elements that have the class "roundedCorners" will be styled.

```
<div class="roundedCorners"></div>
```
HTML This div will implement the "roundedCorner" style definition

```
.roundedCorners{
    border-radius: 20px;
}
```
Selects all elements with the class "roundedCorners"

CSS

GROUPING SELECTORS

If multiple elements are to have the same style, it is not necessary to define them separately. Selectors can be grouped together using a comma. All grouped selectors will have the same style applied to them.

```
h1, h2, h3{
        font-size: 24px;
}
```

<h1>, <h2>, and <h3> tags are grouped and will all have a font size of 24px

Id selector
This selector is used to target a single HTML element with a specified "id" attribute value and is indicated with hash (#) prefix. In an HTML document, an id should be applied to only one element per page.

```
<div id="header"></div>
```
HTML

This div will implement the "#header" style definition

```
#header{
        text-align: center;
}
```
CSS

Selects the single element with the id "header"

221B

Complex selectors
Selectors can also be combined to provide more specific definitions based on the relationships between the elements. You can combine the id, class, or tag type into a complex selector definition.

Child selector
This selector includes all the elements that are children of a particular element (see p.210). Use the greater than (>) symbol between the elements to indicate this selector. For example, `div > p`

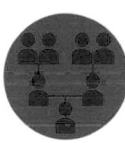

Descendant selector
Indicated by a space, this defines all elements that are descendants of a particular element. This is similar to the child selector, but will include children of the child element. For example, `div p`

General sibling selector
Defines all the elements that are siblings of a particular element. They will all have the same parent element. Use the tilde (~) symbol to indicate this selector. For example, `p ~ div`

Next sibling selector
Defines all the elements that are siblings of and follow on after a particular element. These selectors are indicated by a plus (+) symbol between them. For example, `div + p`

Multiple classes selector
Defines an element that must contain all the classes in the selector. The absence of a space between the class names indicates that all classes must be present. For example, `.roundedCorners.featureBox`

Combine id and class selector
This defines an element that must contain the id and all supplied classes. The absence of a space between the id and class name indicates that both must be present. For example, `#mainContent.minHeight`

CSS styling

CSS style definitions are used to set the background colour, font size, font family, borders, and other elements in a web page. Styles are said to cascade as they are inherited by child elements from the parent elements (the elements they are contained in).

  Styling colour ≡

CSS allows programmers to define the colour of elements on a website, including background colours, borders, and text. The most common colours can be set with a text value of the colour name. For example, white, red, or blue. All modern browsers support 140 HTML colour names. Any other colour value can be described in Hex, RGB, or RGBA format.

HTML COLOUR CODES	
Format	**Values for the colour blue**
Text	color : blue;
Hex full	color : #0000ff;
Hex shorthand	color : #00f;
RGB	color : rgb(0, 0, 255);
RGBA	color : rgba(0, 0, 255, 1);

```
color:rgba(0,0,255, 0.5);
```
RGBA format's alpha channel parameter describes the transparency of a colour

add text

 Font size options ≡

In CSS, font size can be defined in several different ways.
- **Pixels:** This defines the size of the font in pixels. The number is followed by the letters "px".
- **Size:** Keywords such as "large" or "small" are used to define the size of the font.
- **Relative size:** Defines a font size relative to the parent element's font size. Uses keywords such as "larger".
- **Percentage:** Defines size relative to the parent element's font size. For example, "200%" implies twice the parent font's size.
- **Em:** This method is also relative to the parent element's font size. For example, `2em = 2 x parent font-size = 200%`

CSS HELPS MAINTAIN THE DESIGN ACROSS A WEBSITE

Border styling

The CSS border properties allow programmers to specify the style, width, and colour of an element's border. These border styles can be defined in several different ways.

- Define border settings in one line
  ```
  border: 1px solid black;
  ```
- Define border settings in separate lines
  ```
  border-width: 1px;
  border-style: solid;
  border-color: black;
  ```
- Define different vertical and horizontal borders
  ```
  border-width: 1px 0px;
  ```
- Define different width for each side of the border
  ```
  border-width: 1px 0px 3px 2px;
  ```

Animation

The "transition" instruction in CSS allows programmers to create simple animations in modern browsers, such as a button changing size or colour when a mouse hovers over it. To do this, the property to be animated and the duration of the animation should be specified in the CSS file (see p.250).

Cascading styles

An HTML element can have multiple styles applied to it. Many HTML tags also inherit properties from the parent tags that contain them. The browser determines which style to apply based on the rules mentioned below.

Origin
Browsers have built-in default styles that they apply to HTML tags. These are known as user-agent styles. However, styles defined by the programmer, called author styles, will override these user-agent styles.

Importance
A style instruction that is marked with the "!important" declaration will be given priority over other instructions. It will always be applied to an element, regardless of the placement of the instruction in the CSS hierarchy.

Specificity
A style that has a more detailed selector will be applied before a style that is less specific. This means that the greater the number of elements in the selector, the higher the priority that the style will receive.

Instruction order
A style that is defined earlier in a CSS file will be overridden by a style that is defined later, and a style that is defined in the CSS file will be overridden by the styles defined inline by a "style" attribute in an HTML tag.

!IMPORTANT

The !important declaration is an easy way of instructing the browser to prioritize a style definition, but it should only be used as a last resort. It is preferable to make the selector more specific, by including additional classes or id values in the selection criteria. CSS will apply the definition with the most specific selector, avoiding the need to use the !important declaration.

Responsive layouts

A responsive website has a design that can adapt to display correctly on any size screen, from desktop monitors and laptops to smartphones and tablets. This is achieved by a clever combination of HTML, CSS, and JavaScript.

Viewport

The "viewport" declaration tells a browser that a website has a responsive layout. The declaration is placed alongside other metadata. The "content" attribute instructs the browser to set the page width the same as the screen width. It also sets the initial zoom level. These meta instructions allow the page elements to adjust to the maximum width of the screen and improves the user experience by displaying the correct styling and layout for any screen size. Without these instructions, the browser will zoom out to show the whole page, rather than allowing the page elements to reshape to the width of the screen.

MULTIPLE CSS FILES CAN BE **LINKED** TO AN **HTML** DOCUMENT TO MAKE A **RESPONSIVE WEB PAGE**

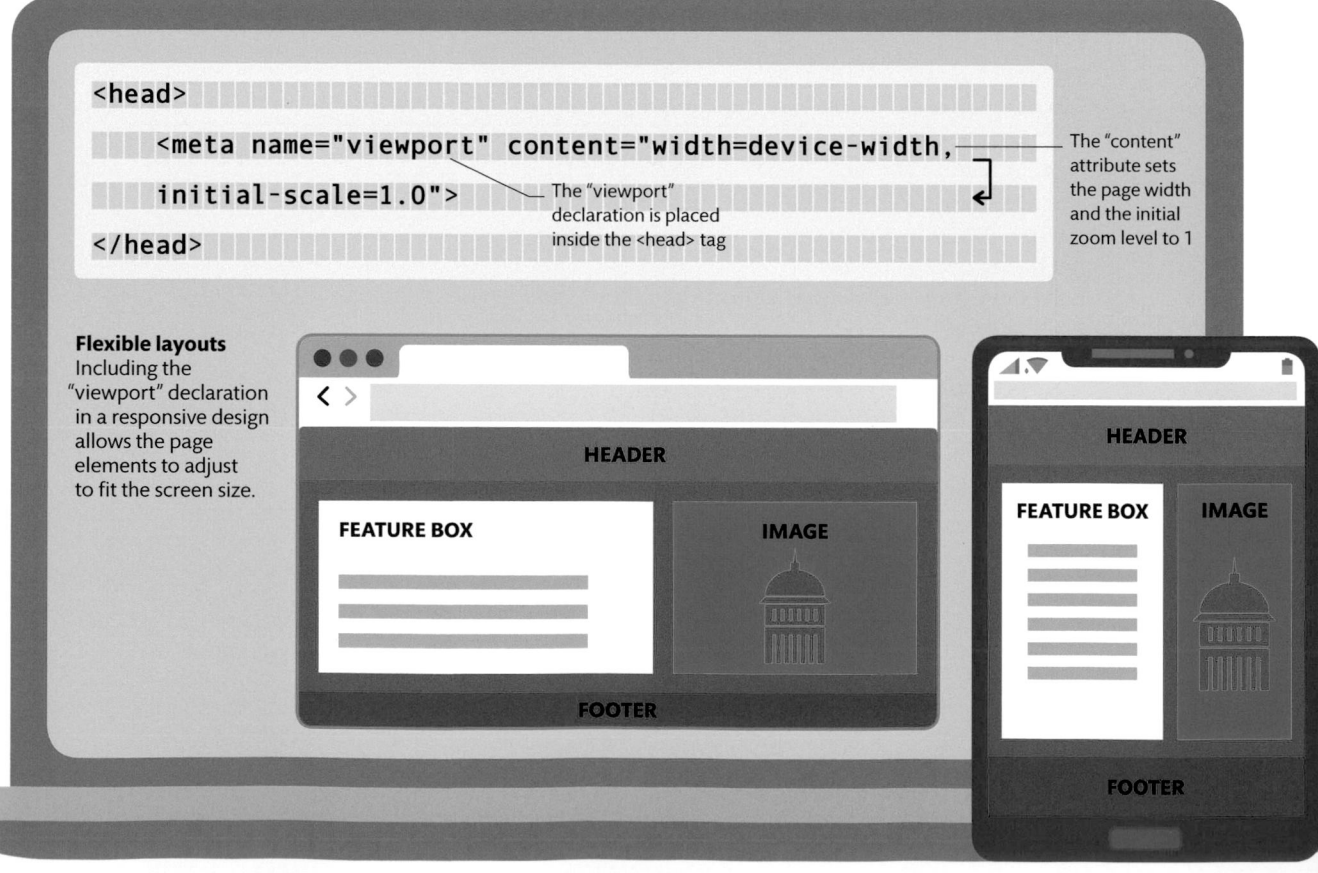

```
<head>

    <meta name="viewport" content="width=device-width,

    initial-scale=1.0">

</head>
```

The "viewport" declaration is placed inside the <head> tag

The "content" attribute sets the page width and the initial zoom level to 1

Flexible layouts
Including the "viewport" declaration in a responsive design allows the page elements to adjust to fit the screen size.

HEADER

FEATURE BOX

IMAGE

FOOTER

HEADER

FEATURE BOX

IMAGE

FOOTER

Why responsive?

When the Web was first created, almost all users viewed websites on a desktop monitor. Early websites were programmed to be viewed at a fixed width of 800px. This width was gradually increased over the years as the average user's screen size increased. The arrival of browsers on smartphones with narrow screens forced programmers to maintain multiple versions of their sites, each designed to display correctly on a different size of screen. Today, there are many different device sizes that can display web pages. The solution to this is to have a single flexible layout that can adjust to any screen size.

Media query

Media queries are used to switch between different layout styles, depending on the width of the page. This is the primary way to create responsive web pages that can scale to fit correctly on any screen size. For example, in the code below, the background colour of elements in the "specials" class will change depending on the width of the screen. The default background colour is red. If the screen is more than 993px wide then the background colour will be blue.

```
.specials {
    background-color: blue;
}


@media screen and (min-width: 993px)   {
    .specials {
        background-color: red;
    }
}
```

Defines the default background colour of the "specials" class

Sets the minimum screen width to 993px

Flexible styles
Media queries fine-tune the CSS styles, so that each element looks its best on any screen size.

HEADER

FEATURE BOX

IMAGE

SPECIALS

CONTACT

FOOTER

HEADER

FEATURE BOX

IMAGE

SPECIALS

CONTACT

FOOTER

Styling the web page

In this part of the project, styling will be applied to the framework created in HTML. CSS allows programmers to have much better control over the layout of their website. The look of the site can be kept consistent by using a single style sheet, which makes the maintenance of a website more efficient. This also saves time and makes it easy to update the design.

What the program does

Use the HTML elements of the web page created in Build a web page (see pp.216–33). You will use CSS to select and style these HTML elements individually in this second part of the project. Each element will be formatted according to its role and function, making the web page easier to navigate.

Project requirements

To add styling to your web page, you will need the HTML file and images folder from the first part of the project. You can continue using Visual Studio as the development environment.

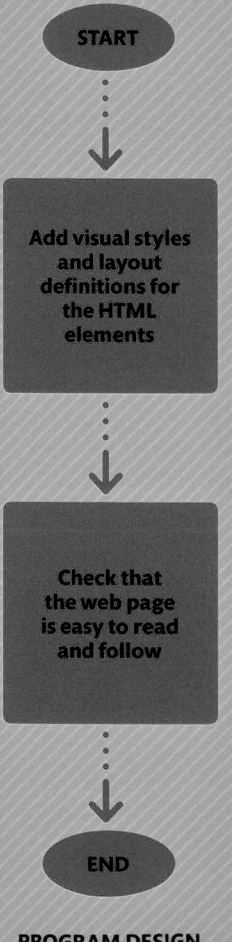

PROGRAM DESIGN

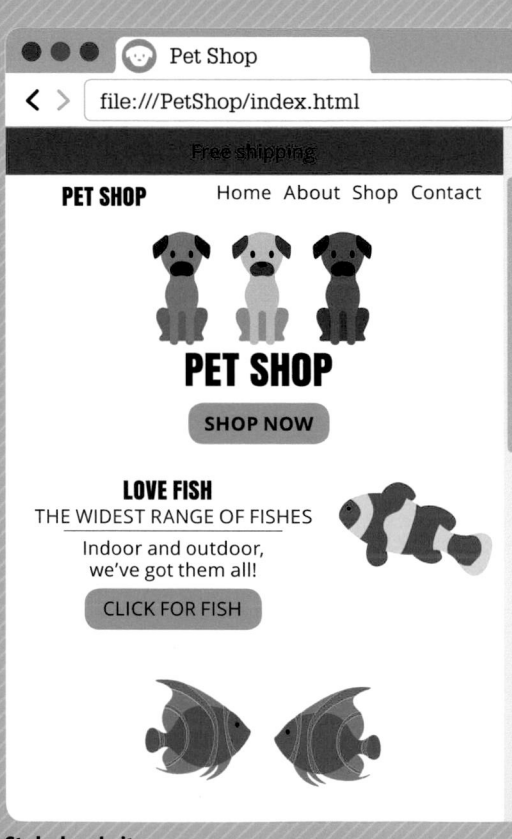

Styled website
The long vertical web page from the HTML part of this project will now appear styled, with clearly defined sections and formatted text and images. Adding CSS makes the web page more visual and individual.

HTML FILE

IMAGES FOLDER

DEVELOPMENT ENVIRONMENT

YOU WILL LEARN

> How to use CSS style sheets

> How to create buttons with rollovers

> How to add CSS animations and transitions

Time: 2–3 hours

Lines of code: 315

Difficulty level
● ○ ○ ○ ○

WHERE THIS IS USED

CSS is used in all modern websites where visual appearance is important. Using CSS, it is possible to give every element of a website a distinct style. A well-presented web page will encourage interaction with the user and will be easier to navigate as well.

1 Setting up

Before you can start styling the website, it is necessary to create a special CSS file to contain the code and link it to the HTML file previously created. The following steps will create a dedicated "styles" folder and the CSS file inside it.

1.1 CREATE A NEW FOLDER

You will first need to create a new folder in Visual Studio to contain the CSS style sheets. In Windows, right-click on the project name "PetShop" in Solution Explorer. Then, select Add and choose New Folder. Name this folder "styles". The full path to this folder should be "C:\PetShop\styles".

On a Mac, open Finder and create a new folder called "styles" inside the website folder "PetShop". The full path should be "Users/[user account name]/PetShop/styles". Then, open Visual Studio, right-click on the project name "PetShop", select Add, and then choose Add Solution Folder.

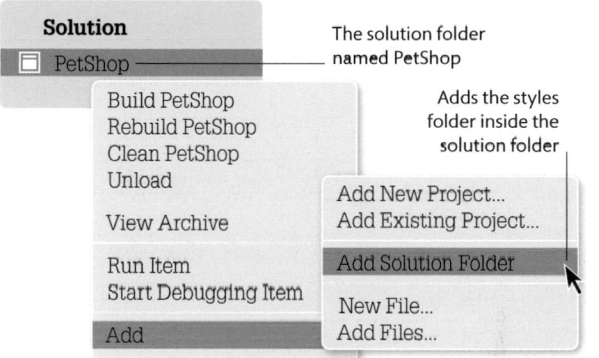

The solution folder named PetShop

Adds the styles folder inside the solution folder

1.2 ADD A CSS FILE

The next step is to create a new CSS file inside the styles folder. Make sure to name the CSS file "global.css". In Windows, the full path to the CSS file should be "C:\PetShop\styles\global.css". On a Mac, the full path to the file should be "Users/[user account name]/PetShop/styles/global.css". The website folder PetShop should now contain the images folder, the styles folder, and the HTML file.

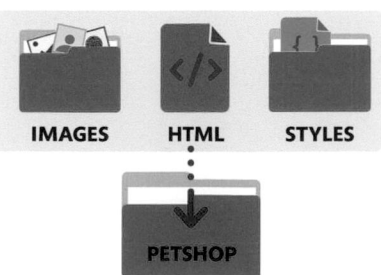

IMAGES   HTML   STYLES

PETSHOP

LOCATING FOLDERS ● ● ●

In Windows, if you would like to see where a folder has been created from inside Visual Studio, go to the "Solution Explorer" window, right-click on the folder you want to locate and select Open Folder in File Explorer. This will open an instance of File Explorer at the location of the folder.

On a Mac, to see the location of a folder from inside Visual Studio, go to the "Solution Explorer" window, command-click on the folder you would like to locate and select Reveal in Finder. This will open an instance of Finder at the folder's location.

1.3 REFERENCE THE CSS FILE

It is necessary to link the newly created CSS file to the HTML document so that the styles can be applied to all its elements. This reference to "global.css" file must be made using a <link> tag within the <head> tag of the "index.html" file. The fonts for this web page will be selected from the options available in Google Fonts. To do this, you will link the Google Fonts website to "index.html", and specify the fonts you want to use. The fonts Anton and Open Sans are used here, but you can pick any other font you like.

HTML

```
<head>

    <meta charset="utf-8" />

    <title>Pet Shop</title>

    <link rel="icon" type="image/png" href="images/favicon.png">

    <link href="styles/global.css" rel="stylesheet" />

    <link href="https://fonts.googleapis.com/css?

    family=Anton|Open+Sans" rel="stylesheet">

</head>
```

Title to be displayed in the browser tab

Link to the custom "global.css" file where all the styles are defined

Link to the CSS style sheets for the Google fonts

1.4 ADD COMMENTS

At the top of the "global.css" style sheet, add a comment with the names of the fonts and the list of colours to be used in the website. Add this information inside a comment block "/* */". Anything inside a comment block will be ignored by the browser. These comments are only included to help the programmer standardize the style of the website and provide an easy reference. Notice that the "font-family" definition contains the name of the primary font being employed, and a secondary font type to use if the first font is not available. You can also choose a different colour scheme for your website if you like.

CSS

```
/*

    font-family: "Anton", cursive;

    font-family: "Open Sans", sans-serif;


    Text color : #333;

    Dark blue : #345995;

    Light blue : #4392F1;

    Red : #D7263D;

    Yellow : #EAC435;

    Orange : #F46036;

*/
```

This font will be used for headings and other prominent text elements

This font will be used for normal paragraph text elements

Hex codes for the colours to be used

2 **Styling the page elements**
Now that the CSS file is ready to contain all the style definitions, you can start by adding the styles that affect elements throughout the page. The next few steps will show you how to do this.

2.1 **DEFINE THE HEADERS**
Start by defining the "h1" and "h2" headers used throughout the website. The styles specified here will be applied to each instance of the two headers. Both headers will be styled the same, but with a separate font-size definition.

The "font-family" property defines the preferred font to use and the fallback font type in case the preferred font is not available

Only "h1" headers will have the font size 110px

Only "h2" headers will have the font size 30px

```
body {

}

h1, h2 {

    margin: 0;

    padding: 0;

    font-family: "Anton", cursive;

    font-weight: normal;

}

h1 {

    font-size: 110px;

}

h2 {

    font-size: 30px;

}
```

The <body> tag appears by default

Applies the style definition to all "h1" and "h2" headers on the web page

The headers will use the Anton cursive font

MARGIN AND PADDING

Margin is the space measured from the border, outside of the element. Padding is the space measured from the border, inside the element. There are different ways to describe the margin and padding styles.

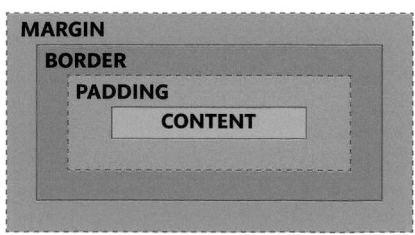

STRUCTURE OF MARGIN AND PADDING IN A WEBSITE

MARGIN STYLES	
Code	**Output**
margin: 40px;	40px on top, bottom, left and right
margin: 20px 40px;	20px on top and bottom 40px on left and right
margin: 10px 20px 30px 40px;	10px on top, 20px on right 30px on bottom, 40px on left
margin: 0 auto;	0 on top and bottom and equal space on the left and right (same as centre align)

STYLING THE PAGE ELEMENTS

Page elements
Every website is made up of various elements serving different purposes. CSS can add unique styles to every element.

2.2 ADD VERTICAL SPACERS
Each section of the web page can be separated with white space to make a website easy to follow. These white spaces are created through standardized vertical spacers throughout this website. In CSS, you can use compound style signatures to associate the required style definitions.

```
.spacer.v20 {
        height: 20px;
}
.spacer.v40 {
        height: 40px;
}
.spacer.v80 {
        height: 80px;
}
```

Compound style signature with the classes "spacer" and "v20"

The height will be 40px if the tag has both "spacer" and "v40" classes

The height will be 80px if the tag has both "spacer" and "v80" classes

2.3 ADDING ELEMENTS ON NEW LINES
Now create a style for "clear". This is required if the previous element does not have a fixed height or is set to float to one side. The "clear" property is used with values such as "left", "right", or "both". It prevents floating objects from appearing on the specified side of the element to which "clear" is applied.

```
.clear {
        clear: both;
}
```

Selects all the elements with the class "clear"

This instruction will place the next HTML element on a new line

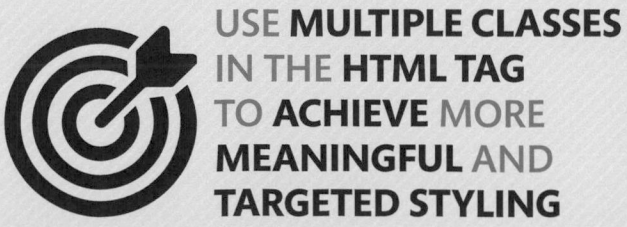

USE **MULTIPLE CLASSES** IN THE **HTML TAG** TO **ACHIEVE** MORE **MEANINGFUL** AND **TARGETED STYLING**

2.4 STYLE THE BODY TAG

Add the style definitions for the <body> tag from step 2.1. The style signature is "body". The style definition will set the values for the margin, padding, font, background colour, and font colour.

```
body {
    margin: 0;
    padding: 0;
    font-family: "Open Sans",
    sans-serif;
    font-size: 15px;
    background-color: white;
    color: #333;
}
```

No space between the browser window and the web page

The default font size for all the text on the web page

The background colour for the web page

Hex code for dark grey, the font colour for the body text

3 Styling the individual elements

In this section, you can add styles to the individual HTML elements from the top of the web page down to the bottom. Each section can be seen as a horizontal layer, with its own visual style and spacing requirements. Start by adding styles to the first element on the web page – the promo bar.

3.1 DEFINE STYLE SIGNATURES

The Promotional Messages, Subscribe, and Footer sections share some of the same style definitions. They all need to be centre aligned, with white text, and a minimum width of 1000px. Add this code below the code added In step 2.3 to give all three style signatures the same definition.

```
    clear: both;
}
#promo,
#subscribe,
#footer {
    text-align: center;
    color: #fff;
    min-width: 1000px;
}
```

The selectors apply the same style definition

Hex code for the colour white

The elements must be at least 1000px wide

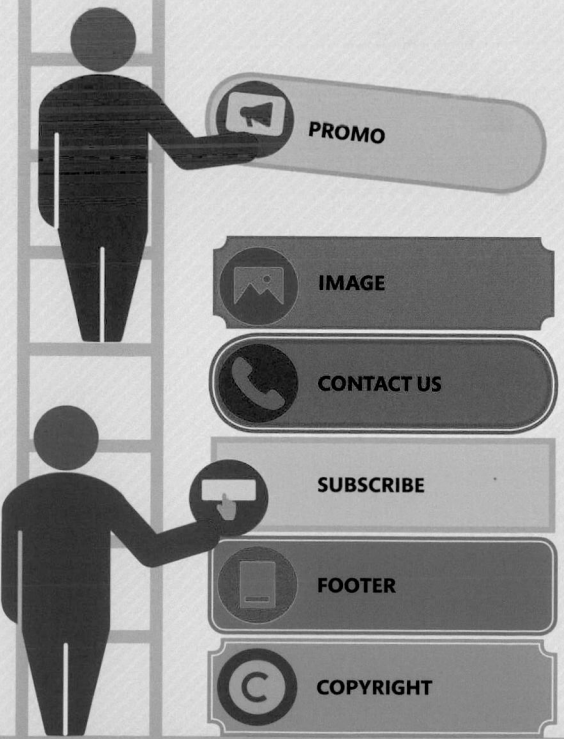

PROMO

IMAGE

CONTACT US

SUBSCRIBE

FOOTER

COPYRIGHT

3.2 BACKGROUND COLOUR FOR PROMO

Next, you will add a background colour to the Promotional Messages section to make it more visible on the web page. This style only applies to the promo section.

```
#promo {
    background-color: #F46036;
}
```

Hex code for orange in the colour scheme

3.3 ADD PADDING TO THE PROMO DIV

Add padding around the text in the Promotional Messages to introduce some space from the border. The style will be applied to all the promotional messages contained within the "promo" div.

```
#promo > div {
    padding: 15px;
}
```

Selects all <div> tags within the <promo> tag

The space between the <div> border and its text content

SAVE

3.4 VIEW THE PAGE

View the page by opening a browser and entering the url into the address bar. In Windows, the url to the file on your local computer will be "file:///C:/PetShop/index.html". On a Mac, the url will be "file:///Users/[user account name]/PetShop/index.html". If the page does not update in the browser when you refresh, the browser may have cached a previous version of the site. Empty the browser cache by going to the history settings and selecting "Clear browsing data". This will force the browser to get the latest files.

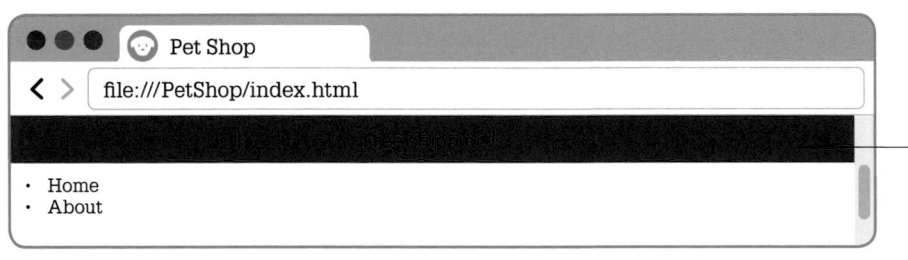

Pet Shop

file:///PetShop/index.html

- Home
- About

The promotional messages will now be displayed with the styles applied

3.5 DEFINE THE WRAP CLASS

Add style definitions for the "wrap" class created in HTML. Most of the website's information is contained in this class. The "wrap" div has a fixed width of 1000px. The horizontal margins adjust automatically to keep the <div> in the centre of the screen if the screen width is more than 1000px wide.

```
    color: #333;
}

.wrap {
    margin: 0 auto;
    padding: 0;
    width: 1000px;
}
```

Add this after the code from step 2.4

Aligns the "wrap" element to the centre of the page

TOP MENU

HOME   ABOUT   SHOP   CONTACT

3.6 DEFINE THE TOP MENU

Now add the style definitions for the Top Menu section. This panel will run across the full screen and will contain the menu items and logo. Set a fixed height for the menu and add padding in all directions for the list of menu items contained in the panel.

```
        padding: 15px;

}

#topMenu {          Add this after the
                    code from step 3.3
    height: 60px;

}

#topLinks {

    float: right;

    padding-top: 20px;

}
```

Space between the "topLinks" border and the list it contains

3.7 DEFINE HORIZONTAL MENU LISTS

The menu lists in both Top Menu and the Footer are horizontal, so you can give them the same style definitions. The menu items should align left within their container lists, so that they appear in a horizontal line with the first item on the left.

The two selectors share the same style definition

No bullet points will be added to the list items

```
#topLinks ul,

#footer ul {

        list-style-type: none;

        margin: 0;

        padding: 0;

        overflow: hidden;

}                           Hides content that
                            overflows the
#topLinks li {              element's dimensions

        float: left;        The element
                            floats to the left
}                           of its container
```

3.8 STYLE THE HYPERLINKS

The hyperlinks in the Top Menu will have one style for their normal state and a different style for when the mouse is hovering over them. The keyword ":hover" is a pseudo-class and instructs the browser to apply that style when the mouse is over the element. Add a "transition" instruction in both style definitions to make the mouse-over effect smoother. Here, three versions of the "transition" instruction have been included, each one intended for a different browser. Including multiple instructions for different browsers is not very common, but is required occasionally.

```
#topLinks li a {

        color: #333;

        text-align: center;         Centre aligns the
                                    hyperlink contents
        padding: 16px;
                                    No underline beneath
        text-decoration: none;      the hyperlink

        -webkit-transition: all 250ms ease-out;     Transition effect
                                                     when a mouse moves
                                                     off the hyperlink
        -ms-transition: all 250ms ease-out;         Transition definition
                                                     required by older
        transition: all 250ms ease-out;             Microsoft browsers,
                                                     such as Internet Explorer
}
```

Transition instruction for Google Chrome browser

```
#topLinks li a:hover {
        color: #4392F1;
        -webkit-transition: all 250ms ease-out;
        -ms-transition: all 250ms ease-out;
        transition: all 250ms ease-out;
        text-decoration: underline;
    }
```

Hex code for the colour blue

Transition effect when a mouse moves over the hyperlink

Underlines the hyperlink when a mouse hovers over it

TRANSITIONS

All major web browsers use different names for the "transition" property, so your CSS style definitions must include all three versions of the "transition" instruction to ensure that the transition effect renders correctly on the browsers. When a browser is implementing the CSS style definition, it will ignore the instructions intended for other browsers and apply the instructions it understands. A warning message about the invalid CSS properties may appear, but these can safely be ignored.

3.9 **STYLE THE LOGO**
The next step is to style the logo in the Top Menu. The logo is used three times on the page (in the Top Menu, the Banner, and the Footer), so you can encapsulate the logo font styles in its own class called "logo". The small logo in the Top Menu is a hyperlink back to the home page, so you will need to define both its normal and hover state.

```
#topMenu .logo {
        float: left;
        padding-top: 13px;
        font-size: 24px;
        color: #333;
        text-decoration: none;
}

        #topMenu .logo:hover {
                color: #4392F1;
        }

.logo {
        font-family: "Anton", cursive;
}
```

Places the logo on the left of the "topLinks" element

Sets the font size to 24px

No underline on the logo hyperlink

This will make the logo appear blue when the mouse hovers over it

The default font for the logo

LOGO STYLES

PET SHOP

PET SHOP

SAVE

3.10 VIEW THE WEBSITE

Save the code and then refresh the page in the browser. The Top Menu section will now be laid out with the small logo on the left and the hyperlinks on the right.

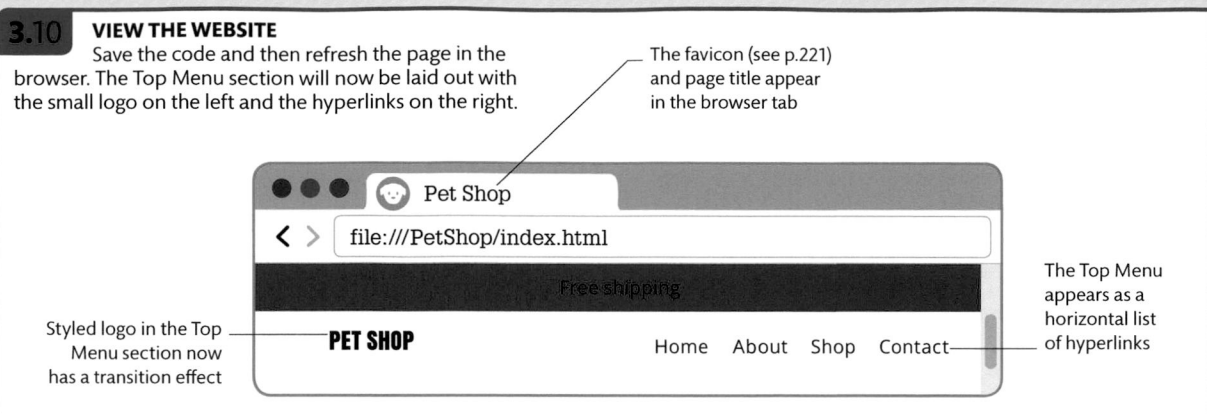

The favicon (see p.221) and page title appear in the browser tab

Styled logo in the Top Menu section now has a transition effect

The Top Menu appears as a horizontal list of hyperlinks

3.11 STYLE THE BANNER

The next section to be styled is the Banner, which will contain the name of the website and an image. First, set the styles for the "banner" div by defining its width, height, and alignment. It should include a background image as well.

Link to the background image for the banner

```
#banner {
    background-image: url("../images/banner.jpg");
    background-repeat: no-repeat;
    background-position: center top;
    width: 100%;
    text-align: center;
    padding-top: 300px;
    color: #333;
}
```

The background image should not repeat vertically or horizontally

Centre aligns the contents of the banner

Hex code for dark grey text

Space between the top border of the banner and the text inside

3.12 STYLE THE BANNER LOGO

Now you can add styles for the logo appearing inside the Banner section. In the HTML document, the logo appearing in the Banner section also has an <h1> tag. So this logo will receive style instructions from both "h1" and "logo" style definitions.

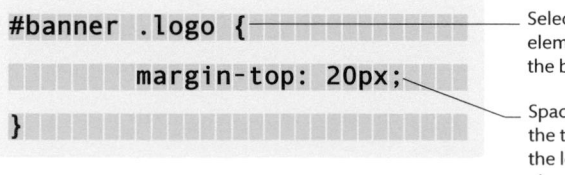

```
#banner .logo {
    margin-top: 20px;
}
```

Selects the "logo" elements inside the banner

Space between the top border of the logo and the element above it

3.13 **ADD STYLES TO THE HYPERLINK**
The next step is to add styles for the "action" div and the "Shop Now" hyperlink. This link style definition will also contain the "transition" instructions to animate the change in styles between the normal and mouse-over states.

```css
#banner #action {
        font-weight: bold;
        width: 200px;
        margin: 20px auto 0 auto;
}


        #banner #action a {
            -webkit-transition: all 250ms ease-out;
            -ms-transition: all 250ms ease-out;
            transition: all 250ms ease-out;
            padding: 20px;
            color: white;
            text-decoration: none;
            border-radius: 30px;
            background-color: #4392F1;
        }


        #banner #action a:hover {
            -webkit-transition: all 250ms ease-out;
            -ms-transition: all 250ms ease-out;
            transition: all 250ms ease-out;
            background-color: #F46036;
            padding: 20px 40px;
        }
```

Style definitions for the div that contains the hyperlink

Three versions of the transition instruction

Hex code for light blue

Transition effect when a mouse moves over the hyperlink

The horizontal padding will increase to 40px when a mouse hovers over the button

Hex code for the colour orange

⬇ **SAVE**

3.14 VIEW THE WEBSITE

Refresh and view the page in the browser. You can now see the background image in the Banner, and the animated rollover effect on the "Shop Now" link.

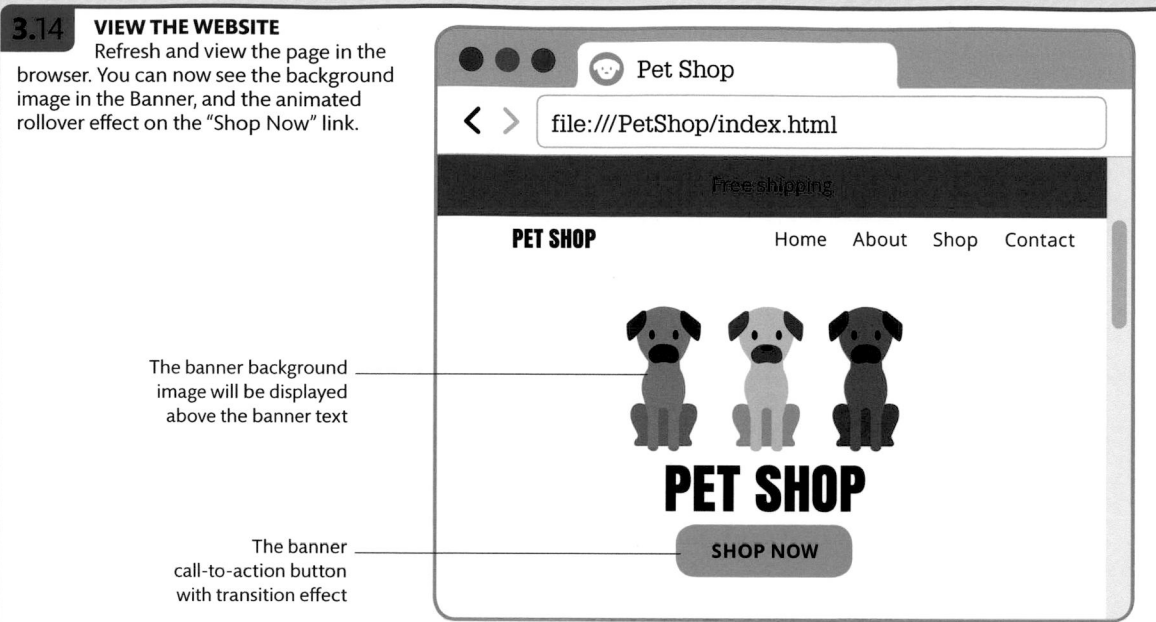

The banner background image will be displayed above the banner text

The banner call-to-action button with transition effect

---

4 Feature box styling

This section will add styles for the "feature box" control, which splits the page into a left column and a right column. The styles for the control are defined as classes and are applied to multiple elements on the web page. The class definitions also allow alternating the position of the images on the page.

4.1 DEFINE THE LEFT COLUMN

First, you will define the left column of the feature box. This will take up half of the space available. By default, every new div occupies a new line. However, since this element must float left, the next element (the right column) will appear on the same line.

Selects all the elements that have both the "feature" and "leftColumn" classes

```
.feature .leftColumn {
    width: 50%;
    float: left;
    text-align: center;
}
```

The width of the left column is set at 50% of the container's width

Aligns the contents to the centre of the left column

4.2 DEFINE THE RIGHT COLUMN

Add the code below to define the right column. This definition instructs the browser to include a margin on the left of the space available, where the left column will sit.

Selects all the elements that have both the "feature" and "rightColumn" classes

```
.feature .rightColumn {
    margin-left: 50%;
    width: 50%;
    text-align: center;
}
```

Aligns the contents to the centre of the right column

4.3 STYLE THE NON-PICTURE ELEMENTS

Now set styles to define the non-picture side of the feature box. In HTML, you used a div with class="text" (see p.225) to indicate the non-picture elements. You can now define the left and the right text columns with the same definition.

```css
.feature .leftColumn .text,
.feature .rightColumn .text {
        padding: 80px 20px 20px 20px;
        min-height: 260px;
}
```

Selectors for the "text" divs in the left and right columns

4.4 DEFINE THE NORMAL AND MOUSE-OVER STATE

Add this code to define the normal and mouse-over state for the hyperlinks that appear in the "text" divs. Similar to the Shop Now button that you styled earlier, this will also be styled as a button that changes colour when the mouse hovers over it.

Selectors for the <a> tags in the "text" div in the left and right columns

"ease-out" defines the speed of the transition effect

```css
.feature .leftColumn .text a,
.feature .rightColumn .text a {
        -webkit-transition: all 250ms ease-out;
        -ms-transition: all 250ms ease-out;
        transition: all 250ms ease-out;
        padding: 20px;
        background-color: #4392F1;
        color: white;
        text-decoration: none;
        border-radius: 30px;
}
        .feature .leftColumn .text a:hover,
        .feature .rightColumn .text a:hover {
            -webkit-transition: all 250ms ease-out;
            -ms-transition: all 250ms ease-out;
            transition: all 250ms ease-out;
            background-color: #F46036;
            text-decoration: none;
            padding: 20px 40px;
        }
```

Transition effect when a mouse moves off the hyperlink

Sets rounded corners for the border of the hyperlink

Transition effect when a mouse moves over the hyperlink

The text is not underlined when the mouse hovers over the hyperlink

4.5 DEFINE THE HORIZONTAL RULE

You will also need to add a style definition for the horizontal rule appearing in the feature box. This rule will separate the heading of the column from the text below it.

Sets the colour for the horizontal rule to dark grey

Sets the width of the horizontal rule

```
.feature hr {
    background-color: #333;
    height: 1px;
    border: 0;
    width: 50px;
}
```

4.6 DEFINE THE IMAGES

Now that you have styled the text columns, it is time to define how the images in the "featureImage" div will be styled.

Selects all <img> tags inside the "featureImage" div

Resizes the image width to 500px. The height will adjust automatically

```
.featureImage img {
    width: 500px;
}
```

SAVE

4.7 VIEW THE STYLE DEFINITIONS

Refresh the browser to see the new style definitions being applied to the web page. All the feature boxes will now have the correct styling, with images alternately appearing on the left and right.

The image will appear in the right column with the correct width

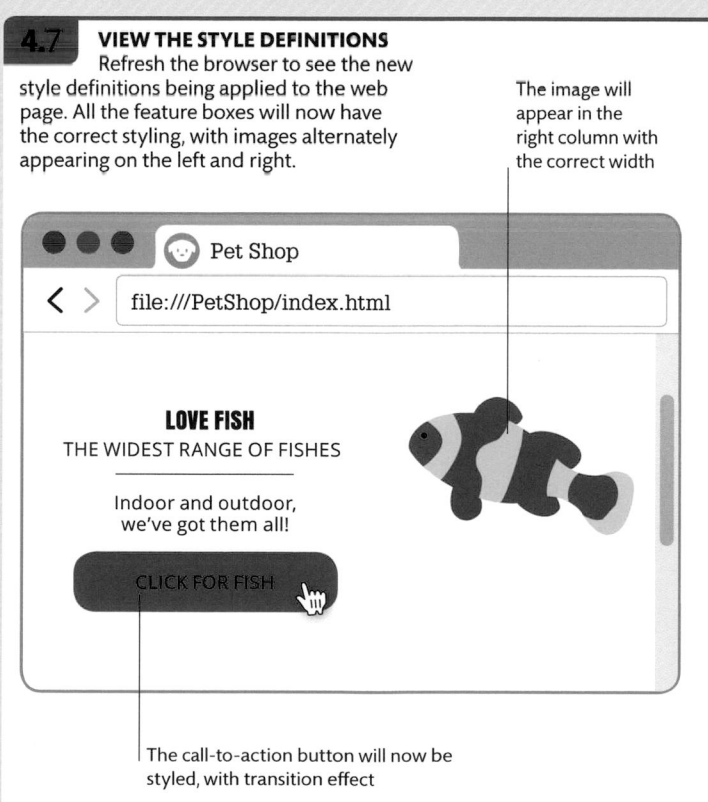

Pet Shop

file:///PetShop/index.html

LOVE FISH
THE WIDEST RANGE OF FISHES

Indoor and outdoor, we've got them all!

CLICK FOR FISH

The call-to-action button will now be styled, with transition effect

BROWSER TEST

New CSS features are constantly being added to browsers. However, there is no point using these features unless you are sure that your website users will be able to take advantage of them. Old browsers will ignore modern CSS instructions and the styling of the HTML document will not conform to the expected layout. Fortunately, all modern browsers accept CSS3, though there may be small differences in the way they process some instructions. It is advisable always to test your web page in several different browsers to find the set of functionality that they all have in common.

4.8 ADD STYLE TO EMAIL HYPERLINK

In the "index.html" file the "feature" class is used not only to advertize the three product categories, but also for the Contact Us section appearing further down. In this step, you will use the "feature" layout definitions to style the Contact Us section, which includes a hyperlink that opens a new email in the user's email program.

```css
.feature .leftColumn .text a.emailLink,
.feature .rightColumn .text a.emailLink {
        color: white;
        text-decoration: none;
        transition: none;
        padding: 10px;
        border: 0;
        background-color: #4392F1;
}
        .feature .leftColumn .text a.emailLink:hover,
        .feature .rightColumn .text a.emailLink:hover {
                -webkit-transition: all 250ms ease-out;
                -ms-transition: all 250ms ease-out;
                transition: all 250ms ease-out;
                background-color: #F46036;
        }
```

Selects the "emailLink" hyperlinks in both the left and right columns

The ":hover" pseudo-class selects the hyperlinks when a mouse hovers over them

Hex code for the colour orange

4.9 DEFINE MIDDLE IMAGES

The next section that needs to be defined are the images that sit in the middle of the page. The "middleImage" div containers must align their contents to the centre of the div, to make them appear in the middle of the page. The <img> tags should also display the images with a consistent maximum width.

```css
.middleImage {
    text-align: center;
}


    .middleImage img {
        max-width: 1000px;
    }
```

Aligns the "middleImage" contents to the centre of the page

Selects all <img> tags inside divs with the "middleImage" class

SAVE

4.10 VIEW THE IMAGES
Save the code and then refresh the browser in order to see the updated web page. The image will now appear centre aligned on the page, just below the feature box.

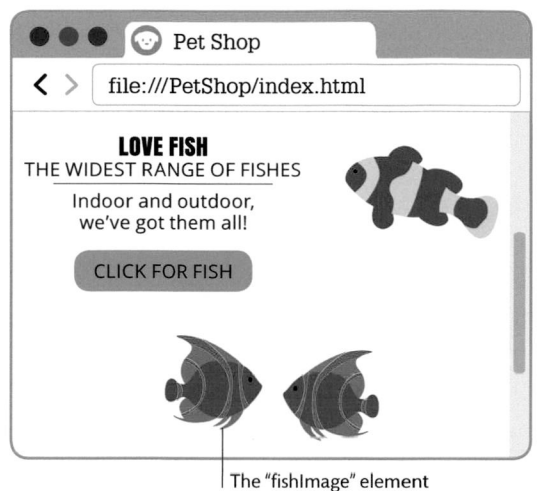

The "fishImage" element will be centre aligned

4.11 CHECK THE IMAGE STYLING
You will notice that the other instances of the "feature" and "middleImage" divs are all styled correctly throughout the page. This is because you defined those styles as classes, so they can be used multiple times on the same page.

The "dogImage" element will be centre aligned

5 Styling the remaining elements
Now that you have defined the styles for the main elements of the web page, you can continue adding style definitions for the remaining sections. In the next few steps, you will style the scroll button, the map, the subscribe section, and the footer.

5.1 STYLE THE SCROLL BUTTON
Now you need to add style definitions to the "Scroll to top" button. The button should have 50 per cent opacity in its normal state, and should display at 100 per cent opacity when the mouse hovers over it. The "Scroll to top" button should be set to invisible when the page opens. The button will be activated in the third part of this project, using JavaScript (see pp.292–95).

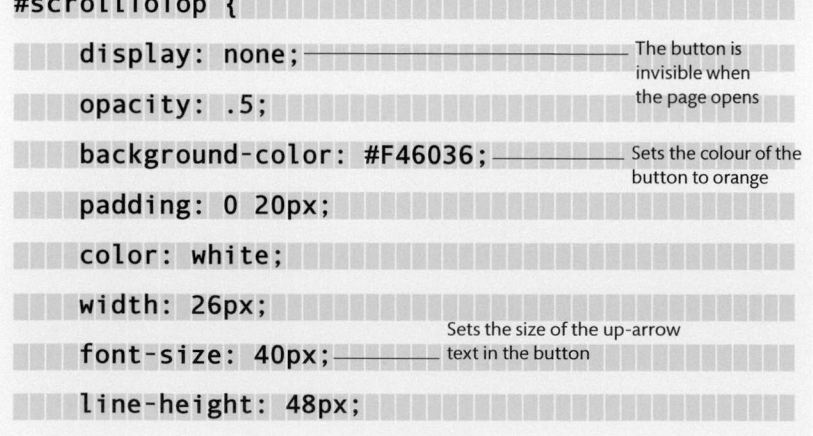

```
#scrollToTop {
    display: none;          The button is
                            invisible when
    opacity: .5;            the page opens

    background-color: #F46036;   Sets the colour of the
                                 button to orange
    padding: 0 20px;

    color: white;

    width: 26px;

    font-size: 40px;        Sets the size of the up-arrow
                            text in the button
    line-height: 48px;
```

```
        position: fixed;
        right: 10px;
        bottom: 10px;
        border: 1px solid white;
        border-radius: 30px;
}
#scrollToTop:hover {
        opacity: 1;
        -webkit-transition: all 250ms linear;
        -ms-transition: all 250ms linear;
        transition: all 250ms linear;
        cursor: pointer;
    }
```

The button stays in a fixed position in the bottom-right corner of the page

A white border around the orange button makes it easier to see

The hover state is active when a mouse moves over the button

The cursor is displayed as a pointer

5.2 STYLE THE CONTACT US SECTION

The next section of the page that needs styling is Contact Us. The "feature" div has previously defined its two columns. The left column contains the text elements while the right has an embedded map from Google Maps. You will need to add an instruction to format the map's "iframe" element correctly. Then, save the code and refresh the browser to check if the section is displaying correctly.

The map width will be **100%** of the space available in the right column

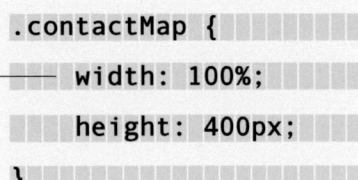

```
.contactMap {
        width: 100%;
        height: 400px;
}
```

SAVE

The email call-to-action button, styled in step 4.8

A dot on the Google map shows the exact location of the address

5.3 STYLE THE SUBSCRIBE SECTION

The next element to be styled is the Subscribe section. This will appear below the Contact Us section on the web page. Add this code to set the style definitions for the Subscribe panel and the heading appearing inside it.

```css
#subscribe {
    background-color: #4392F1;
    height: 160px;
    padding-top: 40px;
}

    #subscribe h2 {
        margin: 15px 0 20px 0;
        color: white;
        font-size: 24px;
        font-family: "Open Sans", sans-serif;
        font-weight: bold;
    }
```

Hex code for light blue. Sets the background colour of the Subscribe section

Distance between the text and the top border of the Subscribe panel

Sets the text to white

Specifies the font used for the "h2" headers

5.4 STYLE THE INPUT FIELD

The Subscribe section has a text field where users can enter their email address. Add styles for this text input field to define its size and appearance, as well as the style of the placeholder text that will appear inside it.

Ensures that only text fields are selected

```css
#subscribe input[type=text] {
    border: 0;
    width: 250px;
    height: 28px;
    font-size: 14px;
    padding: 0 10px;
    border-radius: 30px;
}
```

No border around the email address text input box

Adds space to the sides of the text input box

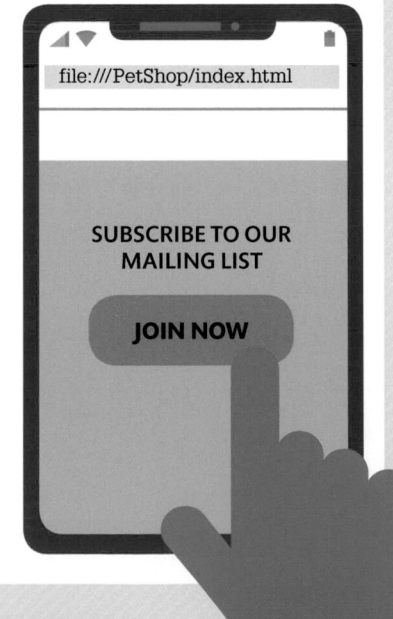

file:///PetShop/index.html

SUBSCRIBE TO OUR
MAILING LIST

JOIN NOW

5.5 **STYLE THE SUBSCRIBE BUTTON**
Add the code below to define styles for the
"subscribe" <input> button and its hover state. The button
will implement a transition on the "background-color"
from dark blue to orange when a mouse moves over it,
and then back to dark blue when the mouse moves off it.

Selects the input button
in the "subscribe" div

```css
#subscribe input[type=submit] {
        border: 0;
        width: 80px;
        height: 30px;
        font-size: 14px;
        background-color: #345995;
        color: white;
        border-radius: 30px;
        -webkit-transition: all 500ms ease-out;
        -ms-transition: all 500ms ease-out;
        transition: all 500ms ease-out;
        cursor: pointer;
}

        #subscribe input[type=submit]:hover {
        background-color: #F46036;
            -webkit-transition: all 250ms ease-out;
            -ms-transition: all 250ms ease-out;
            transition: all 250ms ease-out;

        }
```

Sets the button
width to 80px

Hex code for the
colour dark blue

Transition
instructions

The cursor will be
displayed as a pointer
when the mouse is
over the button

Hex code for orange
in the colour scheme

Repeat the transition
instructions for the
mouse-over effect

SAVE

5.6 VIEW THE WEBSITE

Save the code and refresh the browser to view the updated web page. Ensure that the panel is appearing below the Contact Us section and rendering correctly.

The text is aligned to the centre of the left column

A placeholder text hint inside the email text input box

The button with rounded borders and transition effect will be displayed

5.7 STYLE THE FOOTER

You can now style the footer for the web page. Start by adding styles for the "footer" div, and then add styles for the unordered list and the list items containing the links.

Sets a fixed height for the Footer section

Does not show bullet points in the unordered list

No space between the list border and the list items

Displays as an inline-block element to allow padding and margin

Places the list items next to one another from the left

```css
#footer {
    background-color: #F46036;
    height: 80px;
}

#footer ul {
    list-style-type: none;
    margin: 28px 0 0 0;
    padding: 0;
    overflow: hidden;
    display: inline-block;
}


    #footer li {
        float: left;
    }
```

5.8 **ADD STYLES TO THE FOOTER HYPERLINKS**
Next, you will need to add styles for the hyperlinks that appear within the Footer section. When the mouse hovers over them, the colour of the text will change from white to black.

Styles will be applied to all anchor tags that are inside list items within the "footer" div

```
#footer li a {
        color: white;
        text-align: center;
        padding: 20px;
        text-decoration: none;
        font-size: 18px;
        -webkit-transition: all 250ms linear;
        -ms-transition: all 250ms linear;
        transition: all 250ms linear;
}

        #footer li a:hover {
            color: #333;
            -webkit-transition: all 250ms linear;
            -ms-transition: all 250ms linear;
            transition: all 250ms linear;
        }
```

The footer hyperlink text will appear in white

The hyperlink text will not be underlined

The text colour of the footer hyperlink will change to dark grey

STORE FINDER

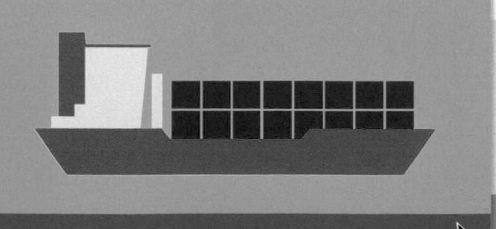

SHIPPING

FAQ

5.9 **STYLE THE COPYRIGHT SECTION**
The last element to style is the Copyright section.
In this step you will add styles for the "copyright" div and the logo
it contains. Add this code and then refresh the browser to check
if the Footer and Copyright sections are displaying correctly.

Aligns the "copyright"
contents to the centre
of the page

Selects the tag
with the id
"copyright"

```
#copyright {
    text-align: center;
    background-color: #345995;
    color: white;
    height: 40px;
    padding-top: 18px;
    font-size: 16px;
}

    #copyright .logo {
        font-family: "Open Sans", sans-serif;
        font-weight: bold;
    }
```

The "copyright" text
will appear in white

Space between the
top border of the
"copyright" section
and its text

Selects the tag with
class "logo" inside the
tag with id "copyright"

Overrides the
default style
definiton for
"**logo**" with a
sans-serif font

SAVE

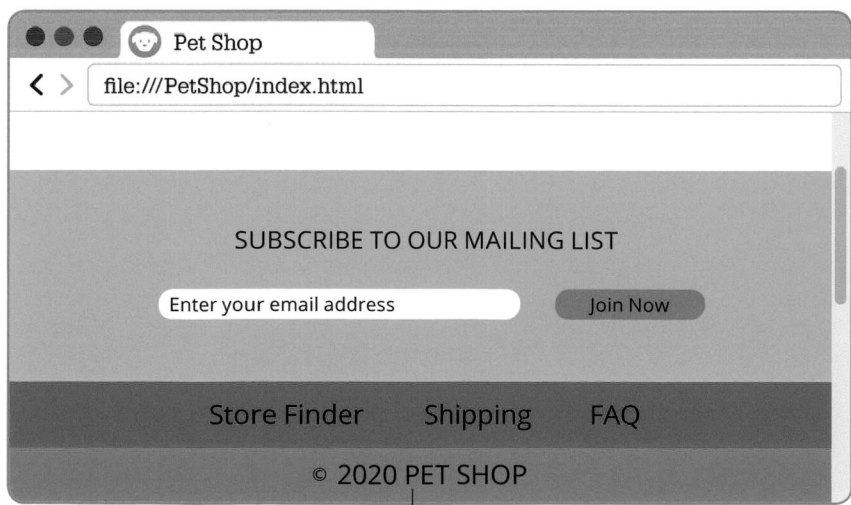

The copyright text appears in the
centre of the page with an HTML
entity for the copyright symbol

What is JavaScript?

JavaScript is one of the most popular modern programming languages for the Web. It is an object-oriented language that is used to enhance HTML pages by adding dynamic and interactive elements to websites. Programs written in JavaScript are called scripts.

Why JavaScript?

JavaScript was invented to implement client-side behaviour in web browsers. Today, however, it is used in many kinds of software and server-side web applications. For example, developers can use a cross-platform run time environment like Node.js (see p.284) to run scripts outside of the browser. This allows for a wide variety of server-side applications, such as generating dynamic HTML pages and sending responses from a Node web server.

Using JavaScript online

All modern web browsers can read and run JavaScript when rendering an HTML page. JavaScript code is interpreted and run by the browser in real time, and does not need to be compiled before it is executed.

The program within a browser that executes a script is called the JavaScript Engine. This engine is an interpreter that first reads the script and converts it into machine code, and then executes the machine code.

On an HTML page

To use JavaScript on an HTML page, simply enclose the script in a <script> tag. This tag can be placed either within the <head> tag or the <body> tag, depending on when the script is run – before, during, or after the HTML.

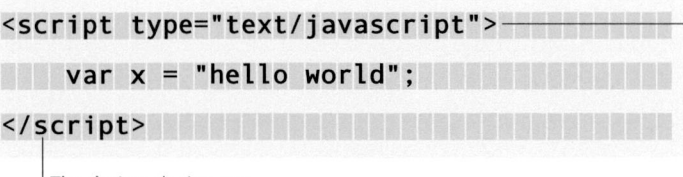

```
<script type="text/javascript">

    var x = "hello world";

</script>
```

The JavaScript instruction must be inside a <script> tag

The closing </script> tag

On an external file

JavaScript can also be placed in an external file and referenced with an "src" attribute in the <script> tag. The external JavaScript file does not need to include the <script> tag as this has already been declared in the calling file.

```
<script src="customScript.js"></script>
```

The "src" attribute points to an external JavaScript file

CUP OF MOCHA

The language currently known as JavaScript was created by Brendan Eich for the Netscape browser. It was called Mocha during the development stage. When it was released, Netscape changed the name of the scripting language to LiveScript, renaming it JavaScript within the first year.

INTERACTION AND FEEDBACK IMPROVES **USER EXPERIENCE** AND PROMOTES EFFECTIVE NAVIGATION THROUGH A **WEBSITE**

Features of JavaScript

JavaScript allows programmers to perform calculations, validate user input, and manipulate and inject HTML elements on the page. It also has a vast library of advanced features that can be easily imported and employed in customized scripts. Even though JavaScript is a flexible language, there are limits to what the JavaScript Engine can do in the browser. For example, it cannot write files to the hard drive or run programs outside the browser.

Dedicated code editor
JavaScript can be written into any standard text file, but it is much easier to use a dedicated code editor to work with it. There are several code editors (see pp.208–209) that can be used to do this.

Scripting language
JavaScript is a dynamic language that is interpreted each time it is run. When a user requests an HTML page, the HTML page and its JavaScript code is sent to a browser where the JavaScript is processed and executed.

Web browser
While all modern browsers can execute JavaScript, each browser implements the language slightly differently. This is why programmers use libraries such as JQuery (see p.284) to code instructions that will be correctly implemented on every browser.

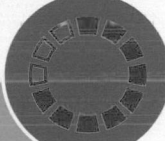

AJAX
AJAX, or Asynchronous JavaScript and XML, can be used to do partial updates of the content in the browser. This prevents the browser from having to do a full page load, allowing the user to stay in the same document while sending requests and receiving responses from the server.

Document Object Model
The Document Object Model (DOM) is a programming interface for HTML documents. It structures a web page so that programmers can easily access and manipulate elements on the page. JavaScript can add, edit, or delete elements in an HTML document by interacting with the DOM.

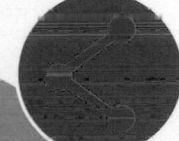

Community sharing
Programmers can share their projects through online communities or by adding to JavaScript's existing libraries. There are several code-sharing websites available online, such as Dabblet, JSFiddle, Codeshare, and Github Gist.

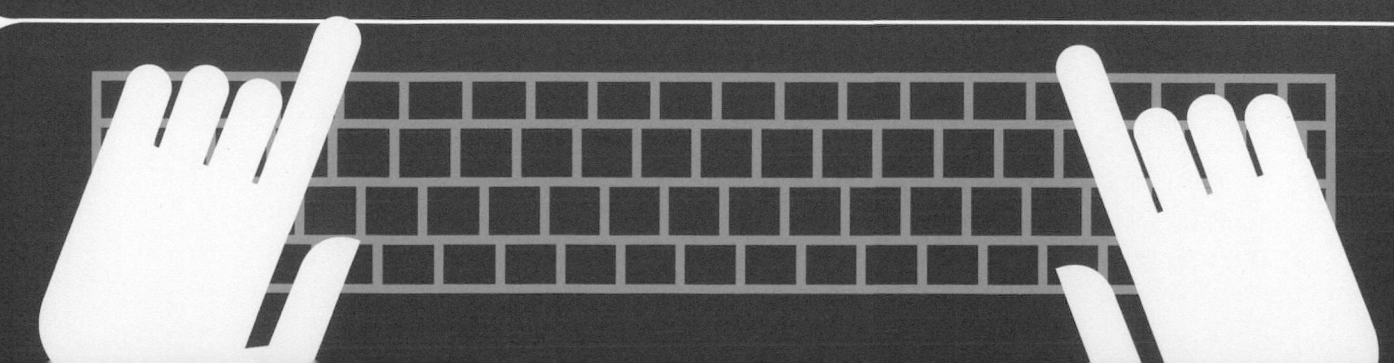

Variables and data types

Variables are containers that store data. When JavaScript code runs, these variables can be compared and manipulated. A variable can contain different types of data, and logical operations (see pp.270–71) should only be performed with variables of the same data type.

Primitive data types

A primitive data type is a simple data value that is not an object or a method. There are three main primitive data types in JavaScript – numbers, Booleans, and strings. Data types do not need to be explicitly stated at the time of declaring a variable (see right); JavaScript automatically infers them from the code.

GOLD   SILVER

$250 $150

Numbers

Unlike other programming languages, JavaScript does not distinguish between integers (whole numbers without a decimal) and floating point numbers (numbers with a decimal). All numbers in JavaScript are treated as floating point numbers.

```
var price = 250;
```

Number values do not have quotation marks around them

Booleans

Similar to Scratch and Python, Boolean variables in JavaScript also contain only two possible values – true or false. As the result of every logical operation is a Boolean value, these variables determine the flow of a program.

```
var isThisGold = true
```

Boolean values do not have quotation marks around them

Declaring variables

It is important to declare and initialize a variable before it can be used in a script. Initialization means to assign a value to the variable. It allows JavaScript to determine the data type that the variable contains and access its value. A variable should only be declared once in a program.

```
var lastName = "Smith";
var fullName = firstName + " " + lastName;
var firstName = "John";
console.log(fullName);
```

Declares the variable `lastName` and sets its value to `Smith`

The variable `firstName` is used before it is declared

Incorrect declaration
In this example, the variable `firstName` is used before it is declared in the code. Since its value is unclear at the time of use, the output displayed will be "undefined Smith".

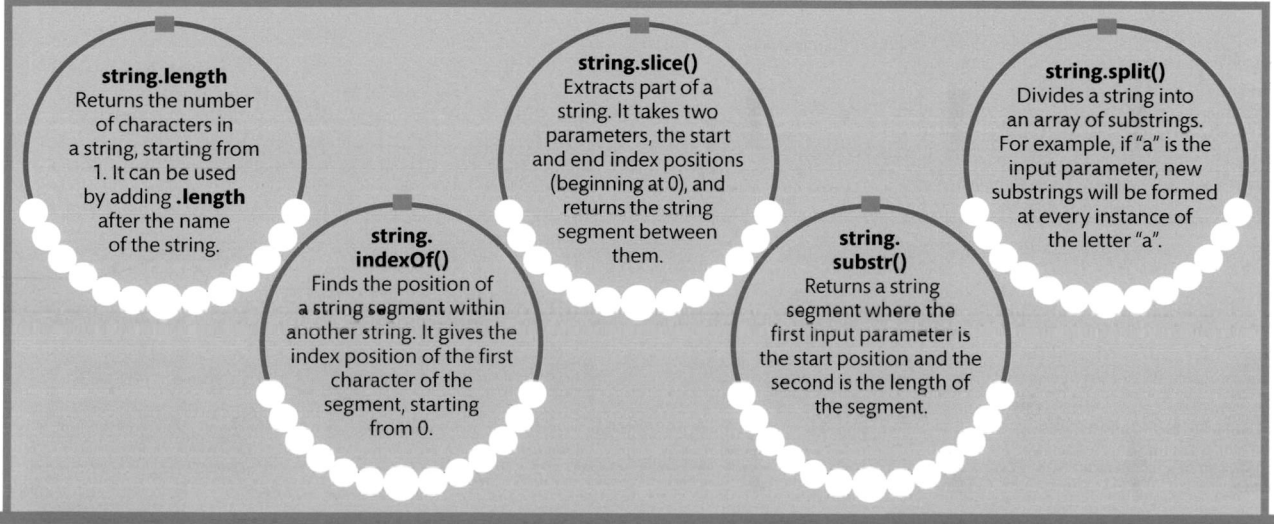

string.length
Returns the number of characters in a string, starting from 1. It can be used by adding **.length** after the name of the string.

string.indexOf()
Finds the position of a string segment within another string. It gives the index position of the first character of the segment, starting from 0.

string.slice()
Extracts part of a string. It takes two parameters, the start and end index positions (beginning at 0), and returns the string segment between them.

string.substr()
Returns a string segment where the first input parameter is the start position and the second is the length of the segment.

string.split()
Divides a string into an array of substrings. For example, if "a" is the input parameter, new substrings will be formed at every instance of the letter "a".

Strings

Strings are data types that can store a series of characters or numbers. They have a number of useful properties and methods that are described above.

```
var myString = "Hello world";
```

String values always have quotation marks around them

Concatenating strings

As in other programming languages, strings in JavaScript can be joined together by using the plus (+) symbol. However, a better way to join, or concatenate, strings is by using the template literal notation (`). This format is easier to read and maintain than using the plus symbol.

```
var myBook = {
    title: "Great Expectations",
    format: "paperback",
};
var myBookDetails = `Title: ${myBook.title}
Format: ${myBook.format}`;
console.log(myBookDetails);
```

`title` is a string value

Template literals are enclosed within back-tick characters instead of quotation marks

Template literals can contain placeholders, indicated by the dollar sign and curly brackets

Logic and branching

Logic is concerned with determining whether a statement is true or false. JavaScript uses logical statements to determine if a variable satisfies a certain condition and then makes decisions based on whether the statement is true or false.

Boolean values

A Boolean data type only has two possible values: true or false. This means that a logical statement will always return one of the two Boolean values. These values allow an algorithm to execute a particular branch of code to produce a desired outcome.

Logical operators

Logical operators combine multiple boolean values into a single Boolean result. The most common logical operators are "And", "Or", and "Not". The "And" operator (&&) demands that both Boolean values are true. The "Or" operator (||) demands that any of the Boolean values are true. The "Not" operator (!) swaps the Boolean value, so true becomes false and false becomes true. For example, "variable1 && !variable2" means, "Is variable1 true And variable2 false? If so return true."

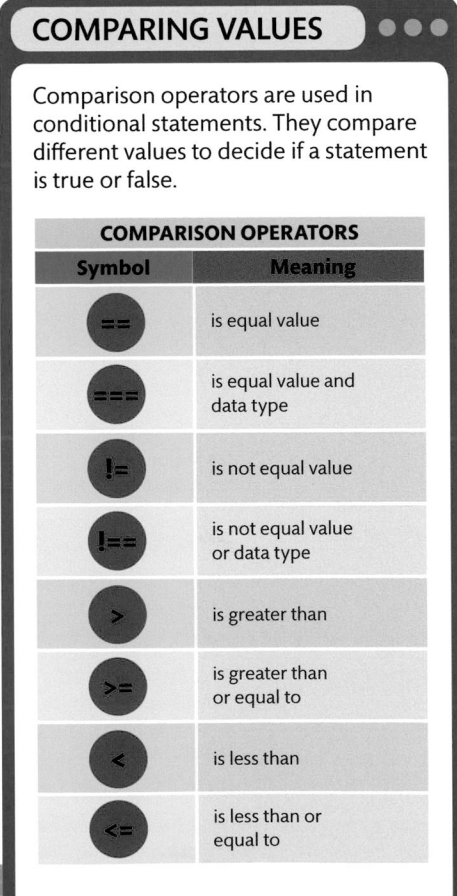

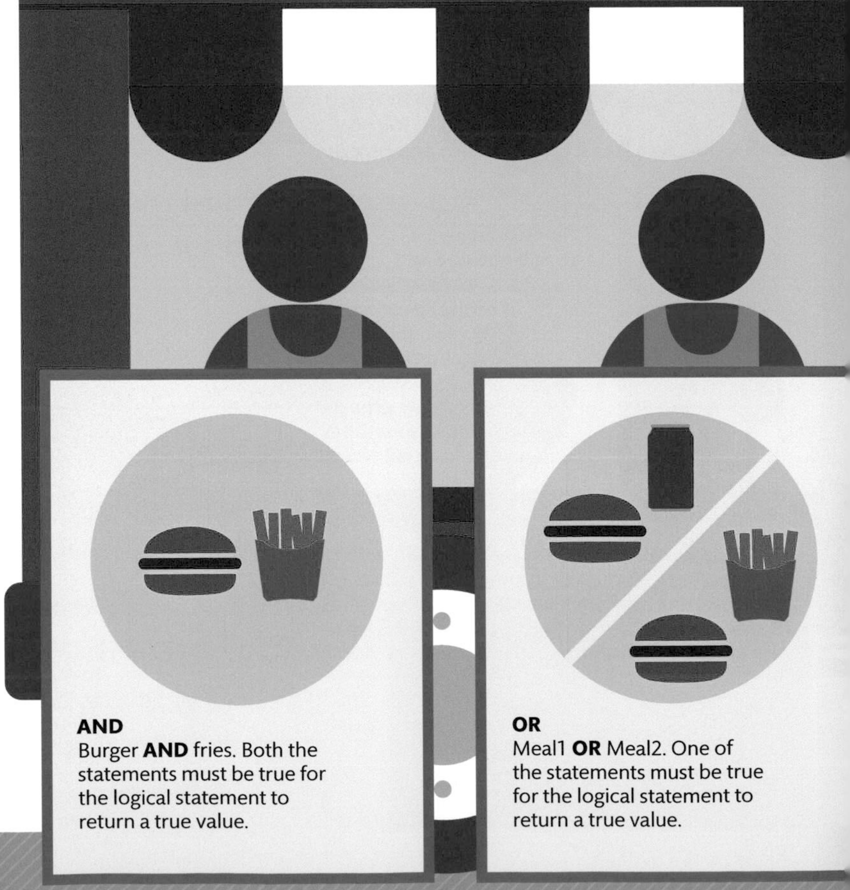

COMPARING VALUES ● ● ●

Comparison operators are used in conditional statements. They compare different values to decide if a statement is true or false.

COMPARISON OPERATORS

Symbol	Meaning
==	is equal value
===	is equal value and data type
!=	is not equal value
!==	is not equal value or data type
>	is greater than
>=	is greater than or equal to
<	is less than
<=	is less than or equal to

AND
Burger **AND** fries. Both the statements must be true for the logical statement to return a true value.

OR
Meal1 **OR** Meal2. One of the statements must be true for the logical statement to return a true value.

Branching in JavaScript

The most commonly used conditional statement is the **if-then** branching statement. This statement instructs the program to execute a block of code only if a logical condition is true. A program (or algorithm) is really a sequence of conditional logical steps that are designed to transform a given input into a desired output. More steps can be added to the conditional logic by using **if-then-else** and **else-if** branching statements.

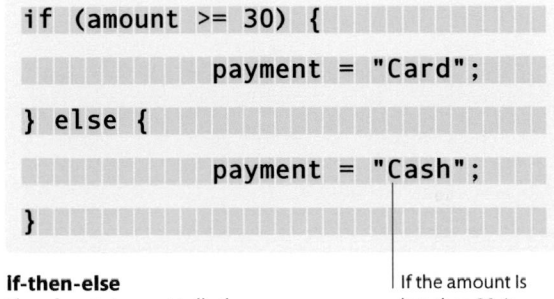

```
if (amount >= 30) {
              payment = "Card";
}
```

if-then
The **if** statement is used to specify a block of JavaScript code to be executed if a condition is true.

If the amount is greater than or equal to 30, it is paid by card

```
if (amount >= 30) {
              payment = "Card";
} else {
              payment = "Cash";
}
```

if-then-else
The **else** statement tells the JavaScript engine to perform an action if the condition is false.

If the amount Is less than 30, it is paid in cash

NOT
Burger and **NOT** onion or tomato. Reverses the logical state, so true becomes false and false becomes true.

SWITCH

A better way to express complex conditional logic is to use the **switch** statement. A single **switch** statement can replace multiple **else-if** statements. Each possible state is represented by a case, and if none of the cases match the condition statement, then a default code block will execute. Each code block is separated by a **break** statement.

Input and output

One of the best features of the Web is that it is interactive. Using JavaScript, it is possible to program a web page to output information to the user in different forms, as well as to accept input from the user in various ways.

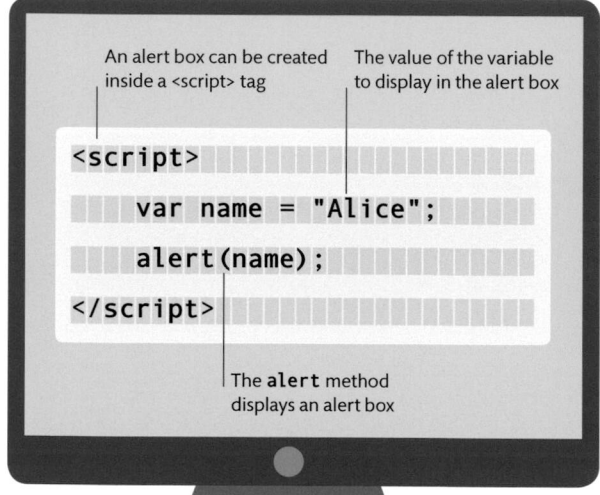

An alert box can be created inside a <script> tag

The value of the variable to display in the alert box

```
<script>
    var name = "Alice";
    alert(name);
</script>
```

The **alert** method displays an alert box

Show a modal alert box
An alert box is a modal window that opens above the normal browser window with a message. Users cannot continue until they dismiss the alert box.

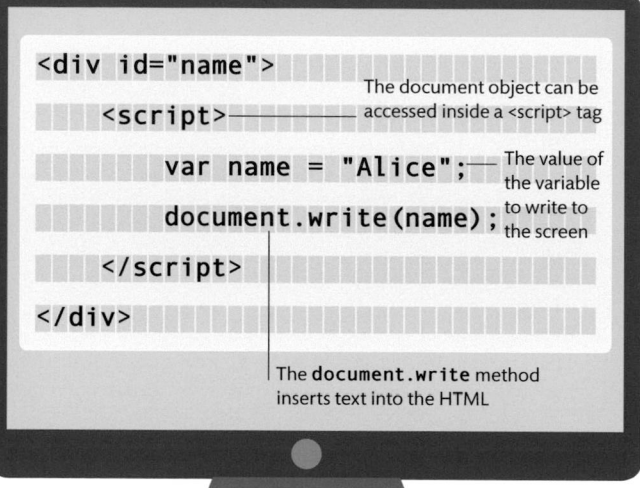

The document object can be accessed inside a <script> tag

The value of the variable to write to the screen

```
<div id="name">
    <script>
        var name = "Alice";
        document.write(name);
    </script>
</div>
```

The **document.write** method inserts text into the HTML

Insert data into the HTML output
This allows programmers to execute JavaScript and output some data into the HTML at the exact location where they want the output to appear on screen.

User input

There are several ways to capture user input and work with the data in JavaScript. The choice of input method depends on the degree of urgency involved in entering the data, whether the input fields need to conform to the visual style of the page, or whether the user must answer the questions in a specific order.

Prompt
A prompt is a modal message box that asks the user for a single line of input. The user must answer the question before doing anything else in the browser. Prompts are helpful in cases where the user must answer questions urgently or in a specific order.

This page says

Please enter your first name

Cancel   OK

Output data on screen

There are four different ways for JavaScript to display data back to the screen. The choice of method to employ is based on the type of information being displayed and whether the output is meant for the developer or the end user. For example, an urgent alert or question should be displayed in a modal window because users must acknowledge it before they can proceed. Debugging information, on the other hand, is intended for the developer and should be displayed in the JavaScript console log.

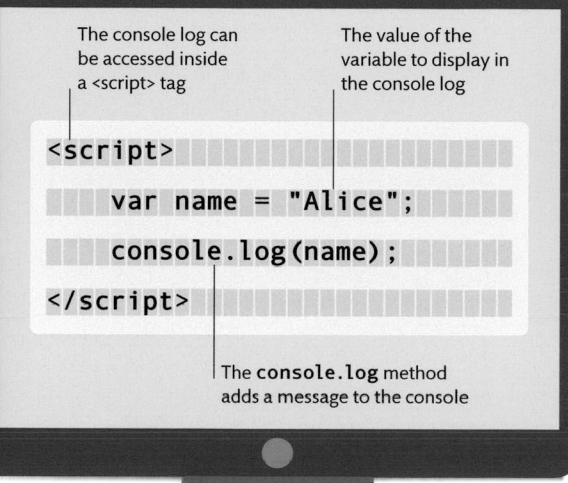

The console log can be accessed inside a <script> tag

The value of the variable to display in the console log

```
<script>
    var name = "Alice";
    console.log(name);
</script>
```

The **console.log** method adds a message to the console

Show data in the console
Information can be output to the JavaScript console log. These log messages are very useful when debugging to see what is happening during the execution of the code.

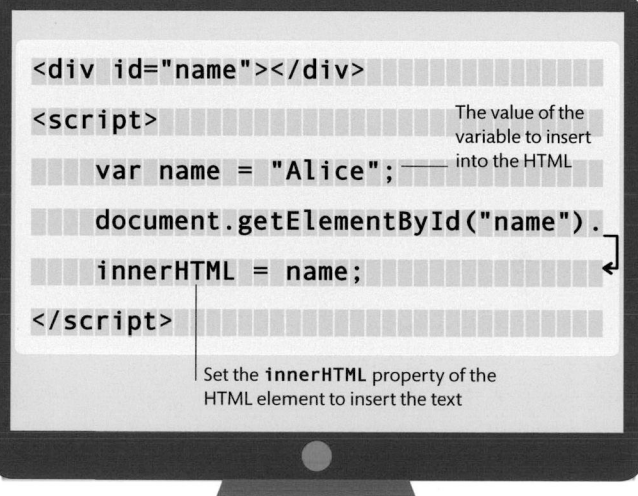

```
<div id="name"></div>
<script>
    var name = "Alice";
    document.getElementById("name").
    innerHTML = name;
</script>
```

The value of the variable to insert into the HTML

Set the **innerHTML** property of the HTML element to insert the text

Insert data into an HTML element
Allows output to be calculated during the execution of a script, and then inserted into the correct location via a placeholder HTML element.

Confirmation box
A confirmation box is a modal dialogue box that is used to verify a user's intention. Users are forced to interact with the confirmation box before they can return to the main page.

This page says
Are you enjoying JavaScript?

Cancel   OK

HTML Input
An HTML <form> tag (see p.212) is usually used to send information entered into the input fields back to the server. However, it is also possible to use this data in JavaScript code. For example, using HTML input controls to get a user's first name and last name.

First Name: John
Last Name: Smith

Click me   This page says
             Hello John Smith

             Cancel   OK

For loop

A **for** loop will repeat a block of code and each time increment a counter until the counter no longer satisfies a given condition. With each increment, the counter can increase or decrease, allowing the loop to run from top to bottom, or vice versa.

```
for (let loopCounter = 0; loopCounter < 5;
loopCounter++) {
    console.log(loopCounter);
}
```

The logical condition appears before the loop

For loop with positive increments
The `loopCounter` is increased by 1 each time the loop repeats the block of code. The loop will stop when `loopCounter` equals 5.

Displays the value of the `loopCounter` variable in the console log

While loop

A **while** loop will repeat a block of code until a condition returns false. This is similar to the **do while** loop, except that the condition runs before the block of code, so it might not run the first time.

Using while loops
This loop is ideal when an instruction must repeat an unknown number of times. However, depending on the condition, the loop may not qualify to execute even once.

```
var numberOfDaysCounter = 0;
var numberOfDays = 3;
var daysOfWeek = ["Monday", "Tuesday", "Wednesday", "Thursday",
"Friday", "Saturday", "Sunday"];
while (numberOfDaysCounter < numberOfDays) {
    console.log(daysOfWeek[numberOfDaysCounter]);
    numberOfDaysCounter++;
}
```

The logical condition defines when the loop is executed. Here it will run if the counter is smaller than the number of days

Loops in JavaScript

In programming, instructions may often need to be repeated a certain number of times or until a condition has been met. Loops allow us to control how many times a set of instructions should be repeated. There are several different kinds of loops, and each loop has it own way of knowing when to stop.

For in loop

A **for in** loop repeats a block of code for each property of an object. Inside the loop instruction, a variable is declared that will hold the value of the property as it is being processed by the loop.

Looping through arrays
This loop is perfect for processing arrays of data. The code block will process each item in the array and stop when there are no more items.

```
var myBook = {
    name: "Great Expectations",
    numberOfPages: 250,
    format: "paperback"
}
for (let property in myBook) {
    console.log(` ${property} ${myBook[property]}`)
}
```

The **myBook** variable has three properties: **name**, **numberOfPages**, and **format**

The **format** property has a string value "paperback"

The **property** variable represents the current property being processed by the loop

Do while loop

Similar to a **while** loop, a **do while** loop will also repeat a block of code until a condition returns false. However, the condition appears after the block of code and will only be checked after the code block has run the first time.

Using do while loops
This loop is used when the block of code must repeat an unknown number of times, but it must be executed at least once.

```
var numberOfDaysCounter = 0;
var numberOfDays = 3;
var daysOfWeek = ["Monday", "Tuesday", "Wednesday", "Thursday",
"Friday", "Saturday", "Sunday"];
do {
    console.log(daysOfWeek[numberOfDaysCounter]);
    numberOfDaysCounter++;
} while (numberOfDaysCounter < numberOfDays)
```

The condition may depend on the state of variables outside of the loop

The block of code will run before the condition is checked

Nested loops

Loops can be nested, or contained, within other loops. This allows us to iterate sequentially through all the items in a list or multidimensional array (an array containing one or more arrays).

Using nested loops

In this example, arrays represent the days of the week and temperature readings taken during that day. Nested loops are used to find the highest temperature. The outer loop represents the days of the week, while the inner loop represents the data for each day.

```javascript
var daysAndTemperature = [
    ["Monday", 26,21,24],
    ["Tuesday", 24],
    ["Wednesday", 28,21],
];
var maxTemperature = 0;
for (let outerCounter = 0; outerCounter < daysAndTemperature.
length; outerCounter++) {
    for (let innerCounter = 0; innerCounter < daysAndTemperature
    [outerCounter].length; innerCounter++) {
        var innerValue = daysAndTemperature[outerCounter]
        [innerCounter];
        if (isNaN(innerValue)) {
            continue;
        } else {
            if (maxTemperature < innerValue) {
                maxTemperature = innerValue;
            }
        }
    }
}
console.log(`Max Temperature ${maxTemperature}`);
```

Each array has a different number of items

The **outerCounter** loop iterates through each day

innerValue will represent each array item inside daysAndTemperature[outerCounter]

If **innerValue** is not a number the code jumps to, the next iteration of the **innerCounter** loop

The **innerCounter** loop iterates through the data for each day

This variable will hold the highest value found in the array items

Displays the value of the highest temperature in the console log

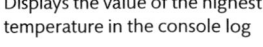

Escaping loops

Sometimes the current iteration of the loop is not worth running, or programmers may have already found the answer they were looking for. To avoid wasting time processing loops that are not required, you can use the **continue** command to stop the current iteration of the loop and begin the next iteration. The **break** command can be used to stop running the loop altogether.

Break

The **break** statement tells the JavaScript Engine to stop running the loop and jump to the next instruction after the loop. This is useful as once the loop has found what it is looking for, it can move on with the rest of the program.

```javascript
var days = ["Monday", "Tuesday", "Wednesday", "Thursday"];
var whenIsWednesday = function (days) {
    let result = null;
    for (let i = 0; i < 7; i++) {
        if (days[i] === "Wednesday") {
            result = i + 1;
            break;
        }
    }
    return result;
};
console.log(`Wednesday is day ${whenIsWednesday(days)}`);
```

This function will return the index of the array item that matches the string **Wednesday**

Each time the loop iterates, the **i** counter will increase by 1

Checks if the value of the array item is equivalent to the string **Wednesday**

Array indexes always start from 0, so often you need to add 1 to get a "human friendly" result

Returns the value of the **result** variable after the loop has been completed

Displays the result of the function in the console log; in this case the result is **Wednesday is day 3**

Continue

This statement tells a loop to stop the current iteration and start running the next iteration. This is useful when you know that the current iteration does not need to be executed, and you can carry on with the next iteration through the loop.

```javascript
for (let i = 0; i < 7; i++) {
    if (days[i] !== "Wednesday") {
        continue;
    }
    result = i + 1;
```

The **whenIsWednesday** function using **continue** rather than **break**

Functions in JavaScript

A function is a block of instructions that performs a task. The code inside the function usually only executes when the function is called. To use a function, it must first be defined somewhere in the scope (local or global) from which it needs to be called.

Input parameters are declared in parentheses. There are none in this example

Declaring functions

A function is declared by providing a name, a list of input parameters, and a block of code enclosed in curly brackets. A value can be returned by the function by using the "return" statement.

Name of the function

```
var firstName = "John";
function getFirstName() {
             return firstName;
}
console.log(getFirstName());
```

Code to be executed

Outputs the result of the getFirstName() function to the console log

Simple function definition
Once a function has been defined, it can be called many times from elsewhere in the code.

Function statement vs function expression

In JavaScript, a function will behave differently depending on how it was declared. Function statements can be called before the function has been declared, while function expressions must be declared before they can be used.

Input parameters for the function getFullName()

Function statement
A function statement begins with the word "function" followed by the function name, the input parameters, and then the code block in curly brackets.

```
function getFullName(firstName, lastName) {
             return `${firstName} ${lastName}`;
}
console.log(getFullName("John","Smith"));
```

The template literal notation `${variable}` returns a string with the variable value embedded in place

Function expression
A function expression begins with a variable declaration and then assigns a function to the variable.

```
var fullName = function getFullName(firstName, lastName) {
             return `${firstName} ${lastName}`;
}
console.log(fullName("John","Smith"));
```

Variable declaration

Nested functions

It is also possible to nest a function within another function. The inner function, however, can only be called by its outer function. The inner function can use variables from the outer function, but the outer function cannot use the variables of the inner function.

A function expression declaration

A nested function expression declared inside the **car** function

```
var car = function (carName) {
            var getCarName = function () {
                    return carName;
            }
            return getCarName();
}
console.log(car("Toyota"));
```

The nested function **getCarName()** can access the variable **carName** from the parent **car** function

Why use nested functions?
Nested functions are only accessible from inside the parent function. This means that the inner function contains the scope of the outer function.

Self-executing functions

Normally a function needs to be called in order to execute its code. However, a function that is surrounded by a self-executing function will run as soon as it is declared. Self-executing functions are often used to initialize the JavaScript application by declaring a global scope variable counter.

```
(function getFullName() {
        var firstName = "John";
        var lastName = "Smith";
        function fullName() {
            return firstName + " " + lastName;
        }
        console.log(fullName());
})();
```

These variables are only accessible within the self-executing function

Using self-executing functions
Variables and functions declared in a self-executing function are only available within that function. In this example, the nested function **fullName()** can access the variables **firstName** and **lastName** from the parent function **getFullName()**.

JavaScript debugging

Programmers spend a lot of time diagnosing and remedying errors and omissions in their code. Debugging slows down the JavaScript execution and shows how data is modified line by line. Since JavaScript is interpreted at run time and executed inside the browser, debugging is performed with tools built in to the browser.

Errors in JavaScript

In JavaScript an error is detected or thrown when a program tries to perform an unexpected or forbidden action. JavaScript uses an Error object to provide information about the unexpected event. JavaScript errors can be viewed in a browser's Developer Tools, inside the Console tab. Every Error object has two properties, a "name" and a "message". The name indicates the type of error, while the message provides further details about the error, such as the location in the JavaScript file where the error was thrown.

SyntaxError
An error in the way the code is written causes a syntax error. This error occurs while the JavaScript Engine is interpreting the code at run time.

TypeError
This error occurs when the wrong data type is used. For example, applying the `string.substring` method to a variable that is a number.

RangeError
When the code attempts to use a number that is outside the range of possible values, JavaScript detects a RangeError.

URIError
Some alphanumeric characters are not allowed to be used in a url. A URIError is thrown when there is a problem encoding or decoding a URI because of the use of a reserved character.

EvalError
This error occurs when there is a problem with the `eval()` function. Newer versions of JavaScript do not throw this error.

ReferenceError
This error occurs when the code refers to a variable that either does not exist or is not in scope (see p.269) for the executing code.

Developer tools

All modern browsers contain a set of Developer Tools to help programmers work with HTML, CSS, and JavaScript. The Developer Tools contain functionality to debug JavaScript and view the state of HTML elements in the browser. To open the Developer Tools for the Google Chrome browser, press Command+Option+I (Mac) or Control+Shift+I (Windows, Linux).

The Console
Web developers can output messages to the console log to make sure their code is executing as expected. The "Console" tab contains two areas:
- **Console Output Log:** Displays system and user messages from the JavaScript execution.
- **Console Command Line Interface:** Accepts any JavaScript instructions and executes them immediately.

JavaScript debugger
The JavaScript debugger can be found under the Sources tab. The debugger makes it possible to step through the code line by line to see what is happening to the variables as the code executes. On the left is a list of all the source files used by the HTML document. Select the file to debug from this list.

Scope
In the "Sources" tab, the window on the right contains the Scope (see p.269). The local and global sections under this show the variables that are defined in the current scope. The Scope pane is only populated with variables when the script is being debugged.

Breakpoints
The JavaScript Engine pauses the execution of code when it hits a breakpoint. This allows programmers to examine it. The execution can proceed in one of the following ways:
- **Resume Script Execution:** Resumes execution until the program hits another breakpoint or the program ends.
- **Step over:** Executes the next line of code in a single step and then pauses on the following line. It steps over a function without debugging the individual steps of the function.
- **Step into:** Executes the next line of code and then pauses on the following line. It will step into a function line by line.
- **Step out:** Executes the remaining code in the current function, and pauses when run time returns to the line of code, after the function was called.

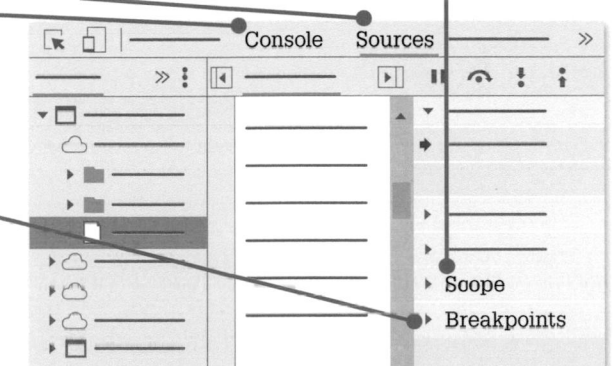

GOOGLE CHROME DEVELOPER TOOLS

Error handling

In JavaScript, the **try...catch** statement allows programmers to handle errors in the code. Normally program execution stops when an error is thrown by the JavaScript Engine. However, if the code is wrapped in a try block, the execution will jump to the catch block if an exception is thrown, and the program will continue as normal. It is also possible to manually raise an error using the "throw" statement.

The error message is displayed in the console

```
try {
        noSuchCommand();          This function
                                   does not exist
}
catch (err) {          The code jumps to the catch block instead
                       of stopping the program execution
        console.error(err.message);
}
console.log("Script continues to
run after the exception");
```
TRY...CATCH STATEMENT

The throw operator generates an error

```
throw("Oops there was an error");
```
THROW STATEMENT

Object-oriented JavaScript

It is common in programming to create many objects of the same type. Object-oriented programming encapsulates properties and methods into classes. Functionality can be reused by creating new child classes.

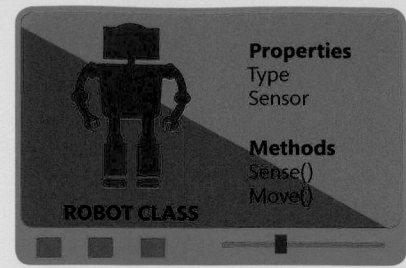

Class inheritance
In JavaScript, an object can be declared as an instance of the class, and it will inherit all the properties and methods belonging to that class. Here, the properties and methods for the class Robot can be inherited by each of its child objects.

Prototypes

Every JavaScript object comes with a built-in variable called a prototype. Any properties or functions added to the prototype object will be accessible to a child object. A child object is created as an instance of the parent object using the keyword "new".

Calls the method in the parent object's prototype from the child object, and returns the child object's "title" property, ABC

```javascript
let parentObject = function() {
    this.title = "123";
}
let childObject = new parentObject();
childObject.title = "ABC";
parentObject.prototype.getTitle = function(){
    return this.title;
}
console.log(childObject.getTitle());
```

Creates a new parent object

Creates a new child object as an instance of the parent object

Sets the child object's title property

Adds a new method to the parent object's prototype

Functions

Just as in prototypes, an object can be declared as an instance of a function with the **new** command. This command acts as a constructor (a method used for initializing the properties of the class). The child object inherits all the properties and methods defined in the function.

```javascript
function Book(title, numberOfPages) {
            this.title = title;
            this.numberOfPages = numberOfPages;
};
let JaneEyre = new Book("Jane Eyre", 200)
console.log(JaneEyre.title);
```

Instantiates the new book

Properties and methods of the function

Defining objects in JavaScript

JavaScript is a prototype-based language, which means that properties and methods can be inherited via the "prototype" property of the object. This differs to the way that other object-oriented languages, such as Python, construct classes (see pp.156–57). There are three ways to define and instantiate a JavaScript object in an object-oriented way: prototypes, functions, and classes.

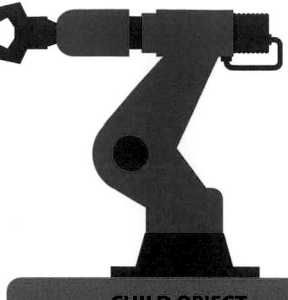

CHILD OBJECT

Properties	Methods
Type: Humanoid	Sense()
Sensor: Temperature	Move()

CHILD OBJECT

Properties	Methods
Type: Industrial	Sense()
Sensor: Light	Move()

Classes

A JavaScript class is a special kind of function that contains a constructor method and the getter and setter methods. The constructor method runs when the object is instantiated with the **new** command, while getters and setters define how a property should be read and written. Similar to functions, classes can be defined in the ways shown below.

Class declaration
A class can be declared with the "class" keyword. The constructor method takes the input parameters necessary to initialize the object properties.

```
class Book {
    constructor(title, numberOfPages, format) {
        this.title = title;
        this.numberOfPages = numberOfPages;
        this.format = format;
    }
}
let JaneEyre = new Book("Jane Eyre", 200, "Paperback")
console.log(JaneEyre.title);
```

Defines the properties and methods of the class Book

Calls the "title" property of the object

Class assigned to the variable **Book**

Class expression
A class can also be assigned to a variable that can be passed around and returned by a function.

```
let Book = class {
    constructor(title, numberOfPages, format) {
        this.title = title;
```

Libraries and frameworks

JavaScript makes extensive use of libraries of prewritten functionality that can be called in the code to make programming easier and faster. Frameworks on the other hand provide a standard way of programming, by calling and using the code as needed.

Types of libraries and frameworks

There are various JavaScript libraries to help with all common programming tasks. For the user interface, there are tools for responsive layouts, manipulating HTML elements, and managing graphics on screen. For data processing, there are libraries to keep data synchronized, to validate user input, and to work with maths, date, time, and currencies. There are even comprehensive testing frameworks to ensure that code runs as expected in the future.

JQuery
JQuery is a framework that contains many useful tools, such as animation, event handling, and AJAX (see p.265). It takes complex JavaScript code and wraps it into simpler methods that can be called with a single line of code.

NODE.JS AND NPM

Node.js is a run time environment that is used to create web server and API applications in JavaScript. It has a large library of JavaScript files that perform all the common tasks on a web server, such as sending requests to a computer's file system and returning the content to a client once the file system has read and processed the requests. The JavaScript files that define the Node.js environment are interpreted by the Google JavaScript Engine outside of the browser.

Node Package Manager (NPM) is a package manager for programs written in JavaScript. It contains a database of both free and paid-for applications. You need to install Node.js before using NPM.

ReactJS
This library is used for building interactive user interfaces (UIs). It allows programmers to create complex UIs from small pieces of code, called "components". ReactJS uses this component model to maintain state and data binding in single-page apps.

RequireJS
This library manages the loading of JavaScript files and modules. It ensures that the scripts are loaded in the correct order and are available to other modules that depend on them.

TypeScript
TypeScript is a scripting language that is used to export simple JavaScript files that can be run inside the browser. It offers support for the latest and evolving JavaScript features to help build powerful components.

Angular
This framework is used for building dynamic single-page apps. It can implement complex requirements of an app, such as data binding and navigating through "views" and animations. Angular provides specific guidelines on how to structure and build apps.

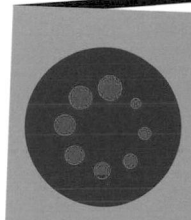

Moment.js
This library makes it easy to work with dates and time in JavaScript. It helps parse, manipulate, validate, and display date and time on screen. Moment.js works both in the browser and in Node.js (see opposite).

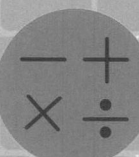

MathJS
MathJS is a library that features extensive tools for working with maths. It supports fractions, matrices, complex numbers, calculus, etc. It is compatible with JavaScript's built-in Math library, and runs on any JavaScript engine.

Bootstrap
This library contains many useful graphical elements and grid layout tools, which are used to create visually appealing websites that can scale to fit screens of any size. Bootstrap is a combination of HTML, CSS, and JavaScript. When applied to a page, it creates an attractive graphic user interface.

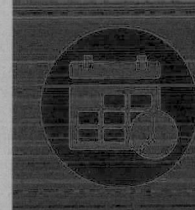

Graphic user interfaces

A web page is a graphic user interface (GUI) through which a user navigates a website. HTML and CSS provide the basis for the graphic design, while JavaScript adds custom logic and business rules to the elements on the page to improve the quality of the interaction.

Working with graphics in JavaScript

In an HTML document, <img/> tags are used to display image files and <svg> tags are used to display vector images. JavaScript can be used to modify the properties of these graphic elements in response to user interaction. The <canvas> HTML element allows JavaScript to draw graphics directly to the screen. JavaScript also has an extensive library of frameworks (see pp.284–85) that can be imported and employed to produce complex graphic applications.

Scalable Vector Graphics (SVG)

SVG is a format that describes two-dimensional graphics in code. These graphics are then drawn by the browser on the screen. SVGs have a small file size and can be scaled to any size without losing quality. They can be drawn and exported from graphic softwares, such as Adobe Illustrator or Gimp. Graphics in SVG can also be styled with CSS and indexed by search engines.

Draw a company logo in SVG

In this example, you can draw a rectangle shape for the background using the <rect> tag. The <text> tag can be used to draw the logo text. You can modify the final drawing with the style attributes.

Draws a red-coloured rectangle with a grey border

```
<svg width="200" height="100">
        <rect style="stroke:grey;stroke-width:10px;fill:red;"
        x="0" y="0" height="100" width="200" />
        <text fill="white" font-size="30" font-family="Verdana" x="20"
        y="60">SVG LOGO</text>
</svg>
```

The closing </svg> tag

Draws the logo text in front of the rectangle

Uses CSS style attributes to define SVG elements

HTML Canvas

The <canvas> element defines a space
on the web page where graphics can be
created using JavaScript. This space is
a two-dimensional grid onto which
JavaScript can draw lines, shapes, and text.
The grid coordinates (0, 0) are measured
from the upper left-hand corner.

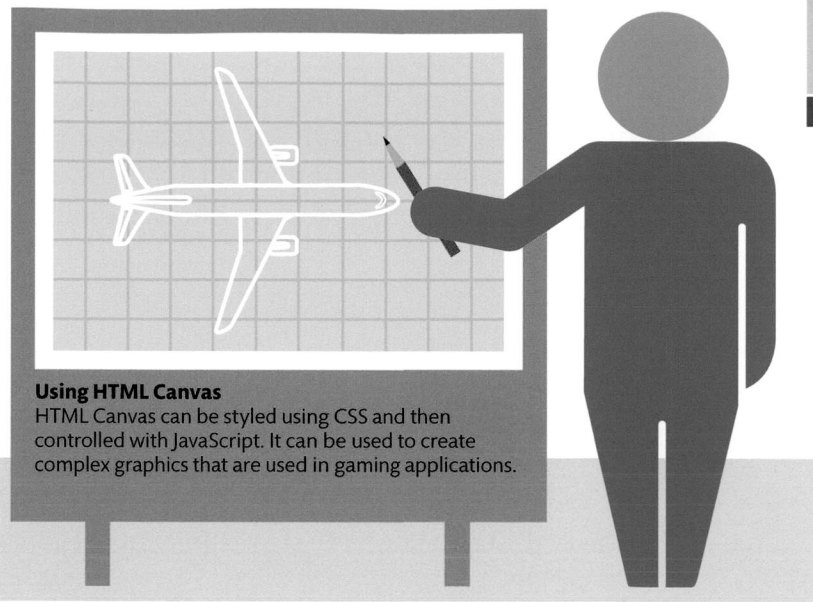

Using HTML Canvas
HTML Canvas can be styled using CSS and then
controlled with JavaScript. It can be used to create
complex graphics that are used in gaming applications.

Graphics libraries

JavaScript has several built-in graphic libraries that make
it easier to work with complex graphics on the Web. Each
library has a specific purpose, such as converting numeric
data into graphs, representing statistical data as infographics,
or mapping a virtual world in a computer game.

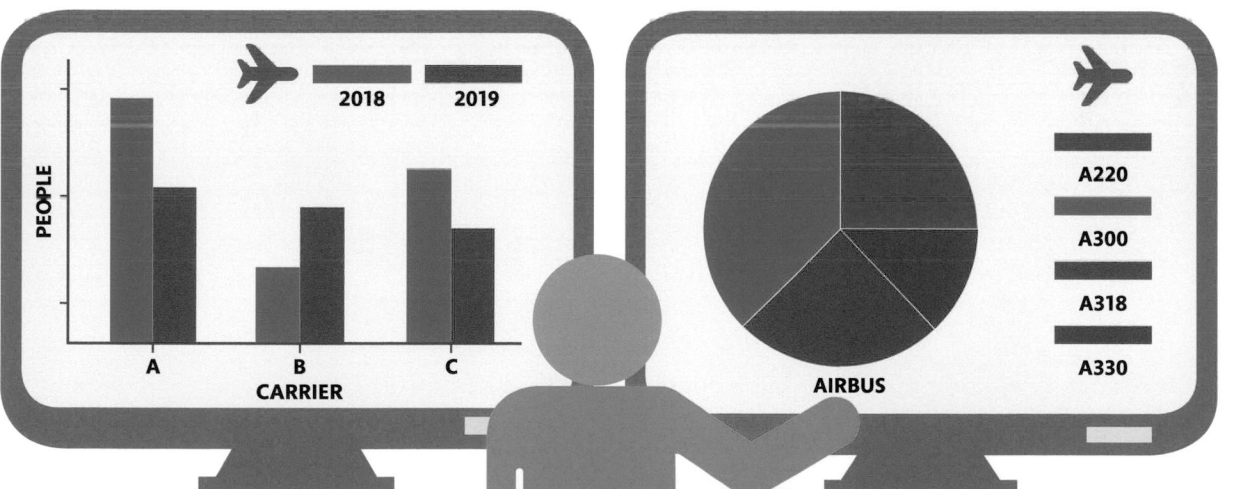

D3.js
Data-Driven Documents or D3.js is used to
create colourful, animated, and interactive
representations of data. It is brilliant for
drawing graphs and organizing data in a
structural manner.

Chart.js
This library allows the programmer to add graphs
and charts to a Web document. It is an open-source
library that works well on tablets and mobile phones.
Bar charts, Doughnut, Line charts, and Area charts
are some of the core charts in Chart.js.

Animating the web page

JavaScript is used to extend the functionality of a website and make it more dynamic. Here it will allow you to add intelligent and interactive behaviours to the existing HTML framework, completing the web page project.

What the program does

In this part of the project, JavaScript is added to the structured and styled web page created in Styling a web page (see pp.242–63). The functionalities added in this part of the project will allow the web page to handle customized user interactions.

Interactive website

The web page will now have interactive elements. The promo bar on top will cycle through four messages, and the scroll button will be visible at the end of the web page. It will scroll up to the top when clicked.

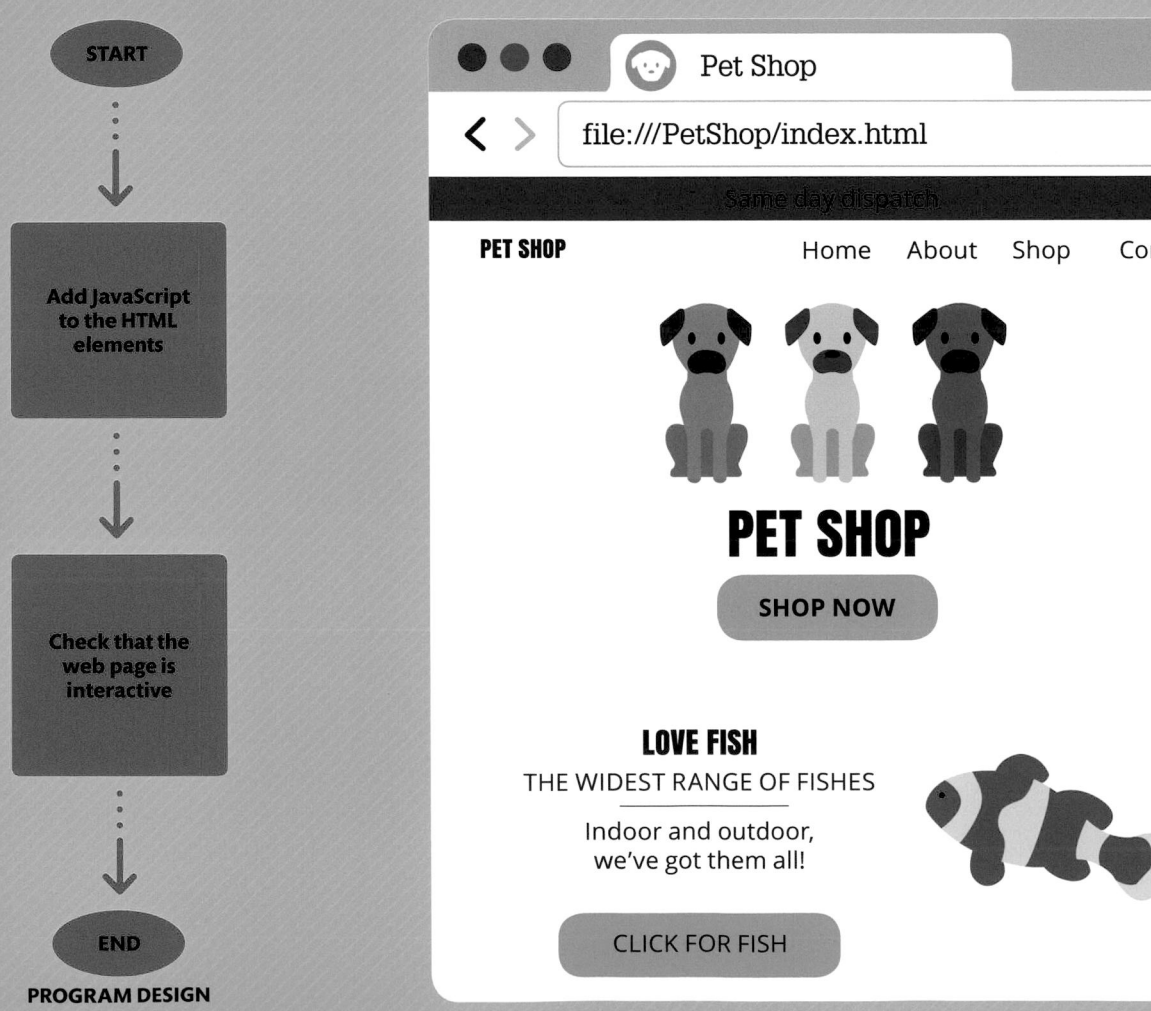

START

Add JavaScript to the HTML elements

Check that the web page is interactive

END

PROGRAM DESIGN

Pet Shop

file:///PetShop/index.html

Same day dispatch

PET SHOP   Home   About   Shop   Contact

PET SHOP

SHOP NOW

LOVE FISH
THE WIDEST RANGE OF FISHES

Indoor and outdoor,
we've got them all!

CLICK FOR FISH

YOU WILL LEARN

> How to create JavaScript files
> How to use JQuery
> How to animate HTML elements

Time: 1 hour

Lines of code: 89

Difficulty level

WHERE THIS IS USED

JavaScript is used in almost all websites. It helps web developers make web pages more attractive and interactive by implementing custom client-side scripts. It even allows the use of cross-platform run time engines, such as Node.js, to write server-side code.

Project requirements

For this project, you will need the previously created HTML and CSS files. You can continue using the same IDE.

HTML FILE

CSS FILE

DEVELOPMENT ENVIRONMENT

1 Getting started

To add the interactive functionality of JavaScript to the website, you will require multiple JavaScript files. You will also link the HTML document to a JavaScript framework (see pp.284–85) to make programming easier.

1.1 ADD A FOLDER

Create a new folder, called "scripts", to contain the JavaScript files. On a Mac, open Finder and create the folder inside the website folder. Then, open Visual Studio, right-click on the project name, select Add and choose Add Solution Folder. In Windows, right-click on the project name in Solution Explorer, select Add and choose New Folder.

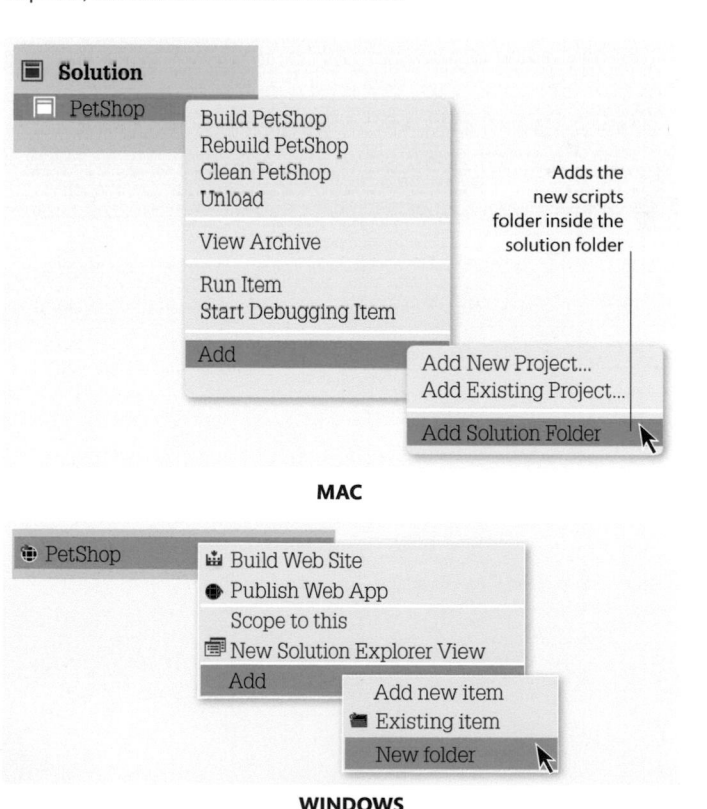

Adds the new scripts folder inside the solution folder

MAC

WINDOWS

HTML

1.2 ADD JQUERY

Before adding the custom JavaScript files, you need to add JQuery (see p.284) to the HTML file. You will use JQuery in the custom scripts to make it easier to target the HTML elements. In the "index.html" file, add a <script> tag inside the <head> tag, pointing to the online location that you can use to retrieve JQuery. This online location is called a CDN (content delivery network). You can download these files and host them in your own site, but it is often easier and quicker to use a CDN.

```
<link href="https://fonts.googleapis.com/css?family=Anton|
Open+Sans" rel="stylesheet">
<script src="https://code.jquery.com/jquery-3.3.1.min.js">
</script>
</head>
```

The "src" attribute points to the CDN for JQuery

Link to retrieve JQuery

2 Adding JavaScript files

The web page in this project needs three custom JavaScript files. In this section, you will create the first two files – one to contain the global scope variables and another to contain functionality for the features of the home page.

APP.JS

HOME.JS

2.1 ADD NEW FILE

The first custom script you need to add is called "app.js". This will add an "app" class/function that you can instantiate to hold all the global scope variables. Right-click on the scripts folder, select Add and choose New File to create a JavaScript file. Name this file "app.js".

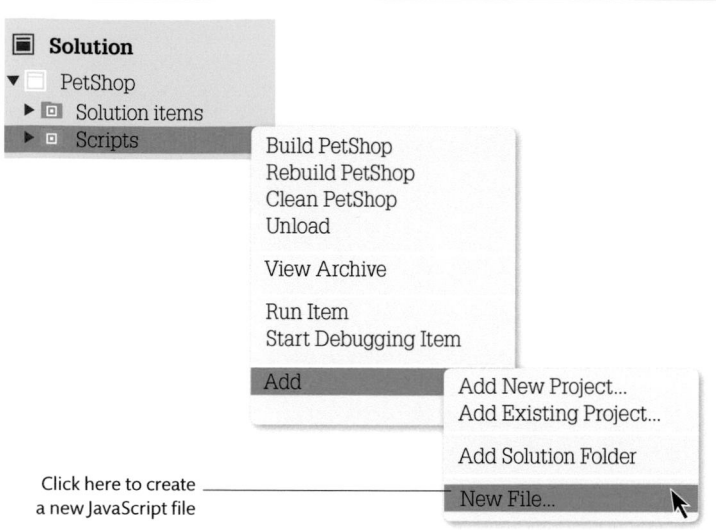

Solution
▼ PetShop
  ▶ Solution items
  ▶ Scripts

Build PetShop
Rebuild PetShop
Clean PetShop
Unload

View Archive

Run Item
Start Debugging Item

Add

Add New Project...
Add Existing Project...

Add Solution Folder

New File...

Click here to create a new JavaScript file

2.2 REFERENCE APP.JS

You now need to link the JavaScript file to the HTML file. In the "index.html" file , add a <script> tag that will point to the newly created JavaScript file. Place this link inside the <head> tag, just below the <script> tag for JQuery. The order in which you declare the JavaScript files is important, because the scripts must be loaded into the JavaScript Engine (see p.264) before they can be called. For example, JQuery must be loaded before you can use any of its methods.

HTML

```
<script src="https://code.jquery.com/jquery-3.3.1.min.js">
</script>
<script src="scripts/app.js"></script>
```
Adds a new <script> tag that points to the new JavaScript file

2.3 CREATE FUNCTION

Inside "app.js", declare a variable called **app** that is a self-executing function (see p.279). Then add a property called "websiteName" and a method called "getWebsiteName" inside the function. This is an example of how to add functionality to the app class.

Code after double slashes (//) or between /* and */ is treated as a comment in JavaScript

```
var app = (function () {

    /* Properties */

    var websiteName = "PetShop";

    /* Methods */

    return {

        getWebsiteName: function () {

            return websiteName;

        }

    }

})();
```

Round brackets instruct the JavaScript Engine to run that function immediately

JS

SAVE

2.4 ADD ANOTHER FILE

Next, add another new custom script with all the logic you will need for the home page. Follow the same steps as before to create a new JavaScript file inside the scripts folder, and name it "home.js".

HOME.JS

2.5 REFERENCE HOME.JS

As before, you will need to reference this new JavaScript file in the HTML document. In the "index.html" file, add a <script> tag that points to the "home.js" file. Ensure that this is placed below the reference for "app.js" added in step 2.2.

HTML

```
<script src="scripts/app.js"></script>
<script src="scripts/home.js"></script>
```

Indicates that the file is inside the scripts folder

SAVE

2.6 ADD FUNCTIONALITY TO HOME.JS

In "home.js", create a function called **HomeIndex()**, which will contain all the functionality required by the home page. Below this function, add a **on document ready()** function. This is a JQuery command that instructs the JavaScript Engine to wait until all the elements on the page have finished loading before running the code within it. Inside the **on document ready()** function, you will instantiate the **HomeIndex()** function as a property of the "app" object, which has already been instantiated in the "app.js" file.

JS

```
function HomeIndex() {

}
$(document).ready(function () {
    /* Instantiate new Home class */
    app.homeIndex = new HomeIndex();
});
```

The dollar sign denotes the JQuery function

Makes a function available after the document is loaded

Comments are ignored, and will not be executed

Links "home.js" to "app.js"

---

3 Managing the Scroll to top button

In the next few steps, you will add functionality to the Scroll to top button. You need to add code to control when the button becomes visible and to make it scroll back to the top of the page when clicked.

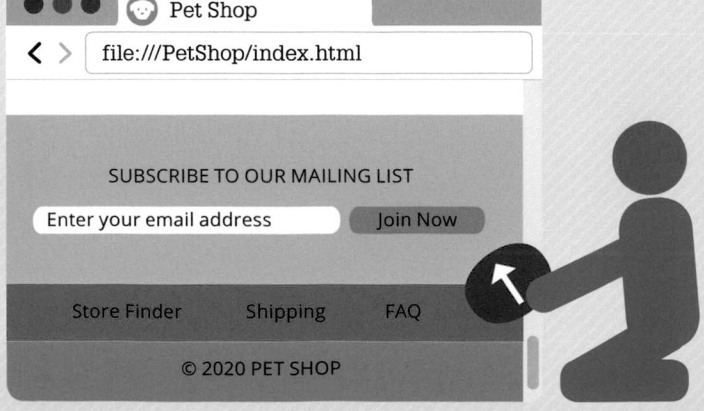

3.1 DEFINE PROPERTIES

Add a property inside the **HomeIndex()** function to set the height from the top of the page at which the Scroll to top button should become visible.

```
function HomeIndex() {

    /* Properties */

    const heightFromTop = 300;

}
```

The height will not change, so it is defined as constant

3.2 DEFINE METHODS

Now add a method to initialize the Scroll to top button. This method will control two aspects of the button. It will add an "on scroll" event handler, so that every time the user scrolls up or down in the browser, the JavaScript Engine checks if the scroll distance is more than the amount defined in the **heightFromTop** value. The button is then made visible or hidden accordingly. The method also adds an "on click" event handler, so that every time the user clicks the Scroll to top button, the page will scroll back to the top. Add this code within the **HomeIndex()** function.

```
    const heightFromTop = 300;

    /* Methods */

    this.initialiseScrollToTopButton = function () {

    }

}
```

The keyword "this" refers to the owner object, in this case the **HomeIndex()** function

3.3 ADD CALL TO INITIALIZE

In the **document ready()** function, add this code below the "app.homeIndex" declaration. This will add the call to run the **initialiseScrollToTopButton** method.

```
$(document).ready(function () {

    /* Instantiate new Home class */

    app.homeIndex = new HomeIndex();

    /* Initialize the Scroll To Top button */

    app.homeIndex.initialiseScrollToTopButton();

});
```

Initializes the Scroll to top button

3.4 SHOW THE BUTTON

Add the "on scroll" event handler in the `initialiseScrollToTopButton()` function. This determines the current scroll distance by using the JavaScript command `scrollTop()`. It then compares the current scroll distance with the "heightToTop" value to see if the scroll button needs to fade in or fade out.

```
/* Methods */

    this.initialiseScrollToTopButton = function () {

        /* Window Scroll Event Handler */

        $(window).scroll(function () {

            /* Show or Hide Scroll to Top Button based on
            scroll distance*/

            var verticalHeight = $(this).scrollTop();

            if (verticalHeight > heightFromTop) {

                $("#scrollToTop").fadeIn();

            } else {

                $("#scrollToTop").fadeOut();

            }

        });

    }
```

This instruction tells JQuery to run the code block every time the user scrolls the page

JQuery selector that targets the "window" object

This selector tells JQuery to use the element that triggered the event: the window object in this instance

This JQuery selector targets the HTML element with id="scrollToTop"

JQuery methods that automatically animate the button

3.5 CLICKING THE BUTTON

Next, you need to add a event handler to manage what happens when the Scroll to top button is clicked. To do this, add the JQuery `click()` function that detects when the button is clicked. Use the `animate()` command to instruct JQuery to animate the "html" and "body" elements when the button is clicked.

```
            $("#scrollToTop").fadeOut();

        }

    });

    /* Scroll to Top Click Event Handler */

    $("#scrollToTop").click(function () {

        $("html, body").animate({ scrollTop: 0 },"slow");

    });

}
```

This code runs every time the button is clicked

Animates the "html" and "body" elements

Stops when the scroll reaches the top of the page

SAVE

3.6 **VIEW PAGE**
Test the Scroll to top button. Open the browser and enter the url for the web page into the address bar. In Windows, the url to the file on your local computer will be "file:///C:/petshop/index.html". On a Mac, the url will be "file:///Users/[user account name]/PetShop/index.html". The Scroll to top button should be visible now. Click on it and make sure that the page scrolls back up to the top.

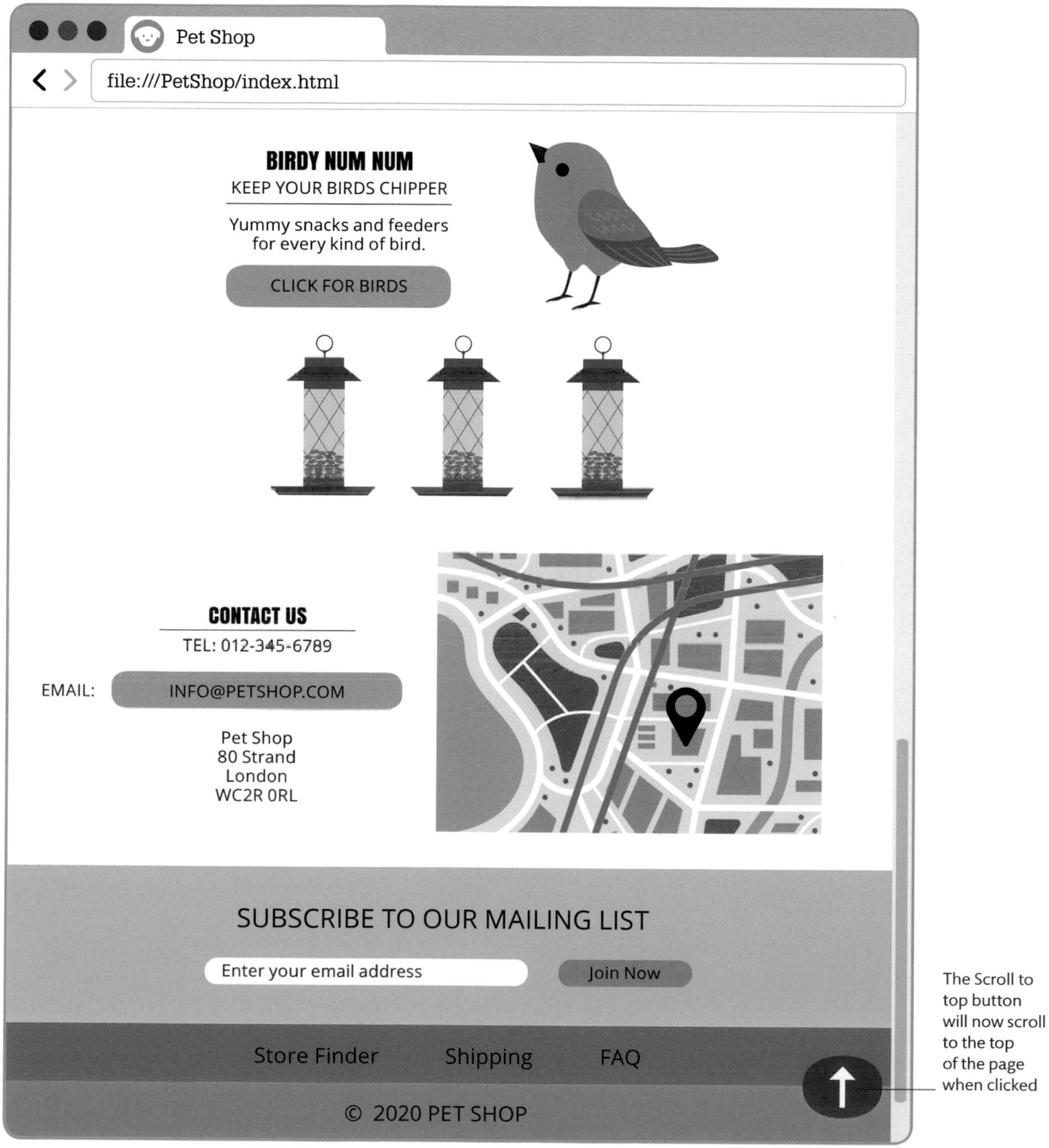

Pet Shop

file:///PetShop/index.html

BIRDY NUM NUM
KEEP YOUR BIRDS CHIPPER

Yummy snacks and feeders
for every kind of bird.

CLICK FOR BIRDS

CONTACT US
TEL: 012-345-6789

EMAIL: INFO@PETSHOP.COM

Pet Shop
80 Strand
London
WC2R 0RL

SUBSCRIBE TO OUR MAILING LIST

Enter your email address   Join Now

Store Finder   Shipping   FAQ

© 2020 PET SHOP

The Scroll to top button will now scroll to the top of the page when clicked

4 **Managing promotional messages**
The next element that needs to be managed is the promotional bar that appears on top of the web page. The promo section in HTML contains four different messages (see p.221). Using JavaScript, you will program the promo bar to cycle through these messages, making them appear one at a time.

New toys
for puppies

Free
shipping

Buy 5 toys
and save 30%

4.1 ADD A NEW CUSTOM SCRIPT
You will want the Promotional Messages to be visible on all pages of the website. Create a new JavaScript file called "common.js". The code in this file will provide functionality for the promotional messages section at the top of the web page. Follow the same steps as earlier to create a new JavaScript file within the scripts folder.

4.2 REFERENCE FILE
Now use a <script> tag to reference the new file "common.js" in the "index.html" file. Add this line of code below the reference for the "home.js" file.

HTML

```
<script src="scripts/home.js"></script>
<script src="scripts/common.js"></script>
```
Links the JavaScript file to the HTML file

SAVE

4.3 CREATE A FUNCTION
Inside "common.js", add a new function called **Common()**. This function will act as a class (see pp.282–83) that can be instantiated as a property of the "app" object defined previously. Add an **on document ready()** function below this to instantiate the "Common" class as a property of the "app" object.

JS

```
function Common() {

}

$(document).ready(function () {

    /* Instantiate new Common class */

    app.common = new Common();

});
```
Instantiates the "Common" class as a property

4.4 ADD PROPERTIES

Next, inside the **Common()** function, add a property called "promoBar". This is a JavaScript object (see p.269) that contains all the variables used by the Promotional Messages section to manage itself.

```
function Common() {

    let self = this;

    /* Properties */

    this.promoBar =

        {

            promoItems: null,

            currentItem: 0,

            numberOfItems: 0,

        };

}
```

Creates a reference to the object that can be used later in its methods

null indicates that the variable has no value

This is the list of <div> tags with messages

This is the index of the <div> that is currently visible

This is the number of <div> tags with messages

4.5 INITIALIZE THE PROMOTIONAL MESSAGES

Add a method to initialize the Promotional Messages section. This method will set the values of the properties contained in the "promoBar" object, and will start the loop to show the next message Item.

```
            numberOfItems: 0,

        };

    /* Methods */

    this.initialisePromo = function () {

        /* Get all items in promo bar */

        let promoItems = $("#promo > div");

        /* Set values */

        this.promoBar.promoItems = promoItems;

        this.promoBar.numberOfItems = promoItems.length;

        /* Initiate promo loop to show next item */

        this.startDelay();
```

This JQuery selector returns an array of all the divs inside an element with id="promo"

Returns the number of elements in this array

```
        }

        this.startDelay = function () {

            /* Wait 4 seconds then show the next message */

            setTimeout(function () {

                self.showNextPromoItem()

            }, 4000);

        }
```

This function instructs JavaScript to repeat the call every 4,000 milliseconds

This function will fade out the current promo message and fade in the next message

4.6 CYCLE THROUGH THE PROMOTIONAL MESSAGES

Add a new method below the `initialisePromo()` function. This method will hide the current message, and then determine the index of the next message before displaying it on screen. If the current message is the last item in the message list, then the next message must be the first message in the list. The array index property (see p.268) will be used here. The value of the variable `currentItem` indicates the index number of the displayed message. As this value changes, the message being displayed will also change.

```
    this.showNextPromoItem = function () {

        /* Fade out the current item */

        $(self.promoBar.promoItems).fadeOut("slow").promise().

        done(function () {

            /* Increment current promo item counter */

            if (self.promoBar.currentItem >= (self.promoBar.

            numberOfItems - 1)) {

                /* Reset counter to zero */

                self.promoBar.currentItem = 0;

            } else {

                /* Increase counter by 1 */

                self.promoBar.currentItem++;

            }

            /* Fade in the next item */
```

This command instructs JQuery to extract the array item with the given index number

Ensures that the `currentItem` never exceeds the index number

Cycles through the promotional messages

```
            $(self.promoBar.promoItems).eq(self.promoBar.currentItem).
        fadeIn("slow", function () {
                /* Delay before showing next item */
                self.startDelay();
            });
        });
    }
}
```

Displays the next promotional
message in the list

4.7 **ADD CALL TO INITIALIZE**
Finally, add a call to start cycling through the promotional messages.
In "common.js", in the **on document ready ()** function, add a call to run
the **app.common.initialisePromo()** function.

```
$(document).ready(function () {
    /* Instantiate new Common class */
    app.common = new Common();
    /* Initialize the Promo bar */
    app.common.initialisePromo();
});
```

SAVE

4.8 **VIEW PAGE**
Now go to the browser and refresh the page. Check that
the orange promotional messages bar on top of the web page is
cycling through the four messages specified in the HTML file.

The promotional
messages appear
one at a time

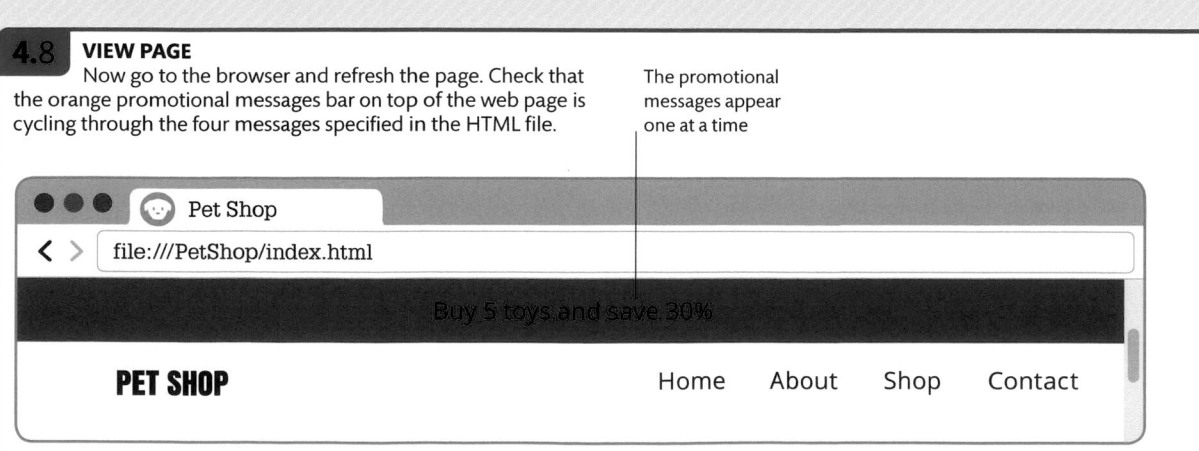

2 **ADD BUTTON**
Now add the Twitter button to the Top Menu. Inside the "topLinks" div unordered list, add a new list item that contains a hyperlink to the Twitter page. If you refresh the browser and view the page on screen, you will see a new social media button in the Top Menu.

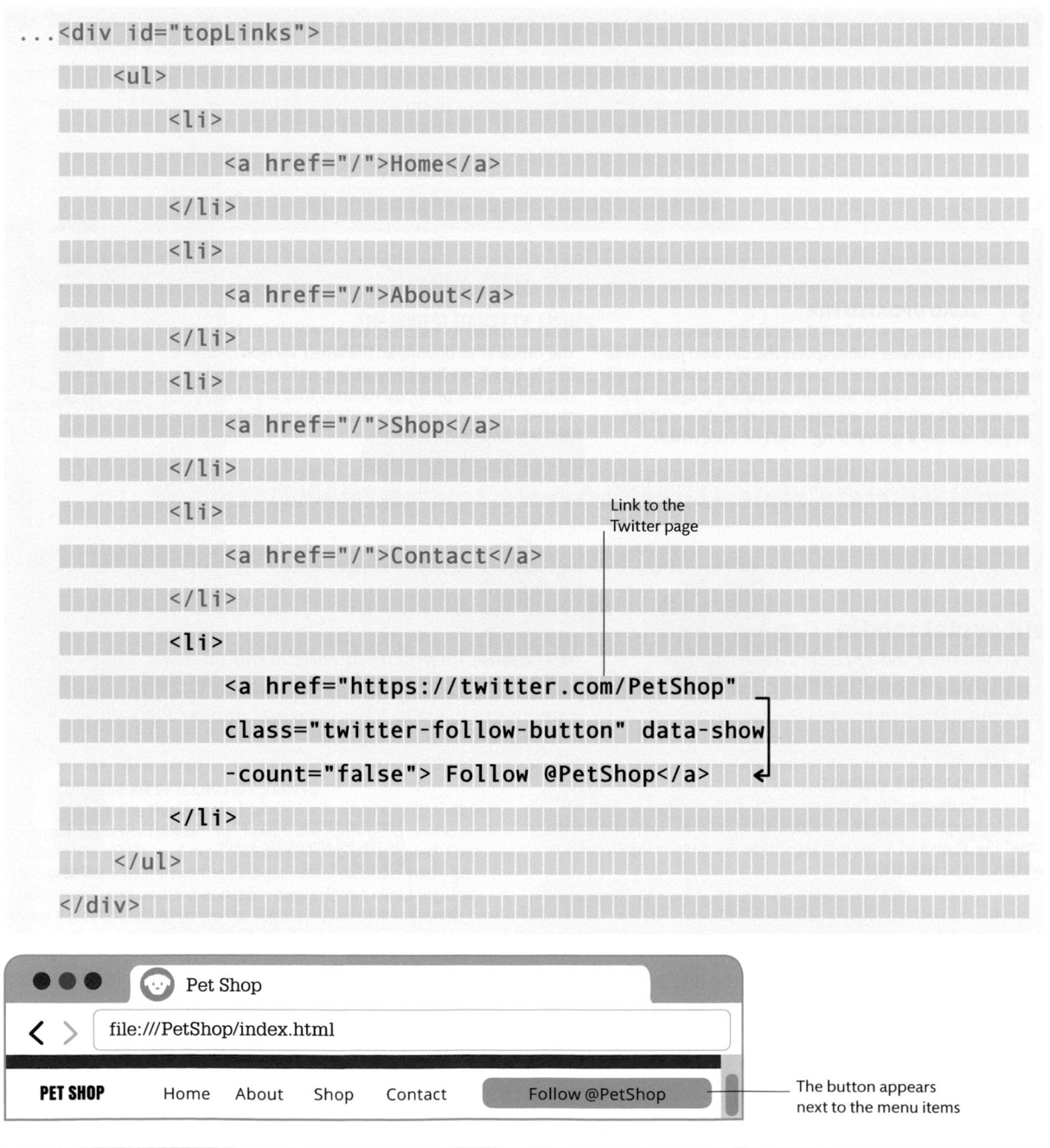

```
...<div id="topLinks">
    <ul>
        <li>
            <a href="/">Home</a>
        </li>
        <li>
            <a href="/">About</a>
        </li>
        <li>
            <a href="/">Shop</a>
        </li>
        <li>
            <a href="/">Contact</a>
        </li>
        <li>
            <a href="https://twitter.com/PetShop"
            class="twitter-follow-button" data-show
            -count="false"> Follow @PetShop</a>
        </li>
    </ul>
</div>
```

Link to the Twitter page

PET SHOP   Home   About   Shop   Contact   Follow @PetShop

file:///PetShop/index.html

Pet Shop

The button appears next to the menu items

Page template

This project only includes code for the website home page. However, other pages, such as About, Shop, and Contact in the Top Menu, are required to make a fully functioning website. In order to create these pages you will need a template, which contains all the elements that are common to every page of the website. This template will include the meta links to the CSS and JavaScript files, along with all the common HTML code.

ABOUT

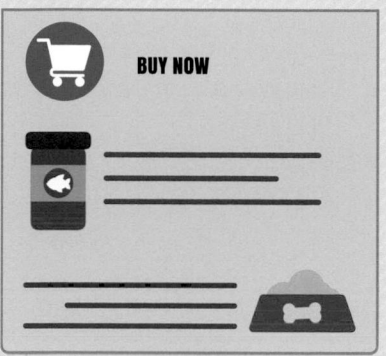

SHOP

CONTACT

1 TEMPLATE HTML FILE

Create a new file called "template.html". Then, copy the HTML from the home page into this new file. Insert the code shown here into the template file.

Now try creating the other pages of the website. Start by copying the content of "template.html" and pasting it into a new file. Rename the file accordingly; for example, "contact.html". Then, using the instructions given for the home page (see pp.220–33), insert the HTML for the "Contact page" into the placeholder "## Insert page content here ###" given in the template code.

```
                        <a href="/Shop">SHOP NOW</a>
                    </div>
            </div>
        </div>
    <div class="clear spacer v80"></div>
    <div class="wrap">
        ## Insert page content here ###
    </div>
    <div id="footer">
```

Replace the code between the Banner section and the Footer section with these lines

Insert HTML for the new page between the div tag with class ="wrap"

2 SERVER-SIDE TEMPLATE OPTIONS

In order to automatically inject the template into each page, you will need to use a server-side language, such as C# MVC or Python Django. In this project, you repeatedly had to include the links to the CSS and JavaScript files into every HTML page on the website. This is obviously difficult to update and maintain, especially if there are lots of pages in the website. You may want to explore the "layout file" concept in C# MVC (*https://www.asp.net/mvc*) and the "template inheritance" feature in Python Django (*https://www.djangoproject. com*) to solve this problem.

Responsive website

Responsive layouts enable programmers to create and publish the same content on any digital platform. This is achieved through a clever use of HTML and CSS. In this project, you will use HTML, CSS, and JavaScript, as well as JQuery and Bootstrap, to create a responsive website.

How it works

The focus of this project is to build a responsive website using JQuery and Bootstrap (see pp.284–85). Each element of the website will be programmed using HTML, CSS, and JavaScript at the same time, to see how they work together to achieve a visual effect. You will use JQuery in the custom scripts to target HTML elements, and then use Bootstrap to add responsiveness to the website.

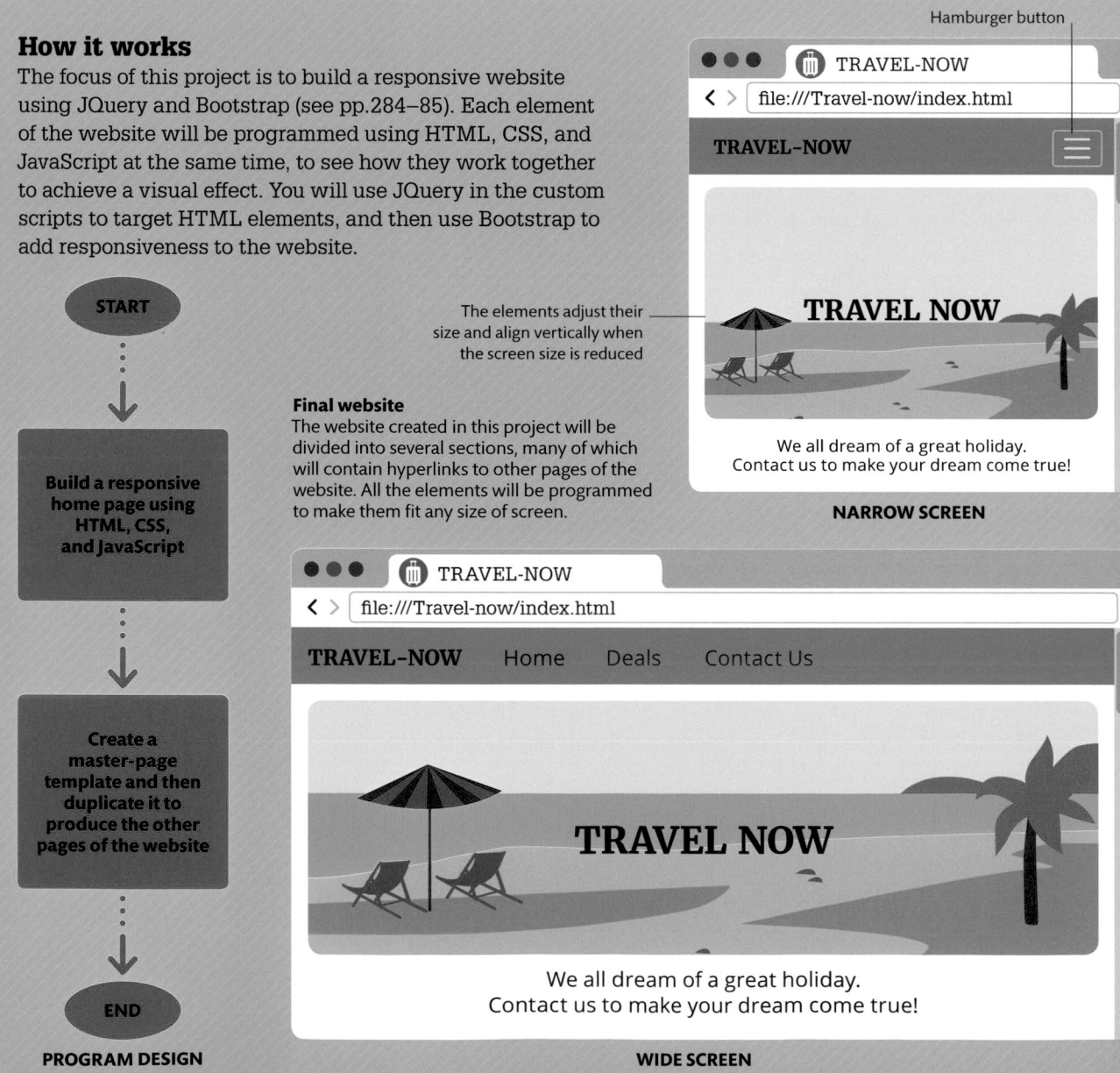

Hamburger button

START

The elements adjust their size and align vertically when the screen size is reduced

Final website
The website created in this project will be divided into several sections, many of which will contain hyperlinks to other pages of the website. All the elements will be programmed to make them fit any size of screen.

Build a responsive home page using HTML, CSS, and JavaScript

Create a master-page template and then duplicate it to produce the other pages of the website

END

PROGRAM DESIGN

TRAVEL-NOW

file:///Travel-now/index.html

TRAVEL-NOW

TRAVEL NOW

We all dream of a great holiday.
Contact us to make your dream come true!

NARROW SCREEN

TRAVEL-NOW

file:///Travel-now/index.html

TRAVEL-NOW   Home   Deals   Contact Us

TRAVEL NOW

We all dream of a great holiday.
Contact us to make your dream come true!

WIDE SCREEN

YOU WILL LEARN

> How to use Bootstrap grid layout
> How to use Bootstrap controls in your website
> How to use JQuery to target HTML elements

TIME:
3–4 hours

Lines of code: 659

Difficulty level
● ● ● ● ●

WHERE THIS IS USED

Responsive layouts allow the website to be programmed once and to render correctly on a variety of devices, such as desktops, tablets, and smartphones. This compatibility with varying screen sizes means that this technology is often used by sites to reach a wider audience.

Project requirements

This project will require several programming elements to build the website.

Text files
You will need HTML, CSS, and JavaScript files to build this website. You can either use a simple text editor to create them or a dedicated IDE like the one used in this project.

Development environment
The IDE (see pp.208–209) "Microsoft Visual Studio Community 2019" is used in this project. It supports a large variety of programming languages and paradigms.

Browser
The Google Chrome browser is used to run the code in this project. Its "Developer Tools" can be used to better understand what you see in the browser. However, you can use any browser you are comfortable with.

Images
Get a copy of the images folder for this project from *www.dk.com/coding-course*. These images will be used to build the website. You can also use your own images if you like.

1 Getting started

To create this project, you first need to install Visual Studio (see p.217). You can then add all the essential folders and files that are required to create the home page of the website.

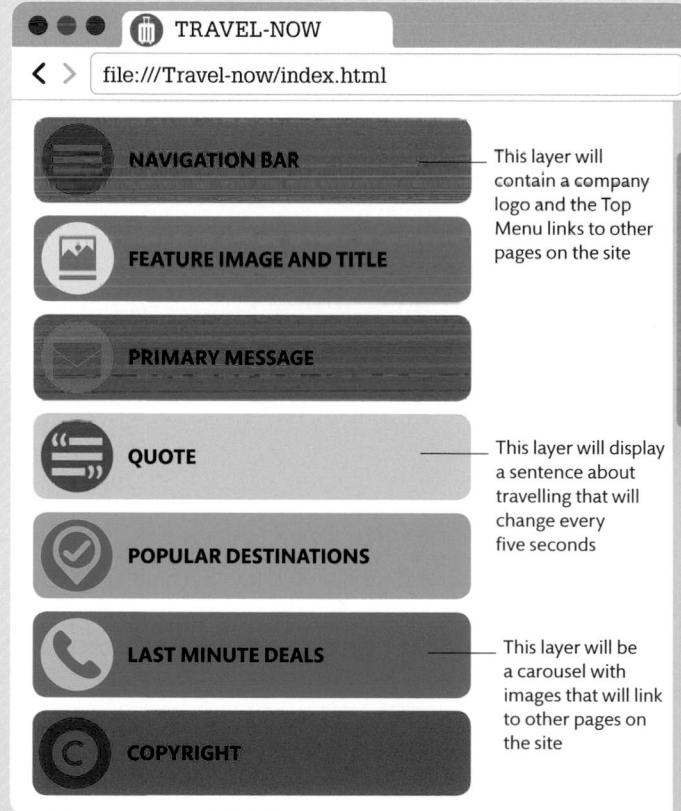

Home page design
The elements of a home page can be understood as a series of horizontal layers that sit one above the other. This home page will have seven layers. Some of its common elements will be repeated on every page of the website.

1.1 CREATE THE FOLDERS

The first step is to create a website folder on your computer to contain all the files for this website. Name the folder "Travel-now". Then, open a new project in Visual Studio and create a solution file called "Travel-now.sln" and save it in the website folder. Follow the steps from Build a web page (see pp.218–19), to do this. Paste the previously downloaded images folder inside the website folder. The path to the website folder on your computer should be as shown below.

Users/[user account name]/Travel-now

MAC

C:/Travel-now

WINDOWS

1.2 ADD AN INDEX FILE

Follow the instructions given in Build a web page (see p.219) to create an "index.html" file. Add this file to the website folder. Visual Studio will create the file with the minimum code required for a valid HTML page (see p.220). If you are using another development environment, you may need to type the code into the new index file.

INDEX.HTML

1.3 ADD A STYLE SHEET

Now add a "styles" folder for the website (see p.243). Then, add a new CSS file called "global.css" inside the styles folder. The styles defined in this file will apply to all the pages of the website. In Windows, right click on the styles folder and select Add. Then, choose Add a new item and select Style Sheet.

On a Mac, right click on the styles folder and select Add, then choose New File. Go to Web and select Empty CSS File and save it. Now add the colour and font references for the website at the top of the CSS file. You can refer to these later when you need them.

CSS

Comments contained within these marks are ignored by the browser

Font used for headings and logos

```
/*

    font-family: "Merriweather", serif;

    font-family: "Open Sans", sans-serif;

    font-family: "Merienda One", cursive;

    Text color : #000;

    Dark blue : #345995;

    Light blue : #4392F1;

    Red : #D7263D;

    Yellow : #EAC435;

    Mauve : #BC8796;

    Silver : #C0C0C0;

    Light gray : #D3D3D3;

*/
```

Font used for normal paragraph text

Font used in the "quote" section

Hex codes for the colours used on the website

1.4 ADD STYLES TO THE BODY

Add the style definitions for the <body> elements below the comment section. This will set the values for the margin and padding (see p.245), font, font colour, and background colour. As these styles are applied to the <body> elements, they will be used for all the text elements in the document. You can override the default font styles for the headings, buttons, and hyperlinks later.

Sets the font and colour definitions

CSS

```css
body {
    margin: 0;
    padding: 0;
    font-family: "Open Sans", sans-serif;
    font-size: 15px;
    color: #000;
    background-color: white;
}
```

Instructs the browser to make the <body> element fit the entire width and height of the screen

1.5 ADD SPACERS

Next, add style definitions for the vertical spacers that will be used throughout the website. These will create standardized white spaces between the various sections of the page.

CSS

Compound style signature with classes "spacer" and "v80"

```css
.spacer.v80 {
    height: 80px;
}
.spacer.v60 {
    height: 60px;
}
.spacer.v40 {
    height: 40px;
}
.spacer.v20 {
    height: 20px;
}
```

This spacer can only be applied to an element that has both "spacer" and "v20" in its "class" attribute value

1.6 STYLE THE HEADERS

The next element to be styled are the headers. Define the font styles for the "h1", "h2", and "h3" headers that will be used throughout the website. All the headers will have the same font, but a different font-size definition. Add this code just after the spacers added in the previous step.

CSS

Font used by all the headers

```css
h1, h2, h3 {
    font-family: "Merriweather", serif;
}
h1 {
    font-size: 60px;
}
h2 {
    font-size: 30px;
}
h3 {
    font-size: 20px;
}
```

This property defines the preferred font to use and a second font type in case the preferred font is not available

Only "h1" headers will have the font size 60px

Only "h2" headers will have the font size 30px

Only "h3" headers will have the font size 20px

1.7 STYLE THE CORNERS

Many elements of the website will require rounded corners. Reuse the "roundedCorners" class so this visual characteristic can be shared by the elements. If only one number is stated in the border-radius definition, then all four corners will exhibit that property. Add this code to "global.css" just after the code from the previous step.

Only the top and bottom corners are rounded

```css
.roundCorners {
    border-radius: 15px;
}

.roundCorners.top {
    border-radius: 15px 15px 0 0;
}
.roundCorners.bottom {
    border-radius: 0 0 15px 15px;
}
```

CSS

This definition applies to all the four corners

These refer to the four corners – topLeft, topRight, bottomRight, and bottomLeft

1.8 ADD A SCRIPTS FILE

Now add a new folder called "scripts" to the website folder. This will hold all the JavaScript files for the project. In the Solution Explorer window, right click on the project name Travel-now to create the folder. Then, create a new JavaScript file called "app.js" and add it to the scripts folder. Follow the instructions given in Animating a web page (see p.291) to create this file.

This file will contain an "app" class function that will be instantiated to hold all the global scope variables

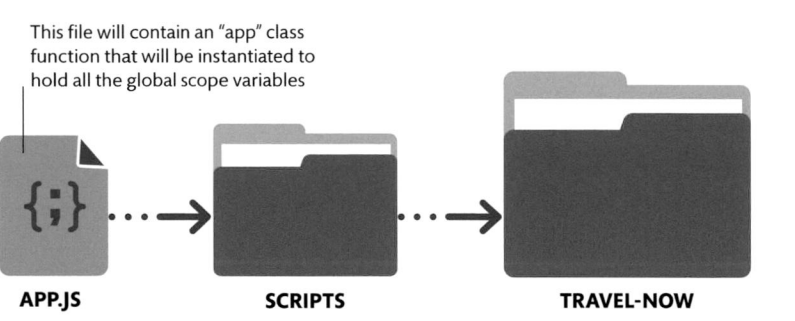

APP.JS   SCRIPTS   TRAVEL-NOW

1.9 MAKE A FUNCTION

Add this code inside the "app.js" file. This will declare a variable called "app" that is a self-executing function. Add a property called "websiteName" and a method called "getWebsiteName" inside it as an example of how to add functionality to the app class.

Round brackets around the function instruct the JavaScript Engine to run that function immediately

```js
var app = (function () {
    /* Properties */
    var websiteName = "TRAVEL-NOW";
    /* Methods */
    return {
        getWebsiteName: function () {
            return websiteName;
        }
    }
})();
```

JS

Name of the website

2 Creating the navigation bar

The first element to be created is the navigation bar on the home page. This bar will appear on all the pages of the website. In this section, you will program the navigation bar and then add some hyperlinks to it that will connect to all the other pages of the website.

2.1 ADD THE TITLE AND FAVICON

Go to the "index.html" file. Inside the <head> tag, add a <meta> tag with the "viewport" definition as shown. This allows the HTML document to adjust its content to fit the screen. Without the viewport meta definition, a browser with a narrow screen will zoom out to try and show the whole page on the screen. Next, add a <title> tag and then the favicon (see p.221) definition.

HTML

```
<head>
    <meta charset="utf-8" />
    <meta name="viewport" content="width=device-width,
    initial-scale=1, shrink-to-fit=no">
    <title>TRAVEL-NOW</title>
    <link rel="icon" type="image/png" href="images/favicon.png">
</head>
```

Instructs the browser to display the HTML document at the correct resolution

This text will appear as the tab title in the browser

This attribute points to the "favicon.png" file in the images folder

2.2 ADD THE MODULES

Now add references to the JQuery and Bootstrap JavaScript files in the HTML file. Inside the <head> tag, add the <script> tags and <link> tags just below the <link> tag to the favicon. The "src" attributes in the <script> tags point to the online location of the modules from where they can be retrieved.

This <script> tag for Bootstrap contains an "integrity" attribute that ensures the downloaded file has not been manipulated

HTML

```
    <link rel="icon" type="image/png" href="images/favicon.png">
    <script src="https://code.jquery.com/jquery-3.3.1.min.js">
    </script>
    <script src="https://stackpath.bootstrapcdn.com/bootstrap/
    4.2.1/js/bootstrap.min.js" integrity="sha384-BOUglyR+jN6Ck
    vvICOB2joaf5I4l3gm9GU6Hc1og6Ls7i6U/mkkaduKaBhlAXv9k" cross
    origin="anonymous"></script>
```

Reference to the JQuery file

```
<script src="scripts/app.js"></script>
```
The "src" attribute in this tag points to the "scripts/app.js" file

```
<link rel="stylesheet" href="https://stackpath.bootstrap
cdn.com/bootstrap/4.2.1/css/bootstrap.min.css" integrity=
"sha384-GJzZqFGwb1QTTN6wy59ffF1BuGJpLSa9DkKMpODgiMDm4iYM
j70gZWKYbI706tWS" crossorigin="anonymous">
```
Link to the Bootstrap CSS file

```
<link href="https://fonts.googleapis.com/
css?family=Merienda+One|Merriweather|Open
+Sans" rel="stylesheet">
```
Imports the fonts used in the website

```
<link href="styles/global.css" rel="stylesheet" />
```

Link to the custom CSS file – global.css

The custom CSS file is added at the end as it must overwrite the default Bootstrap CSS definitions

ORDER OF TAGS

The order in which you declare the JavaScript files is important. This is because JavaScript functions must be loaded into the JavaScript Engine before they can be called. For example, JQuery must be loaded before Bootstrap because Bootstrap uses JQuery to execute its functions. This is also true for your custom JavaScript files. They must be added to the HTML after the JQuery and Bootstrap files in order to call their functions.

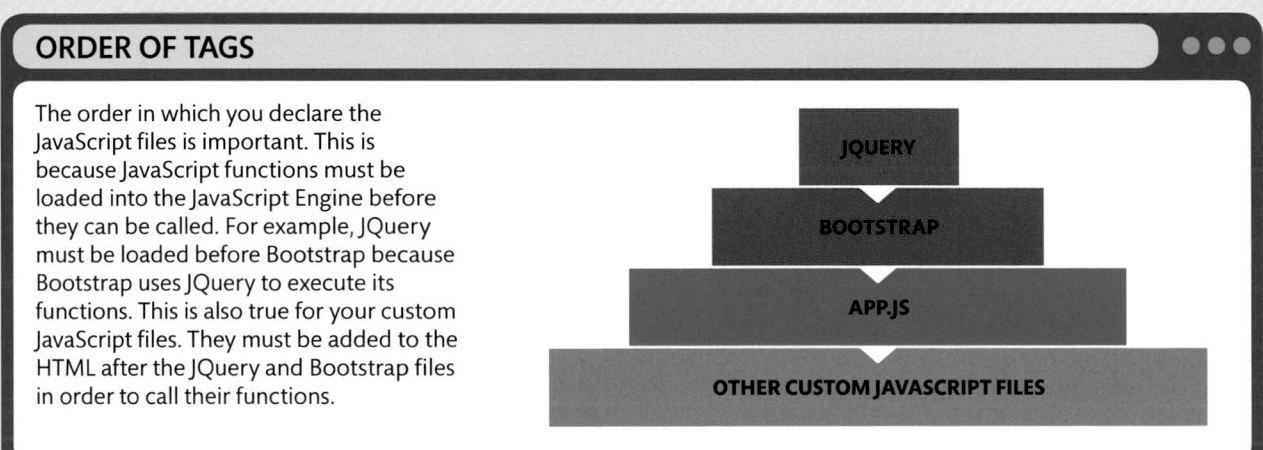

JQUERY

BOOTSTRAP

APP.JS

OTHER CUSTOM JAVASCRIPT FILES

2.3 ADD A BOOTSTRAP NAVIGATION BAR

Next, inside the <body> tag, add a <nav> tag to contain all the Bootstrap navigation bar elements. If the screen is wide enough, it will display the Top Menu list horizontally along the top of the page. If the screen is narrow, then the Top Menu will be replaced by a "hamburger menu" button – a button resembling a hamburger, used to toggle a menu or navigation bar. When this button is clicked, the Top Menu will display a vertical list.

Tells the navbar when to collapse to a hamburger menu button

HTML

```
<body>
    <nav class="navbar navbar-expand-md
    navbar-dark fixed-top bg-mauve">
    </nav>
</body>
```

Fixes the navbar position at the top

Sets the background colour to mauve

2.4 ADD A BOOTSTRAP CONTAINER

The navbar must run across the full width of the screen, but the Top Menu logo and hyperlinks must only occupy the centre of the page where all the page contents will go. Add a <div> with class = "container" inside the <nav> tag. This Bootstrap class defines the margins on the left and right of the element. Then, inside the "container" div, add an <a> tag to display the company logo. When clicked, this will hyperlink to the home page.

HTML

```html
<nav class="navbar navbar-expand-md navbar-dark fixed-top
bg-mauve">
    <div class="container">
        <a class="navbar-brand logo" href="index.html">TRAVEL-NOW
        </a>
    </div>
</nav>
```

Contains all the HTML elements that need to appear centred on the page

This Bootstrap CSS class specifies that the element must appear inline with some padding and margins

This custom CSS class defines the font to be used for the logo

2.5 DEFINE THE HAMBURGER BUTTON

Inside the "container" div, below the "navbar-brand" </a> closing tag, add the "navbar-toggler" <button> tag. This element will perform the "hamburger menu" button functionality. When clicked, the button displays the Top Menu as a vertical drop-down list.

HTML

This attribute manages the state of the drop-down menu

```html
        <a class="navbar-brand logo" href="index.html">TRAVEL-NOW
        </a>
        <button class="navbar-toggler" type="button" data-toggle=
        "collapse" data-target="#navbarCollapse" aria-controls=
        "navbarCollapse" aria-expanded="false" aria-label=
        "Toggle navigation">
            <span class="navbar-toggler-icon"></span>
        </button>
    </div>
```

This class contains display properties, such as margin and padding

The "aria" classes are used by assistive technologies, such as screen readers for the blind, to make sense of the complex HTML

2.6 ADD HYPERLINKS TO THE NAVBAR

Next, add the "navbarCollapse" div, which will contain an unordered list of the actual hyperlinks that will appear in the Top Menu of the website: Home, Deals, and Contact Us. Place it inside the "container" div, just below the closing tag for the "navbar-toggler" </button>. Then add a spacer div after the </nav> closing tag.

HTML

```
          </button>
          <div class="collapse navbar-collapse" id=
          "navbarCollapse">
              <ul id="topMenu" class="navbar-nav mr-auto">
                  <li class="nav-item active">
                      <a class="nav-link" href="index.html">
                      Home <span class="sr-only">(current)
                      </span></a>
                  </li>
                  <li class="nav-item">
                      <a class="nav-link" href="deals.html">
                      Deals</a>
                  </li>
                  <li class="nav-item">
                      <a class="nav-link" href="contact.html">
                      Contact Us</a>
                  </li>
              </ul>
          </div>
      </div>
  </nav>
  <div class="spacer v80"></div>
```

Indicates whether the navbar is in the "collapse" or "full-screen" state

Contains style definitions for the unordered list

Contains style definitions for the list items that will appear as a horizontal or vertical list, depending on the width of the screen

Anchor tags hyperlink to other pages on the website

Each <a> tag is a member of the "nav-link" class, which specifies mouse-off and hover style definitions for the navbar hyperlinks

Closing tag for the "navbarCollapse" div

Closing tag for the "container" div

Closing tag for the "navbar" div

Adds a vertical height of 80px between the navbar and the next element

SAVE

2.7 SPECIFY THE BACKGROUND COLOUR

Now go to the "global.css" style sheet to set the background colour of the navigation bar. Add this code immediately after the lines added in step 1.7 to set the style definition for this bar.

```
.bg-mauve {
    background-color: #BC8796;
}
```

CSS

2.8 STYLE THE LOGO

The next step is to style the logo that appears in the Top Menu. Add the "logo" class to specify the font to use for the company logo. Then add style definitions for the logo that appears in the navbar. The navbar logo is a hyperlink, so you will need to define both its normal and hover states. If you are unsure what CSS style definitions are acting on an element, use the Developer Tools (see p.281) in Chrome to view the styles.

CSS

```css
.logo {
    font-family: "Merriweather", serif;
    font-weight: bold;
}
.navbar-brand.logo {
    color: white;
}

    .navbar-brand.logo:hover {
        color: white;
    }
```

The default font for the logo

Normal state of the hyperlink

Hover state of the hyperlink

This will ensure the logo remains white when the mouse hovers over it

SAVE

2.9 RUN THE PROGRAM

Now test the code to see if the navigation bar renders correctly. In the Solution Explorer window, right click on "index.html" and open the file in the browser of your choice. You can also open the browser and type the website's url into the address bar. In Windows, the url will be "file:///C:/Travel-now/index.html". On a Mac, the url will be "file:///Users/[user account name]/Travel-now/index.html".

● ● ● 🧳 TRAVEL-NOW
< > file:///Travel-now/index.html
TRAVEL-NOW   Home   Deals   Contact Us

WIDE SCREEN

● ● ● 🧳 TRAVEL-NOW
< > file:///Travel-now/index.html
TRAVEL-NOW ☰
Home
Deals
Contact Us

NARROW SCREEN

3 Adding a feature image

The next element of the home page that needs to be managed is the feature image. Each page on the website will have a "feature image" banner that will cover the entire width of the page and contains the page title.

3.1 CENTRE THE CONTENTS

Go to "index.html", and after the "spacer v80" </div> closing tag, add a "container" div so that all the contents appear centred on the page, regardless of the width of the screen.

HTML

```html
<div class="spacer v80"></div>
<div class="container">
</div>
```

3.2 ADD THE FEATURE IMAGE BANNER

Now, inside the "container" div, add the feature image for the home page and an "h1" header with the title of the page. You can even use a different image on each page of the website if you like. The "homeIndex" and "featureImage" classes are used to specify the background image for the home page.

HTML

```
<div class="container">

    <div class="featureImage roundCorners homeIndex">

        <div class="text">

            <h1>

                TRAVEL-NOW

            </h1>

        </div>

    </div>
```

The "featureImage" div will appear on every page

The "homeIndex" class specifies the background image to be used for the home page

Text that appears in front of the image — TRAVEL-NOW

Closing tag for the "featureImage" div — </div>

Closing tag for the "text" div

SAVE

3.3 CENTRE THE IMAGE

Open the "global.css" file and add some styles to specify the position of the feature image on a page. These styles allow the browser to automatically fit the image to any size of screen. Add this code to the end of the CSS file.

CSS

```
.featureImage {

    width: 100%;

    position: relative;

    height: 400px;

    background-size: cover;

    background-position:

    center;

}

.featureImage.homeIndex {

    background-image: url

    (../images/

    feature.jpg);

}
```

Specifies the width and height of an image

Specifies the actual image file that will be displayed on the page

3.4 STYLE THE IMAGE TEXT

Now add some code to style the text that will appear in front of the image. The "text" div defines a space in the middle of the "featureImage" div, which will contain the heading.

CSS

```
.featureImage .text {

    margin: 0;

    color: black;

    position: absolute;

    top: 50%;

    left: 50%;

    width: 80%;

    color: #000;

    text-align: center;

    -webkit-transform: translate

    (-50%,-50%);

    transform: translate

    (-50%,-50%);

}
```

Specifies the text colour

Positions the text to start in the middle of the page

Repositions the text so that it fits in the middle of the page

3.5 ADD RESPONSIVENESS

The name of the website needs to be displayed at different font size, depending on the width of the screen. Use the "@media screen" instructions to tell the browser which definitions to apply according to the size of the screen.

CSS

```
@media screen and (max-width: 400px) {

    .featureImage .text h1 {

        font-size: 22px;──────── Size of the "h1" header at
                                 the minimum screen width
    }
}
```
Instructs the browser to change the font size depending on the width of the screen

```
@media screen and (min-width: 401px) and (max-width: 767px) {

    .featureImage .text h1 {

        font-size: 32px;──────── Size of the "h1" header when
                                 the screen width is changing
    }

}

@media screen and (min-width: 768px) {

    .featureImage .text h1 {

        font-size: 80px;──────── Size of the "h1" header at
                                 the maximum screen width
    }

}
```

SAVE

3.6 RUN THE PROGRAM

Save all the files and refresh the web page in the browser to see what the website looks like at this point. The feature image and its text should resize according to the width of the screen.

WIDE SCREEN

NARROW SCREEN

4 **Adding a message**
The next step is to manage the "primary message" section of the website. This message is a paragraph of text that will display the main intention of the page in a prominent font.

4.1 **ADD THE MESSAGE TEXT**
Open "index.html". Then, within the "container" <div> add another <div> tag with class="primaryMessage". Place this new <div> immediately after the closing tag for the "featureImage" </div>. This will contain the paragraph of text you want to display on the website.

HTML

```
        </div>───────── Closing tag for the
                          "featureImage" div
   <div class="primaryMessage">

      <p>─────────── The paragraph tag

          We all dream of a great holiday.

          <br />

          Contact us to make your dream come true!

      </p>

   </div>─────────── Closing tag for the
                       "primaryMessage" div
```

Contents of the primary message

SAVE

4.2 **STYLE THE MESSAGE**
Now go to the "global.css" file and add some style definitions to the message. These styles will apply to both wide and narrow screens.

CSS

```
        font-size: 80px;

    }

}

.primaryMessage {

    color: #000;                    "auto" sets the
                                    horizontal margins
    margin: 0 auto;───── at equal width

    text-align: center;

    padding: 60px 0;

    max-width: 80%;

}
```

The width of the "primaryMessage" cannot be more than 80% of the parent "container" div

4.3 **ADD RESPONSIVENESS**
The message will be displayed with different font sizes, depending on the width of the screen. Add this code below the ".primaryMessage" style definition.

CSS

```
@media screen and (max-width:
575px) {

    .primaryMessage {

        font-size: 18px;

    }                        Sets the size of the font
                             when the screen width
}                            is less than 576px wide

@media screen and (min-width:
576px) {

    .primaryMessage {

        font-size: 23px;

    }                        Sets the size of the font
                             when the screen width
}                            is more than 575px wide
```

4.4 VIEW THE MESSAGE

Save all the files and then refresh the web page in the browser to see if the message is rendered correctly. The primary message will be displayed immediately after the feature image, and its text will resize according to the width of the screen.

WIDE SCREEN

Displays the message with the larger font size

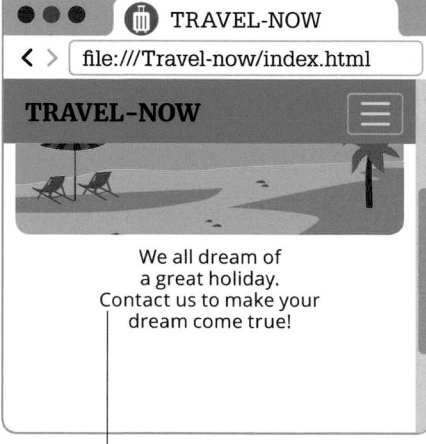

NARROW SCREEN

The font size changes according to the width of the screen

5 Adding a quote

The next element to be added is a Quote section. You will structure the section using HTML, and then add style definitions in CSS to specify the basic layout properties and colours. Finally, using JavaScript, you will make this section cycle through the quotes, making them appear one at a time.

5.1 ADD A SCRIPT TAG

In the <head> section of the "index.html" file, add a <script> tag to link a custom JavaScript file to the HTML file. Add this code below the closing </script> tag for "app.js". This instructs the browser to include the "home.js" file when the page is loading. The new custom file will be created later using JavaScript.

HTML

```
<script src="scripts/app.js"></script>

<script src="scripts/home.js"></script>
```

The "src" attribute points to the external "home.js" file

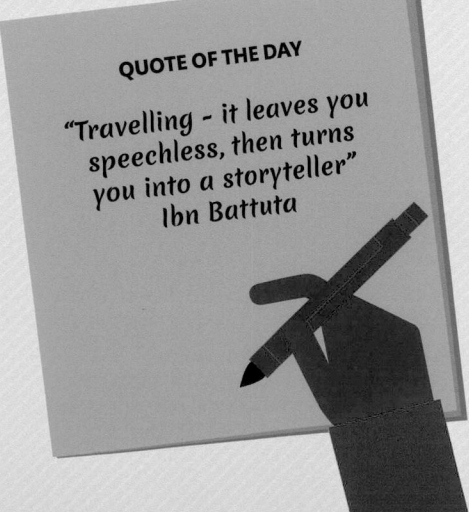

QUOTE OF THE DAY

"Travelling - it leaves you speechless, then turns you into a storyteller"
Ibn Battuta

HTML

5.2 ADD THE QUOTE TEXT

Now add the "quote" div just after closing </div> tag for the "primary message". This will contain the text for all the quotes, including names of the people who made them. All the quote items, except the first, will have an inline style definition "display:none", so that when the page loads, only the first quote item is visible.

```
</div>                                   Closing tag for the
                                         "primaryMessage" div

<div class="quote roundCorners">

    <div class="quoteItem" >

        <p>                              This tag contains
                                         the quote text

            The journey not the arrival matters.

        </p>

        <span>T.S. Eliot</span>          This tag is used for applying
                                         styles to inline elements

    </div>

    <div class="quoteItem" style="display:none;">     The second
                                                      "quoteItem"
        <p>                                           will not be
                                                      visible when
            Jobs fill your pocket, but adventures     the page
                                                      appears
            fill your soul.              ↵

        </p>

        <span>Jaime Lyn Beatty</span>

    </div>

</div>                                    Adds a vertical height of
                                         40px between the "quote"
<div class="spacer v40"></div>           div and the next element
```

SAVE

5.3 STYLE THE QUOTE

Next, open the "global.css" file and add the style definitions for the "quote" div. These styles will specify the text alignment, padding, background colour, and text colour of the quotes. Add this code immediately after the "@media screen" instructions for the primary message.

CSS

```
.quote {

    text-align: center;          Aligns the contents
                                 to the center of the
    padding: 60px 20px;          "quote" div

    background-color: #4392F1;

    color: white;                Hex code for
                                 light-blue colour
    height: 180px;

    position: relative;

}
```

Defines the vertical space occupied by the quote section

5.4 ADD RESPONSIVENESS

The quote section needs to be displayed at a different size, depending on the width of the screen. Add a style definition for the "quote" div that will only apply when the screen width is more than 766px wide.

CSS

```css
    position: relative;
}
@media screen and (min-width: 767px) {
    .quote {
        height: 220px;
    }
}
```

Adjusts the vertical space occupied by the quote section ——— height: 220px;

5.5 POSITION THE TEXT

Now add some style definitions for all the "quoteItems" elements, below the code for step 5.4. These will define the basic layout properties of all the text elements in the quotes.

CSS

```css
.quote > .quoteItem {
    max-width: 60%;
    margin: 0;
    color: white;
    position: absolute;
    top: 50%;
    left: 50%;
    text-align: center;
    -webkit-transform: translate(-50%,-50%);
    transform: translate(-50%,-50%);
}
```

The width of the "quoteItem" cannot be more than 60% of the width of the parent "quote" div

Positions the top-left corner of the "quoteItem" element in the middle of the parent "quote" div

Repositions the "quoteItem" up by 50% of its height and left by 50% of its width, so that it aligns exactly in the middle of the "quote" section

5.6 DEFINE THE FONTS AND MARGINS

The <p> element style definition declares the font styles to be used for each quote item. It also sets the margin that appears below each paragraph. Add these lines just below the code from step 5.5.

CSS

```css
.quoteItem p {
    font-family: "Merienda One", cursive;
    font-size: 20px;
    font-weight: normal;
    margin-bottom: 5px;
}
```

Vertical space between the paragraph and the <span> element below it

Displays the quote text in a cursive font

5.7 INSERT QUOTATION MARKS

Now use CSS selectors to instruct the browser to insert quotation marks automatically around the <p> element. The "content" definition specifies which quotation mark is to be inserted.

Specifies the basic layout properties of the quotation marks

```css
.quoteItem p:before {
    color: #EAC435;
    content: open-quote;
    font-size: 40px;
    line-height: 20px;
    margin-right: 5px;
    vertical-align: -13px;
}

.quoteItem p:after {
    color: #EAC435;
    content: close-quote;
    font-size: 40px;
    line-height: 20px;
    margin-left: 5px;
    vertical-align: -13px;
}
```

CSS

Instructs the browser to insert the "open-quote" character

Hex code for the colour yellow

Instructs the browser to insert the "close-quote" character

Lowers the element by 13px below the baseline

5.8 STYLE THE QUOTE MARKS

You can now add style definitions to adjust the font size for the quote text and the spacing of the quotation marks, depending on the width of the screen. Then, set the styling for the <span> tag that contains the name of the source of the quote.

```css
@media screen and (max-width: 766px) {
    .quoteItem p {
        font-size: 14px;
    }
    .quoteItem p:before {
        vertical-align: -12px;
    }
    .quoteItem p:after {
        vertical-align: -17px;
    }
}
```

CSS

Adjusts the size of the quote font

Adjusts the vertical alignment of the "open-quote" character

Adjusts the vertical alignment of the "close-quote" character

```
.quoteItem span {

    color: #EAC435;

    font-size: 18px;

}
```

Font size of the <span> text when the width of the screen is more than 766px

SAVE

5.9   **CREATE A JAVASCRIPT FILE**

You will need a new custom JavaScript file to contain the functionality required by the home page. To create this file, go to the Solution Explorer window, right click on the scripts folder, select Add and then select Add New Item in Windows, and New File on a Mac. Name the file "home.js". Then, add a **Home()** function and another **on document ready()** function below it. This function is a JQuery command that will tell the JavaScript Engine to wait until all the elements on the page have finished loading before running the code in the **$(document).ready()** function.

Instantiates the **Home()** function as a property of the "app" object

```javascript
function Home() {
}
$(document).ready(function () {
    /* Instantiate new Home class */
    app.home = new Home();
});
```

{;}
JS

The "app" object has already been instantiated in the "app.js" file

---

5.10   **APPLY PROPERTIES TO THE QUOTE**

Just below the **Home()** function, add a property called "quoteControl" that contains all the variables used by the quote section to manage itself.

Index of the "quoteItem" div that is currently visible

Holds a reference to the JavaScript "setInterval" command, which instructs the JavaScript Engine to repeatedly call the function to show the next quote

This object has four properties

Contains the list of <div> tags with quotes

Number of <div> tags with quotes

```javascript
function Home() {
    /* Properties */
    this.quoteControl =
        {
            quoteItems: null,
            currentItem: 0,
            numberOfItems: 0,
            interval: null,
            repeatPeriod: 5000
        };
}
```

{;}
JS

5.11 INITIALIZE THE QUOTE

Inside the **Home()** function, add a method below the "quoteControl" declaration to initialize the quote section. This function can be accessed as a property of the "app.home" instance declared in te **$(document).ready()** function.

JS

```
};
/* Methods */

this.initialiseQuoteControl = function () {

    /* Get all items in quote bar */

    let quoteItems = $(".quoteItem");

    /* Set values */

    this.quoteControl.quoteItems = quoteItems;

    this.quoteControl.numberOfItems = quoteItems.length;

    /* Initiate quote loop to show next item */

    let self = this;

    this.quoteControl.interval = setInterval(function () {

        self.showNextQuoteItem(self);

    }, this.quoteControl.repeatPeriod);

}
```

Sets the values of the properties contained in the "quoteControl" object and starts the loop to show the next quote item

The variable **quoteItems** is defined as the array of all the <divs> that have the class "quoteItem"

The variable **self** retains the reference to the instance of the "Home" class

Instructs the JavaScript function to repeat the call to the **showNextQuoteItem()** function every 5,000 milliseconds

5.12 ANIMATE THE QUOTE

Now add the **showNextQuoteItem()** function below the code from step 5.11. This method will hide the current quote item, and when that is complete, it will determine the index of the next quote item and make it visible. If the current quote item is the last item in the list, then the next quote item will be the first quote item in the list.

JS

```
this.showNextQuoteItem = function (self) {

    /* fade out the current item */

    $(self.quoteControl.quoteItems).eq(self.quoteControl.

    currentItem).fadeOut("slow", function () {

        /* Increment current quote item counter*/

        if (self.quoteControl.currentItem >= (self.

        quoteControl.numberOfItems - 1)) {

            /* Reset counter to zero */
```

Hides the current quote item

Determines the index of the next quote item

```
            self.quoteControl.currentItem = 0;
```
This is the index number
of the current quote item

```
        } else {
            /* Increase counter by 1 */
            self.quoteControl.currentItem++;
```
Increases the index by
one and moves to the
next quote item

```
        }
        /* fade in the next item*/
        $(self.quoteControl.quoteItems).eq(self.quoteControl.
        currentItem).fadeIn("slow");
    });
}
```
Gets all the message items

This command instructs
JQuery to target a specific
quote item with the index
number **currentItem**

5.13 CALL A FUNCTION

Finally, add a call to the **initialiseQuoteControl()** function to start cycling through the quote Items. Add thls code inside the **on document ready()** function that you added in step 5.9.

```
    app.home = new Home();
    /* Initialize the Quote bar */
    app.home.initialiseQuoteControl();
});
```

Calls the **initialiseQuoteControl()** function to animate the quote items

SAVE

5.14 VIEW THE QUOTE SECTION

Refresh the web page in the browser to see what is being rendered on screen. The "quote" div will resize according to the width of the screen, and the quote text will change every five seconds.

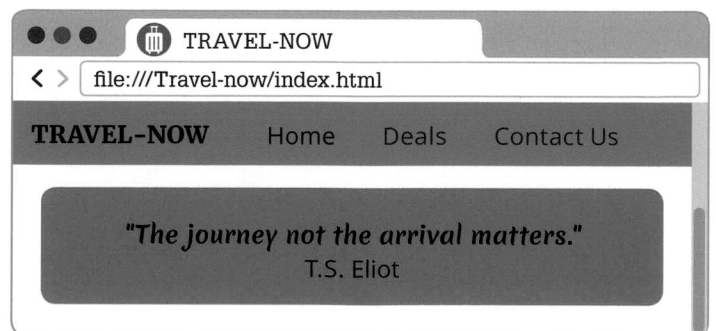

WIDE SCREEN

NARROW SCREEN

6 Adding popular destinations

The next element to be managed is the "popular destinations" section, which will showcase three featured holiday destinations. Within a wide screen, Bootstrap's column definitions will make the section appear as three side-by-side horizontal columns. Columns will appear one on top of the other when the screen width is narrow.

6.1 ADD THE CONTENT

Go to the "index.html" file. Within the quote section in the "container" div, add the "popularDestinations" div and all its contents below the closing tag for the "spacer" div. You will have to use the Bootstrap grid system, which contains 12 columns across the page, to group the destination items in separate columns on the screen. These columns automatically adjust to display correctly on any screen size.

HTML

```
<div class="spacer v40"></div>
<div class="popularDestinations">
    <div class="heading">
        POPULAR DESTINATIONS
    </div>
    <div class="row">
        <div class="col-md-4 destinationItem">
            <a href="deals.html" class="subHeading">
                <img src="images/France.jpg"
                class="image" /><br />France
            </a>
        </div>
        <div class="col-md-4 destinationItem">
            <a href="deals.html" class="subHeading">
                <img src="images/Egypt.jpg"
                class="image" /><br />Egypt
            </a>
        </div>
        <div class="col-md-4 destinationItem">
            <a href="deals.html" class="subHeading">
                <img src="images/Africa.jpg"
                class="image" /><br />Africa
            </a>
```

"md" is a Bootstrap column definition that defines how the columns behave when the width of the screen changes

The first "popular destinations" item

The second "popular destinations" item

The third "popular destinations" item

The "src" attribute points to the location of the image file on the computer

The class "col-md-4" forces the columns to change from a horizontal lay out to a vertical layout when the screen is of medium width

```
                </div>
            </div>────── Closing tag for
                            the "row" div
            </div>────── Closing tag for the        Adds a vertical height
                            "popularDestinations" div   of 60px between this
        <div class="spacer v60"></div>────── section and the next
```

SAVE

6.2   ADD RESPONSIVENESS

Now go to the "global. css" file and add style definitions for the "destinationItem" divs. This will require a definition for narrow screens and another definition for when the screen size is more than 575px wide.

Defines the size of the bottom margin for a destination item depending on the width of the screen

CSS

```
    font-size: 18px;
}
.popularDestinations .row
.destinationItem {
    text-align: center;────── Sets the alignment
                                 of the contents of
}                                destinationItem
@media screen and (max-width: 575px) {
    .popularDestinations .row
    .destinationItem {
        margin-bottom: 20px;────── Sets the space between
                                      the bottom border of
    }                                 the destinationItem
}                                     and the element below
                                      it to 20px
```

6.3   DEFINE THE FONTS

Next, add the font style definitions for the "heading" and "subHeading" elements just below the code for step 6.2.

CSS

Defines the height between lines of text, which is important to specify as the heading can sometimes appear on multiple lines

```
.popularDestinations .heading,
.popularDestinations .subHeading {
    font-family: "Merriweather", serif;
}                                 Default font for the
                                  heading and subHeading
.popularDestinations .heading {
    font-size: 30px;
                                  Specifies the style definitions for
    line-height: 35px;            the heading in "normal" state
}
```

6.4 STYLE THE IMAGE AND SUBHEADING

To set the styles for the "subHeading" hyperlink, you will require definitions for the "normal" and "hover" states. You will then instruct the browser to display the image at the maximum width available to it.

CSS

```
.popularDestinations .subHeading {
    font-size: 36px;
    color: #345995;
}
```

Specifies the style definitions for the subHeading in "normal" state

Hex code for dark-blue colour

```
.popularDestinations .subHeading:hover {
    text-decoration: none;
    color: #D7263D;
}
```

The text is not underlined when the mouse hovers over it

Sets the colour of the hyperlink to red

Defines the "hover" state when a mouse moves over the subHeading

```
.popularDestinations .image {
    width: 100%;
}
```

Displays the image at 100% of the width available to it

SAVE

6.5 RUN THE PROGRAM

Save the file and then refresh the page in the browser. The popular destinations section will resize according to the width of the screen. All the destination items will be displayed horizontally if the screen is wide, and vertically if the screen is narrow.

In a wide screen, the **destinationItems** appear as a horizontal list of images with hyperlinks

In a narrow screen, the **destinationItems** appear as a vertical list of images with hyperlinks

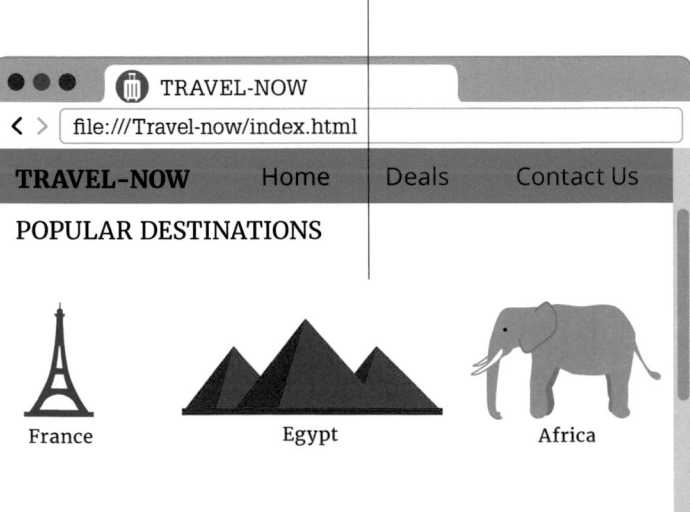

WIDE SCREEN

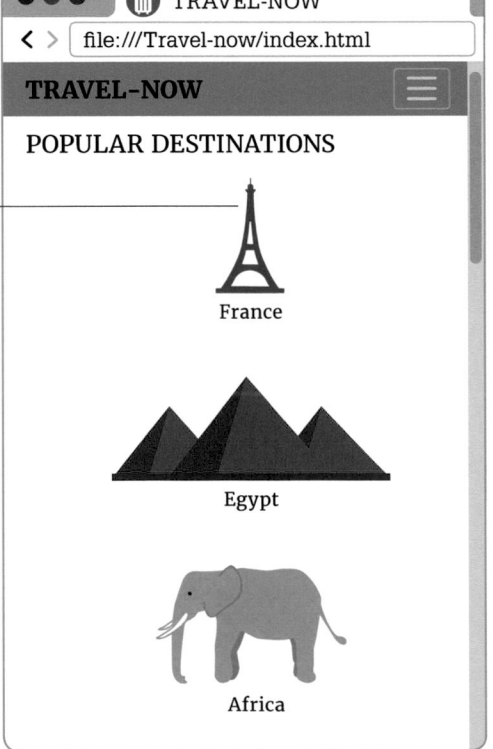

NARROW SCREEN

7 Adding last minute deals

The next element is the "last minute deals" section. This
section will use a carousel to show a slideshow of two images. Each
slide is a hyperlink that will take the user to the "deals.html" page.
Bootstrap contains all the functionality required to create a carousel.

7.1 DEFINE THE ELEMENTS OF THE CAROUSEL

In the "index.html" file, just below the "spacer v60"
</div> closing tag of the popular destinations section, add
the "featuredDeals" div and all its contents. This will include
a header for the section and an ordered list of place markers
that will show users which slide they are currently viewing.

The "h2" header contains
the name of the section

HTML

```
<div class="spacer v60"></div>

<div class="featuredDeals">

     <h2 class="heading">LAST MINUTE DEALS</h2>

     <div id="dealsCarousel" class="carousel slide " data-ride=
     "carousel">

          <ol class="carousel-indicators">

               <li data-target="#dealsCarousel" data-slide-to=
               "0" class="active"></li>

               <li data-target="#dealsCarousel" data-slide-to=
               "1"></li>

          </ol>

     </div>

</div>
```

The two attributes – "id" and "data-ride" – are used to manage the behaviour of the carousel

These classes are used to style the contents of the <div>

These classes are used to style the place-marker indicators

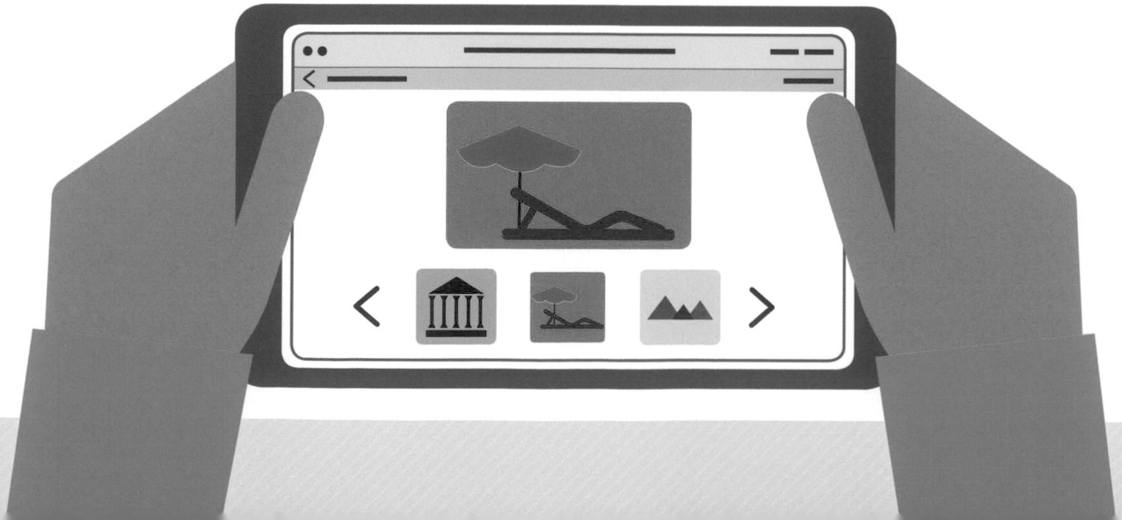

7.2   **ADD THE CONTENTS**
Below the "carousel-indicators" closing </ol> tag, add the "carousel-item" content for the slides. Make sure to add the class "active" to the first carousel item. This will instruct the JavaScript Engine to start the slideshow on that particular item. When the next slide shows, the "active" class

will be removed from the first carousel item and will be added to the next carousel item. You also need to add two classes –"d-block" and "w-100" – to the <img/> tag to specify the size of the images. There are two carousel items being added here, but you can add more if you like.

HTML

Closing tag for the "carousel-indicators" ordered list

The slideshow starts with this carousel item

```
...</ol>

    <div class="carousel-inner">

        <div class="carousel-item active">

            <a href="deals.html">

                <img class="d-block w-100 roundCorners"

                src="images/Serengeti_Safari.jpg"

                alt="Serengeti Safari">

                <div class="carousel-caption d-block">

                    <h3>SERENGETI SAFARI</h3>

                </div>

            </a>

        </div>

        <div class="carousel-item">

            <a href="deals.html">

                <img class="d-block w-100 roundCorners"

                src="images/Taj_Mahal.jpg"

                alt="Taj Mahal">

                <div class="carousel-caption d-block">

                    <h3>TAJ MAHAL</h3>

                </div>

            </a>

        </div>

</div>
```

Instructs the browser to display the image as a "block" element

Provides alternate text for an image if the image cannot be displayed

Defines the header of the first slide

Contains the second slide of the carousel

Instructs the browser to scale the image to 100% of the width available to it. The size of the slide increases according to the width of the screen

Adds a caption to the slide

Closing tag for the "carousel-inner" div

Defines the header of the second slide

7.3 CREATE THE BUTTONS

Now add the "next" and "previous" buttons for the carousel so that the user can move forward and backward through the slideshow. Type this code after the "carousel-inner" </div> closing tag from step 7.2.

The "href" attribute is used by Bootstrap to manage the carousel button behaviour

HTML

```
...</div>
    <a class="carousel-control-prev" href="#dealsCarousel"
role="button" data-slide="prev">
        <span class="carousel-control-prev-icon"
        aria-hidden="true"></span>
        <span class="sr-only">Previous</span>
    </a>
    <a class="carousel-control-next" href="#dealsCarousel"
role="button" data-slide="next">
        <span class="carousel-control-next-icon"
        aria-hidden="true"></span>
        <span class="sr-only">Next</span>
    </a>
```

The <a> tag defines the button as a hyperlink

The "sr-only" class specifies that the <span> element will only be visible on a screen-reader client

This <span> element will not be visible if the client is a normal web browser

7.4 ADD A HYPERLINK

Next, within the "featureDeals" div, add a call-to-action hyperlink below the "dealsCarousel" </div> closing tag. This hyperlink will take the user to the "deals.html" page. Then, add a "spacer v60" div to include vertical distance before the next element on the web page.

Name of the call-to-action button that links the home page to the deals page

HTML

```
                </a>
            </div>
        <div class="link">
            <a href="deals.html">VIEW ALL LAST
            MINUTE DEALS</a>
        </div>
    </div>
    <div class="spacer v60"></div>
```

Closing tag for the "dealsCarousel" div

Closing tag for the "featureDeals" div

Adds a vertical space of 60px between this element and the next

SAVE

7.5 ADD RESPONSIVENESS

As the carousel functionality is already built in to Bootstrap, you will only need to define the font styles for the text you want to display. Start by adding the style definitions for the "h3" element in the "global.css" file.

CSS

```
    width: 100%;
}

@media screen and (max-width:
575px) {
    .carousel-caption h3 {
        font-size: 24px;
    }
}

@media screen and (min-width:
576px) {
    .carousel-caption h3 {
        font-size: 40px;
    }
}
```

Sets the font size for the header when the screen is narrow

Sets the font size for the header when the screen is wide

7.6 STYLE THE TEXT

Next, define the styles for the "carousel-caption" element that contains the "h3" header text in the slide. Add this code just after the code from step 7.5.

CSS

```
.carousel-caption {
    margin: 0;
    color: black;
    position: absolute;
    top: 50%;
    left: 50%;
    width: 80%;
    color: #000;
    text-align: center;
    -webkit-transform: translate
(-50%,-50%);
    transform: translate
(-50%,-50%);
}
```

The "h3" header will appear in black

Positions the top-left corner of the "carousel-caption" to the middle of the parent "carousel-item" div

Centre aligns the contents on the slide

Repositions the caption to centre it in the "carousel-item" div

7.7 STYLE THE HYPERLINK

Finally, add styles for the "View all last minute deals" hyperlink that appears just after the carousel. This will require definitions for both "normal" and "hover" states.

CSS

```
.featuredDeals .link {
    text-align: right;
}
.featuredDeals a {
    color: #000;
}
    .featuredDeals a:hover {
        text-decoration: none;
        color: #D7263D;
    }
```

Sets the "normal" state colour of the hyperlink to black

Right-aligns the hyperlink contained in the "link" div

Sets the hyperlink "hover" state colour to red

SAVE

7.8 TEST THE PROGRAM

Save all the files and then refresh the page in the browser to see the updated website. The carousel will animate the slideshow and the text will resize according to the width of the screen. You should be able to move forward and backward through the slideshow using the next and previous buttons.

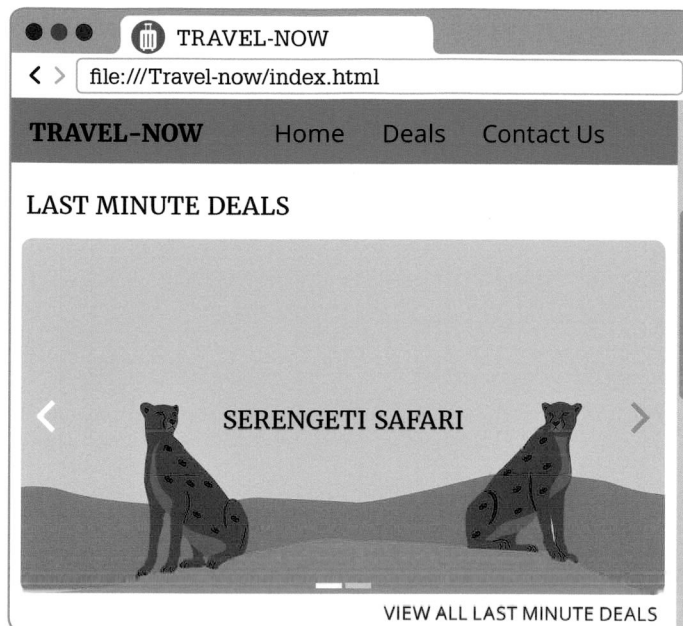

WIDE SCREEN

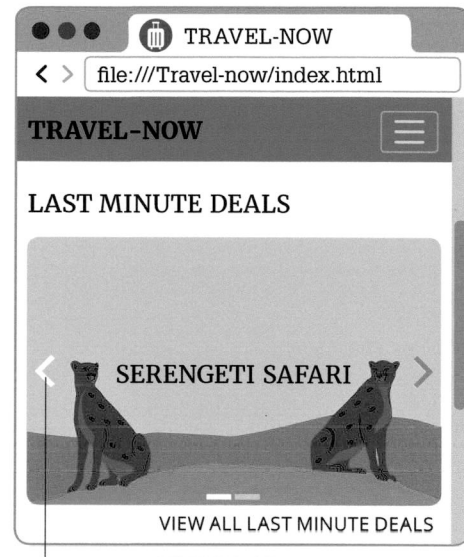

NARROW SCREEN

Click this button to move through the slideshow

8 Adding the copyright

The last element of the home page is the "copyright" section. This will contain a footer with the copyright text. Just like the navigation bar, the footer will also be repeated on every page of the website.

8.1 DEFINE THE COPYRIGHT

The "copyright" div simply contains a copyright notice with the specified year. Add this after the "container" </div> closing tag towards the end of the "index.html" file.

Links the footer to the index page of the website

HTML

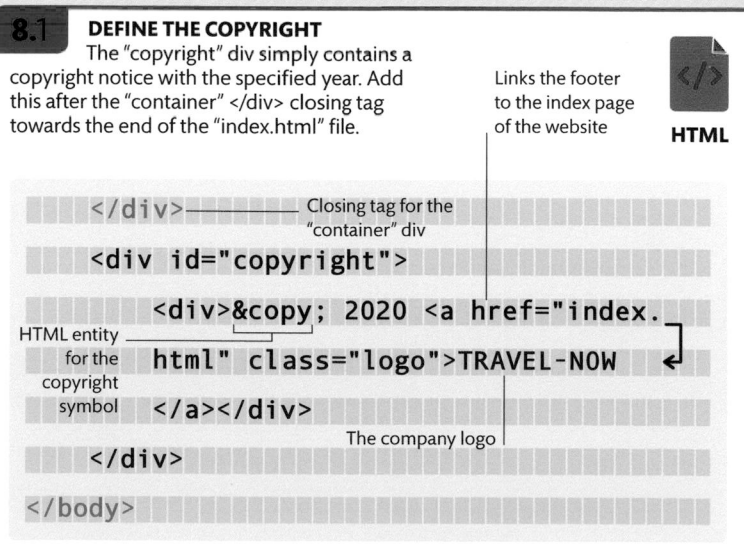

```
    </div>                    Closing tag for the
                              "container" div

    <div id="copyright">

        <div>&copy; 2020 <a href="index.
        html" class="logo">TRAVEL-NOW

        </a></div>

    </div>

</body>
```

HTML entity for the copyright symbol

The company logo

8.2 STYLE THE COPYRIGHT

Go to the "global.css" file to define the "copyright" div. Then, add styling for the hyperlink that appears in the "Copyright" section. This will require definitions for the "normal" and "hover" states. Type this code just below the code added in step 7.7 and save the file.

CSS

```css
            color: #D7263D;

    }

#copyright {

    text-align: center;

    background-color: #345995;

    color: white;

    height: 58px;

    padding-top: 18px;

    font-size: 16px;

}

    #copyright a {

        color: white;

        cursor: pointer;

    }

        #copyright a:hover {

            color: #D7263D;

            text-decoration: none;

        }
```

Sets the colour of the footer to blue

Defines the height of the container with the copyright information

Sets the font size of the copyright text

Sets the colour of the copyright text in "normal" state

The cursor is displayed as a pointer

Colour of the hyperlink in "hover" state

Hex code for the colour red

SAVE

8.3 RUN THE PROGRAM

Save all the files and then refresh the page in the browser. The "Copyright" section will display at the bottom of the page for both wide and narrow screens.

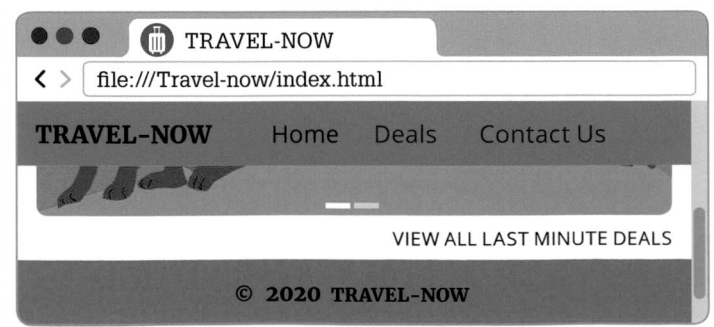

WIDE SCREEN

NARROW SCREEN

9 Creating a template

Almost all websites use an HTML template to add CSS, JavaScript, and common graphical elements to their pages. The template usually includes common elements, such as a navigation bar, menus, footers, and buttons that are used throughout the site. In order to achieve a standard look and feel for this project, you will create a "template.html" file and then modify it for all the subsequent pages on the website.

9.1 CREATE AN HTML FILE

Start by creating a new HTML file, just as you did in step 1.2 of this project. Name this new file "template. html". Visual Studio creates the file with the minimum code required for a valid HTML page. Now copy the entire <head> tag from the "index.html" file and paste its contents into the <head> tag of the "template.html" file. Replace the text in the <title> tag with some asterisks (*) and remove the <script> tag for "home.js".

HTML

```
<meta name="viewport" content="width=device-width,
initial-scale=1, shrink-to-fit=no">
<title>******</title>
```
Replace the asterisks with the correct page title when you use the template to make a new page

```
<script src="scripts/app.js"></script>
<script src="scripts/home.js"></script>
```
Delete this entire line of code from the "template.html" file

9.2 COPY ELEMENTS TO THE TEMPLATE PAGE

Now copy the entire <nav> tag from the "index.html" file and paste its contents into the <body> tag of the "template.html" file. Within the <nav> tag, find the <a> hyperlink to "index.html". Remove the "active" class from the <li class="nav-item"> and the "<span class="sr-only">(current)</span>" class from the hyperlink.

HTML

```
...<ul id="topMenu" class="navbar-nav mr-auto">
    <li class="nav-item">
        <a class="nav-link" href=
        "index.html">Home</a>
    </li>
```
Remove the "active" class from this line

Remove the "sr-only" span from this line as it indicates the active menu item for the screen reader

9.3 ADD A CONTAINER TAG

Next, add a "spacer" and a "container" div after the </nav> closing tag in the "template.html" file. The spacer will add a vertical gap between the navbar and the next element in the template.

HTML

```
</nav>
<div class="spacer v80"></div>
<div class="container">
</div>
```
Closing tag for the "navbar" div

Contains all the HTML elements on the page

CREATING A TEMPLATE

9.4 EDIT THE HEADER

Copy the "featureImage" div from the "index.html" file and paste its contents inside the "container" div in the "template.html" file. Replace the text in the "h1" header with asterisks.

HTML

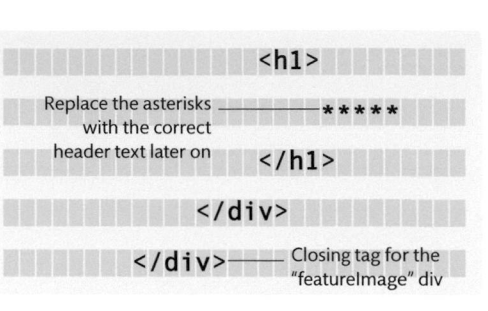

```
                    <h1>
Replace the asterisks ——————— *****
with the correct
header text later on    </h1>

                </div>

            </div>—— Closing tag for the
                        "featureImage" div
```

9.5 ADD THE CONTENT

Within the "container" div, add a "spacer" div below the "featureImage" </div> closing tag. Then add a "pageContent" div with a row of asterisks inside it.

HTML

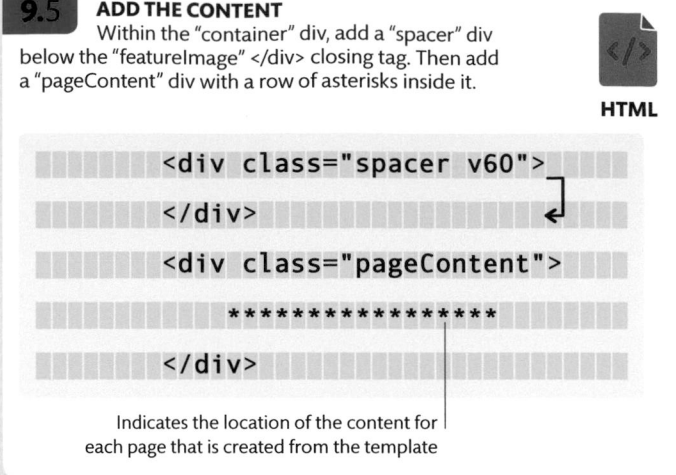

```
        <div class="spacer v60">

        </div>                    ⤶

        <div class="pageContent">

            ******************

        </div>
```

Indicates the location of the content for each page that is created from the template

9.6 ADD THE COPYRIGHT

Finally, add another "spacer" div after the "container" </div> closing tag. Then, copy the "copyright" div from the "index.html" file and paste its contents into the "template.html" file. Save the file.

The copyright text is copied onto the template page

HTML

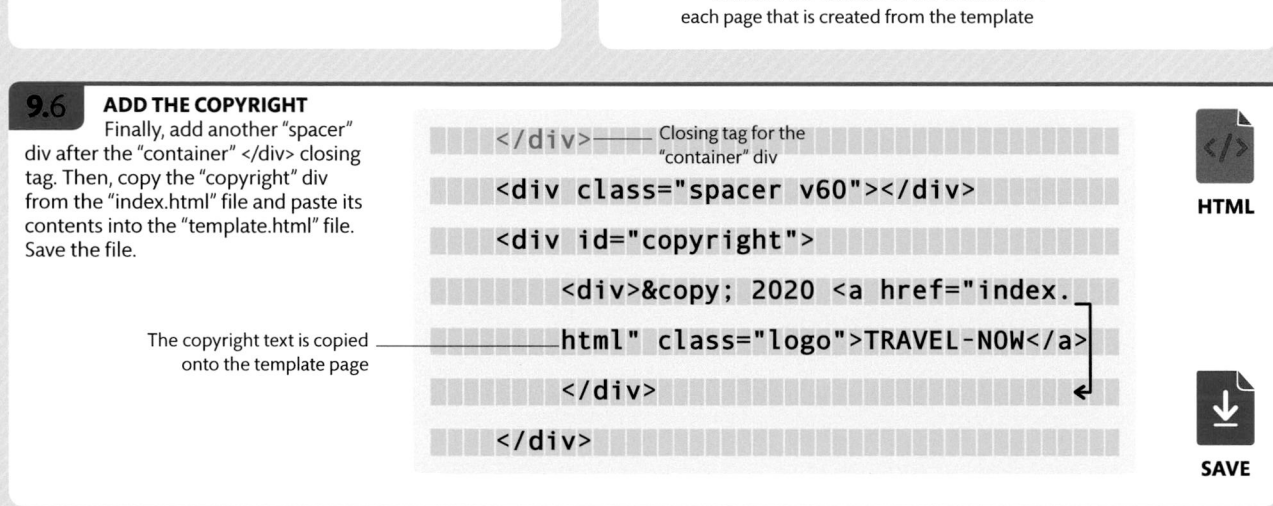

```
    </div>—— Closing tag for the
                "container" div
    <div class="spacer v60"></div>

    <div id="copyright">

        <div>&copy; 2020 <a href="index.
        html" class="logo">TRAVEL-NOW</a>

        </div>                              ⤶

    </div>
```

SAVE

9.7 RUN THE PROGRAM

Now, open the browser and type the url for "template.html" into the address bar. The url will be "file:///C:/Travel-now/template.html" in Windows and "file:///Users/[user account name]/Travel-now/template.html" on a Mac.

Asterisks will appear in place of the page title

WIDE SCREEN

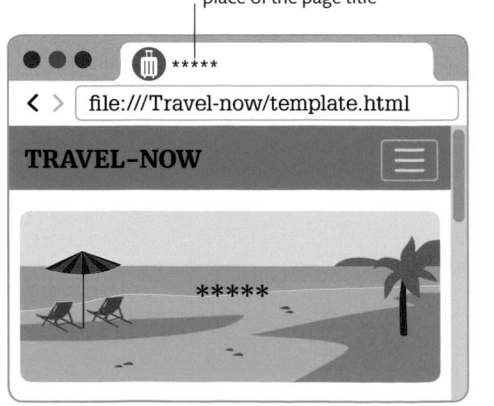

NARROW SCREEN

10 Creating a new page

In this section, you will create the "last minute deals" page using the template page created earlier. The new page will display a table of items that will be styled using Bootstrap's column definitions.

10.1 ENTER THE PAGE TITLE

First, you need to make a copy of the template page. In the Solution Explorer window, right click on "template.html" and select Copy. Then, right click on Travel-now and choose Paste to create a copy of the template page "template(copy).html". Right click on this file and select Rename to change its name to "deals.html". Open the "deals.html" page and replace the asterisks in the <title> tag with the page title.

HTML

```
<meta name="viewport" content="width=device-width,
initial-scale=1, shrink-to-fit=no">
<title>LAST MINUTE DEALS</title>
```

Find the <title> tag inside the <head> tag and enter the page title

10.2 UPDATE THE CODE

Inside the <nav> tag, find the <a> hyperlink to "deals.html". Add the class "active" to the <li> tag that surrounds the "deals.html" hyperlink and then append <span class="sr-only">(current)</span> to the hyperlink content.

HTML

```
...</li>
    <li class="nav-item active">
        <a class="nav-link" href="deals.html">Deals
        <span class="sr-only">(current)</span></a>
    </li>
```

Add the "active" class to indicate the current page in the Top Menu

The "sr-only" span is not visible in a normal web browser. It indicates the current page for a screen reader client

10.3 ADD THE CONTENT

In the "featureImage" div, replace the "homeIndex" class with the "deals" class to display a different feature image on the deals page. Then, go to the "text" div and update the content for the "h1" header.

Replace "homeIndex" with "deals" in the "deals.html" file

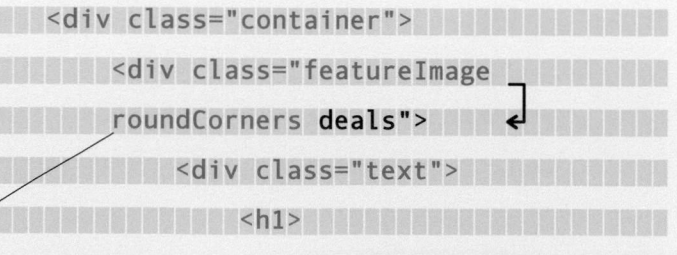

HTML

```
<div class="container">
    <div class="featureImage
    roundCorners deals">
        <div class="text">
            <h1>
                LAST MINUTE DEALS
            </h1>
```

Replace the asterisks with the header text for the deals page

10.4 UPDATE THE PAGE CONTENTS

Go to the "pageContent" div and replace the asterisks inside it with an "h2" header, a "spacer" div, and a new "lastMinuteDeals" div, as shown here.

Creates a horizontal rule between the "h2" header and the table of "deal" items

This <div> contains the various "deal" items arranged in rows

HTML

```
<div class="pageContent">          This header contains
                                   the page title
    <h2>LAST MINUTE DEALS</h2>

    <hr>

    <div class="spacer v20"></div>

    <div class="lastMinuteDeals">

    </div>
```

10.5 ADD THE FIRST DEAL

Now add the first "deal" item inside the "lastMinuteDeals" div. Each "deal" item will be a hyperlink that contains a Bootstrap "row" and four Bootstrap "columns". These columns will appear horizontally when the screen width is wide, and vertically when the screen width is narrow.

HTML

```
...<div class="lastMinuteDeals">

    <div class="deal">

        <a href="deals.html">

            <div class="row">

                <div class="col-sm name">

                    Taj Mahal

                </div>

                <div class="col-sm depart">

                    21 July 2020

                </div>

                <div class="col-sm length">

                    10 days

                </div>

                <div class="col-sm price">

                    $1000

                </div>

            </div>

        </a>

    </div>
```

This outer <div> acts as a container for the hyperlink that surrounds the row contents of the first "deal" item

There are four Bootstrap columns in each row

Content in the first Bootstrap column – name of the destination

Content in the second Bootstrap column – date of departure

Content in the third Bootstrap column – duration of the trip

Content in the fourth Bootstrap column – price of the deal

10.6 ADD THE SECOND DEAL

Below the first "deal" </div> closing tag, add the second "deal" item. You can add as many "deal" items to this page as you like, but make sure to add an equivalent number of "carousel-items" to the "featuredDeals" div in the "index.html" file (see pp.327–29).

HTML

```
...        </div>
        <div class="deal">
            <a href="deals.html">
                <div class="row last">
                    <div class="col-sm name">
                        Serengeti Safari
                    </div>
                    <div class="col-sm depart">
                        27 July 2020
                    </div>
                    <div class="col-sm length">
                        7 days
                    </div>
                    <div class="col-sm price">
                        $800
                    </div>
                </div>
            </a>
        </div>
</div>
<div class="spacer v60"></div>
```

- Closing tag for the first "deal" div
- Container for the hyperlink that surrounds the row contents of the second "deal" item
- Contents of the second "deal" item placed in individual Bootstrap columns
- Closing tag for the "lastMinuteDeals" div
- Add a vertical space between this item and the next

SAVE

10.7 DEFINE THE BACKGROUND IMAGE

Now go to the "global.css" file and define the "featureImage" that will appear as the background image for this section. Type this code just below the code added in step 8.2.

```
.featureImage.deals {
    background-image: url(../images/
    deals.jpg);
}
```

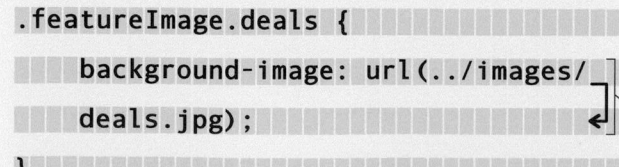

CSS

- Sets a new feature image for the deals page

10.8 STYLE THE ROW

Next, define the styles for the rows that will apply to each "deal" item. Specify that the row with the class "last" should have a different border, and the row should change colour when the mouse hovers above it. Add this code below the code added in the previous step.

```css
.lastMinuteDeals .row {
    padding-bottom: 15px;
    margin: 0;
    border-width: 1px 0 0 0;
    border-style: solid;
    border-color: #888;
}
.lastMinuteDeals .row.last {
    border-width: 1px 0 1px 0;
}
.lastMinuteDeals .row:hover {
    background-color: #BC8796;
    color: white;
}
```

CSS

Defines the style of the row's four borders

Sets a different border width for the last row

Sets the width of the border surrounding a row

Sets the border colour to a shade of grey

Hex code for the colour mauve

Changes the text colour from dark grey to white when the mouse hovers above the row

10.9 ADD RESPONSIVENESS TO THE ROWS

The rows must appear vertically when the screen width is narrow. To do this, instruct the browser to apply a different padding definition to the "row" divs.

Defines a different padding for the row when the width of the screen is less than 576px

CSS

```css
        color: white;
    }
@media screen and (min-width: 1px) and (max-width: 575px) {
    .lastMinuteDeals .row {
        padding: 0px 15px 20px 15px;
    }
}
```

Adds spacing between the content and the container boundary

10.10 STYLE THE HYPERLINK

Now add style definitions for the "link" div that contains the hyperlink for the rows, including the "normal" and "hover" states for the anchor tag.

CSS

```
.lastMinuteDeals div {
    text-align: left;
}
.lastMinuteDeals a {
    color: #333;
}
    .lastMinuteDeals a:hover {
        text-decoration: none;
        color: white;
    }
```

Defines "normal" state

Defines "hover" state

10.11 ALTERNATING THE ROW COLOURS

Make the "deal" items table more visual by adding styles that alternate the background colour of the "deal" div. Use the "nth-child(odd)" and "nth-child(even)" selectors to specify which deal divs qualify for the style definition.

CSS

```
.lastMinuteDeals .deal:nth-child(odd) {
    background-color: #C0C0C0;
}
.lastMinuteDeals .deal:nth-child(even) {
    background-color: #D3D3D3;
}
```

Sets the colour of every odd-numbered row to silver

Sets the colour of every even-numbered row to light grey

10.12 ADD RESPONSIVENESS TO THE COLUMNS

Now add styles to define the Bootstrap columns. Specify the styles for both wide and narrow screen widths, then add a style definition for the name column so that the "name" field appears in a bold font. Then, save the file.

Sets the spacing between the content and the column boundary

CSS

```
.lastMinuteDeals .col-sm {
    padding: 15px 0px 0px 15px;
    margin: 0;
}
@media screen and (min-width: 1px) and (max-width:575px) {
```

Defines a different padding for the column when the width of the screen is less than 575px

CREATING A NEW PAGE

```
    .lastMinuteDeals .col-sm {
        padding: 15px 15px 0px 15px;
    }
}
.lastMinuteDeals .name {
    font-weight: bold;
}
```

The "name" column text displays in bold font

SAVE

10.13 **RUN THE PROGRAM**
Open the browser and type the url for "deals.html" into the address bar. The url will be "file:///C:/Travel-now/deals.html" in Windows and "file:///Users/[user account name]/Travel-now/deals.html" on a Mac. You can also refresh the "index.html" page in the browser and then select "Deals" on the navigation bar to see what this page looks like.

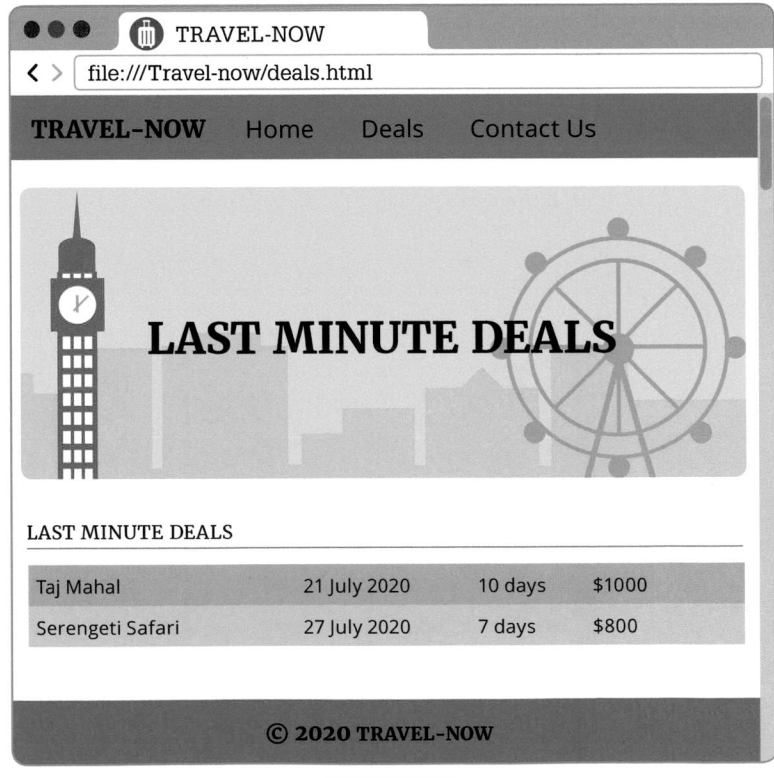

WIDE SCREEN

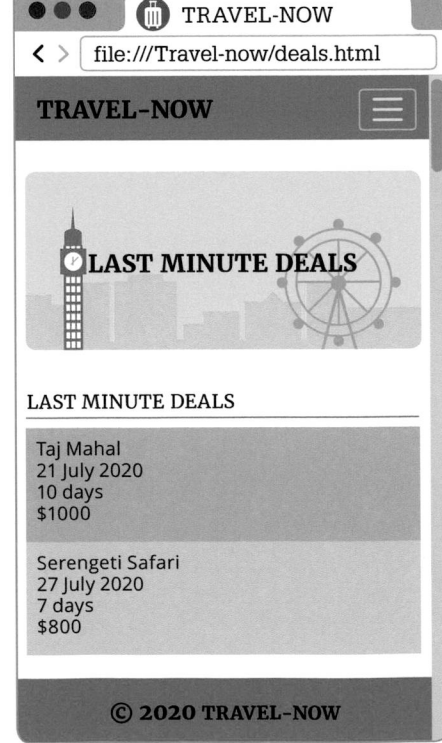

NARROW SCREEN

Hacks and tweaks

Google fonts

This project uses Google Fonts (*https://fonts.google.com/*) to provide the text fonts. You can explore this library and use different fonts and icons to enhance the look of your website. You can even go to Google Material Icons (*https://material.io/*) and search for more options for a favicon.

Updated line of code in the <head> tag with the new font names

```
<link href="https://fonts.googleapis.com/css?family=
Suez+One|Oswald|Niconne" rel="stylesheet">
```

INDEX.HTML

```
font-family: "Suez One", serif;
font-family: "Oswald", sans-serif;
font-family: "Niconne", cursive;
```

Update the fonts in the comment section and use them wherever applicable in the code

GLOBAL.CSS

The font "Oswald" is used for the "navbar" items

The font "Suez One" is used for the "featureImage" text

Bootstrap SASS

This project points to a Content Delivery Network (CDN) version of the CSS file, which contains all the default styles used by Bootstrap. While programming, you will need to override these default styles with your own style definitions. To avoid doing this every time, you can simply modify the default Bootstrap files so that they produce your custom styles without the need to override them. This can be achieved by downloading the Bootstrap source files, editing the SASS variables (variables that define a value and can be used in multiple places), and compiling the final CSS file.

https://getbootstrap.com/docs/4.0/getting-started/theming/

https://sass-lang.com/

PayPal "Buy Now" buttons

It is quite simple to allow users to make payments on your website. You can do this by adding a PayPal "Buy Now" button to the deal items on the "deals.html" page. To receive money via PayPal, it is necessary to open a PayPal account and verify your bank account details. The email address that you register as the login for your PayPal account will be used to identify you as the intended recipient of the payment. The code below creates a button that allows users to buy a deal. Clicking on the button will redirect users to a secure page on the PayPal site, where they can make the payment.

www.paypal.com

This form allows the user to make a payment to the Travel-Now website via PayPal

```
...<div class="col-sm price">

    $1000

</div>                              Closing tag for the
                                    "col-sm price" div

<div class="col-sm buy">            Content in the fifth Bootstrap
                                    column – "Buy Now" button
    <form method="post" target="_blank" action=

    "https://www.paypal.com/cgi-bin/webscr">

        <input type="hidden" value="_cart" name="cmd" />

        <input type="hidden" value="yourpaypalemailaddress

        @example.com" name="business" />

        <input type="hidden" name="upload" value="1" />

        <input type="hidden" name="charsetmm" value="US-ASCII" />

        <input type="hidden" value="1" name="quantity_1" />

        <input type="hidden" value="Taj Mahal"

        name="item_name_1" />

        <input type="hidden" value="1000" name="amount_1" />

        <input type="hidden" value="0" name="shipping_1" />

        <input type="hidden" value="USD" name="currency_code" />

        <input type="hidden" value="PP-BuyNowBF" name="bn" />

        <input type="submit" value="Buy Now" class="roundCorners" />

    </form>

</div>
```

Email address of the PayPal account that receives the payment

The name of the item being purchased will be passed to the PayPal page

Clicking this input button submits the form data to the PayPal url

This class defines the shape of the "Buy Now" button

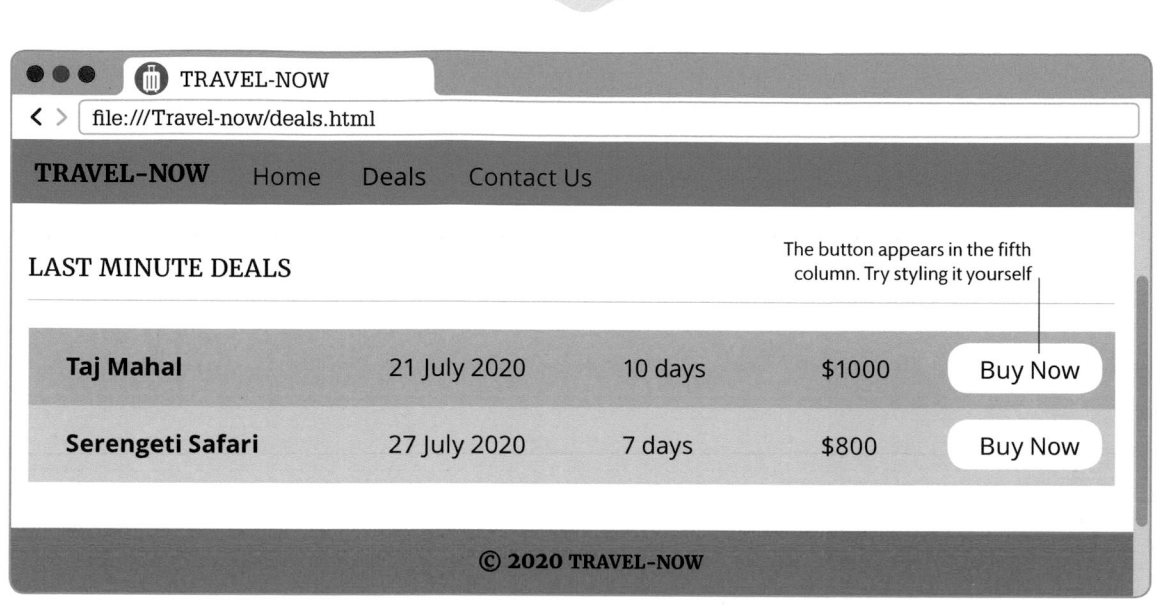

● ● ● 🧳 TRAVEL-NOW

‹ ›   file:///Travel-now/deals.html

TRAVEL-NOW   Home   Deals   Contact Us

LAST MINUTE DEALS

The button appears in the fifth column. Try styling it yourself

| Taj Mahal | 21 July 2020 | 10 days | $1000 | Buy Now |
| **Serengeti Safari** | 27 July 2020 | 7 days | $800 | Buy Now |

© 2020 TRAVEL-NOW

Web page templates

A website usually has a common template that is repeated on every page of the site. This template includes links to the CSS files, JavaScript files, and the common HTML elements, such as the header and footer elements that appear on each page. Unfortunately, there is no way to employ a template using only HTML and JavaScript. You would need to use a server-side language, such as C# MVC or Python Django to inject the header and footer into each page automatically.

This project also uses a template that is used to create the other pages of the website. It will be very difficult to maintain this process if there are a lot of pages. Explore the "layout file" concept in C# MVC and the "template inheritance" feature in Python Django to solve this problem.

Try creating this page using the concepts from a server-side language

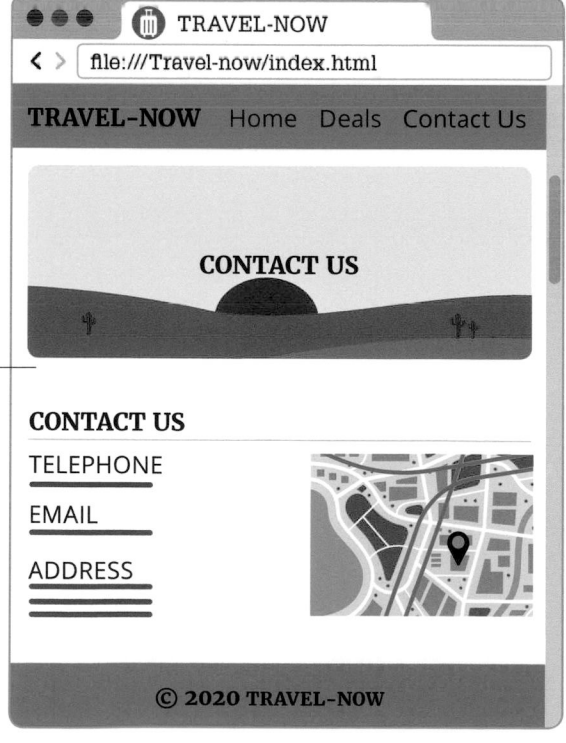

● ● ● 🧳 TRAVEL-NOW

‹ ›   file:///Travel-now/index.html

TRAVEL-NOW   Home   Deals   Contact Us

CONTACT US

CONTACT US

TELEPHONE

EMAIL

ADDRESS

© 2020 TRAVEL-NOW

https://www.asp.net/mvc

https://www.djangoproject.com

Other programming languages

Every profession has its own vocabulary and ways to describe common problems and solutions. Programming languages were developed to help humans communicate with computers. Most languages are designed for a specific task or domain, but are often adapted for other purposes.

Grouping programming languages

Human languages are grouped into families (such as Germanic or Dravidian) that use similar alphabets, vocabulary, and structures. If you know one language in a family, it is easier to learn others.

Programming languages are also grouped into families, and often borrow words and structures from each other. For example, C, C++, Objective-C, Java, C#, Go, and Swift are all related, so developers who know one of them can learn the other languages more easily.

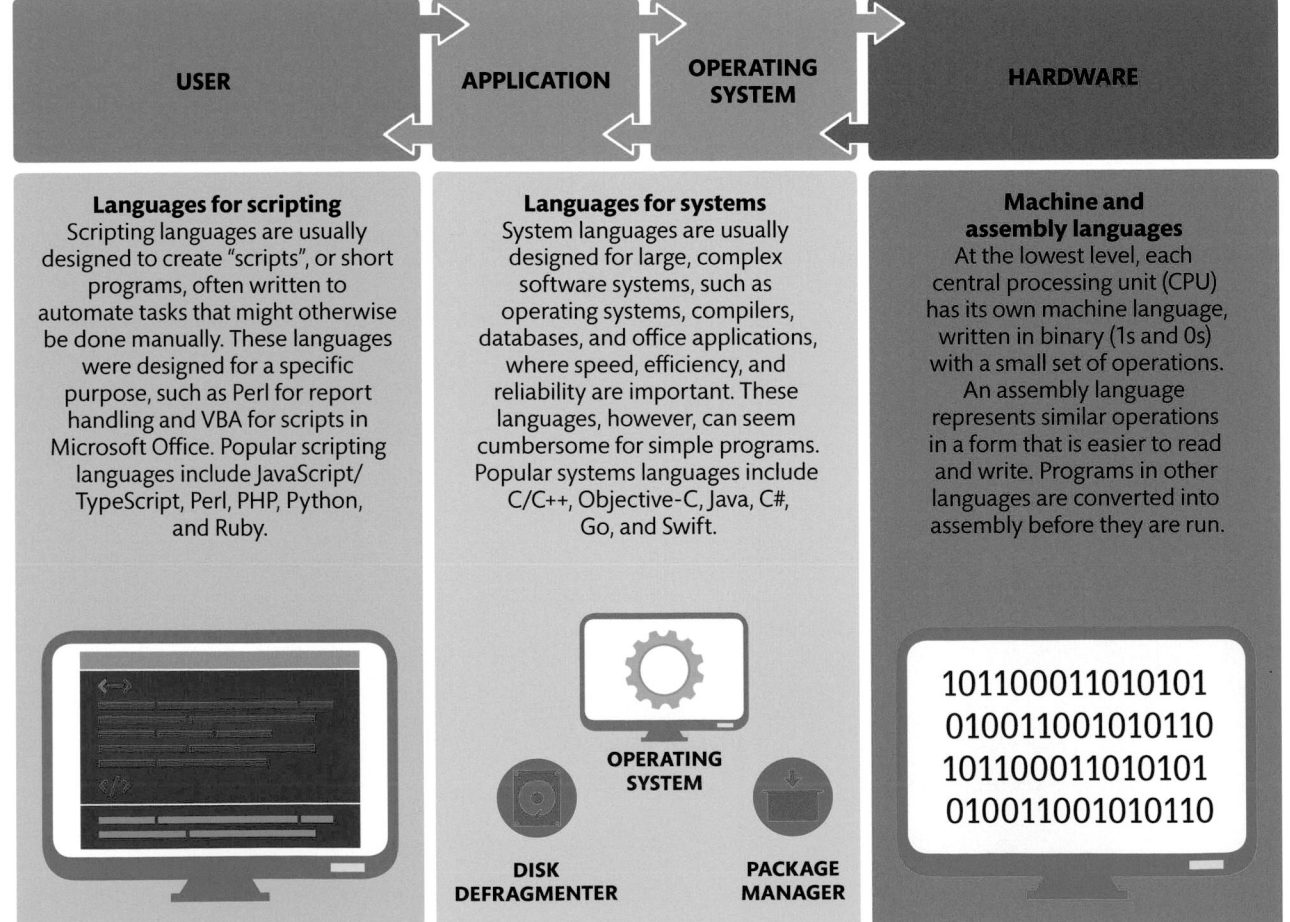

USER → **APPLICATION** → **OPERATING SYSTEM** → **HARDWARE**

Languages for scripting
Scripting languages are usually designed to create "scripts", or short programs, often written to automate tasks that might otherwise be done manually. These languages were designed for a specific purpose, such as Perl for report handling and VBA for scripts in Microsoft Office. Popular scripting languages include JavaScript/TypeScript, Perl, PHP, Python, and Ruby.

Languages for systems
System languages are usually designed for large, complex software systems, such as operating systems, compilers, databases, and office applications, where speed, efficiency, and reliability are important. These languages, however, can seem cumbersome for simple programs. Popular systems languages include C/C++, Objective-C, Java, C#, Go, and Swift.

OPERATING SYSTEM

DISK DEFRAGMENTER

PACKAGE MANAGER

Machine and assembly languages
At the lowest level, each central processing unit (CPU) has its own machine language, written in binary (1s and 0s) with a small set of operations. An assembly language represents similar operations in a form that is easier to read and write. Programs in other languages are converted into assembly before they are run.

```
101100011010101
010011001010110
101100011010101
010011001010110
```

Languages for data

Some languages are designed to work with large sets of data. The data might come from experiments, monitoring systems, sales, simulations, and other sources in science, engineering, business, education, or other areas. People may want to process this data to reduce noise, analyse trends or patterns, and compute statistics. Languages to manipulate and analyse data include APL, MATLAB, and R.

MATLAB/ OCTAVE FOR NUMERICAL COMPUTATION

APL FOR DATA HANDLING

S/R FOR STATISTICAL COMPUTING

Languages for special purposes

Some programming languages are designed to solve specific problems, and might not be useful in other areas. PostScript, TeX, and HTML describe the content and layout of pages with text, images, and other information. SQL is used to manage databases. Maple and Mathematica are used for symbolic mathematics. LISP and Scheme are useful for AI (artificial intelligence). Prolog is used for logic programming.

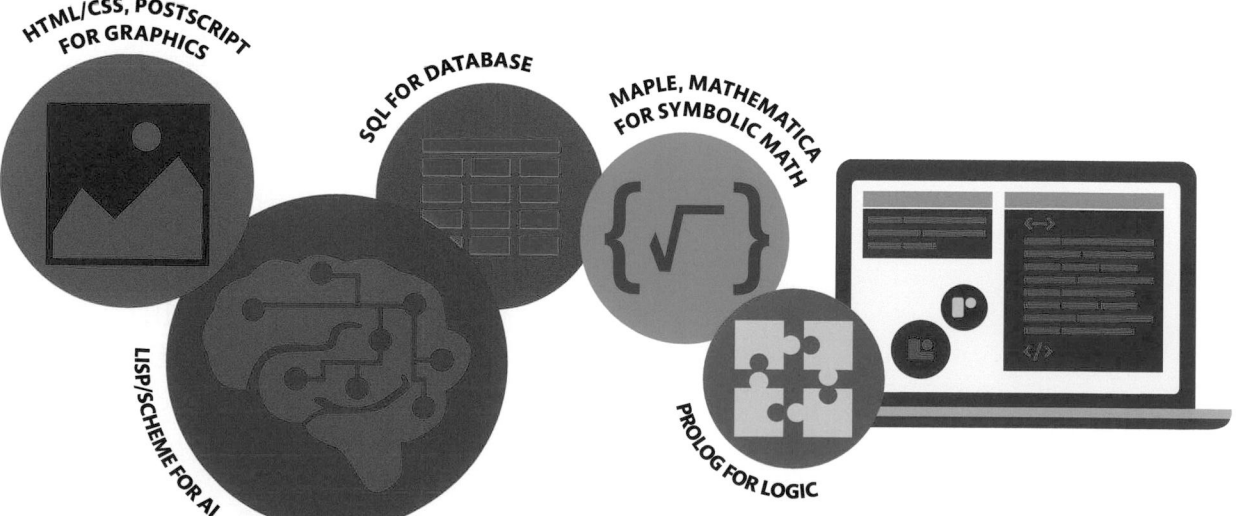

HTML/CSS, POSTSCRIPT FOR GRAPHICS

SQL FOR DATABASE

MAPLE, MATHEMATICA FOR SYMBOLIC MATH

LISP/SCHEME FOR AI

PROLOG FOR LOGIC

Early programming languages

There are other widely used languages, some with a long history. Fortran was created in the 1950s for scientific and engineering applications. COBOL was created around 1960 for business applications. BASIC was an easy language created in the mid-1960s for students. Pascal was created around 1970 to encourage structured programming practices, and was widely used in education. Ada was created around 1980 to reduce the number of different languages used across the US Department of Defense (DoD).

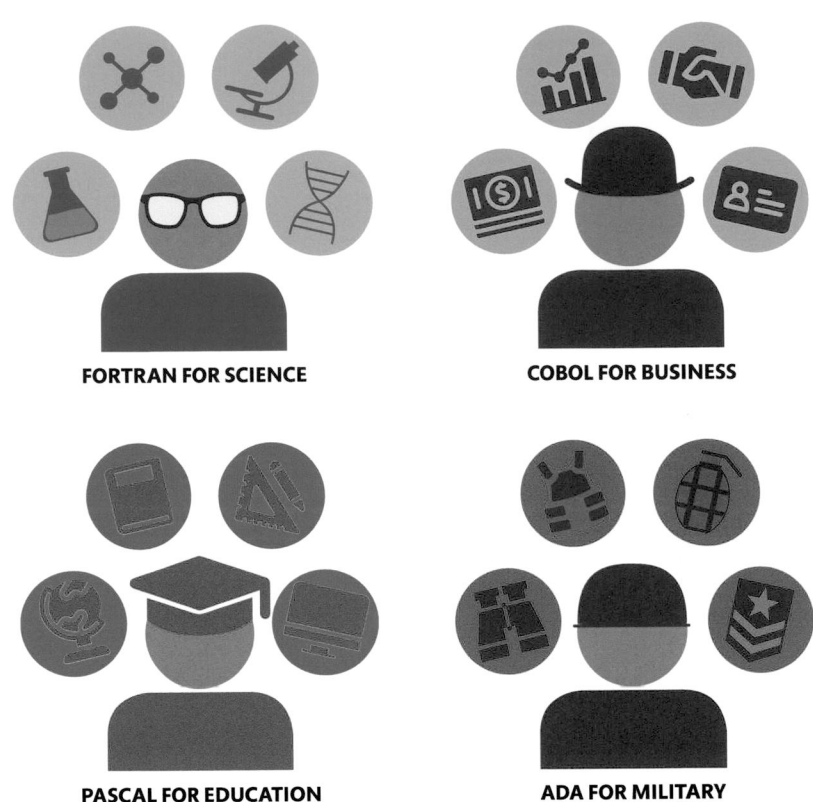

FORTRAN FOR SCIENCE

COBOL FOR BUSINESS

PASCAL FOR EDUCATION

ADA FOR MILITARY

Visual languages

In visual (or block-based) languages, programs are created graphically rather than with text. For example, a user might drag elements into position, connect them, and then type in number values or text messages. Such languages are often designed for non-programmers in specific areas, such as education, multimedia, and simulation. Popular visual languages include Blockly, Alice, and Scratch in education, and Kyma, Max, and SynthEdit for music.

BLOCKLY

SCRATCH

Other programming languages

There are hundreds of programming languages, and most developers are proficient in a few, familiar with more, and expect to learn new languages throughout their careers. The table below lists some of these programming languages, with information on when they were first developed, the lead creator, and a brief summary of key ideas and major uses.

POPULAR PROGRAMMING LANGUAGES	
Language, date, and creator	**Key ideas and major uses**
C (1972) Dennis Ritchie	Designed to be concise, portable, and to generate efficient machine code. It is widely used for operating systems, compilers, interpreters, and large applications. Many other languages have adapted features and syntax from C.
C++ (1983) Bjarne Stroustrup	Designed to add object-oriented features to C (in C, "C++" adds 1 to the variable c). Widely used for operating systems, compilers, interpreters, and large applications.
Java (1995) James Gosling	Designed to be an object-oriented language based on C and C++. Java was meant to be a "write once, run anywhere" programming language – code written on one type of computer can be run on other types. Widely used for desktop applications and browser-server applications.
Python (1991) Guido van Rossum	Designed for readability, and to support multiple programming styles. Uses a small core language with libraries that add more specialized functions. Widely used in web applications, scientific computing, and for scripting in other software products.
PHP (1994) Rasmus Lerdorf	Designed for web development ("PHP" originally meant "Personal Home Page"), where it is widely used.
JavaScript (1995) Brenden Eich	Designed to create interactive web pages and applications, where is it widely used. JavaScript is also used in some web servers, so that a web application can use the same language in the browser and server.
Fortran (1950s) John Backus	Designed at IBM (International Business Machines Corporation) for scientific and engineering applications, which often involve many numeric calculations. Named from "FORmula TRANslation".
COBOL (1959)	Designed for data processing, COBOL was based on the earlier work of Grace Hopper. It was supported by the US Department of Defense, which led to its wider adoption. Named from "COmmon Business-Oriented Language".
BASIC (1964) John Kemeny and Thomas Kurtz	Designed to be easy to use for students in many fields, not just science and mathematics. It expanded into Microsoft Basic (1975) and Visual Basic (1991). Named from "Beginner's All-purpose Symbolic Instruction Code".
Ada (1980s) Jean Ichbiah	Designed for embedded and real-time systems and to reduce the number of languages used across the US Department of Defense (DoD). Named after Ada Lovelace, often described as the first computer programmer.
SQL (1970s) Donald Chamberlin and Raymond Boyce	Designed to edit and search databases, especially "relational databases" (when data is stored in tables that are related to each other in various ways). SQL is short for "Structured Query Language".

Glossary

algorithm
A sequence of steps or instructions that complete a task or solve a problem. In programming, an algorithm often includes repeated steps, decisions between two or subsequences of steps, and steps that refer to other algorithms to do subtasks or solve subproblems.

API (Application Programming Interface)
A set of definitions that programmers can use to access another system without having to understand all of its details. The definitions might include functions, classes, data structures, and data values. Originally named because it defines an interface for programmers to develop applications using an underlying system. See also *library*.

array
A collection of items stored in adjacent locations in the system's memory, using a single name and a numeric index. The index usually starts at 0. Often, all elements in the array have the same type. For example, all integers, or all strings of characters. An array is one way to store a list. See also *list*.

attribute
A specific piece of information associated with a data object. For example, an image would have attributes for height and width, and a sound would have attributes for length and sampling rate.

binary
A numbering system, used by computers, that has only two digits (0 and 1), not the usual decimal system with ten digits (0 to 9). In binary, each position is two times the position to its right, rather than ten times in decimal. For example, 101101 = 1*32 + 0*16 + 1*8 + 1*4 + 0*2 + 1*1 = 45.

bit
Shortened from "binary digit", it is the basic unit for information or communication. The value of a bit can be either 0 or 1. Thus, an eight bit device mostly uses storage elements with 8 bits, which can store 2^8 = (256) different values.

block element
An HTML element that breaks the flow of text and changes the layout of the page. For example, paragraphs (<p>), lists (<ul>, <ul>, <li>), and tables are all block elements. See also *inline element*.

branching statement
A program statement that chooses one of several possible paths or sets of steps, usually based on the value of an expression. For example, an "if-then-else" statement takes the "then" path if an expression is true, and the "else" path if an expression is false. Also called a conditional statement.

Boolean
A value that can be either true or false. Named after George Boole, who defined a logic system based on such values.

bug
A defect, or an error, in a program or other system that prevents it from working correctly. The term was used in engineering long before computers, but is often associated with a story told by Grace Hopper about a moth stuck in an early computer, causing wrong results.

call
A program statement that causes the computer to run another function, and return to the original function when done.

carousel
A software component in Bootstrap that cycles through a set of elements, like a slideshow.

CDN (Content Delivery Network)
A network of servers spread across different places that can deliver the same content (data or services). For example, when a web browser loads content for a page, the CDN can deliver content from nearby servers, which reduces the wait time and the network traffic.

child object
An object created from a prototype in a parent object. The child shares (inherits) all functions and properties of the parent, but can override them. For example, the parent might define functions and properties for any book, and each child would define the author, title, publisher, and date for a specific book.

class
(1) A definition or description of a category, which usually includes data and functions, and is used to create (instantiate) objects in that category. For example, the class for employees might specify that every employee has a name,

phone, and email address, and provide functions to set or display them. (2) In CSS, a style definition that can be added to any number of elements.

cloud
A set of Internet servers that can be used instead of a local computer. Cloud storage stores files and other data, and cloud computing does computation.

compiler
A program that analyses a computer program and converts (compiles) it into machine code so it runs faster. See also *interpreter*.

composite data
Data that is created by combining other simpler data. For example, a string of characters, an array of numbers, or an object. See also *primitive data*.

concatenate
To combine items, usually character strings, one after another. For example, concatenate "snow" and "ball" to get "snowball".

conditional statement
See *branching statement*

constructor
A special function used to create new objects of a class. Typically, the constructor allocates memory, initializes variables, and does other setup.

data
Any information stored in or used by a computer.

data binding
Connecting (binding) the data values in two or more objects or systems so that changing one also changes the others. For example, binding a GUI element to a data object ensures that changes to the object appear in the GUI, and GUI changes also change the object.

debug
To remove bugs in a program. This might involve running the program with different inputs, adding statements to print or store values

as the program runs, or watching memory values and how they change. See also *bug*.

directory
(1) Also called a folder; a structure to store files, and sub-directories with other files. (2) A list of resources and how to access them.

ECMAScript
The official definition for the scripting language used in browsers and servers, to provide a standard that could be used by JavaScript, JScript, ActionScript, and other Web languages.

element
(1) A single value in a larger set, such as an array. (2) In HTML, a part of a document, often with a start tag, content, and a stop tag. For example, "DANGER" is an element that shows "DANGER" as emphasized text.

event
A description of something that has happened, often used as a signal to trigger responses in a program. For example, a mouse-click event could submit a form or display a menu.

execute
Also called run; the command to start a program.

file object
An object that describes or gives access to a file stored in the system's memory.

float
A number with a decimal point in it. It allows a computer to store very large and very small numbers more efficiently. Also called a floating point number.

flowchart
A graphical way to show the steps, branches, and loops in an algorithm.

framework
A collection of software elements that can be combined and customized in various ways, usually to create user applications. For example, Angular, Django, Express, jQuery, React, and Ruby on Rails are all frameworks used for websites and web applications.

function
Code that carries out a specific task, working like a program within a program. Often, a function has a name, a set of input parameters to give information to the function, and a result for the code that called the function. Also called procedures, subroutines, and methods (especially in object-oriented languages).

git
A popular version control system, used to track changes in a set of files, so that users can easily collaborate and access different versions of the same file. See also *version control system*.

global variable
A variable that can be used anywhere in a program. See also *local variable, variable*.

GUI (Graphical User Interface)
Often pronounced "gooey", a user interface is the name for graphical elements, such as buttons, menus, text fields, and checkboxes that make up the part of the program that a user can see and interact with. It is different from a command line interface where everything is displayed as text.

hardware
The physical parts of a computer such as the processor, memory, network connectors, and display. See also *software*.

hack
(1) An ingenious change to code that makes it do something new or simplifies it. (2) To break into other computer systems.

hosting
Also called web hosting; providing server and Internet access to clients for their own websites. In dedicated hosting, each client gets their own server; in shared hosting, many clients share a single server.

hover state
The appearance of a GUI element when the cursor or pointer hovers above it. For example, a button or text field might have a different colour or border when the mouse hovers above it, to indicate that it is active or ready to use. Also called "mouseover" state. See also *normal state*.

hyperlink
A text or graphical element that can be clicked, tapped, or otherwise selected to access other information, often using a url. The other information can be in the same document, another document, or on another website.

index number
A number indicating the position (index) of an element in an array. Many programming languages use square brackets with arrays, so "myArr[3]" means the element in position "3" of array "myArr".

inline element
An HTML element that does not break the flow of text or change the layout of the page. See also *block element*.

input control
A part of a user interface, such as a button, checkbox, or text field, that allows a user to provide input to a program.

instantiate
To create a new object, usually using its class definition.

integer
A number without a fractional part, also called a whole number. Usually, a computer can represent a large, but not infinite, set of integer values.

interface
A boundary between two parts of a system. Thus, a user interface (UI) is how a user interacts with the system, and an API (Application Programming Interface) is a set of definitions to help programmers develop applications using an underlying system.

Internet
The global computer network, which is actually a network of networks. Shortened from "interconnected network".

interpreter
A program that executes computer programs one statement at a time, without first converting (or compiling) the program to machine code.

iterate
To execute a task or set of statements repeatedly. Most programming languages have special syntax to make it easier for programs to iterate, either a set number of times, or until some condition is met. For example, a program might iterate through an array to perform the same actions on each element.

iteration
The general process of iterating, or the process of repeatedly going through a set of statements in the code.

library
A set of resources that can be reused in other projects. These resources might include functions, classes, data structures, and data values. A library is similar to an API. For example, a math library might have a constant value for pi and functions to compute the sin, cosine, and tangent of an angle. See also *API*.

literal
A fixed value written in source code. In most programming languages, integer and real number literals are written normally, and strings of characters are written between quotation marks.

list
A set of data values, where each value has a specific position in the list. One way to store a list is as an array. See also *array*.

local variable
A variable that can only be used with a particular function or other limited part of a program. See also *global variable*, *variable*.

loop counter
A variable that counts (tracks) the number of times a loop has been repeated.

machine code
The set of instructions that is used by a computer processor. It is difficult for users to read or write machine code, so other programming languages are used with a compiler or interpreter to convert them to machine code.

malware
Short for "malicious software"; any software designed to gain illegal access to a computer or system. Malware includes viruses, worms, spyware, and ransomware.

memory
Storage used by a computer, using a wide range of technologies, including ROM (read-only memory), RAM (random access memory), solid states drives (SSDs), hard disk drives, and optical drives (e.g., CDs or DVDs). In general, faster technologies are much more expensive, so most computers use smaller amounts of expensive memory (RAM) and larger amounts of cheaper memory (hard disk drives).

metadata
Data that describes other bits of data. For example, web pages use metadata to specify the page title, language, and HTML version, while music files use metadata to specify the composer, performer, title, date recorded, style of music, copyright status, and other information.

module
A package of ready-made code that can be imported into a program, making lots of useful functions available.

network
A set of computers connected together to allow the sharing of data and resources.

normal state
The way a GUI element (for example, a button) appears normally. See also *hover state*.

object
In object-oriented programming, an object is a component that consists of data and code to manipulate the data.

object-oriented
An approach to coding where programs are organized into classes and objects, which typically contain data values and functions that use or change those values.

opcode
Part of a machine code instruction that specifies the operation rather than other information (such as the memory locations) to use. Shortened from "operation code". See also *operand*.

operand
Parts of a machine code instruction that do not specify the operation, but other information such as the memory locations to use. More generally, a parameter passed to a function. See also *opcode*.

OS (operating system)
The underlying software system that manages resources (both hardware and software) and provides services used by other software. For example, Microsoft Windows, Apple's macOS, and Linux.

output
The result of a program, which might be displayed on a screen, stored in a file, or sent to another program or computer.

parameter
An input for a function. In most languages, a function definition includes a name for each input. For example, the function "sum(x,y)" has two formal parameters "x" and "y".

parent object
An object used to create child objects. The parent has a prototype with functions and properties that can be used by each child. See also *child object*.

parse
To take text or other input data and create a more useful structure out of it. For example, a browser parses a file of characters and creates a data structure (called the Document Object Model, or DOM) that shows which elements contain which other elements.

payload
The actual message within a larger communication. For example, when a browser loads a web page, the payload is the actual HTML that will be displayed.

port
(1) A virtual connection point used to contact a specific service or process. (2) To adapt software to run on another operating system or on other hardware.

primitive data
The basic data type that is used to build more complex data types. For example, characters, integers, and real numbers. See also *composite data*.

primitive variable
A variable that contains primitive data. See also *reference variable*.

processor
The hardware that actually executes a program. Also called the central processing unit or CPU.

protocol
A set of rules that define how something works. For example, HTTP is a high level protocol that describes how a browser and a web server communicate using lower level protocols that handle other details.

prototype
In JavaScript, a built-in variable with functions and properties that can be used by each child object.

pseudo-class
In CSS, a way to define a special state of an element. For example, the pseudo-class ":hover" defines an element's hover state.

reference variable
A variable that does not contain primitive data, but refers to a location in the system's memory where the data is stored. Typically used for arrays, strings, and other composite data. See also *primitive variable*.

run
See *execute*

run time
(1) The period of time during which a program runs. (2) Software that is used to help programs run.

SASS variable
A variable defined using SASS (Syntactically Awesome Style Sheet). SASS is an extension to CSS and adds features, including variables, that make it easier to develop style sheets.

scope
The parts of a program in which the specific name of a variable, function, or class has meaning. For example, a global variable's scope is the entire program, while a local variable's scope is a single function.

screen reader
A program that finds text on the screen and reads it aloud, to assist users with limited vision.

script
A program written in a scripting language, usually intended for an interpreter rather than a compiler. Originally, scripts were short programs that performed very specific tasks, but over time scripting languages have been used for many other purposes.

semantic
The part of code that is focused on the underlying meaning of text, rather than the rules it follows (the syntax). Most HTML tags focus on the meaning and role of the data, not the appearance. For example, <h1> marks a heading and <em> marks emphasized text, but neither describes how the text should be displayed.

server
A hardware or software system that provides services to other systems or clients. Software servers include database servers, mail servers, and web servers. A hardware server can run more than one software server.

software
A set of instructions or data that tells a computer what to do, including the operating system, libraries, server software, and user applications. See also *hardware*.

source code
The set of instructions that is read and written by users. Source code can also be intended for an interpreter or a compiler.

state
The way a GUI element (a button or a text field) looks, which may change over time. For example, a button might be in its normal state most of the time, but may switch to its hover state when a cursor or pointer moves over it.

string
A sequence of characters that are stored together. This includes letters, numbers, and punctuation. In most languages, literal strings are written within quotation marks.

style definition
In CSS, the definition of a specific style for a category of text. For example, the style definition for a list might include what type of bullets to use and how much to indent.

subset
A group of items taken from another set.

syntax
The part of code that is focused on the rules followed by text rather than its underlying meaning (the semantics). For example, the syntax for emphasized text requires an <em> tag, the text, and an </em>.

tag
In HTML, the text marking the start and end of an element, usually using angle brackets. For example, <em> and </em> are tags used for emphasizing a piece of text.

template literal
A way to write a string that can span multiple lines and insert the values of other variables.

tuple
A short list of items or values; a 2-tuple has two items, and an n-tuple has n items.

URL (Uniform Resource Locator)
A consistent way to refer to the location of some resource and how to access it via the Internet.

variable
The name associated with a value stored in the system's memory. In computing, a variable can have different values at different times.

version control system
A system that keeps track of files, so that users can easily collaborate and access different versions of the same file. Often, but not necessarily, used in software development.

view
In the Angular framework, a set of screen elements that control what the users can see.

virus
A type of malware that inserts its code into other programs, creating more copies of itself.

web page
A document that can be accessed over the Internet. It is displayed in a web browser.

website
A set of related resources, such as web pages, images, sounds, and videos that are stored and accessed together over the Internet using a web browser.

Index

Page numbers in **bold** refer
to main entries.

32-bit processors 96, 97
64-bit processors 96, 97
@media screen 315
$(document).ready function
(home.js) 293, 321
.NET Core + ASP.NET Core 217
!important declaration **239**

A

About Menu 303
accessibility (websites) **214-15**
Actor class (Pygame Zero) 179, **183**,
    184, 186, 197-98
Ada 346, 347
Adobe Illustrator 286
agile model 21
Agile Software Development **181**
AI see artificial intelligence
AJAX (Asynchronous JavaScript)
    265
alert box 272, 273
algorithms 53, 270
Alice 346
analysis (software development) 20
anchor property (Python) 183
and (logical operator) 270
and block (Scratch) 45
Angular **285**
animate() command (JQuery) 294
animate() function (Pygame Zero)
    197, **198**, 202
animating the web page **288-303**
    adding JavaScript files 290-92
    adding social media 301-2
    exploring fonts and icons
        300-301
    getting started 289-90
    hacks and tweaks 300-303
    managing promotional messages
        296-99
    managing the scroll to top button
        292-95
    page template 303
    program design 288
    project requirements 289
    what the program does 288

animation (CSS) 239
answer blocks (Scratch) 47
APL 345
append() (Python) 113
app.js 290, 291, 308
application layer protocol 207
applications software 17
architecture, computer 96, 97
Arduino 23
area charts 287
arithmetic operators 43, **102**,
    104, 199
arrays 268, 298
    and loops 122, 275, 276
arrow keys 80, 84, 178, 185, 186
artificial intelligence (AI) 345
artists 18
ask blocks (Scratch) 47, 55, 59,
    62, 63
ASP.net and web development
    217
assembly languages 22, 344
Asteroid dodge (Scratch) **80-91**
    code the rocketship 83-86
    create the asteroids 86-89
    hacks and tweaks 90-91
    how the game works 80
    prepare the launch 82-83
    program design 81
Atom (code editor) 208

B

backdrop (Scratch)
    changing 54, 64, 78, 82
    colour cycling 90
    designing 66-68
    Sounds tab 79
    switching 85
Backdrop Library (Scratch) 78
    background colour
    canvas widget 147
    CSS styling 235, 238, 241, 247,
        307, 339
    promo bar 248
    specifying 312
    subscribe section 259
background images 251, 337
background music (Scratch) 79
background (Pygame Zero)
    chequerboard 199-201
    drawing 181
Backus, John 347

banner 221, 224
    logo 251
    styling 251
bar charts 134, 287
BASIC 346, 347
Basic Input/Output System (BIOS) 17
binary digits 23, 344
BIOS see Basic Input/Output
    System
bitmap mode 33, 57, 67, 68, 82
blind people 214
block-based languages 346
Blocks Palette (Scratch) 30, 35, 55
    Add Extension section 35, 37, 39,
        58-59
    Events section 40
    Looks section 38
    Variables section 42, 43, 58, 69,
        70, 72
blocks (Scratch)
    colour-coded **34-35**
    defining your own 51
    dragging and dropping 74
Blocky 346
body, styling 307
body tag 247, 310
Boolean expressions **44**, 104, 105
    combining **45**
    using **45**
Boolean operators 104, 270-71
Boolean values 270
Boolean variables (JavaScript) **266**
Bootstrap **285**, 341
    column definition 305, 335, 336
    container 311
    creating a carousel 327-31
    grid system 324
    order of tags 310
    responsive layouts 304, 309
    SASS 341
border styling 239, 245
Boyce, Raymond 347
Brackets (code editor) 208
braille 214, 215
branching
    JavaScript **271**
    Python **105**, 119
break command (Python) 110
breakpoints 281
break statement 271
broadcast blocks (Scratch) 48, 85
broadcasts **48-49**
    uses of 49

browsers 217
    CSS features **255**
    Developer Tools 281, 305
    and screen size 240
    transitions 249-50
Brush tool (Scratch) 67, 88
Budget manager **158-75**
    adding a budget 161-64
    converting the code into a class
        169-72
    hacks and tweaks 174-75
    program design 159
    setting up 160
    tracking expenditure 164-68
    tracking multiple budgets 172-73
    what the program does 158-59
building (software development)
    20
build a web page **216-33**
    adding a contact section 230-31
    adding the copyright notice 233
    adding the footer 232
    adding more feature boxes
        226-29
    adding the subscribe section 232
    feature box control 224-26
    getting started 218-20
    how it works 216
    HTML stage 216
    installing an IDE 217-18
    program requirements 217
    scrolling to the top 230
    structure the home page 220-24
business
    applications 95
    programming languages 346
buttons
    button widgets 147, 148
    call-to-action 220, 224, 258, 329,
        330
    carousel next/previous 329, 331
    clear 155
    creating in Scratch 56, 60-61
    hamburger menu 310, 311
    Open project 135, 153
    PayPal "Buy Now" 342
    radio 212
    with rollovers 243, 253, 254
    scroll 257-58
    scroll to top 257, 292-95
    Shop Now 253, 254
    subscribe 260
    templates 333

C

C 94, 344, 347
C# 303, 344
C# MVC 303, 343
C++ 344, 347
calculations 43, 102
calling (functions) 112, 113, 310
  scheduling 194
call-to-action button 220, 224, 258, 329, 330
cameras 17
canvas widget, Tk 147, **150**
carousels 327–31
cars 16
Cascading Style Sheets see CSS
case sensitivity 99
casting 103
catch block 281
CDN (content delivery network) 290
central processing unit (CPU) 344
centring 247, 313
Chamberlain, Donald 347
characters 103
  disallowed see entities
Chart.js **287**
charts
  area 287
  doughnut 287
  flowcharts 53, 144
  Gantt charts 134, 135, 149, 151, 152
  JavaScript 287
  line 287
  Python 146–51
cheat codes 90
checkboxes 212
Check Module (IDLE) **131**
child elements 237, 238
child objects 282, 283
child selector 237
child tags 210, 211, 221
choice() function (Python) 122
Chrome see Google Chrome
class attribute 225
classes
  HTML tags 211, 246
  JavaScript 282, **283**
  Python **156–57**, 158, 159, 168–72, 283
class inheritance 182
class selector (CSS) 236

Clean up Blocks (Scratch) 76
clear property 246
click() function (JQuery) 294
client/server model 206, 207
client-side scripting **209**, 264, 289
clock events 179
clock object **194**
COBOL 346, 347
Code Area (Scratch) 30, 35
code editors **208–9**, 265
CodePen 209
coders
  becoming a coder **16**
  in the real world **18–19**
Codeshare 265
code sharing websites 265
collision detection 47
colour
  background 235, 238, 241, 247, 307, 312
  font 235, **247**
  Pygame Zero 190
  rows 339
  styling 238
  text 262
  website style sheet 244
colour-matching games 179
columns
  adding responsiveness 339–40
  Bootstrap 305, 335, 336
  column headers 149
  column numbers 182
  column values 137, 138, 160
  feature box styling 253
combine id and class selector 237
comma-separated values see CSV
communication protocols 206, 207
community sharing 265
company logo 220, 223, 224, 286, 305, 311, 313
comparison operators 270
compilers 23
  programming languages 344
complex logic 64
concatenation 103, 130
config method 154
confirmation box 273
console log 273, 281
constructor method 282, 283
Contact Us 220, 230–31, 256, 300, 303, 312
  styling 258

container tags 333
content attribute 240
Content Delivery Network see CDN
content organization (websites) 214
continue command (Python) 110, 111
Control blocks (Scratch) 40
coordinates 36, 69, 70, 72
  canvas widgets 150
  grid and screen **182**
copyright 220, 233, 305, 331–32, 334
  styling 263
corners, styling 308
costumes (sprites) 30–31, 33, 38, 57, 61, 78, 85, 91
cross-platform run time engines 289
CSS 23, **234–39**
  animating the web page 288, 289, 301, 303
  building a web page 216, 218, 222, 233
  debugging 281
  and graphics design 286, 287
  meta links 303
  new features on browsers **255**
  responsive layouts **240–41**, 304, 306–8, 312–16, 318–21, 325–26, 330, 332, 337–40, 341
  selectors 236–37
  styling 238–39
  styling the web page 242–46, 250
CSV files 135
  creating and reading 136–43
  Python library 136, 138, 139
csv.reader object 138, 139
current year Sensing block (Scratch) 45

D

D3.js (Data-Driven Documents) **287**
Dabblet 265
data
  adding to web page 221
  programming languages for 345, 347
  reading from files 135, 138
databases, programming languages 344, 345
data centers 16

Data-Driven Documents see D3.js
data types
  converting 139
  non-primitive **268**
  primitive **266–67**
datetime module (Python) 116
deaf people 214
Deals hyperlink 312
debugging
  checklist 133
  code editors **208–9**
  debuggers 22, 106, **133**, 281
  JavaScript 273, **280–81**
  Python 94, 106, **130–33**
decisions (Scratch) **44–45**
declarative programming 24
default code block 271
delay, introducing **41**
Department of Defense (US) 346, 347
descendant selector 237
design
  program 53
  software development 20
desktop computers 16, 215, 240, 241, 305
Developer tools **222**, 280, **281**, 305, 313
development environment 217, 305
dictionaries, Python 138, 145, 158, 159, **160**, 174
DNS (Domain Name Systems) protocol 207
Document Object Model (DOM) 265
DOM see Document Object Model
Domain Name Systems see DNS
doughnut charts 287
do while loops (JavaScript) 275
drag and drop interfaces 25
  Scratch 28, 30, 35, 74, 76, 84
draw_actors() function (Pygame Zero) 184, 188, 191
draw_background() function (Pygame Zero) 199, 200
draw_chart function (Python) 149, 151
draw() function (Pygame Zero) 186
draw_game_over() function (Pygame Zero) 196, 197
draw_handler function (Pygame Zero) 179

drawing (Scratch) 67
draw interface 179
draw_scenery() function
    (Pygame Zero) 183, 202
drop-down lists 212
    vertical 311
dungeon crawl games 178, 179
duplication
    code 62
    sprites 60

E

ECMA Script 264
Edge 222
editing, code **208-9**
editor window (IDLE) 98, 99
education, programming languages
    346
Eich, Brenden 347
elastic cloud computing 215
element selector (CSS) 236
elements (HTML tags) 210, 211,
    234, 235
elif see else-if
else branch (Python) 105
else-if branch
    JavaScript 271
    Python 105
email
    hyperlink 256
    id 259
embeddable scripts 95
engineering, programming
    languages 346
entities **233**
equality 104
equals signs (Python) 104
error messages
    code editors 209
    Python 99, **132-33**, 162, 163-64
errors
    in JavaScript 280
    in Python 130-31, 162, 163-64
    see also debugging
escaping loops (Python) 109,
    110-11
EvalError (JavaScript) 280
event-driven programming 24, 40
event-handler function (Python)
    185, 186
event handlers (JavaScript) 294
event loop programs 178, 179

Events blocks (Scratch) 40, 46
exceptions (Python) **162**
expenditure, tracking 159-75
explosions, painting 88
Extension blocks (Scratch) 35, 37,
    39, 58-59
external files 264
    CSS 234
external hyperlinks 213
external information 46

F

factories, automation 17
false value 270-71
favicon **221**
    definition 221, 309
    images 300
feature boxes 220, 224-29
    styling 253-57
feature images 305, 313-15
    banner 314
fields (objects) 156, 157
File Explorer 243
filename labels 154
file objects 107
files
    input from 107
    output to 107
File Transfer Protocol see FTP
Fill tool (Scratch) 57, 68, 82, 88
financial planning 158-75
Fintech (financial technology)
    95
firmware 17
floats (floating point numbers)
    102, 139, 266
FLOSS (free/libre and open
    source software) 94
flowcharts 53, 144
folders
    creating 160, 180, 218, 243, 289,
    306, 308
    locating **243**
fonts
    canvas widget 150
    changing 57, 300, 301
    colour 247, 307
    company logo 313
    default 307
    Google Fonts 244, 300, 341
    list of website 244
    prominent 316

fonts continued
    setting/defining 235, 244, 259,
    319, 325
    size 190, 238, 315
footer section 220, 232, 247, 249,
    331, 333
    styling 261-62
footers, table 167-68
forever blocks (Scratch) 41, 84, 86
forever loops 79, 86
for loops
    JavaScript 268, 274
    Python 108, 110, 122, 145
for in loops (JavaScript) 275
Format menu (Python) 169
format strings (Python) 159, **166**
forms, HTML **212-13**
Fortran 346, 347
frame container widget 147
frameworks (JavaScript) 284-85,
    286, 289
FTP (File Transfer Protocol) 207
functions **51**
functions (JavaScript) 269, **278-79**,
    282, 283, 291
    creating 296, 308
    declaring 278
    function statement vs function
        expression 278
    nested 279
    self-executing 279, 291
functions (Python) **112-15**, 161,
    164-65
    built-in 113
    calling 112, 113, 117, 159
    creating 114-15
    defining 112, 114-15
    importing 117
    methods 169, 170
    methods for scheduling calls 194
    naming **114**, 117
functions (Scratch) **50-51**

G

Game Over message 89, 190, 195, 196
Game_over variable 189
games 23
    Asteroid dodge (Scratch) 80-91
    consoles 17
    development 80, 95
    gaming apps 134, 137
    Knight's quest (Python) 178-203

Gantt charts 134, 135, 149, 151, 152
Gap Time 86
general sibling selector 237
getters 283
Gimp 286
Github Gist 265
global positioning system see GPS
global variables
    JavaScript 290, 291, 308
    Python 115, 160, 163, 189, 195
Go 344
GoDirect Force & Acceleration 59
Google Chrome 217, 222, 281,
    305, 313
Google Fonts 244, 300, 341
Google Maps 258
Google Material Icons 341
Google Translate API 52
Gosling, James 347
GPS 16
graphics
    graphical modules (Python) 134,
    146-51
    graphic user interfaces (GUI)
        147, **286-87**
    programming languages for
        345
graphs and charts 287
grid
    coordinates **182**, 185-87
    HTML Canvas 287
    moving on the **187**, 192
    width and height 203
GUI see graphic user interfaces
guidelines, compliance with
    website 215

H

hamburger menu button 310, 311
hard-coding 100
hardware 17
    machine and assembly languages
        344
headers
    carousels 327
    defining 245, 249
    styling 307
    tables 167-68
hex code 150
hidden fields (web pages) 213
high-level programming languages
    22

hobbyists 18
home automation 23
Homebrew package manager 176–77
Home() function (home.js) 321
Home hyperlink 312
Homeindex() function (home.js) 292, 293
home.js 290, 292, 317, 321
Home Menu 300
home page
  copyright section 331–32
  design 305
  feature image 313–15
  navigation bar 309–13
  primary message 316–17
  quote 317–23
  responsive 304
  slideshow 327–31
Hopper, Grace 347
horizontal borders 239
horizontal layers 220, 247, 305
horizontal margins 248, 316
horizontal menu lists 249, 251
horizontal rule 225, 255, 336
hosting, web **215**
household appliances 16
hover state 249, 252, 254, 258, 260, 262, 313, 326, 330, 332, 338, 339
HTML (Hypertext Markup Language) 23, 206, 207, 209, 345
  animating the web page 288, 289, 290–92, 296, 300–303
  building a better website **214–15**
  building a web page **216–33**
  colour codes 238
  common entities **233**
  and CSS 234–39
  debugging 281
  document structure 211
  exploring basic **210–11**
  forms and hyperlinks **212–13**
  and graphics design 286, 287
  and JavaScript 264, 265, 272–73, 286, 288
  responsive layouts 240, 304, 305, 309–14, 316–18, 324–25, 327–29, 331, 333–37
  styling the web page 242, 246, 247–53, 254
  tags and attributes **210–11**, 214, 215, 234, 239

HTML continued
  template file 303
  templates 333–34
HTML Canvas **287**
HTTP (Hypertext Transfer Protocol) 206, **207**
hyperlinks **212–13**
  adding to navigation bar 312
  call-to-action 329, 330
  copyright section 332
  email 256
  footer 262
  home page 220, 304, 309
  list 223, 232
  styling 249–50, 252, 254, 256, 330, 339
  Top Menu 250

I

IBM 347
Ichbiah, Jean 347
icons 300, 341
IDEs (Integrated Development Environment) **23**, 132, 208, **209**, 289, 305
  installing 217–18
IDLE (Integrated Development and Learning Environment) 95, 96, 97, 113, 120, 121, 136, 160, 180, 182
  Check Module **131**
  colours in the code **98**, 132
  creating a CSV file in 136
  debugging 130, 131, 133
  editor window 98
  shell window 98
  using **98–99**
id selector (CSS) 237
if branch (Python) 105, 118
if-then block (Scratch) 44, 59, 62, 63, 72, 73, 74, 75, 77–79, 84–87
if-then branch (JavaScript) 271
if-then-else block (Scratch) 44, 73, 75, 77
if-then-else branch (JavaScript) 271
images
  adding to web page 221, 228, 229, 305
  background 227, 251
  centring 314
  feature 255, 257, 305, 313–15
  folder 180, 217, 218, 242, 306

images continued
  middle 256, 257
  styling 257
image tile grids 178, 179
imperative programming 24
importing (Python) 117
indentation
  errors 130
  Python 99, 108, 109, 130, 169
  tags 211
indexes (Python) 122
index file 218, 219, 306
indexing (search engines) 214
index strings 179
infinite loops (Python) 109
infographics 287
information processing 46
Initialisers (Python) 169
inline CSS 234
input
  JavaScript **272–73**
  Python **106–7**
  Scratch 34, **46–47**
  types of 46
input blocks (Scratch) 34
input events 179
input fields 212
  styling 259
input() function (Python) 106, 113
input validation (web pages) 213
instance variables 170
Instructions, computer programs as 17
integers **102**, 139, 140, 141, 266
Integrated Development Environment see IDEs
Integrated Development and Learning Environment see IDLE
integrity attribute (Bootstrap) 309
interactive behaviours 216, 272, 273, 288
Internet 206
Internet Explorer 217, 222
interpreters 23
int function (Python) 140
IP (Internet Protocol) 207
  IP address 207
  IP routing **206**
issubset set method **145**
iterations 108–11, 118, 181, 182, 197, 276–77
iterative model 21

J

Java 25, **264**, 344, 347
JavaScript 23, 24, 25, **264–87**, 347
  animating the web page **288–303**
  building a web page 216, 218, 221, 233
  debugging **280–81**
  features of **265**
  functions in **278–79**, 310
  graphic user interfaces **286–87**
  input and output **272–73**
  interactive functionality 289
  libraries and frameworks **284–85**, 289
  logic and branching **270–71**
  loops in **274–77**
  object-oriented **282–83**
  order of tags 310
  responsive layouts 240, 304, 308, 321–23
  using online 264
  variables and data types **266–69**
  what it is **264–65**
JavaScript Engine 264, 277, 284, 291, 293, 308, 310, 321, 328
JQuery 265, **284**, 289, 294, 298, 305
  adding 290
  order of tags 310
  responsive layouts 304, 309
JSFiddle 265
Json data format 269

K

Kemeny, John 347
keyboard control 46, 186, 214
keys 187, **188**
  dictionary 138, 140, 160
keywords 210
  class 156, 283
  Pygame Zero keyword arguments 198
Knight's quest **178–203**
  adding the keys 187–88
  adding messages 196–97
  animating the actors 197–98
  creating the guard actors 191
  creating the player 184
  hacks and tweaks 202–3
  how to play 178–79
  moving the guards 192–94
  moving the player 185–87

Knight's quest *continued*
setting up 180–84
tracking the result 194–97
Kurtz, Thomas 347
Kyma 346

L

labels 212
label widget 154
labyrinthine environments 178
languages
foreign 52–63
programming *see* programming
languages
laptops 240
layers, horizontal 247, 305
layout styles, different 241
left column elements 225
LEGO BOOST 59
LEGO Education WeDo 2.0 59
LEGO Mindstorms EV3 59
len() function (Python) **103**, 113
Lerdorf, Rasmus 347
less than 104
libraries
Google fonts and icons 341
graphics 287
JavaScript 265, 284–85, 286, 287
Python 94, 95, 114, 116–17,
136, 138, 139, 146, 159, 173
Scratch 39, 54
Lifelong Kindergarten group (MIT)
29
lightweight editors **208**
line charts 287
link layer protocol 207
Linux 29
LISP 345
lists
of lists 111
loops with 108
Python **103**, 111, 113, 118, 119,
121, 122, 129
Scratch **43**
sets compared with 140
shuffling 121
splitting **122**
tuples compared with 137
within lists 111
list widget 147
local variables 115, 269
location (Contact Us section) 258

logic
errors 131
JavaScript **270**
Python **104–5**, 140
Scratch **44–45**
task ordering 144–45
logical operators 104, 270–71
logic programming 345
logic puzzle (Scratch) **64–79**
adding more sprites 74–77
adding a new sprite 71–73
adding the rules 78–79
getting started 66–70
hacks and tweaks 78–79
program design 65
the puzzle 64
logo
company 220, 223, 224, 286,
305, 311, 313
styling banner 251
styling Top Menu 250, 313
loops
continuous 135, 144, 145
do while loops 275
escaping 109, 110–11, 277
infinite **109**
JavaScript **274–77**
with a list 108
loop conditions 108
for loops 108, 110, 122, 145, 268,
274
loop variables 108, 111
nested **110–11**, 179, 276
Pygame Zero game loop **179**
Python **108–11**, 118, 119, 122, 125
Scratch **41**, 45, 65, 73, 75, 79, 81
while loops 108, 109, 110, 125, 274
Lovelace, Ada 347
low-level programming languages
22

M

Mac computers
locating folders 243
Pygame Zero 176–77
Python on 97
Scratch on 29
machine code 23, 264, 347
machine languages 344
main loop function 147
Makey Makey blocks (Scratch) 59
managers 18

map() function (Python) 140
Maple 345
maps
Contact Us section 258
virtual worlds 287
margins **245**
setting 247, 307, 311, 319
Mathematica 345
mathematics, symbolic 345
MathJS **285**
MATLAB 345
Max 346
media queries 241
messages
displaying (Scratch) 38
naming 49
primary (websites) 309, 316–17
sending (Scratch) **48–49**
metadata 221, 240
meta links 303
methods
calling (Python) 113
JavaScript 282, 293, 297, 298
Python 113, 157, 169, 170, 174
micro:bit 59
microprocessors 23
Microsoft Basic 347
Microsoft Visual Studio
Community 2019 *see* Visual
Studio Community 2019
Microsoft Windows 17
locating folders 243
Pygame Zero 176–77
Python on 96
Scratch on 29
military, programming languages
for 346
modal windows 272, 273
modules
adding 309–10
built-in 116
importing and using 117
Python **116–17**
modulo (remainder) operator
(Python) **199**
Moment.js **285**
money, Budget manager project
158–75
Monty Python's Flying Circus 96
Motion blocks (Scratch) 36–37
mouse 214
mouse-over state 230, 249, 252,
254, 258, 260, 262

move_guard() function
(Pygame Zero) 193, 194, 197
movement
illusion of 81, 87
logic 185
move_player() function
(Pygame Zero) 186, 188, 189,
193, 195, 198, 202
multimedia 206
multiple classes selector 237
multiview function 208
Music blocks (Scratch) **39**, 59
music, programming languages
346

N

named tuples (Python) 135,
142–43
name errors 131
NASA, Mission Control Centre
95
navigation bar 305
creating 309–13
templates 333
nested functions (JavaScript)
279
nested loops
JavaScript 276
Python 110–11, 179
NetBeans 209
network protocols 207
new projects (Scratch) 54, 66
next sibling selector 237
Node.js 264, **284**, 285, 289
Node Package Manager
see NPM
noise reduction 345
non-primitive data types
268
normal state 254
not (logical operator) 271
not block (Scratch) 45
not equal 104
Notepad 208, 218
NPM **284**
numbers
computation 345
in JavaScript **266**
list of 129
in Python **102**, 129, 139
random 43, **121**, **201**
in Scratch **43**

O

Objective-C 344
object-oriented programming
 25, 156–57, 264, 347
 JavaScript **282–83**
objects
 JavaScript 269, 282–83, 297
 Python **156–57**, 188
office applications, programming
 languages 344
office workers 18
on document ready() function
 (home.js) 292, 321, 323
on_key_down() function (Python)
 186
opcode 23
Opera 222
operands 23
operating systems 17
 installing Python 96–97
 programming languages 344
 updates 177
Operator blocks (Scratch) 42–43,
 44, 64
or (logical operator) 270
or block (Scratch) 45
outline colour (Pygame Zero) 190
output
 JavaScript **272–73**
 Python **106–7**
 Scratch **35**
output blocks (Scratch) 35

P

package managers 176–77
packets **206–7**
packet sequence 207
packet switched networks 206
padding 235, 245, **245**, 247, 248,
 249, 252, 307, 311
page elements, styling 244–53
Paint Editor (Scratch) 33, 57, 61, 64,
 66–68, 78, 88
pandas 95
parent elements 237, 238
parent function 279
parent objects 282
parent tags 210, 211, 239
parent widgets 147
Pascal 346
PayPal 342
pen blocks (Scratch) 37, 59

Perl 344
pet shop website project
 animating the web page **288–303**
 Build a web page **216–33**
 styling the web page **242–63**
PHP 209, 344, 347
pip package managers 176–77
pixels 150, 182, 215, 238
placeholder text 261
place markers 327
planning (software development)
 20
plugins 209
pos property (Python) 193
PostScript 345
prerequisites
 as sets of numbers 140
 tasks 134, 141, 144, 145
preview windows 208
primary messages 305, 316–17
primitive data types **266–67**, 268,
 269
print() function (Python) 106, 113
printing (code editing) 208
probability **201**
problem-solving 65
procedural programming 25
processing blocks (Scratch) 34–35
program flow 34–35, 50
 managing **40–41**
programming **16–17**
programming languages 16, **22–25**,
 344–47
 choosing **25**
 for data **345**
 early **346**
 families of **344**
 popular **347**
 for specific purposes **345**
 types of **24–25**
 visual **346**
 website construction 216
 see also JavaScript; Python;
Scratch
programs 17
Project planner **134–55**
 creating and reading the CSV file
 136–43
 drawing the chart 146–51
 hacks and tweaks 152–55
 how it works 134
 ordering the tasks 144–46
 program design 135

Prolog 345
promo bar 247–48, 287, 288, 296,
 299
promotional messages 220, 221,
 296–99
 cycling through 298–99
 initializing 297–98
 styling 247–48
prompts 272
protocols **207**
prototype-based languages 283
prototypes (JavaScript) **282**, 283
push() method (JavaScript) 268
puzzles 64–79
PyBrain 95
Pygame **117**
Pygame Zero 95, 117, **176–77**
 Actor class 178, **183**
 animations **198**
 drawing text with **190**
 game loop **179**
 initializing 180
 library 117
 updates **177**
PySoy 95
Python 22, 24, 25, **92–203**, 347
 applications **95**
 Budget manager project **158–75**
 common errors 99
 data in **102–3**
 debugging **130–33**
 dictionaries **160**, 174
 exceptions **162**
 features 94–95
 format strings **166**
 functions **112–15**, 159, 161,
 164–65
 how it works 95
 input and output **106–7**
 installing **96–97**
 Knight's quest project **178–203**
 libraries 94, 95, 114, **116–17**, 136,
 138, 139, 146, 159, 173
 logical operators and branching
 104–5
 loops in **108–9**
 on a Mac 97
 objects and classes **156–57**
 Project planner project **134–55**
 Pygame Zero **176–77**
 sets **140**
 Team allocator project **118–29**
 tuples **137**

Python *continued*
 using IDLE **98–99**
 variables **100–101**, 115, 121, 125,
 160, 163, 169, 170, 189, 195
 versions 96
 on Windows 96
Python Django 303, 343
Python Standard Library 116

Q

quotation marks 103, 320–21
quotes 305, 317–23
 animating 322–23
 applying properties to 321
 initializing 322

R

R 345
radio buttons 212
randint() function (Python) 201
random allocation 118, 119
random blocks (Scratch) 87
random module (Python) 116, 118,
 119, 120, 121, 200
random numbers 43, **121**, **201**
RangeError (JavaScript) 280
range function (Python) 108
Raspberry Pi 23
ReactJS **284**
readability, code 94
readable content (websites) 214
read_tasks() function (Python)
 141, 143
ReferenceError (JavaScript) 280
reference variables 268
repeat blocks (Scratch) 41, 45, 75
repeat until blocks (Scratch) 45
RequireJS **285**
researchers 19
response variable 125
responsive layouts (websites) 215,
 240–41, 304
responsive website **304–43**
 adding the copyright 331–32
 adding a feature image 313–15
 adding last minute details 327–31
 adding a message 316–17
 adding the modules 309–10
 adding popular destinations
 324–25
 adding a quote 317–23

responsive website *continued*
  adding the title and favicon 309
  creating the navigation bar
    309–13
  creating a new page 335–40
  creating a template 332–33
  getting started 305–8
  hacks and tweaks 341–43
  how it works 304
  program design 304
  project requirements 305
result, tracking 195
right column elements 226
Ritchie, Dennis 347
robotics 23, 179
rollover effect 253
root folder 218, 219
root window widget 147
rounded corners 308
round() function (Python) 113, 186
routers 206–7
rows
  adding responsiveness 338
  changing colours 339
  row numbers 182
  styling 338
Ruby 344
run time environment 284
runtime errors 130

S

Safari 217, 222
SASS variables 341
Scalable Vector Graphics *see* SVG
scenery (Python) 182–83
Scheme 345
science, programming languages
  for 346
scientific computing 95
scientists 19
scope, variables **269**
Scratch 25, **26–91**, 346
  Asteroid dodge project **80–91**
  backdrops 55
  coloured blocks and scripts **34–35**
  features **28–29**
  getting Scratch 29
  hardware support 29
  input **46–47**
  interface **30–31**
  logic and decisions **44–45**
  logic puzzle project **64–79**

Scratch *continued*
  loops **41**, 45, 65, 73, 75
  managing program flow **40–41**
  manipulating data **42–43**
  output using looks and sounds
    38–39
  output using movement **36–37**
  sending messages **48–49**
  sprites **32–33**
  travel translator project **52–63**
  using functions **50–51**
  variables **42**, 44, 58, 69, 70, 72,
    74–77, 79, 83
  versions of **30**
screen coordinates **182**, 183
screen_coords() function (Python)
  186
screen.draw.text() function
  (Python) 190
screen size 215, 240–41, 304, 305,
  309, 315, 316, 319, 325, 326,
  338, 339
  adding responsiveness 315, 316,
    319, 325, 330, 338, 339–40
  centring contents 313, 314
scripting, client- and server-side
  209
scripting languages 344
scripts
  creating 35, 344
  JavaScript 264, 265
  Python 95
  Scratch 34, 35
scripts file 308
scroll button, styling 257–58
scrolling 214
scroll to top 230, 257, 288, 292–95
search engines 214
selectors, CSS 235, **236–37**
  complex 237
  grouping 237
self-executing functions
  (JavaScript) 279
semantics **215**
sensor input 46
servers 206–7
  dedicated 215
server-side scripting **209**, 264, 289
  template options 303, 343
set() constructor function (Python)
  140
sets (Python) 134, **140**
  issubset set method **145**

setters 283
setup_game() function (Python)
  187, 189, 191, 195, 196
shape-matching games 179
shared hosting 215
shell window (IDLE) 98, 99, 120,
  161, 163
Shop Menu 303
Shop Now link 253, 254
Shopping Cart 300
shuffle() function (Python) 121
shuffling 118, 119, 121
side-scrolling games 80, 81
simulations 65
slideshows 327, 328, 331
smartphones 179, 215, 240, 241, 305
social media, adding to websites
  301–2
socket module (Python) 116
software 16, 18
  developers **20–21**
  engineers 19
software systems, programming
  languages 344
Solution Explorer 243, 289, 313,
  321, 335
solution file 218, 219
Solution Folder 243, 289
sound, Scratch 39
space applications 95
spacers 246, 307
spaces, vertical 224, 246
spacing settings 235, **245**
special effects (Scratch) 38
specificity 239
split method (Python) 140
sport, team allocator project **118–29**
spreadsheet applications 135, 136
spread syntax **268**
Sprite Library (Scratch) 54, 68, 71,
  74, 76, 78, 82
Sprite List (Scratch) 30, 54, 83
sprites (Scratch) **32–33**
  adding buttons 56, 60–61
  adding new 54, 71–77, 82
  broadcasts 48–49
  changing appearance 38
  collision detection 47
  costumes 32, 33, 57, 61, 78, 85, 91
  creating 32, 54, 68
  deleting the cat 54, 66
  drawing with pen blocks 37
  duplicating 60

sprites *continued*
  moving using coordinates 36
  moving using directions 37
  naming/renaming 56, 68
  speech/thought bubbles 38
SQL 345, 347
Stage (Scratch) 30
  changing backdrop 55
  coordinates 36
  designing backdrop 66–68
Stage Info (Scratch) 30
statistical computing 345
steering controls 84
strings
  combining 103
  concatenating 267
  format **166**
  JavaScript 266, **267**
  Python 100, **103**, 138, 139, 140,
    141, 166, 190, 198
  Scratch **42**
Stroustrup, Bjarne 347
style definitions, CSS 235, **238–39**,
  250, 252, 255, 319, 325
styles folder 243
style sheets 242, 243, 306
styling
  body elements 307
  carousel 330
  Contact Us section 258
  copyright 263, 332
  corners 308
  CSS **238–39**
  and ease of navigation 243
  email hyperlink 256
  encourages interaction 243
  feature box 253–57
  footer 261–62
  headers 307
  hyperlinks 252, 256, 262, 330, 339
  image and subheading 326
  image text 314
  input field 259
  logo 313
  margin and padding **245**
  non-picture elements 254
  page elements 245–53
  primary message 316
  quotation marks 320–21
  quote 318
  rows 338
  scroll button 257–58
  standardization 244

styling *continued*
styling the webpage project **242–63**
Subscribe section 259
text 306–8, 314, 330
Tk canvas widget 150
styling the web page **242–63**
feature box styling 253–57
program requirements 242
setting up 243–44
styling the page elements 245–53
styling the remaining elements 257–63
what the program does 242
sub-elements 210
subheadings 325–26
Sublime Text (code editor) 208
subscribe button 260
subscription link 220, 232, 247
styling 259–60
subsets 122, 145
substrings 267
SVG **286**
Swift 344
switch statement **271**
symbolic mathematics 345
synchronization 49
syntax 94
errors 130, 131, 132
highlighting 208
spread **268**
SyntaxError (JavaScript) 280
SynthEdit 346
system languages 344

T
tables
footers 167
headers 167
tablets 215, 240, 305
tabs 209
tags, HTML **210–11**, 234
attributes 211
container 333
indenting 211
order of **310**
TCP (Transmission Control Protocol) 207
Team allocator **118–29**
create a team 120–21
hacks and tweaks 127–29
how it works 118

Team allocator *continued*
pick new teams 125–26
pick teams 122–24
program design 119
templates
creating new pages from 305, 333–34, 335
literals 267
master page 303, 304
renaming 335
web page **343**
testing (software development) 20
TeX 345
text
adding to web page 221
drawing with Pygame Zero **190**
feature images 314
placeholder 261
positioning 319
quote 318
styling 253–54, 306–8, 314, 330
text alternatives (website) 214
text area (web pages) 212, 213
text-based languages 94
TextEdit 218
text editors 208, 305
IDLE 95
text fields (web pages) 212, 213
text files 305
text input, users 47
Text tool (Scratch) 57, 61, 88
Text to Speech blocks (Scratch) 59, 63
throw statement 281
ticker tape 215
tiles 179, 199, 200
time management, Project planner **134–55**
time module (Python) 116
TK Canvas widget 147, **150**
Tk Frame widget 153
Tk GUI **147**
tkinter (Python) 116, 146, 148, 150
TK module (Python) 146–51
top-down 2D view 178
top-down coding **114**
top-level window widget 147
Top Menu 220, 222, 223, 303, 310, 311
styling 249, 250–51
touching mouse-pointer block (Scratch) 47

tournaments, sporting 128
traceback error messages (Python) 130
transitions **250**
transition instruction 249–50, 252, 254
Translate blocks (Scratch) 56, 59, 60, 63
translation apps, travel translator project **52–63**
transport layer protocol 207
travel translator (Scratch) **52–63**
adding a language 56–60
adding more languages 60–62
hacks and tweaks 63
how the app works 52
program design 53
setting the scene 54–56
travel website project **304–43**
trend analysis 345
true value 270–71
try block 281
tuples (Python) 134, **137**, 138, 142–43
calling 143
turtle module (Python) 116
tween keyword arguments **198**
Twitter 301–2
two-dimensional games 178, 179
TypeError (JavaScript) 280
type errors 130
TypeScript **285**

U
UDP (User Datagram Protocol) 207
underscores 114
Uniform Resource Locator
see URL
Unix operating system 94
update game state (Pygame Zero) 179
update handler function (Pygame Zero) 179
updates, Pygame Zero **177**
upper() method (Python) 113
URIError (JavaScript) 280
URL (Uniform Resource Locator) 206
hyperlinks and 213
User Datagram Protocol
see UDP

tournaments, sporting 128

user input
Java Script 265, **272**, 284
Python **106**
Scratch 40
user interactions 46

V
value
Boolean 270
comparing **270**
functions producing 115
sets 140
of variables 100, 101, 109, 268, 269
van Rossum, Guido 94, 96, 347
variables
arrays 268
and Boolean operators 104, 266
class assigned to 283
declaring **101**, 267, 269
global **115**, 160, 163, 189, 195, 269
initializing 267
instance 170
JavaScript **266–69**, 278, 279, 298, 308
local **115**, 269
naming 101, 188
non-primitive data types 268
primitive data types 266–67
Python **100–101**, 115, 121, 125, 160, 163, 169, 170, 189, 195
SASS 341
scope of **269**
Scratch **42**, 44, 58, 69, 70, 72, 74–77, 79, 83
and sets 140
using **101**
values 100, 101, 109, 268, 269
VBA 344
vector images 286
vector mode 33, 57, 61
vertical alignment 321
vertical borders 239
vertical lists 311, 312, 326
vertical spaces 224, 225, 230, 231, 246, 307, 319, 329, 333
video sensing blocks (Scratch) 59
viewport 240
viewport meta definition 309
Virtual Private Server *see* VPS
virtual worlds, mapping 287
Visual Basic 347